To the Memory of
George S. Tomkins

scholar, mentor and friend

Schools in the West
Essays in Canadian Educational History

Editors

Nancy M. Sheehan
J. Donald Wilson
David C. Jones

Detselig Enterprises Limited
Calgary, Alberta

Nancy M. Sheehan
The University of Calgary
J. Donald Wilson
The University of British Columbia
David C. Jones
The University of Calgary

Canadian Cataloguing in Publication Data

Main entry under title:

Schools in the West

ISBN 0-920490-57-3

1. Education — Canada, Western — History — Addresses,
essays, lectures.   I. Sheehan, Nancy M., 1935-
II. Wilson, J. Donald.   III. Jones, David C., 1943-
LA411.S36   1986   370'.9712   C85-091012-1

© 1986 by Detselig Enterprises Limited
P.O. Box G 399
Calgary, Alberta T3A 2G3

SAN 115-0324

Printed in Canada

ISBN 0-920490-57-3

Contents

Contributors

Jean Barman is a lecturer in the Departments of History and Social and Educational Studies at the University of British Columbia. She is the author of *Growing Up British in British Columbia: Boys in Private School* (1984) and co-editor of *Indian Education in Canada* in two volumes to be published by UBC Press, and of a special issue of *BC Studies* on Vancouver (Spring 1986). Her research interests include the changing relationship between families and schools in twentieth-century Canada.

John Calam has recently retired as professor in the Department of Social and Educational Studies at the University of British Columbia. Besides *Parsons and Pedagogues: The SPG Adventure in American Education* (1971) he has many journal articles to his credit and has edited *"A Decennial Festschrift," The Study of Education: Canada, 1982.*Currently he is completing a study on teacher education in British Columbia between 1925 and 1956.

Lawrence W. Downey is professor and director of the Centre for Policy Studies in Education at the University of British Columbia. He is involved in the development of the Centre and in the production of a regular publication, *Policy Explorations*. Five issues of *Explorations* have now been produced. Dr. Downey's most recent study is *The Anatomy of a Policy Decision: Bill 33 — BC's Independent Schools Support Act.* (1984).

Thomas Fleming is an assistant professor in the Department of Administrative, Adult and Higher Education at the University of British Columbia. Recent articles have appeared in *The Journal of Educational Thought, Canadian Journal of University Continuing Education* and *Journal of Business Administration*. He was prominently involved in the BC government report *Let's Talk About Schools* (1985). He has recently authored the book *Management By Consensus,* and co-authored *Educational Administration: Developments in Thought and Practice,* both under review by publishers.

Stella Hryniuk is a sessional assistant professor in the Department of History, University of Manitoba. She is the author of articles on the experiences of Ukrainians in Canada. Dr. Hryniuk's most recent publication is "Peasant Agriculture in East Galicia in the Late Nineteenth Century," in *Slavonic and East European Review,* April 1985.

David C. Jones, an associate professor at the University of Calgary, is the author of *Midways, Judges and Smooth-Tongued Fakirs* (1983). He has co-edited *Shaping the Schools of the Canadian West* (1979), *Schooling and Society in 20th Century British Columbia* (1980), with J. Donald Wilson, which won the CHA award for excellence in regional history, *Approaches to Educational History* (1981) and *Building Beyond the Homestead* (1985). His articles have appeared in several Canadian and international journals. He is at present completing a study of the prairie dry belt called "Empire of Dust."

John Lyons received his B.A. and B.Ed. from the University of Manitoba, his M.A. in Education from the University of Calgary, and his Ph.D. from the University of Alberta. He taught high school in Manitoba and British Columbia and is currently an associate professor in Educational Foundations and Assistant Dean of the Secondary Program in the College of Education at the University of Saskatchewan. His research interests are in minority groups and education and nationalism and education.

Bill Maciejko has an M.Ed. from the University of Manitoba and is currently enrolled in a Ph.D. program in Social and Educational Studies at UBC. His interests are in the area of education and social change, particularly labour and ethnic history. "'Social Disharmony': Public Schools and the Winnipeg Workers' Movement, 1912-1919" was presented at CSSE (1985). A monograph, "The Politics of Progress: Ukrainians and Public Education: An Historical Perspective on the Manitoba Experience" is in press.

Neil G. McDonald is a professor in the Faculty of Education at the University of Manitoba. He has co-edited *Canadian Schools and Canadian Identity* (1977), *Egerton Ryerson and His Times* (1978) and *Approaches to Educational History* (1981), and has written several articles on the development of schooling in western Canada. He has recently initiated a major research project on the immigrant experience in Manitoba schools.

Morris Mott is assistant professor of history at the University of Manitoba. His interests include the history of sports, especially the history of hockey, and the social and political history of the West. He has published in *Manitoba History, Journal of Sport History, Urban History Review, Prairie Forum, Journal of the West* and *The Canadian Journal of History of Sport*. Currently he is editor of *Manitoba History*.

Robert S. Patterson is Dean of Education and professor in the Department of Educational Foundations at the University of Alberta. His research interests include progressive education, the history of teachers, especially rural teachers and the development of normal schools. Articles on these topics appear in a variety of texts and journals. "Go, Grit and Gumption: A Normal School Perspective on Teacher Education" was his McCalla Lecture delivered at the University of Alberta (1983).

Nancy M. Sheehan is an associate professor and Associate Dean (Academic Programs) in the Faculty of Education at the University of Calgary. Her research interests are directed toward voluntary organizations and their influence on the school curriculum. She has co-edited *Shaping the Schools of the Canadian West* (1979), *Approaches to Educational History* (1981) and a special issue of *The Journal of Educational Thought* (1980), and has published in major Canadian and international journals.

E. Brian Titley teaches in the Department of Educational Foundations, the University of Alberta. He is the author of *Church, State and the Control of Schooling in Ireland, 1900-1944* (1983) and co-editor of *Education in Canada: An Interpretation* (1982). His most recent articles have appeared in the *Oxford Review of Education, Revue des sciences de l'éducation* and *Prairie Forum*. He is currently completing a book on Duncan Campbell Scott and the administration of Indian Affairs in Canada.

Harro Van Brummelen is Education Coordinator for the Society of Christian Schools in British Columbia. His doctoral dissertation, "Molding God's Children: The History of Curriculum in Christian Schools Rooted in Dutch Calvinism," is being published. He co-edited and wrote chapters in *Shaping School Curriculum: A Biblical View* (1979), and is co-author of *The Story of Numbers and Numerals* (1984). His current interests include ideology and curriculum as well as alternative schooling.

Clinton O. White is a professor of history, Campion College, University of Regina. He has published *Power for a Province,* a history of Saskatchewan electrical utilities, and a number of articles dealing with prairie subjects, including an earlier one on German Catholics. From 1978 to 1982 he held a seat in the Saskatchewan Legislature where he served as chairman of the Crown Corporation Committee and Minister of Culture and Youth under Premier Allan Blakeney.

J. Donald Wilson is professor of educational history at the University of British Columbia. He has written widely in the area of Canadian educational, immigration and ethnic history. His recent publications include a contribution to the *Dictionary of Canadian Biography* and articles in various journals. He has co-edited seven books, the most recent of which is *An Imperfect Past: Education and Society in Canadian History* (1984). His current focus is on schooling and society in rural British Columbia in the 1920s.

1

Introduction: Schools in the West

J. Donald Wilson

At the Canadian Historical Association annual meeting in Montreal in 1985, at which educational history was a major theme, Chad Gaffield in a keynote address spoke of the need for "a fresh agenda" for the history of Canadian education. This was a timely suggestion considering that the bitter debates between the moderate and radical revisionists of the mid-seventies now seemed of another era, and no new direction had seized the field.[1] Gaffield's prescription was simple:

> . . . it is time for historians of education to go "back to school" although in ways that Charles Phillips would hardly recognize. The topics of books, pupils, teachers and schools may have long traditions in the scholarly literature but analyses of issues such as conflict, diversity, and the character of relationships are indeed a recent development. These analyses suggest ways in which the study of education can continue to mature as a field of social history. . . . By specifically examining topics such as the "culture of the classroom," historians can examine the actual ways in which factors [such as gender, class and ethnicity] have determined the everyday experience of education.[2]

Significantly, another keynote speaker at the same conference, Richard Aldrich from the University of London, reported that controversy in English history of education "is now coming to focus as much upon the *actual nature of the educational process itself* as upon the historical procedures by which it must be examined and defined."[3]

It is probably true that not enough of our writing of late in Canadian educational history has been concerned with the content of schooling and the responses and resistances which it engendered; and some important relationships, such as that between the working class and education, have received little or no attention. One historian, R. J. Carney, is blunt in his criticism of recent scholarship:

> What is needed . . . is a dialectic in which those who doubt the entire wisdom of the radical critique are more given to determining what has occurred in schools and to advancing the implications of their findings with the same zeal and openness which the radicals have shown. . . . Whatever benefits the move by educational historians to social history have been, it has also provided a sanctuary which some have used to avoid historical inquiry into the practices of schools.[4]

1

The articles that compose this book were solicited before either of these critiques or challenges was delivered. Nonetheless, it is perhaps significant that many of them treat the very subjects and issues advocated by Gaffield and Carney. There are, for example, entire sections on teachers and school curriculum, including one chapter on textbooks. Clinton White and Brian Titley discuss in detail two very different types of schools — industrial schools for Indians and German Catholic schools in Saskatchewan. The diversity of views between parents on the one hand and teachers and school trustees on the other are treated in chapters by Bill Maciejko, and Stella Hryniuk and Neil McDonald. In both cases serious conflict resulted. The character of relationships, both bureaucratic and political, is addressed in chapters by Thomas Fleming and Lorne Downey.

Several new topics and methodologies are also evident in the book. As to topics, consider sports and physical education in the twentieth century curriculum (Mott); the assimilation process as seen this time from the perspective of the recipients rather than the school board trustees, inspectors and teachers (Hryniuk and McDonald); working-class views on the public school system, a much neglected topic (Maciejko); and a comprehensive article on Indian industrial schools in the Canadian west (Titley). As to innovative methodologies, consider Patterson's oral history perspective on rural teachers in the inter-war period[5] and Maciejko's Marxist perspective on working-class culture.

Although most chapters treat aspects of public schooling, a few continue the interest historians have shown in outside organizations whose influence impinged upon both school and curricula. Nancy Sheehan's article on the WCTU and John Lyons' on the Saskatchewan Teachers' Federation are representative of this genre. Since the 1970s Canadian historians have been fascinated by the external factors that have influenced public school decision-making. Sheehan has been in the vanguard of this type of history, having completed numerous studies on the WCTU, the IODE and the Junior Red Cross as active lobbyists in school matters.[6] In her treatment of the WCTU in Alberta and Saskatchewan, Sheehan highlights the divergence between their rhetoric about educational progress and what actually happened in the classroom. The organizational framework, the women's limited experience in dealing with educational bureaucracies, and their household responsibilities set up constraints on their ability to deal with educational matters. The author concludes that schools and other educational agencies had little direct influence on effecting either prohibition or its defeat.

The impact of social history on the writing of educational history in Canada has drawn the attention of educational historians away from the culture of the classroom to the "big" questions of power relationships on the one hand and client concerns about schooling as reflected in "family strategies" approaches.[7] As a result, studies in the history of curriculum have been neglected over the past two decades. Historians' current awareness of being sensitive to social context while avoiding a "schools-in-isolation" approach has only made them more hesitant to attempt curriculum histories. Nonetheless, studies in the history of curriculum can provide powerful insights into the dialogue between schooling and society.[8] As the late George Tomkins concluded:

> Cultural conflict in Canadian education has typically expressed itself in bitter social, political and religious controversies which ultimately have hung on the objectives and content, including the materials, of the curriculum. In a word, cultural conflict in the schools is characteristically curriculum conflict centering upon the basic curriculum question of what the schools should teach.[9]

Over the course of the history of Canadian schooling there has been a continuous battle over "what knowledge is of most worth." Sides have formed up over whether the literary-humanistic cultural heritage going back to Greece and Rome should be stressed, or whether the more practical and "useful" subjects such as science, technology and job-related skills should form the core of the curriculum. In Canada a third strain, concern over cultural survival, has suggested at various times that Canadian school children should be deeply conscious of the Imperial connection, the dangers of Americanization, and the development of a distinct Canadian identity. These questions are addressed in the section on "Curriculum," especially in the chapters by Nancy Sheehan on Alberta and Harro Van Brummelen on British Columbia.

Van Brummelen's study of early British Columbia textbooks underlines the particular vision which the province's anglophone leadership placed before students from 1872 to 1925. It was a British, Protestant vision of life and society, a combination of social myth and national feeling. That vision, reflected in the textbooks adopted, was rooted in a strong moral imperative. At first, this was closely intertwined with the beliefs of traditional Christianity, but gradually it loosened itself, though far from completely, from its religious roots. From a literal interpretation of the Bible and a strong sense of sin and need of redemption in Jesus Christ, religion came to be viewed in terms of promoting morality and social justice. Virtue was rewarded, evil punished. By 1925 children were more encouraged to draw their own conclusions, but living a moral life nonetheless remained a powerful idea. The traditional virtues were now those of good citizenship rather than of obedience to God. Happiness could be achieved if children had loyal hearts, constant minds and the courage to be true. Loyalty to and love of Britain and its empire were vigorously encouraged. Only gradually did a separate Canadian identity, still associated with Britain, become recognized as important. Throughout the period, therefore, textbooks continued to enforce both clear-cut standards of individual responsibility and a sense of how life in the larger community was to be understood.

In her chapter on curriculum in Alberta Nancy Sheehan focuses on three curricular areas: nationalism, progressive education and vocational/technical education which areas suffice to demonstrate the kinds of traditions and constraints that have moulded developments over the years. Despite the vast demographic and technological changes which Alberta experienced throughout the twentieth century, Sheehan concludes that the academic program remained central in a provincial school system that has not changed in fifty years.

Morris Mott presents a case history of the introduction of one subject in Manitoba's school curriculum before World War I. The subject in question, physical education, is of particular interest because it was non-academic as well as a typical progressive education subject. Insight is offered into the social reasons for promoting it (improving levels of health and fitness) as well as for opposing it (a "play" or "soft" subject that interfered with the real purpose of schooling). But physical education had additional merit having to do with the assimilation of the "foreign element." As one spokesman reported, play "leads to the heart of the foreign child as readily as [to that of] the British-born." Consequently "Canadian" games such as baseball and soccer could bring "foreign" youngsters to think and act like Canadians, to see the world in a "Canadian" way. Here we see another example of the curriculum serving the imperative of cultural survival.

But such important matters were not left exclusively to the schools. Churches also played their part in developing character through organized play, and municipalities began to organize playgrounds, supervised skating rinks and swimming pools. Local branches of the YMCA, boy scouts and various boys' clubs joined in. The ideal product of all this was summed up in 1908 by a YMCA secretary:

> He is hard as nails and wiry as a cat . . . and he can put boys larger than himself flat on the mats. Saturday morning he teaches a Bible class and Sunday finds him in his Sunday school class . . . . His evenings are spent in study . . . and when bed time comes it finds him tired and ready for . . . sleep. In the morning he starts for school with clear eye, ruddy cheek, and quick step. . . . The Devil has no show with a boy like this.[10]

Teachers were an essential ingredient of the schooling process and so their training was of the utmost importance. Although normal school training in central and eastern Canada had been a fact of life since the mid-nineteenth century, such formal institutions did not appear in western Canada until the turn of the century. John Calam's chapter traces the first fifteen years of normal school instruction in British Columbia. The preparing of effective elementary school teachers was carried out with meticulous attention to detail through both lectures by master teachers and practice-teaching sessions. Things seemed to be moving smoothly until the mid-twenties when the Putman-Weir Report criticized the two normal schools for inadequate staffing, outmoded curricula, boring lectures, low admission standards, and artificial practice-teaching arrangements. The commissioners, themselves noted progressive educators, advocated the immediate implementation of various features of the progressive education movement based upon recent findings in child study, social psychology, and educational psychology such as IQ testing.

The great disparity between the theoretical goals of progressive educators such as Putman and Weir and the realities of elementary-school teaching in western Canada is well borne out in Robert Patterson's chapter on rural school teachers in Alberta and Saskatchewan. One empathizes with the difficulties they faced: isolation, loneliness, uncooperative parents and school trustees, large classes, authoritarian inspectors, inadequate resources, insensitive departmental directives, threat of abrupt dismissal, and general insecurity of tenure. All these aspects weighed much more heavily on teachers' minds, as Patterson illustrates, than whether they were following the precepts of Donalda Dickie's *The Enterprise in Theory and Practice*. Incidentally, the predominance of young females among rural teachers (in the order of four to one) remains an unwritten chapter in the history of women in Canada.

Paradoxically, a large proportion of male teachers who eventually rose to the lofty rank of school inspector began their careers in rural schools. As Tom Fleming points out, until recent years there was an accepted *cursus honorum* in Department of Education bureaucracies which often began in rural schools, led to town and city schools through the positions of vice-principal and principal, and in a few cases on to the honoured and powerful post of inspector. In the period from 1887 to 1958 only one woman in British Columbia held this office. Patterson, speaking from the perspective of the retired teachers he interviewed, concludes that the services of inspectors "often left much to be desired." Fleming, on the other hand, paints a much more favourable picture of the "Department's men-in-the-field." "Many inspectors," he writes, "were known for their acts of kindness to teachers in various kinds of trouble, as well as their willingness to bring news of the outside world [including the latest World Series scores] to those in isolated schools." There is little question, however, that until the last generation school inspectors in western Canada served as the instruments of centralized control and the most visible symbols of the government's presence in schools. More recently, the men and now women who became the first generation of superintendents to be locally employed inherited, as Fleming states, "an educational world in turmoil, a world often in disagreement over the direction schools should take." They had to find ways "to cope with more restless public and professional constituencies." No longer part of a close-knit group as some of them once were, they are isolated, caught somewhere between the levels of government they serve and, at the same time, alienated to some extent from the professionals they supervise.

Patterson's account of the rural teaching experience helps us, as he puts it, "to appreciate why the establishment of a teachers' organization was so essential to teacher well-being and the improvement of schooling." John Lyons' chapter renders a specific case study of the evolution of such an organization, in this case the Saskatchewan Teachers' Federation. He sets this organization firmly into the province's educational and political history during the decade and a half between the onset of the Depression and the coming to power of the CCF Party under T. C. Douglas in 1944. The main objectives of the STF were to achieve a statutory salary schedule to offset declining salaries, security of tenure in the face of arbitrary layoffs, revisions to superannuation legislation, and the formation of larger units of school administration. The chapter highlights the growth of professionalism among Saskatchewan teachers, and establishes a pattern of professionalization which was duplicated elsewhere in English Canada during these years.

As Gerald Friesen reminds us in his prize-winning book, "schools have always been the crucial battleground for cultural ideals in western Canada. . . ."[11] Several chapters analyze the dialectic between recipients and promoters of public education. This is particularly evident in those treating the education of religious and ethnic minorities and in one chapter on working-class attitudes toward the public schools. The education of minority groups figures prominently in three chapters. The Hryniuk-McDonald article on Ukrainians and the public schools gives us quite a different picture from the traditional account of an ignorant and backward peasant folk suffering from cultural shock on the Canadian Prairies. Instead we encounter parents who were excited about public education and willing to tax themselves for what they believed was the best possible education. Of course, there were tensions over the language question, especially after the outbreak of World War I, but Ukrainian parents were generally happy with the bilingual system in Manitoba while it lasted. The article is innovative in at least three respects: it establishes the sort of mental baggage and schooling experience Ukrainian immigrants brought with them from the homeland; it details the immigrants' view (not just the assimilators') of formal education here in Canada/Manitoba; and it specifies in what respects parents made accommodations with the authorities, resisted them, or went off on their own to make educational provisions for their children, usually supplementary to the public system. All was not, however, trouble-free for the Ukrainians. The abolition of bilingual schooling in Manitoba in 1916 followed by wartime persecution of the Ukrainians as enemy aliens and the rise of socialism and communism among their ranks after the Bolshevik Revolution inaugurated a period of serious tension and conflict between Ukrainian settlers and government authorities in health, education and law enforcement.[12]

The story of a German Catholic community in Saskatchewan at approximately the same time follows in the next chapter. Like Hryniuk and McDonald, Clinton White examines the tension between popular and official culture. He seeks to write history from the inside out, to get at the process of schooling from the perspective of the recipients, or at least of their parents. His study of Saskatchewan's German Catholics presents an entirely different picture from that of previous scholars. The latter suggested that this religio-ethnic group favoured separate and private schools, often poorly run; that German and religion received great emphasis; that teachers were generally German or fluent in German; and that unilingual English-speaking teachers avoided the area. Relying upon such primary sources as school district and teachers' records, local newspapers, and diaries of early residents, White provides a new interpretation. German Catholic residents, in fact, relied upon quite a different educational structure, a pluralistic system containing many more public than private or separate schools, hiring as their most common type of teacher a unilingual Irish Catholic from the East, and promptly adopting the provincial curriculum for use in practically all their schools. This is an example of revisionist history at its best.

Brian Titley's chapter on Indian industrial schools in the Canadian West reveals another dimension of the clash between school promoters, in this case the federal Department of Indian Affairs, and the objects of their plans, the Indian people themselves. Industrial schools for the Indians of western Canada were first created in the 1880s as joint ventures between the major Christian churches and the federal Department of Indian Affairs. Residential in character, they offered a joint program of academic studies and instruction in trades and agriculture. They were deliberately designed to sever the Indian children's connection with their ancestral culture and prepare them for integration into the dominant society. But parental opposition provided the experiment with a persistent stumbling block. The schools were rarely filled to capacity, and few children remained in attendance long enough to undergo the intended transformation. By the first decade of the twentieth century, rising costs and disappointing results had prompted Indian Affairs to seek alternative methods of promoting assimilation. Some of the more inefficient industrial schools were closed, and they vanished as an administrative category in 1922-23. The industrial school experiment was a monument to the folly of educating children in open defiance of parental wishes.

Similarly, Bill Maciejko's chapter on working-class attitudes to public education in Winnipeg also gives us an "inside-out" view of the public system in that city. What did working-class parents think of that system and what actions did they take to change it? Even though their efforts fell short of their reach, the story of their struggle to attain the sort of system they wanted for their children and for all Canadians bears telling. Despite the rash of recent books, some prize-winning, and articles, most often in *Labour/Le Travail*, on the subject of working-class history, workers' attitudes to public schooling have tended to draw a blank from historians.[13] The points of variance over schooling between working class and "bourgeois" (middle-class) culture are Maciejko's subject. The public school, product of dominant bourgeois views, valued deference to authority — to God, king and country — and the dominant ethos — respect for order and bourgeois morality. Social conformity, productivity and the work ethic, nationalism and militarism permeated school texts, curriculum and classroom practices. Many workers, however, valued some degree of class autonomy, some retention of working-class culture, including independent social and political organizations, and anti-militarism.[14] The ideals of socialism, cooperation and internationalism provided the underpinnings for these values. Once again, it is the resistance offered and the accommodations made by the supposed object of the school system's moral regulation which is of interest, not whether the radical workers were in fact victorious in their struggle for change. It is undoubtedly true that there was more opposition to the form and practice of schooling over the years than historians would have us believe. One is reminded of Kenneth McNaught's "discovery" some fifteen years ago that indeed Canada has had a violent history and was not always "the peaceable kingdom."[15]

Maciejko reminds us that it is not enough to simply record the experience of disadvantaged groups — blacks, women, workers; analysis of both experience and structures of power is required. In their effort to right the balance between politics and society, social historians often run the risk of leaving out the politics altogether. It is now almost a decade since Eugene Genovese and Elizabeth Fox-Genovese first pointed up this danger in a powerful critique of the new social history. Although they admitted the best of these studies afforded "a healthy and much-needed corrective to the narrower view that emphasized working people, as well as women and children, as mere objects of the attention of their betters," they admonished historians to pay due attention "to the rulers as well as the ruled and to the political antagonism between them." After all, political structures do set the boundaries of public discourse. Put briefly, history for the Genoveses is "primarily the story of who rides whom and how."[16]

A young Canadian historian has recently argued in a similar fashion in a study on the origins of mass public education in Upper Canada/Canada West. Critical of the "family strategies," bottom-up approach of the late Douglas Lawr and Robert Gidney, Bruce Curtis insists, "however much local residents, students among them, may have embraced particular pedagogical initiatives, however much they may have opposed particular pedagogical initiatives, after the organization of public education pedagogical space became a form of state space and this space had its own structure of powerfulness."[17] The bureaucratic framework got established early thanks to Ryerson's efforts, and the local initiative and popular demands in reaction to it (the focus of Lawr and Gidney's work) led only to a new and greater bureaucracy, not a diminution of the one already in place. Thus the common or public schools in Canada were from their beginnings in the 1840s part of a framework established by a small but effective bureaucracy. It was this framework against which the populace reacted, forcing the bureaucracy in turn to resort to a new and greater bureaucratic structure. All this began almost half a century later in the case of western Canada, but nonetheless the pattern remained common across the nation and remains so even today.

It has been said that history is that which one age finds interesting and relevant in another. The fascination a decade ago with colonial education, school promoters, and church-state relations in education is replaced in this volume with discussion of the actual process of schooling, the changing role of teachers and inspectors, and an examination of some policy issues such as public funding of independent schools in British Columbia (Downey). The distinguished British historian Harold Silver has concerned himself of late with the role of history in policy studies. Many chapters of his book *Education as History* point up the applicablility of history to policy studies in education. Quoting from *Unpopular Education: Schooling and Social Democracy in England Since 1944* (1981) by Steve Baron *et al.*, he reiterates the need of writing and thinking more historically. The best historical work contains "first, a concern with close and detailed description and analysis, firmly set in time and place, and second, a preoccupation with continuity and especially with change, with crisis and with transformations."[18] Lorne Downey's study of British Columbia's Bill 33 and Tom Fleming's examination of the changing role of B.C.'s school inspectors over a century underline the value of "detailed description and analysis, firmly set in time and place." The same may be said of David Jones' study of the relationship between social disintegration and schooling in southeastern Alberta in the twenties. The new policy studies orientation of many former "Foundations" departments in Canadian faculties of education seems to hold attraction for both scholars and administrators alike. As support for "educational foundations" diminishes, such departments often find themselves renamed or restructured into units of educational policy studies, often in tandem with educational administration faculty. Canadian historians of education have been somewhat ambivalent about these recent developments. While a sense of being engaged in "practical" research can have its rewards, there remain nagging concerns about a headlong rush into policy studies. As Harold Silver reminds us, "the concerns of historians about too close an involvement with policy issues . . . include the nature of social science models, levels of generalisation, and the claims and status of social science knowledge." There is also the danger that policy analysis is "inevitably conservative in direction and effect."[19] Since the questions asked are present-oriented and often government-initiated, the studies done tend to be present-minded and within the context of the current political and economic system. Books such as Grubb and Lazerson, *Broken Promises: How Americans Fail Their Children* (1982), however, make clear that this danger can be overcome. Their study, strongly historical in approach, is extremely critical of U.S. state and federal government policies directed towards children and youth, and recommends radical policy shifts. Policy studies from a historical perspective, as Part IV shows, are likely to attract the attention of a good proportion of Canadian historians. Such a trend would be in keeping with an apparent renewed interest in "going-back-to-school" issues.

Unlike works of a decade ago, most chapters in this section concern the twentieth century, and especially the first half of this century. Only one chapter, Jean Barman's, is entirely about the nineteenth century and colonial education. This marks a considerable shift from the preoccupation with colonial education of a decade ago. The chapter differs in another respect: it discounts the notion of public education being imposed by a small minority on an unwilling or uninformed population. Her study makes it clear that the important decisions moving British Columbia toward a system of free non-denominational public education were taken with the acquiescence of the major segments of the colonial and provincial population. Thus in this case the fashionable social control thesis of ten years ago is reversed.[20]

Rural school problems and solutions predominate in two chapters, Fleming's and Jones'. The latter is a study of social dislocation in southeastern Alberta in the twenties and its attendant effects on the public schools. The divisive tendencies within the school system mirrored the community's sense of anxiety and breakup. Teacher training programs were not equal to preparing rural teachers, curricular reforms intended to aid agriculture failed dismally, and teachers' living and working conditions highlighted an alien existence. The teacher, already an outsider, was hardly capable, Jones concludes, of "integrating a society which the school itself had done so much to fracture." In Fleming's chapter the focus is on the role played by the school inspector and later superintendent to suggest and implement solutions for B.C.'s rural school problems. As in Alberta's case the main solution was found in school-district and school amalgamation. The same trend was observable in Saskatchewan and as set out in Lyons' chapter, especially the teachers' role in promoting larger school units. As elsewhere, larger units of administration did not become common, however, until after World War II. Nonetheless the cooperation of teachers, inspectors, and departmental officials in times of severe financial restraint provides a lesson for today's troubled educational scene. The role of the STF as a vehicle for changing public opinion is particularly instructive.

David Jones' chapter is typical of a trend observable in educational history over the last decade, that is, the work of a number of educational historians has moved right out of educational history *per se* and into related areas of social history: for example, Neil Sutherland into history of childhood, Alison Prentice into women's history, J. D. Wilson into ethnic history, and Jones himself into agricultural history. If we take Jones' case as exemplary, we can see how this process has evolved. Beginning with an interest in agricultural education as an aspect of the New Education, he moved progressively into non-school rural education and recreational history with his book *Midways, Judges and Smooth-Tongued Fakirs: The Illustrated Story of Country Fairs in the Prairie West* (1983). Herein the country life movement in Canada formed the central focus, but another important context was accorded the attention it deserves, the disaster in the dry belt of Alberta after World War I. A common theme running through all Jones' work has been the crucial interaction between experts and the common folk with the advice of the experts often coming out second best, a sort of history of "miseducation."[21]

A second major suggestion coming from Gaffield's important paper mentioned at the outset was for educational historians to avoid trying to write "coherent national syntheses," such as *Canadian Education: A History* (1970). Rather a "lower level of explanation" is still in order such as seeks to chart the "diverse experiences, competing ambitions, and contradictory phenomena" inherent in Canadian education.[22] The editors of this volume believe that such a goal can be attained by examining a region of Canada, in this case western Canada, within the time frame of a century. In a sense this book is intended to replace two earlier volumes with which the editors were involved: *Shaping the Schools of the Canadian West* (1979) and *Schooling and Society in Twentieth Century British Columbia* (1980). In this volume fully two-thirds of the articles are original, and the re-published ones are both recent and innovative. It is our contention that regional syntheses of this sort will provide the grist eventually for the coherent national synthesis which Gaffield quite rightly asserts Canadian educational historians are not yet ready to write.[23]

In their recent comprehensive "state of the art" report on social history in Canada, David Gagan and H. E. Turner pointed to an overemphasis in English-Canadian social history on the period 1850-1914 and on developments in central Canada, as well as the ignoring of the 1920s and 1940s. Chapters in this book go some distance in meeting these three objections. Gagan and Turner also asserted that "studies of rural society are out of fashion." Though this may be generally true, several chapters in this book concentrate in whole or in part on rural developments. In the past decade and a half educational history has been one of the most vibrant sub-fields in Canadian social history, and in a small way we feel this book contributes to the social history of Canada which, as Gagan and Turner maintain, "still requires . . . continued support and ministrations."[24]

Notes

[1]J. Donald Wilson, "From Social Control to Family Strategies: Some Observations on Recent Trends in Canadian Educational History," *History of Education Review* (Australia), XIII: 1 (1984): 10.

[2]Chad Gaffield, "Going Back to School: Towards a Fresh Agenda for the History of Education," paper read at the Canadian Historical Association Annual Meeting, Montreal, 1985, pp. 40-41. The same suggestion is offered by Robert J. Carney in "Towards a History of Schooling," *Curriculum Inquiry*, XIV: 3 (1984): 348-56, wherein he speaks of the need to study "in-school environments."

[3]Richard Aldrich, "History of Education in England: An Historiographical Perspective," paper read at the Canadian Historical Association Annual Meeting, Montreal, 1985, p. 14. Italics added.

[4]Carney, "Towards a History of Schooling," p. 355.

[5]See also Neil Sutherland, "The Role of Memory in the History of Childhood," paper read at the Canadian Historical Association Annual Meeting, Montreal, 1985.

[6]See, for example, Nancy M. Sheehan, "National Pressure Groups and Provincial Curriculum Policy: Temperance in Nova Scotia Schools, 1880-1930," *Canadian Journal of Education*, IX: 1 (1984): 73-88; "The IODE, the Schools and World War

I," *History of Education Review,* XIII: 1 (1984): 29-44; "The Junior Red Cross Movement in Saskatchewan, 1919-1929: Rural Regeneration Through the Schools," in David C. Jones and Ian MacPherson, eds., *Building Beyond the Homestead: Rural History on the Prairies* (Calgary: University of Calgary Press, 1985), pp. 66-86.

[7]J. Donald Wilson, "Some Observations on Recent Trends in Canadian Educational History," in Wilson, ed., *An Imperfect Past: Education and Society in Canadian History* (Vancouver: UBC Centre for the Study of Curriculum and Instruction, 1984): 7-29.

[8]For examples of some of the best work currently being done in curriculum history see three books written or edited by Ivor Goodson: *School Subjects and Curriculum Change* (London: Croom Helm, 1983); *Social Histories of the Secondary Curriculum: Subjects for Study* (London: Falmer Press, 1985); *The Making of Curriculum: Essays in the Social History of Education* (London, Falmer Press, forthcoming). For a discussion of problems associated with writing curriculum history, see Goodson, "Towards Curriculum History," in *Social Histories* , pp. 1-9. For university level curriculum problems, see Patricia Jasen, "Rhetoric and Reform: The Liberal Arts Curriculum in the English-Canadian University," paper read at the Canadian Historical Association Annual Meeting, Montreal, 1985.

[9]George S. Tomkins, "Stability and Change in the Canadian Curriculum," in J. Donald Wilson, ed., *Canadian Education in the 1980s* (Calgary: Detselig, 1981), p. 135. See also his forthcoming *A Common Countenance: Stability and Change in the Canadian Curriculum* (Toronto: Prentice-Hall).

[10]Quoted in David Macleod, "A Live Vaccine: The YMCA and Male Adolescence in the United States and Canada, 1870-1920," *Histoire sociale/Social History,* XI (May 1978): 24.

[11]Gerald Friesen, *The Canadian Prairies: A History* (Toronto: University of Toronto Press, 1984), p. 269.

[12]See John H. Thompson, *The Harvests of War: The Prairie West, 1914-1918* (Toronto: McClelland and Stewart, 1978); Donald Avery, *'Dangerous Foreigners': European Immigrant Workers and Labour Radicalism in Canada 1896-1932* (Toronto: McClelland and Stewart, 1979); Frances Swyripa and John H. Thompson, eds., *Loyalties in Conflict: Ukrainians in Canada During the Great War* (Edmonton: Canadian Institute for Ukrainian Studies, 1983): Bill Maciejko, *Educating Ukrainian-Canadians: Ethnicity and Hegemony in the Schools of Manitoba, An Historical Perspective* (Winnipeg: University of Manitoba, Monographs in Education series, forthcoming).

[13]Wilson, "Observations," p. 17.

[14]See Bryan D. Palmer, *Working-Class Experience: The Rise and Reconstitution of Canadian Labour, 1800-1980* (Toronto: Butterworth, 1983).

[15]Kenneth McNaught, "Violence in Canadian History," in John S. Moir, ed., *Character and Circumstance: Essays in Honour of Donald Grant Creighton* (Toronto: Macmillan, 1970), pp. 66-84.

[16]Elizabeth Fox-Genovese and Eugene D. Genovese, "The Political Crisis of Social History: A Marxian Perspective," *Journal of Social History* , 2 (Winter 1976): 213, 219.

[17]Bruce Curtis, "Policing Pedagogical Space: Educational Administration in Canada West," paper read at the Canadian Historical Association Annual Meeting, Montreal, 1985, p. 23.

[18]Harold Silver, *Education as History* (London: Methuen, 1983), pp. 239-40.

[19]Harold Silver, "Historian in a Policy Field: a British Chef in Paris?" *History of Education Review*, XIV: 1 (1985): 4,5.

[20]For another example of a school system that evolved as a product of social demand, see François Furet and Jacques Ozouf, *Lire et écrire: l'alphabétisation des Français de Calvin à Jules Ferry*, 2 vols. (Paris: Editions de Minuit, 1977).

[21]Jones' evolution can be traced through such representative works as "'We Cannot . . ;. Allow it to be Run by Those Who Do Not Understand Education': Agricultural Schooling in the Twenties," *B.C. Studies*, 39 (Autumn 1978): 30-60; "The *Zeitgeist* of Western Settlement: Education and the Myth of the Land," in J. D. Wilson and D. C. Jones, eds., *Schooling and Society in Twentieth Century British Columbia* (Calgary, Detselig, 1980), pp. 71-89; *Midways, Judges and Smooth-Tongued Fakirs* (Saskatoon: Western Producer, 1983); *We'll All Be Buried Down Here: The Prairie Dryland Disaster, 1917-1926* (Edmonton: Alberta Historical Society, forthcoming); "The Canadian Prairie Dryland Disaster and the Reshaping of 'Expert' Farm Wisdom," *Journal of Rural Studies*, I: 2 (1985): 135-46.

[22]Gaffield, "Going Back to School," p. 41.

[23]For the prairie West as a distinctive region, see Gerald Friesen, "The Prairie West Since 1945: an Historical Survey," in A. W. Rasporich, ed., *The Making of the Modern West: Western Canada Since 1945* (Calgary: University of Calgary Press, 1984), pp. 1-10. For a new history of Manitoba education, see Alexander Gregor and Keith Wilson, *The Development of Education in Manitoba* (Dubuque: Kendall Hunt, 1984).

[24]David Gagan and H. E. Turner, "Social History in Canada: A Report on the 'State of the Art,' *Archivaria*, 14 (Summer 1982): 34.

Curriculum

2

Shifting Perspectives:
Early British Columbia Textbooks from 1872 to 1925*

Harro Van Brummelen

Authorized textbooks have played an important role in determining British Columbia's school curriculum. A relatively small number of textbooks have been used to shape children's views of their society. These textbooks have reflected the popularly-approved religious, moral, political, economic, social and cultural ideas of the dominant societal group; therefore an analysis of them gives us insight into the mores and attitudes of Canadian anglophone leadership during the late nineteenth and early twentieth centuries.

This chapter traces how the world view, i.e., the set of assumptions held about the basic makeup of the world and of society, gradually shifted in B.C.'s textbooks between 1872 and 1925 — a period that set the stage for Canada's entry into modern society. As McKillop has pointed out, this was a period during which the universal moral authority of Christianity gradually gave way to more liberal, secular and critical views of society — but ones that were still rooted in a strong sense of cultural moralism.[1] This development was clearly evident in Canadian textbooks. Using all the readers, many of the history and geography books, and a selection of the science, health and mathematics texts prescribed during the half century following the passing of B.C.'s first Public School Act, this chapter analyzes the extent of change in the views of religion and morality, of Canada as a nation, of science, culture and progress, and of the child and his society. The 1925 cut-off date was the year the landmark progressive Putman-Weir report on education was released — a time when the impact of modern industrialization was making itself felt, when Canadian consciousness was being promoted by political and cultural leaders, and when social gospel thinking was resulting in such things as the founding of the United Church of Canada and the institution of old-age pensions.

In the 1840s Egerton Ryerson had already prescribed standard textbooks in Ontario, hoping to create a common set of values among those who would use them. John Jessop, B.C.'s first superintendent of education, copied Ryerson's pattern of province-wide prescription in his efforts to promote social harmony and homogeneous citizenship. Within three weeks of his appointment in 1872, he approved a list of prescribed textbooks.[2] Almost all were books on the Ontario list, with the first prescribed readers being the *Canadian*

---

*This chapter is reprinted from *B.C. Studies,* 60 (Winter 1983-84); 3-27, with permission.

Series of Reading Books,[3] popularly known as *The Red Series* — books that were Canadian revisions of the Irish National Readers that Ryerson in 1846 had introduced as an antidote to the various American readers in use in Ontario at that time.[4] However, Jessop was more successful than Ryerson in imposing uniform textbooks, both because most schools in British Columbia were new and because there were few books of any kind in the frontier settlements outside of Victoria. Moreover, Jessop regularly visited all the schools himself, publishing charts showing which textbooks were used by each school. Already in his fourth annual report he could show that all schools used the prescribed books in all subject areas.[5] The pattern was set: even today British Columbia uses prescription of textbooks as a major curriculum constraint on its schools.

The practice of using specifically Ontario texts did not, of course, continue. Richardson in his 1921 survey of Canadian schools reported that only two of Ontario's books were then adopted in British Columbia.[6] There remained, nonetheless, a great deal of similarity in content and approach among texts used at any one time in English Canada. Many of the observations and conclusions of this chapter also, therefore, apply to textbooks used in other provinces, and thus extend Sheehan's critique of the reading books authorized in Alberta from 1908 to 1947.[7]

Thanks to Canada's tightly-knit anglophone cultural leadership and its centralized school systems, a relatively small group of educators and intellectuals directly influenced the writing and choice of textbooks. Ryerson had been principal of Victoria College and had close ties with the intellectual community of his day. Philosophy professor George Paxton Young had not only been school inspector but for some time was chairman of Ontario's Central Committee of Examiners, which gave advice about textbook adoption.[8] Writer and professor Goldwin Smith was involved in revising Colliers' histories to remove religiously offensive passages.[9] McGill's principal Sir John William Dawson wrote a number of science textbooks that were widely used in Canadian schools at the end of the nineteenth century. With some time lag, many of the textbooks prepared or selected by men such as these found a place in the British Columbia school system.

Religion: Thy Will Alone Let All Enthrone [10]

British Columbia's first prescribed textbooks all assumed a literal interpretation of the Bible and a belief in orthodox Christian doctrines. Colliers' *Outlines of General History*, for example, held that the world was created in 4004 B.C. and that Adam's fall into sin, the deluge, and the story of the Tower of Babel were all literal world history events.[11] Lennie's *Grammar* used many Scriptural texts and maxims such as "Were they wise, they would read the Scriptures daily."[12] It was made clear that faith and religion should be central in a person's life: children were enjoined to lean upon the Lord every hour.[13] All people lived by God's kindness, and hymns to the Creator taught children gratefully to celebrate the praises of God, the fountain of mind and of intellect.[14]

Man's fall into sin, these books argued, caused our current state of decay, and it was only by doing God's will that children could avoid the ignominious death of the wicked. Christ's salvation delivered them not only from sin and death but also from ignorance and from the calamities of life.[15] At the same time, the books were careful to remain non-sectarian, as the first Public School Act demanded, and perhaps it was the Presbyterian emphasis of the grammar book that was authorized in 1872 that contributed to Jessop pointedly choosing Lennie's *Grammar* instead.[16]

In the 1880s and 1890s, Christian beliefs were still assumed to be necessary for a productive life. An 1894 composition book stated that faith in God led to cheerfulness and that almost the only certain truth was the existence of God.[17] While geography books of the time contained only a few explicit references to religion, some insisted that belief in the Bible as God's Word resulted both in fear of God and in loyalty to the Crown.[18] Happy, therefore, was the family where Mother told a Bible story every night.[19] While selected Scripture passages, too, were presented in the readers of the 1880s, references to religion nonetheless became on the whole less frequent: the Canadian Reader's *Second Primer* contained just two.[20] Moreover, the emphasis of such references shifted from honouring God to more direct moral concerns: "The true calling of a Christian is not to do extraordinary things, but to do ordinary things in an extraordinary way."[21] In the same way, the Methodist revival no longer was held to have returned the people to serving God, but to have brought about moral reforms and efforts to lessen the misery and ignorance of the poor and oppressed.[22] There was a gradual but distinct move towards social gospel thinking.

As the new century began to unfold, there were even fewer religious allusions. The 1901 *Second Primer* contained only a picture of the infant Samuel, without any explanation.[23] Religion and the church were still considered useful, but for such reasons as preventing lawlessness among the native people and helping them become part of civilized society.[24] A secular wake-up song replaced the traditional morning prayer or hymn in a 1916 reader, though it still contained an occasional hint of the existence of a God: "I only know I cannot drift / Beyond His love and care."[25] The transition to a secular view of society was almost complete, however. The new temple had become "home, home! sweet, sweet home!" Christmas and Thanksgiving had become family festivals with no religious significance.[26] By the early 1920s, despite the continued inclusion of several psalms and Bible stories in the prescribed readers, the basic beliefs and doctrines of Christianity were not considered all that important or relevant. The church was now deemed important for the enrichment of national life and the development of the ideals of right living. Its work was not to convert people to Christianity but to improve the moral and social conditions of society and in this way to be a great civilizing force.[27]

Thus the content of textbooks gradually changed from an acceptance of the fundamentals of traditional Christian beliefs in 1872 to the approval of religious institutions as useful social service agencies in 1925. It is significant that the influential Queen's philosophy professor John Watson over this same period (1872-1922) taught that the church was an organization for making men better, a view that had been accepted by textbook writers of the mid-1920s.[28]

Morality: Honour, Truth, and Self-Command

In the late nineteenth century, textbooks indicated a close relationship between religion and morality. Because God made children breathe the breath of life, they must always do His will. This meant speaking the truth, not being wild or rude, and listening to the conscience God had implanted in them. Such obedience would result in God's taking them as lambs to His fold.[29] Bible stories were told for their moral dimension. The point of the story of Joseph was not God's care for His people but Joseph's nobility in forgiving his brothers.[30] The story of Moses emphasized the importance of knowing the Ten Commandments.[31] A morning prayer in one reader summed up not only the moral-religious relationship but also the characteristics of the moral imperative for children: "Father, help thy little child / Make me truthful, good, and mild, / Kind, obedient, modest, meek, / Mindful of the words I speak."[32]

These stories exhibited the Golden Rule and were unambiguous about what was right and wrong.[33] Children were encouraged to work hard and use their time well, and to be humble, prudent and courageous. Passions such as indolence, disobedience, miserliness and envy would have immediate catastophic results. Cleanliness truly was next to godliness and lack of it went hand-in-hand with other evils. One ne'er-do-well thus turned out to be not only black as a crow but also a dunce at school and a thief.[34] True repentance was required to overcome such evils.

Students were taught moral lessons through frequent aphorisms used to end stories, to fill empty spaces in readers, and as examples in grammar books: You are happy, because you are good; Indolence undermines the foundation of every virtue; When asked to do right, never say, "I don't want to."[35] Thus students were taught a vision of life that lauded the work ethic, the moral law, and love for other people. It was assumed that parents and others in authority always knew best, and that therefore children should give blind obedience to their elders.

True greatness was the moral greatness displayed by heroes like Wolfe and Nelson — a greatness based on love of virtue and truth, on devotion to duty, freedom and religion, and on defiance of peril.[36] All school subjects were to do their part in encouraging such moral greatness. History, for example, teaches us to admire and esteem the brave, the honest, and the self-denying; and to despise and condemn the cowardly, the base, and the selfish. We are led to see that virtue preserves and strengthens a nation, while vice inevitably causes decay and weakness. . . . History, then, is a great teacher of morals.[37]

Gradually, however, the number of explicit moral injunctions lessened. By the 1920s authors hoped that children would draw their own moral conclusions from the selections. It was now through the stories themselves that children were taught that procrastination led to various evils, that pride went before a fall, and that the disadvantaged must be loved.[38] By this time, moreover, the bond between religion and morality had been cut. Morality was no longer seen as being a consequence of serving God or as a way of avoiding the wrath of God. Rather, the virtues of courage, unselfishness, loyalty, patience and justice were characteristics of good citizenship.[39] It now was not God but the Union Jack that told pupils to be brave, pure and true.[40] It now was as much the government as the church that protected the morals of the community. And the cause of moral decadence and misdeeds no longer lay with children themselves and their sinfulness, but with their environment, particularly lack of good home training and bad companionship. To have the wayward become good and useful citizens did not, in consequence, require repentance as it did in the 1870s and 1880s, but simply an alteration in the circumstances that produced their wrong-doing.[41]

Morality in the textbooks had thus been severed from its religious roots. Piety was now seldom mentioned. However, virtue was still held to be a keystone of good citizenship. But by whom and how that virtue was to be defined had become uncertain. The stage had been set for the ethical relativism of the late twentieth century.

Children and Their World: the Loyal Heart, the Constant Mind, the Courage to be True.

Throughout the period from 1872 to 1922, an ideal of personhood was held before children that changed little except with respect to the importance of personal piety. Children were to develop their God-given abilities by showing backbone and working diligently.[42] Individualism was stressed, with events often being grouped about men of strong personality who overcame hardship and adversity through sheer determination.[43] Students were to develop character by sticking to what they were doing and following the moral law.

Idleness and ignorance produced many vices for children, and the glorious privilege to labour was man's most noble dower. In 1867 the main reason given for studying Latin and Greek was to make the life of a young student what it ought to be, a life of considerable labour.[44] In 1925 not only idleness but also lawlessness and privation could still, it was thought, be remedied by the schools since it was ignorance caused by a lack of education which led to laziness, poverty and crime.[45] Particularly during the nineteenth century, success was always shown to be the result of hard work. Children were, however, taught to accept their lot in life. If Providence sent them a cross, they were to take it up willingly and accept it with contentment. While, texts thus insisted, it was possible to achieve personal well-being through determination, children were also, in some circumstances, to endure poverty without its affecting their happiness.[46]

The importance of a happy family life was emphasized throughout these decades, but for changing reasons. In 1872 mothers were important because they taught children godliness and obedience.[47] Children were considered miniature adults, and were expected to contribute to the work of the family: "I must be learning / To hem and to sew, / And to dress my dear brother."[48] Animals and birds were used to present ideal family life: "Mother keeps you warm, / Father brings you food, / Safe within your nest, / Happy little brood."[49] Around the turn of the century, the idealized version of middle-class family life was presented as one with two or three children of different genders, where Mother stayed at home and regularly played with the children and taught them charity for the poor, where Father helped with school work, and where pets formed an integral part of the family.[50] By 1925 emphasis was placed much more heavily on the way in which good family life was the prerequisite for children becoming useful citizens. Togetherness in discussions, songs, games, picnics and entertainment would lead to such marks of good citizenship as truthfulness and honesty, thoughtfulness and unselfishness, and obedience and self-control.[51]

In the meantime the relationship between parents and their children had gradually changed; by 1915 children were sometimes portrayed in situations where they in a good-natured way showed up their parents — in contrast with the unquestioned deferential distance between parents and children of the Victorian age:

> Mother: "Where did you get that fish?" Tom: "Ha! Ha! You said I couldn't catch a fish, mother. But you see I did."[52]

In 1895 philosopher John Watson wrote that the moral life was the gradual realization of the ideal life. The ideal of humanity, he continued, was therefore not a *mere* ideal: it was an ideal continually in process of realization. Hence, Watson held, the individual could find himself and could become moral only by contributing his share to its realization.[53] Textbook writers around the turn of the century were influenced by such idealism, and therefore it became important to show children the ideal world for which all should strive and to which all could contribute. Everything was good, pleasant and beautiful in the situations the readers presented. Little disrupted the perfect harmony: cows were friendly, blossoms were pretty, brooks were happy, children were healthy and spotlessly dressed, and the environment was serene and idyllic. Milkmaids liked their sanitized work, and farms always reaped plentiful crops. Children brought fine red flowers to their mammas. The dog protected even the little kittens! Slight flaws were soon set straight: "What is the matter with Dick's foot? He has a thorn in it . . . He will soon get the thorn out. Then he will drive home the six cows."[54] Children were to do their part in establishing this ideal by avoiding laziness, loving their parents and friends, and being obedient so that order could reign in home and school.[55] The only grating note was the warning on the inside covers of some of the supplementary readers that they were not to be taken away from the school-house and kept in the bookcase. During this time, David Wilson, in charge of textbook distribution in British Columbia, had difficulty both with such books disappearing and with school boards not providing proper locked bookcases.[56] The ideal, though presented, had not yet been reached.

Closely related to this idealism were two other themes. First, while around the 1880s life in large cities was featured as part of society's scientific and material progress,[57] in the beginning of this century country life was roman-ticized both in story and in art. Country life was beautiful and invigorating: things were better in the country, and it would be a blessing if every man were to do some farm work.[58] Also, the children's environment was given more attention. Pure water and sunlight and open air overcame pale cheeks and languid manners, and bathing was invigorating and prevented disease. If a child lived in the city, s/he should at least go to the country for holidays and there sleep in the open air.[59] Even though by the 1920s pictures had become more realistic, the peace and tranquillity of country life were stressed, and life, in the readers at least, was devoid of cities, industries and cars.[60]

A second theme that confronted children around the turn of the century concerned the importance of alcohol and tobacco temperance. Readers labelled alcohol a formidable vice that was a great source of crime and want.[61] Rich-ardson's *Public School Temperance* emphasized that it was clear that water was the one fluid provided for men by Providence and Nature, and its use instead of alcohol was to cause children to become wise, industrious and happy. Alcohol and tobacco resulted in dull minds and stupidity as well as in stunted growth.[62] It was claimed that scientific evidence showed that total abstainers at age twenty had a life expectancy three times that of moderate drinkers, that children of intemperate parents inherited disordered bodies and minds, and that Americans were more alert than Germans and Englishmen because of their more moderate drinking habits.[63]

Children, to sum up, could construct an ideal world for themselves. As long as they worked hard, obeyed the moral law, contributed to family life, were diligent in their studies and shunned the evils of alcohol and tobacco their lives were to be happy even if they were not wealthy. During the nine-teenth century family life was formal, especially the relationship between Father and his children. Later, a small friendly family that lived in the coun-try, or, at least, was able to sojourn there from time to time, and whose members cared for each other and for animals and plants, was held before children as the ideal. What remained constant was that children were to have loyal hearts, constant minds and the courage to be true.

The Evolution of Science: Proving Once More the Dreams
of Men Divine

Science in 1872 was intended to lead to an understanding of the infinite wisdom and goodness of Providence: every part of Creation was in harmony with a plan of absolute benevolence.[64] The theme that physical objects, plants and animals were witnesses of the one plan of Creative Wisdom recurred again and again.[65] William Dawson emphasized in an 1883 reader that true scientific explanations would be in harmony with the Biblical creation account.[66]

However, science textbooks tended to be less explicit than readers: scientists were being caught up in the spirit of critical inquiry. Both Macadam's 1872 chemistry text and Dawson's 1886 *Handbook of Zoology* were devoid of religious references until the very last section when, almost as an afterthought, it was mentioned that man owed everything to God, and that he was the only moral, religious and responsible being who could comprehend the plans of the Creator.[67] Gradually a sense of God's handiwork was replaced with awareness of the wonders of nature. J. W. Robertson's 1909 preface to an agriculture and nature study book had distinct pantheistic overtones: "We are all part of Nature. Our lives — the transient and the eternal, the human and the divine in us — are sustained by natural processes under natural laws."[68] Robertson still manifested a tendency to see agriculture and nature study in religious terms: "We are all trustees of life and its opportunities for the children. The main thing in the trust is to have the next generation of trustees ready for their duty and privilege. 'Of such is the Kingdom of Heaven.'"[69] As late as 1916, indeed, science textbooks were still careful to avoid evolution controversies. Darwin's influence was nonetheless evident in such things as the chapter headings of a *Beginners' Botany* textbook: *The Struggle to Live* and *The Survival of the Fit*.[70] Science, despite some obvious reservations, was being transformed from the handmaiden of religion to a field of investigation in which Darwin's basic approach was implicitly accepted.

What kind of science was taught? In the 1870s, both readers and science books contained a great deal of factual, descriptive material about physical and biological objects and phenomena. Usually the emphasis was on everyday applications of science. Students were taught not to hurt or mutilate animals and plants.[71] And, while science was shown to have led to astounding progress, there were already some ecological concerns: "Country places generally," noted one text, ". . . even in the New World, no doubt get a share of the bad gases evolved from our populous towns."[72] Yet it was stressed that every department of human knowledge had benefited from the influence of the scientific spirit and its methods of inquiry.[73] Twentieth-century books included more investigations and questions for the students to answer: "Try," a text enjoined its young readers, "to find a seed that will float on the water. How might that seed be carried from one place to another?" The way the material was presented thus gradually manifested the spirit of critical inquiry.[74]

The Concept of Progress: Star of the North, Where Justice Rules from Shore to Shore

The advance of science was looked upon by nineteenth-century textbooks as one of the measures of progress. One 1867 reader lauded the inestimable benefits of the applications of the steam engine. The trans-Atlantic telegraph cable was held to have created a golden, God-given bond between nations. Further examples of the march of science included ships, telephones, phonographs, photographs and electricity.[75]

Progress was being made on other fronts, too. In Canada, a hardy and vigorous population was making wilderness into bountiful farmland and progressive industrial towns; the education system was leading to literary and social advance; and governments were passing wise and sane legislation.[76] Truly, with her magnificent resources and vital people, with her pure and healthy domestic life, and with her excellent forms of government and education, Canada gave ample evidence that the promise of a great nation was being realized.[77] British Columbia was, moreover, in many respects the most progressive of all Canadian provinces.[78] Optimism was boundless, progress inevitable. Utopia seemed just around the corner. Western civilization would reach its apex in twentieth-century Canada.

This concept of progress rested on two main pillars of support: first, a confidence in the continued economic development of Canada; and, second, the belief that Canada was the true inheritor of the British ideals of justice and liberty. Economically the early twentieth century knew few limits: British Columbia had unbounded potential in mineral, lumber and agricultural wealth and could take pride in its fine harbours and steamships; great advances had been made in the grain industries and the up-to-date cities of the Prairies; and the building of the railroad symbolized the rapid progress being made.[79] Such progress was rooted in the power and wisdom of great companies like the Hudson's Bay Company as well as in individual honesty, intelligence, foresight and strength.[80] Mathematics books showed Canadians actively engaged in all manner of commercial and industial enterprise.[81] Despite occasional disputes between labour and management (caused in part, these books encouraged their readers to think, by the Chinese who, though industrious, worked for cheaper wages[82]), and a recognition that society's members were not always rewarded according to their merit, Canada was held to be rapidly taking its place as one of the great producing countries of the world.[83] This faith in continuous material progress, apparent soon after 1872, did not abate even with World War I.

The other great pillar of progress was British justice and liberty. Its basis was the spirit of British law. It was England that championed truth, righteousness and freedom. She still led all peoples in the struggle against vice and tyranny, and from her all lands derived hope and encouragement.[84] Canada, textbooks proclaimed, was the full beneficiary of this remarkable heritage. Little progress had been made by New France because of the French love of absolutism, monopoly and feudalism. Where, however, the sons of France had failed, the sons of Britain were to succeed, thanks to their happy familiarity with conditions of toleration, freedom and equality.[85]

Canada's potential would, the texts insisted, come to fruition only if its vast wealth and its capacity to grow morally were developed in association with high ethical standards on the one hand and a zeal for work on the other.[86] A progressive future depended on a firm devotion to morality and religion. Prosperity and happiness were contingent on Canadian energy, ambition, self-reliance, skill and enterprise.[87] In this way, within the framework provided by Canada's economic potential and British principles of justice and liberty, Canada would be able to combine the very best of the Old and New Worlds. Her continuing development would ensure that the twentieth century would belong to Canada: *that* was the message for all students.

Our Canada: Part of Our Wide-Extending Empire

"Canada is one of the brightest gems in the British crown," the grammar book in use in Ontario in 1872 declared.[88] British Columbia's John Jessop seemed, however, more impressed with the crown than with the gem. He prescribed a British Empire history book that limited its discussion of Canada to little more than half a page. While B.C.'s first readers gave individual histories of the Maritime provinces, Quebec, Vancouver Island and British Columbia,[89] not until the mid-1880s were British Columbia students presented with a systematic treatment of Canadian history or geography. It was as if the last spike at Craigellachie in 1885 not only fulfilled the promise that made British Columbia enter Confederation but also made educational leaders decide that British Columbia was finally and truly part of the Dominion.

That Dominion, the textbooks emphasized, was rooted in British traditions. While Canada's origin in New France was acknowledged, one of the main early heroes was General Wolfe: the well-known painting of his heroic death after the capture of Quebec was given full-page treatment in many books. While Montcalm was recognized as a brave soldier, the French retreat from Quebec was called disgraceful.[90] From that day on, the books indicated, the hand of Providence entrusted to the British the destiny of the New World, and through them, true progress materialized.[91]

Loyalty to and love of Britain and its empire were vigorously encouraged in the textbooks from Confederation to the 1920s. Canada's link with England would keep Canada safe from tyranny, Sir John A. Macdonald was quoted as saying.[92] When students were asked to memorize Sir Walter Scott's "Love of Country," it was not Canada but England that was hailed.[93] It was the honour of England that demanded the defence of Canada: "The meteor flag of England / Shall yet terrific burn."[94] As late as 1922 the Empire continued to have emotional appeal: "Children of the Empire, you are brothers all; / children of the Empire, answer to the call; / Let your voices mingle, lift your heads and sing, / God save dear old Britain, and God save Britain's king!"[95]

Patriotism was held in high esteem, but it consisted of loyalty to the British constitution and laws since they best secured liberty and prosperity and linked children with the proud and noble traditions of Canada's national history.[96] Only within this context were children charged to love their country, believe in her, honour her, work for her, and live and die for her. Queen's Principal George Grant, writing in a text widely used in B.C., summed up this dualistic approach to patriotism when he said that loyalty to the Dominion involved seeking a common imperial citizenship with common responsibilities and a common inheritance.[97]

Only gradually did a separate Canadian identity become recognized as important. Gammell's 1907 *Elementary History of Canada* saw as yet no sign of separation from the motherland; Canada could still be presented as subordinate to Britain; she might be mistress of her own house, but she was still very much her mother's daughter.[98] By 1921, however, this sentiment had disappeared. "In her relations with the foreign countries," one text noted, "Canada has become less and less dependent upon the motherland. . . ." As an independent member she signed the Treaty of Peace and was enrolled in the League of Nations.[99] The apron strings to the motherland were slowly being loosened. After World War I, in fact, the "Dominion Hymn" ("God bless our wide dominion") and "Canada! Maple Land!" started to appear alongside "God Save the King," while the Union Jack had to share its glory with the Canadian red ensign.[100]

Although war was thought cruel,[101] it was considered necessary at times in order to uphold British ideals. The many selections about British war heroes made clear that there was little doubt that God was always on the side of the British. The typical British officer was clean-cut, frank, fearless and kindly, and he showed love of honour, contempt of danger and pride of race.[102] Moreover, the British showed their inherent magnanimity and love of freedom and justice in granting a great deal of self-government to conquered people soon after their defeat, as they had done in Quebec and South Africa.[103] World War I resulted in renewed idolization of war and its heroes, and teachers were instructed to let the class play soldiers, carrying the flag.[104] For the first time, Canadian war heroes were also described, although in the context of British valour and imperial manhood.[105]

In characterizing Canada, texts often found it necessary to come to grips with two special problems. One was the United States; the other the country's indigenous population. Matters, in both cases, were resolved in the same way: Americans and Indians alike found themselves dismissed as possessing little in the way of redeeming features.

Only grudgingly did textbooks during this period admit the existence of the United States. Robertson dealt with the inglorious American War of Independence in a few lines, carefully pointing out that British misfortune in North America was balanced by victories at sea over the fleets of France and Spain.[106] Reference to the injustice of slavery was accompanied by reminders that the Canadian provinces had abolished it in 1793 and 1803.[107] Discussion of the War of 1812 gave opportunity not only to make the point that the Americans had been beaten, but also to say that they had attacked an unoffending people, justly ruining their own commerce and losing their national honour. Canada, by contrast, was shown to have been greatly strengthened by the glorious part that Canadians had taken in this unprovoked war.[108] The Civil War was looked at by one book solely in terms of its effect on Britain: "In 1861," it reported, "a civil war broke out in the United States of America, which led to great suffering among the operatives in the cotton factories of Lancashire."[109] While, in sum, the relationship of Canada to the Empire was described in terms of imperial unity and general progress, Canada's involvement with America focused only on disputes and problems. The Americans were little more than a troublesome and self-centred offshoot from the British Empire. Truly great Americans like George Washington were citizens of the world, and no country could appropriate them. Breaking with England could only have harmed the cause of true liberty, justice and progress in the United States.[110]

The views given of Canada's native people were, generally speaking, negative ones. The native people were at best noble savages, with an emphasis on the savage, throughout the period under discussion: Gammell's 1921 revision of Robertson's 1892 *Public School History of England and Canada* left his descriptions of native people and their activities untouched. Indians, by and large, were portrayed as cruel and revengeful, spending their time gambling, smoking and feasting. Even though the treachery of the French (not the English!) *vis-à-vis* Iroquois chiefs was admitted, the Iroquois were singled out as filled with hate, revenge and bitterness in committing many lawless acts of aggression in their fierce and stealthy warfare.[111]

The native peoples of British Columbia were generally described as being friendly, though one reader claimed that the irresponsible behaviour of some of them during the gold rush naturally provoked reprisals.[112] Their culture was, however, portrayed in unsympathetic terms: totem poles were singled out as rude, imperfect monuments, while the culture as a whole was bound to collapse before the advance of civilization.[113] Their religion, too, was inferior since it, unlike Christianity, moved them only through fear or selfishness.[114]

A few more balanced accounts did exist. One text concluded that native people were always ready to help each other, that they lived peaceably with each other, and that they were hospitable and sociable. It also indicated that the settlers were not always just in their treatment of native people and that this may have been a contributing factor to the horrors of Indian warfare.[115] One of the first readers in British Columbia was, indeed, more moderate than some later ones, for it conceded that how one saw a culture very much depended on his own vantage point: "Savages we call them, because their manners differ from ours, which we call the perfection of civility; they think the same of theirs."[116] Generally, though, the argument asserted the superiority of white civilization. Indians might be indolent, but a benevolent white person could show them the value of their labour.[117] The only wise and brave and humane and noble Indians were those who became Christians or associated themselves with white civilization, such as Joseph Brant and Tecumseh. Except for drawings of men of this sort, pictures made native people look backward at best, brutal and savage at worst.[118] What more, textbooks thus combined in arguing, could anyone desire than to become a British subject, and to be part of the glorious Empire that stood for truth, courage, liberty and freedom?

Culture and Literacy: Sons Must Follow Where Their Sires Have Led

Until World War I, readers beyond the initial primers contained a rich treasury of British literature, including works of Shakespeare, Milton, Swift, Coleridge, Burns, Sir Walter Scott and Wordsworth.[119] Both readers and history books lauded the nineteenth century as one of the richest in English literature, and the higher-level readers made use of works by Dickens, Browning, Matthew Arnold, Robert Louis Stevenson and, especially, the Poet Laureate of the last half of the nineteenth century, Alfred Lord Tennyson. While gradually more American selections were introduced, it continued to be emphasized that there was no more priceless legacy than the heritage of English language and literature.[120] By the 1920s, however, the number of British selections outnumbered American ones only slightly, and Canadian selections comprised only one-fifth of one commonly used anthology.[121] Earlier books pointed out, quite correctly, that little Canadian literature was available, and during the nineteenth century most Canadian selections involved historical or geographical descriptions of regions of Canada, or transcripts of speeches. Anything British was not, of course, considered foreign. In fact, there were suspicions that anything Canadian could not quite live up to the standards set in Britain.

While the readers in the higher grades gradually incorporated more American and Canadian selections, those at lower levels began to include more fairytales and fables, as well as stories with a plot that appealed to children such as the Pied Piper of Hamelin and selections from Heidi. The beginning primers started to show a trend towards greater emphasis on decoding skills and less on meaningful content. In the nineteenth century even the first stories presented had had some meaning — even if it consisted of narrow moral maxims without much literary value. Now the content became more repetitive and superficial: "One kitten plays. Two kittens play. Three kittens play. Three little kittens play, play, play." [122] This particular primer, in fact, boasted that it contained nearly six thousand word repetitions, with a base vocabulary of only 258 words.[123]

Some of the books published early in the century did attempt to generate interest in art and aesthetics. The *Art-Literature Readers*, provided free to every rural school in British Columbia, showed many two-tone reproductions of paintings. While the choice reflected the idealism of the age (e.g., paintings of Paul Peel, Dupré and Millet), it was the first time most pupils were familiarized with the characteristics of various schools of art. The children were encouraged to interpret the art: there were questions about the paintings as well as biographical sketches of some of the artists. While this series gave the most comprehensive treatment of art, other books described such things as the beauty of Westminster Abbey and the way in which Beethoven's Moonlight Sonata came to be written.[124] In addition, some books tried to engender a general appreciation of aesthetics: "Even," suggested one of them, "a happy home or school is made more attractive, and dearer to the hearts of its members, if the grounds about it are tastefully adorned with trees, shrubs, flowers, and grassy lawns."[125]

And We Will Guard Our Own

Textbooks between 1872 and 1925 were compiled and chosen by a relatively small group of educational leaders. Such leaders ensured that the books presented how they believed children should act and what they should think. Canada's future was to unfold within a well-defined framework based on a British, Christian heritage. Of course, with a vast and only sparsely-settled expanse, with the constant threat of American annexation, with an often hostile native population, with a plurality of nationalities and religions, with poor communication and transportation, and with an almost non-existent sense of national identity, it would have been surprising if textbooks, and consequently schools, had not held before the students a common Canadian vision of life and society that the leaders wanted to inculcate.

That vision, as we have seen, was rooted in a strong moral imperative. At first, this was closely intertwined with the beliefs of traditional Christianity, but gradually it loosened itself, though not completely, from its religious roots. From a literal interpretation of the Bible and a strong sense of sin and need of redemption in Jesus Christ, religion came to be viewed in terms of promoting morality and a sense of social justice. God was seen less as a stern taskmaster with an all-seeing eye and more as a gracious Lord of Love. The Golden Rule nonetheless continued to be held before the children. Virtue was rewarded; evil was punished. By 1925 the moral dimension might be less explicit with children being involved in drawing their own conclusions. Living a moral life nonetheless remained a powerful ideal.

The model of Canada that was to shape young citizens also changed. Canada was shown to have unlimited resources, and, as such, to have the potential for unrivalled economic prosperity. Canadian Confederation was solidly grounded in the tradition of British parliamentary government, and in the British ideals of justice and liberty. It combined the best of both the Old and the New Worlds: for instance, it had internal self-government and a kind of democratic equality but at the same time stood one with the whole British Empire. Children were thus confronted with a picture of a government that was benevolent and that gave its citizens more freedom and justice than any other nation except Britain, and with a society that had a bright future if its people would continue to be upright and diligent.

In time the country was portrayed as having become more independent, drawing away from the Empire and managing its own destiny. It was also, however, seen as having remained very much committed to British principle of tradition, and so, in the political as in the moral sphere, continuities were much in evidence. The texts thus continued to do what they had always done: they attempted simultaneously to enforce clear-cut standards of individual responsibility and a sense of how life in the larger community was to be understood.

While, then, the concept of nationhood has always been a difficult one for Canada to define and develop, the textbooks tried to do so, first exclusively in terms of the British heritage and later, in terms of combining what was considered the best of the old and the new:

> And we will guard our own,
> Our Canada,
> From snow to sea,
> One hope, one home, one shining destiny.[126]

Notes

[1] A. B. McKillop, *A Disciplined Intelligence: Critical Inquiry and Canadian Thought in the Victorian Era* (Montreal: McGill-Queen's University Press, 1979).

[2] F. Henry Johnson, *John Jessop: Gold Seeker and Educator* (Vancouver: Mitchell Press, 1971), p. 82.

[3] *Canadian Series of School Books*, originally published in 1867 by several publishers. The volumes used for this paper were *First Book of Reading Lessons, Part I*; *First Book, Part II; Second Book* (Toronto: Warwick, 1867, 1880); *Third Book* (Toronto: Canada Publ. Co. 1867, 1880); *Fourth Book* (Toronto: James Campbell, 1867) and *Fifth Book* (Toronto: Gage, 1867, 1869, 1881). Unless otherwise indicated, all textbooks referred to in this chapter were prescribed or authorized in British Columbia. The dates I have used throughout the chapter are the dates indicated in the copies of the books examined. If I show two dates, they are the earliest and latest dates shown in the book. Often, revisions will have been made between the earlier and later dates. Many nineteenth-century readers were printed by different publishers at slightly different times — and sometimes under different titles. Nor are the dates always reliable; I found two instances where a speech or event was recorded that occurred *after* the indicated date of publication or printing.

⁴E. T. White, *Public School Text-Books in Ontario* (London: Chapman, 1922), p. 9.

⁵This is indicated in a chart in the *Fourth Annual Report of the Public Schools of British Columbia* (Victoria, 1875), p. 37.

⁶William Leeds Richardson, *The Administration of the Schools in the Cities of the Dominion of Canada* (Toronto: J. M. Dent, 1922), p. 189.

⁷Nancy Sheehan, "Character Training and the Cultural Heritage: An Historical Comparison of Canadian Elementary Readers," in G. S. Tomkins, ed., *The Curriculum in Canada in Historical Perspective*, Sixth Yearbook of the Canadian Society for the Study of Education (Edmonton and Vancouver: CSSE, 1979), pp. 77-84. It was Sheehan's article that stimulated this analysis of B.C.'s textbooks.

⁸White, *Public School Text-Books in Ontario*, p. 11.

⁹Ibid., p. 62.

¹⁰The phrases for the headings are taken from two typical patriotic hymns that appeared in readers and literature anthologies in the 1920s and 1930s. The first one is "Lord of the Lands" by Albert Durrant Watson, printed as the last selection in *The Ryerson Book of Prose and Verse*, Book I (1927), and the second is "Star of the North" by Marjorie Pickthall, published in the revised edition of the same volume, *The Canada Book of Prose and Verse, Book I* (1932).

¹¹William F. Colliers, *Outlines of General History* (Toronto: Campbell, 1869).

¹²William Lennie, *The Principles of Grammar* (Toronto: Miller, 1869), p.62. This edition was a reprint of a book published since early in the nineteenth century.

¹³Ibid., p.54.

¹⁴See, for example, *Canadian Series of School Books, First Book of Reading Lessons, Part II*, p. 9, and *Fifth Book of Reading Lessons*, p. 379.

¹⁵*Canadian Series of School Books, Fourth Book of Reading Lessons* , pp. 349-50.

¹⁶The Ontario grammar contained examples from the Westminster Catechism such as "Man's chief end is to glorify God." See *An Analytical and Practical Grammar of the English Language* (Toronto: Miller, 1868, 1869), p. 207. Though part of the Canadian National Series of School Books, this text was actually a Canadian printing of an American text that had already been used for many years in Ontario without authorization.

¹⁷W. J. Alexander and M. F. Libby, *Composition from Models* (Toronto: Copp Clark, 1894), pp. 324-25. This book was only used as a reference in British Columbia.

¹⁸See, for example, *Lovell's Introductory Geographys* (Montreal: Lovell, 1896), p. 32. While this edition was not authorized in British Columbia, William Ellis Topping described related examples from J. George Hodgins' *Lovell's Easy Lessons in Geography* (Montreal: Lovell, 1876). For a more detailed description of early geography textbooks, see W. E. Topping, "The Historical Development of the Teaching of Geography in British Columbia," (M.A. thesis, University of British Columbia, 1963).

¹⁹*The Canadian Readers, The Second Primer* (Toronto: Gage, 1881), p. 64.

²⁰Ibid., pp. 20, 64. Other readers in this series were *Books III, IV, V* and *VI*. For examples of Bible passages, see, for example, *Book III*, pp. 101 ff.

²¹*The Canadian Readers, Book III* (Toronto: Gage, 1881), p. 131.

²²W. J. Robertson, *Public School History of England and Canada* (Toronto: Copp Clark, 1902), p. 143. The same quotation is found in the 1886 and 1892 editions. This 1902 British Columbia edition contains a fifteen-page appendix on B.C.'s history by R. E. Gosnell.

[23]*New Canadian Readers, A Second Primer*, Twentieth Century Edition (Toronto: Gage, 1901), frontispiece. Other volumes of this prescribed series included *A First Primer* and *Books I, II, III, IV.*

[24]D. M. Duncan, *The Story of the Canadian People* (Toronto: Morang, 1904, 1905), p. 387; Maria Lawson, *History of Canada* (Toronto: Gage, 1906, 1908), p. 58; and Maria Lawson and Rosalind Young, *A History and Geography of British Columbia (Toronto: Gage, 1906), pp. 64-67.* The latter two books were likely the first ones written by British Columbians. Journalist Maria Lawson was the eldest daughter of *Daily Colonist* editor Henry Lawson; Rosalind Young was Mrs. Henry Esson Young. See *Daily Colonist*, Dec. 7, 1968, p. 11.

[25]*The British Columbia Readers, Third Reader* (Toronto: Gage, 1916), pp. 9, 146. Other volumes of the latter series included the *Beginner's, First, Second* and *Fourth* Readers.

[26]*New Canadian Readers, A Second Primer*, p. 69; and *The British Columbia Readers, First Reader*, p. 54.

[27]For typical inclusion of passages from the Bible, see, for instance, *The Canadian Readers, Book V* (Toronto: Nelson and Gage, 1922). Other volumes in this series consulted for this chapter were *Books II, III* and *IV.* For the way in which the Christian church was viewed, see I. Gammell, *History of Canada* (Toronto: Gage, 1921, 1922), p. 285 and James McCaig, *Studies in Citizenship* (Toronto: Educational Book Co., 1925, 1931), p. 68.

[28]McKillop, *A Disciplined Intelligence*, p. 216. Of course, the views of teachers did not necessarily always correspond with those of the textbook authors. To what extent teachers reflected, for example, this view of the church in their classrooms is a separate question, one among others of this type that deserve further investigation.

[29]*Canadian Series of School Books, First Book of Reading Lessons, Part I*, pp. 9-11; *Part II*, p. 9; *Fifth Book of Reading Lessons*, p. 349.

[30]*Canadian Series of School Books, Second Book of Reading Lessons*, pp. 39-43.

[31]Ibid., p. 111.

[32]*New Canadian Readers, Book I*, p. 127.

[33]See, for example, the *Canadian Series of School Books, First Book of Reading Lessons, Part I*, esp. p. 33.

[34]*Canadian Series of School Books, First Book of Reading Lessons, Part II*, p. 14.

[35]Lennie's *The Principles of Grammar, The Canadian Series of School Books*, and the *New Canadian Readers* contain these and numerous other examples.

[36]*Canadian Series of School, Fifth Book of Reading Lessons*, p. 239.

[37]G. Mercer Adam and W. J. Robertson, *Public School History of England and Canada* (Toronto: Copp Clark, 1886), p. iii.

[38]*The Canadian Readers, Book II* (Toronto: Nelson and Gage, 1924), pp. 9, 16, 31.

[39]McCaig, *Studies in Citizenship*, p. 1.

[40]*The British Columbia Readers, Beginner's Reader*, last page.

[41]McCaig, *Studies in Citizenship*, p. 44.

[42]For example, see C. H. Stowell, *The Essentials of Health* (Toronto: Educational Book Co., 1909), p. 263, and *The British Columbia Readers, Third Reader*, p. 259.

[43]Duncan, *The Story of the Canadian People*, p. v.

[44]*Canadian Series of School Books, Fifth Book of Reading Lessons*, pp. 356, 369.

[45]McCaig, *Studies in Citizenship*, p. 59.

[46]*Canadian Series of School Books, First Book of Reading Lessons, Part I*, pp. 19, 51; *The Ontario Readers, Fourth Reader* (Toronto: Gage, 1884), p. 154; *The British Columbia Readers, Third Reader*, p. 130; *The Canadian Readers, Book II (Nelson and Gage, 1924), pp. 35-37.*

[47]*Canadian Series of School Books, Second Book of Reading Lessons*, p. 143.

[48]*Canadian Series of School Books, First Book of Reading Lessons, Part I*, p. 19.

[49]*New Canadian Readers, Primer I*, p. 32.

[50]See, for example, *The First Reader* of *The British Columbia Readers* in which stories with pets predominate.

[51]McCaig, *Studies in Citizenship*, p. 53.

[52]*The British Columbia Readers, First Reader*, p. 92.

[53]McKillop, *A Disciplined Intelligence*, p. 199.

[54]*British Columbia Phonic Primer* (Toronto: Educational Book Co., 1902), p. 34.

[55]John Brittain, *Elementary Agriculture and Nature Study* (Toronto: Educational Book Co., 1909), p. 181.

[56]For such labels, see, for instance, Eulalie Osgood Grover's *The Art-Literature Readers: A Primer* (Toronto: Educational Book Co., 1904). Wilson described his frustrations in the *Forty-sixth Annual Report of the Public Schools of British Columbia* (1917), p. 86.

[57]See, for example, *The Canadian Readers, Book V* (Gage, 1882).

[58]J. Halpenny and L. Ireland, *How to Be Healthy* (Toronto: 1911), p. 44.

[59]*Gage's Health Series for Intermediate Classes, Part II* (Toronto: Gage, 1896), pp. 88-90; Stowell, *The Essentials of Health* , pp. iii, 174, 177. Also see Halpenny and Ireland, *How to Be Healthy.*

[60]*The Canadian Readers, Book II* (Nelson and Gage, 1924), pp. 120-27. *Book V* (Nelson and Gage, 1922), pp. 184 ff.

[61]*The Canadian Readers, Book IV* (Gage, 1883), p. 5.

[62]B. W. Richardson, *Public School Temperance* (Toronto: Gage, Grip, 1887), pp. 18, 97; *Gage's Health Series for Primary Classes, Part I* (Toronto: Gage, 1896), pp. 19, 91; Halpenny and Ireland, *How to Be Healthy*, p. 130. Teachers' certification examinations also included questions on temperance. See, for instance, the *Eighteenth Annual Report of the Public Schools of B.C.* (Victoria, 1889), p. xciii.

[63]*Gage's Health Series for Intermediate Classes, Part II*, pp. 158-61; Stowell, *The Essentials of Health*, p. 38.

[64]*Canadian Series of School Books, Fifth Book of Reading Lessons*, pp. 19-20.

[65]Ibid., p. 93; *The Canadian Readers, Book IV* (Gage, 1883), p. 221.

[66]*The Canadian Readers, Book IV* (Gage, 1883), p. 195.

[67]S. Macadam, *The Chemistry of Common Things* (London: Nelson, 1872), p. 178; Sir J. William Dawson, *Handbook of Zoology* (Montreal: Dawson Brothers, 1886), p. 273.

[68]Brittain, *Elementary Agriculture and Nature Study*, p. iii.

[69]Ibid., p. v.

[70]L. H. Bailey, *Beginners' Botany* (Toronto: Macmillan, 1915, 1916), pp. 4, 7. Used only as a reference in British Columbia.

[71] *British Columbia Phonic Primer*, p. 17; Bailey, *Beginner's Botany*, p. 57.

[72]Macadam, *The Chemistry of Common Things*, p. 171.

[73]Robertson, *Public School History of England and Canada*, p. 194.

[74]*New Canadian Geography, British Columbia Edition*, p. 28. The title page of the only available copy was missing; however, the book was on the authorized list in British Columbia in and around 1908. Again, whether such a spirit of critical inquiry was actually implemented in, for example, the many one-room rural schools in B.C. at that time is a separate question.

[75]*Canadian Series of School Books, Fifth Book of Reading Lessons,* p. 206; *The Canadian Readers, Book IV* (Gage, 1883), p. 34; Robertson, Public School History of England and Canada, p. 194.

[76]*Canadian Series of School Books, Fifth Book of Reading Lessons,* p. 273; Duncan, *The Story of the Canadian People*, pp. 3, 314, 319; Lawson and Young, *A History and Geography of British Columbia*, p. 7; I. Gammell, *Elementary History of Canada*, with British Columbia Supplement (Toronto: Educational Book Co., 1907, 1912), chapters 33 and 40: Gammell, *History of Canada*, p. 285; McCaig, *Studies in Citizenship*, pp. 2-3.

[77]Robertson, *Public School History of England and Canada*, p. 280.

[78]Gammell, *History of Canada*, p. 45.

[79]See especially Lawson and Young, *A History and Geography of British Columbia*; Lawson, *History of Canada*,, chapter 44; and the British Columbia supplement of *New Canadian Geography.*

[80]*Lawson, History of Canada*, p. 231; Brittain, *Elementary Agriculture and Nature Study*, p. 274; McCaig, *Studies in Citizenship*, p. 80.

[81]A typical mathematics textbook was W. J. Milne's *Progressive Arithmetic, Third Book* (Toronto: Morang, 1906, 1915).

[82]Lawson and Young, *A History and Geography of British Columbia*, p. 73.

[83]McCaig, *Studies in Citizenship*, p. 80; *New Canadian Geography*, p. 76.

[84]Robertson, *Public School History of England and Canada*, p. 195.

[85]Duncan, *The Story of the Canadian People*, p. 202.

[86]*The Canadian Readers, Book IV* (Gage, 1883), p. 273.

[87]*Canadian Series of School Books, Fifth Book of Reading Lessons*, p. 388.

[88]*An Analytical and Practical Grammar*, p. 7.

[89]See the *Fourth* and *Fifth Books of Reading Lessons* of the *Canadian Series of School Books*. See Note 107 for the British Empire history book chosen by Jessop.

[90]Duncan, *The Story of the Canadian People,*p. 196.

[91]*The Ontario Reader, Fourth Reader,* p. 237; *The Canadian Readers, Book III* (Gage, 1881), pp. 164-65. *The Ontario Readers* were somewhat more grating in this respect than B.C.'s *Canadian Readers.* [92]*The Canadian Readers, Book V* (Gage, 1882), p. 362.

[93]*The Canadian Readers, Book IV* (Gage, 1883), p. 46.

[94]Ibid., p. 25.

[95]*The Canadian Readers, Book IV* (Nelson and Gage, 1922), p. 47.

[96]*The Canadian Readers, Book IV* (Gage, 1883), p. 244.

⁹⁷Ibid., pp. 9-10, 46, 168; *The Canadian Readers, Book V* (Nelson and Gage, 1922, p. 48).

⁹⁸Gammell, *Elementary History of Canada*, p. 318.

⁹⁹Gammell, *History of Canada*, p. 6. This book replaced W. L. Grant's *History of Canada*, which was banned from the province's schools in January 1920 because it had been accused of being anti-British, pro-French Canadian, and pro-Catholic. See Charles W. Humphries, "The Banning of a Book in British Columbia," *BC Studies* (Winter 1968-69): 1-12.

¹⁰⁰See, for example, *The British Columbia Readers, Third Reader,* and *The Canadian Readers, Book IV* (Nelson and Gage, 1922).

¹⁰¹Lawson, *History of Canada*, p. 85.

¹⁰² *The Canadian Readers, Book V* (Nelson and Gage, 1922) p. 73.

¹⁰³W. Stewart Wallace, *A New History of Great Britain and Canada* (Toronto: Macmillan, 1925, 1926), p. 128.

¹⁰⁴*The British Columbia Readers, Beginner's Reader*, last page.

¹⁰⁵*The Canadian Readers, Book V* (Nelson and Gage, 1922), p. 73.

¹⁰⁶Mercer and Robertson, *Public School History of England and Canada*, p. 113.

¹⁰⁷See, for example, George Brown's speech in *Book V* of *The Canadian Readers* (Gage, 1882), or J. George Hodgins' *History of Canada and of Other British Provinces in North America* (Montreal: John Lovell, 1865). The latter was a popular book but not prescribed in British Columbia, with Jessop opting for William F. Colliers' *History of the British Empire* (Toronto: Campbell, 1868) instead.

¹⁰⁸Lawson, *History of Canada*, p. 170. Also see Duncan, *The Story of the Canadian People* and Gammell, *Elementary History of Canada*.

¹⁰⁹Robertson, *Public School History of England and Canada*, p. 188.

¹¹⁰See, for example, *Wallace, A New History of Great Britain and Canada*, p. 73. A Nova Scotia reader, *The Advanced Reader No. VII* of the *Nova Scotia School Series* (Halifax: Mackinlay, 1865) especially emphasized that no country could claim persons like Washington (p. 61).

¹¹¹. Typical selections were found in Hodgins, *History of Canada and of Other British Provinces in North America*, pp. 67-69; Adam and Robertson, *Public School History of England and Canada*, p. 143; and Gammell's *Elementary History of Canada*, p. 29.

¹¹²*Canadian Series of School Books, Fifth Book of Reading Lessons*, p. 175.

¹¹³Lawson, *History of Canada*, p. 227.

¹¹⁴Duncan, *The Story of the Canadian People*, p. 17; Gammell, *Elementary History of Canada*, p. 29.

¹¹⁵Duncan, *The Story of the Canadian People*, pp. 14-17.

¹¹⁶*Canadian Series of School Books, Third Book of Reading Lessons*, p. 172.

¹¹⁷*Canadian Series of School Books, Fifth Book of Reading Lessons*, p. 356.

¹¹⁸Hodgins, *History of Canada and of Other British Provinces in North America*, pp. 135-36; Lawson, *History of Canada*, p. 166. Interestingly, except for the years immediately after the two Riel-led outbursts, there was little if any inflammatory description of Riel and the Métis. Gammell came closest by saying that Riel fomented agitation, but even he added that there was no doubt that the government and its officials were careless and indifferent about the matter. Duncan and Lawson both

described the legitimate land title grievances of the Métis, and tried to balance those grievances with the government's need to restore its authority.

[119]The 1916 *Third Reader* of *The British Columbia Readers* put in its preface: "As must always be the case in books of this kind, the selections are, for the most part, drawn from the great storehouse of English literature, the works of the writers of Britain."(p. iv).

[120]Wallace, *A New History of Great Britain and Canada*, p. 257.

[121]*The Canadian Readers, Book V* (Nelson and Gage, 1922).

[122]Grover, *The Art-Literature Readers: A Primer*, p. 7.

[123]. Ibid., p. 106.

[124]See, for example, *The New Canadian Readers, Book IV*.

[125]Brittain, *Elementary Agriculture and Nature Study*, p. 181.

[126]Last four lines of Marjorie Pickthall, "Star of the North." See Note 10.

Textbook References

Except where indicated, all books listed were prescribed for schools in British Columbia.

1. Readers and Composition
The following five series of prescribed readers were used:
Canadian Series of School Books ("The Red Series"), first published in 1867 in Toronto by various publishers such as Warwick, James Campbell, and Gage.
The Canadian Readers. Toronto: Gage and Company, 1881.
New Canadian Readers, 20th Century Edition. Toronto: Gage, 1900.
The British Columbia Readers. Toronto: Gage, 1915.
The Canadian Readers Toronto: Nelson and Gage, 1922.
Also examined were the following:
British Columbia Phonic Primer. Toronto: Educational Book Co., 1902.
Eulalie Osgood Grover. *The Art-Literature Readers: A Primer*. Toronto: Educational Book Co., 1904. This volume was one of a series made available as supplementary readers to all rural schools in B.C.
William Lennie. *The Principles of Grammar*. Toronto: Miller, 1869. W. J. Alexander and A. Mowat. *Elementary Composition with Grammar*. Toronto: Gage, 1912, 1922.
2. History and Geography
J. George Hodgins. *History of Canada and of Other British Provinces in North America*. Montreal: John Lovell, 1865. Used as a reference only in British Columbia.
William F. Colliers. *The History of the British Empire*. Toronto: Campbell, 1868.
William F. Colliers. *Outlines of General History*. Toronto: Campbell, 1869.
G. Mercer Adam and W. J. Robertson. *Public School History of England and Canada*. Toronto: Copp Clark, 1886.
Gage's New Primer of Map Geography. Toronto: Gage, 1883, 1892.
W. J. Robertson. *Public School History of England and Canada*. Toronto: Copp Clark, 1902. This revision of Adam and Robertson's 1886 textbook contains a supplement on B.C.'s history.

D. M. Duncan. *The Story of the Canadian People*. Toronto: Morang, 1904, 1905.

I. Gammell. *Elementary History of Canada* (with British Columbia Supplement). Toronto: Educational Book Co., 1907, 1912.

Maria Lawson. *History of Canada* Toronto: Gage, 1906, 1908.

Maria Lawson and Rosalind Young. *A History and Geography of British Columbia*. Toronto: Gage, 1906.

New Canadian Geography, British Columbia Edition (my copy's title page was missing; however, the book was on the authorized list in British Columbia in and around 1908). The original 1899 Gage edition gives no author but states that the book is based on the geographies of Alex. E. Frye.

I. Gammell. *History of Canada*. Toronto: Gage, 1921, 1922.

W. Stewart Wallace. *A New History of Great Britain and Canada*. Toronto: Macmillan, 1925, 1926.

James McCaig. *Studies in Citizenship*. Toronto: Educational Book Co., 1925, 1931.

3. *Science and Agriculture*

S. Macadam. *The Chemistry of Common Things*. London: Nelson, 1872.

Sir J. William Dawson. *Handbook of Zoology*. Montreal: Dawson Brothers, 1886.

John Brittain. *Elementary Agriculture and Nature Study*. Toronto: Educational Book Co., 1909.

L. H. Bailey. *Beginners' Botany* Toronto: Macmillan, 1915, 1916. Used only as a reference in B.C.

4. *Health, Hygiene, and Temperance*

B. W. Richardson. *Public School Temperance*. Toronto: Grip, 1887.

Gage's Health Series for Primary Classes, Part I. Toronto: Gage, 1896.

Gage's Health Series for Intermediate Classes, Part II. Toronto: Gage, 1896.

C. H. Stowell. *The Essentials of Health*. Toronto: Educational Book Co., 1909.

J. Halpenny and L. Ireland. *How to Be Healthy*. Toronto: Gage, 1911.

5. *Mathematics*

T. Kirkland and W. Scott. *Elementary Arithmetic on the Unitary System* . Toronto: Gage, 1880.

B. Smith and A. MacMurchy. *Advanced Arithmetic for Canadian Schools* Toronto: Copp Clark, 1871, 1882.

W. J. Milne. *Progressive Arithmetic, Third Book*. Toronto: Morang, 1906, 1915.

The Dominion High School Arithmetic. Toronto: Gage, 1914, 1921.

J. A. Smith and R. H. Roberts. *British Columbia Public School Arithmetic, Book II*. Toronto: Gage, 1920, 1922.

3

Education, the Society and the Curriculum in Alberta, 1905-1980: An Overview

Nancy M. Sheehan

"What knowledge is of most worth?"   Spencer

"What would you have a woman know?"   *Punch*

With apologies to Spencer and *Punch*, their questions might be combined to ask: "What knowledge is of most worth to whom?" The curriculum, both overt and hidden, as detailed in policy and as implemented in classrooms is the vehicle society has used to pass on its heritage and to prepare its citizens for the present and future. This dual responsibility in a pluralistic society results in a curriculum that is constantly evaluated, defined, defended and changed. The twofold purpose to preserve and to cultivate is reflected in the constant interaction between stability and change on the one hand and among the various users of the school system on the other. The changes made in the curriculum in Alberta between 1905 and 1980 have been one province's attempt to answer the questions, *who* should learn *what, why* should they learn and *how* should this learning take place. They have also been a means of adjusting the ready-made program of studies adopted in 1905 to the maturation needs of the people and to developments taking place in educational research.

With Confederation in 1905, Alberta inherited a school organization, a program of studies, and a financing arrangement from the North-West Territories. The curriculum and textbooks, inspectors and examinations, as well as teacher education and certification were centralized in a department of education under a minister. Locally, an elected board of trustees had the responsibility of building, equipping and operating the school. Outside the cities and towns, this usually meant a one-room school incorporating six to eight grades, a young, inexperienced, female teacher, and school funds collected from local property taxes supplemented by small government grants. In the cities, graded schools, specialized instruction and high school opportunities developed fairly quickly. The program of studies was academic, bookish, and memory-oriented. It was a curriculum developed in nineteenth-century Ontario, and transplanted to the North-West Territories by David C. Goggin, an Ontario educator who became superintendent in 1893. Goggin's ideas on the role of schools as cultural transmitters, as keepers of morality and as agents of the crown were translated into the Territories via the textbooks.[1] Curriculum-making in these early years was really an exercise in textbook selection. With the science of education in its infancy, with undereducated teachers in classrooms and with the belief that truth was absolute and knowledge finite, the textbook became the centre of the course of study. It was the one undisputed authority upon which the child and the teacher could rely. It taught not only the content to be learned for the ever-present provincial examinations, but also an unquestioning belief in society and one's place in that society. This "hidden curriculum" stressed the morals and values of a Christian, British-oriented heritage.[2]

During Alberta's first decade, federal immigration policy, railroad expansion and the development of an early-ripening wheat caused settlement to push northward and into "dry" areas in the southeast. A boom economy enhanced by record wheat production and sales meant a rapid increase in population accompanied by the need to supply services and institutions. The department of education was required to provide more schools and more teachers for a population that was concerned with the basic necessities of life, that included large numbers of non-English speaking peoples settled in bloc colonies, and that did not place a high monetary value on the work of the teacher. Given problems of this magnitude, the curriculum of the school was directed by the need for teachers and by an Anglo-Saxon fear of the immigrant. Textbooks with British-oriented content, English-only schools and a classical, literary curriculum at the secondary level were the results.[3]

The number of pupils attending Alberta schools in the first decades underwent a phenomenal increase from 24,254 pupils in 1905 to 134,750 in 1920.[4] The majority of these were in the lower grades. Statistics for 1915 show only 5.38 percent in the high school grades. Of these about two-thirds attempted provincial examinations, and of this group again about two-thirds passed.[5] The high drop-out rate, and the number of failures on examinations suggested to educators that the curriculum was too academic, too difficult, and irrelevant to the increasing population in the province. This chapter will explore the factors at work over the years in Alberta to make that curriculum more appropriate to the needs of the ever-increasing numbers of students who opted to stay in school for longer periods of time.

Adjustments to the program of studies have not been linear over the years, and they have been fraught with indecision and inconsistency. An incremental growth in the tasks and the clientele of the school has occurred and has been affected by a number of factors such as national and international developments, economics, politics and changing technology. Strategies employed by the federal government, the use of public input to educational commissions, and the attitude of local residents to change have been a part of the picture. The multiplicity of stakeholders in the educational arena has contributed to the slow process of change. A more detailed look at three curricula areas will highlight the link between societal input and curriculum change.

Nationalism

In the years prior to World War I, the society and the schools looked to Britain and the Empire for leadership, for trade and for heroes.[6] Alberta, although a new province, was not any different from the older, eastern provinces. D. C. Goggin, the first superintendent of schools in the North-West Territories, had set an imperialistic tone from the outset. The program of studies, the textbooks and the atmosphere of the school were ones which incorporated British values of loyalty, honesty, respect for authority and obedience. Teachers who were British subjects, schools which used English as the only language of instruction, and a program of studies which stressed British events, places and people contributed to a lack of a Canadian identity. The celebration of Queen Victoria's diamond jubilee, the war in South Africa and an influx to Alberta of non-English speaking immigrants tended to focus attention on the Empire and Canada's role in it rather than on Canada as an independent country with its own national character.[7] The Alexandra Readers, the first free text distributed to all schoolchildren in Alberta, suggested to the reader that the British Empire was progressive, powerful and the most enlightened of civilizations and that the British people were brave, intelligent and moral. This is not to suggest that there was not a Canadian presence. Canadian selections tended to be descriptive stories of growing wheat on the prairies or were characterized by British criteria — selected because, like "Flander's Fields," they spoke of Canadian love and loyalty for the Mother Country.[8] Cadet Corps, funded by the Strathcona Trust to ready school children and Canada to aid Britain in the event of war, were established in urban schools in Alberta. In Calgary, Captain Alex Ferguson, a veteran of the Boer War, was hired to head the physical education program and develop marching and shooting skills in the young cadets. Empire Day celebrations found children in Alberta's schools reading about Lord Nelson, identifying member countries of the Empire, singing "Rule Britannia" and listening to patriotic addresses on the glory of the Empire.[9]

As Arthur Lower concluded, this daily dose of flag waving and empire saluting meant that in 1914 Canadians, including Albertans, were ready, willing and able to contribute to the war in Europe.[10] However, the culmination of this pre-1914 interest in Britain — actual participation in the war effort — was also the beginning of a nationalistic shift in the country and in the schools. The conclusion of the war found Canadians with pride in their contributions, some heroes to acknowledge, and acceptance in the international world as an independent country. Interest in Canada, pride in Canadian accomplishments and knowledge of Canadian communities began to grow. Over the next decade, changes to the curriculum mirrored that Canadian trend. A new series of texts replaced the Alexandra Readers. Titled the Canadian Readers, this series used frontispieces featuring the Canadian Ensign and the Parliament Buildings in Ottawa as well as members of the Royal Family, included "O

Canada" and "The Dominion Hymn," and contained more stories with both Canadian settings and Canadian heroes.[11]

Interest in militarism and readiness to defend Britain faded as peace efforts grew after World War I, and eventually both Calgary and Edmonton School Boards cancelled their Cadet Programs.[12] Although the celebration of Empire Day continued, it also lost some of its fervour and reliance on British-only materials. Canadian content was incorporated into the program suggestions. The Imperial Order Daughters of the Empire (IODE), which had been founded to promote imperialism and Canada's role in the Empire, shifted its educational activities. Donations of books to school libraries included Canadian history and geography texts, and the titles for essay contests also took on a Canadian emphasis.[13] This gradual change in focus to Canada and its peoples and communities was enhanced by the activities of the Junior Red Cross with its twin goals of improving the health of children and developing a civic or community spirit. One method of teaching the children about their communities and their country was to have them design and complete a portfolio for presentation to a Junior Red Cross class in another country. The portfolio included information about the area's history, inhabitants, industry, schools, climate, and geography. Pictures, items from the local newspaper, the children's written submissions and their artwork were a part of the portfolio.[14] In 1927 schools everywhere celebrated the diamond jubilee of Confederation with plays, pageants and course material which looked at the growth of the Dominion from 1867. The twenties, then, for the schools of Alberta as elsewhere, were a time of growing Canadianization.

In 1968, fifty years after the end of World War I., A. B. Hodgetts published his Canada-wide survey *What Culture? What Heritage?*, a ringing indictment of both the kind of content and the methodology involved in Canadian history, geography and civics courses.[15] What had happened to the promises of post-World War I and the thrusts toward a Canada-oriented curriculum of the twenties? Robert M. Stamp suggests that the long reliance on Britain created a vacuum which a growing American culture filled. American resource materials and textbooks were more attractive, and cheaper, and there was a far greater variety. The lack of a well-developed Canadian culture meant that Canadian selections were fewer.[16] Depression, drought and World War II had a profound effect on Alberta's schools. The Banff School of Fine Arts was founded in 1932 and developed Alberta artists and musicians who presented their accomplishments in churches, halls and theatres across the province. The impact of this on the schools awaited better economic conditions. The introduction of the "enterprise" brought social studies into the course of study, and World War II saw the return of Empire Day. Although social studies had the potential to promote Canadianization, a lack of resources hampered the process.

In Alberta a long-standing policy of granting sabbaticals to professional educators as they moved up the career ladder meant that American ideas found their way into the province. In particular, Columbia Teachers' College, the University of Chicago, and Stanford attracted many departmental officials. A sizeable American population did not hamper this movement of people and ideas between the United States and Alberta. Even in the sixties when nationalism drew more attention, American textbooks in science and technology were found in Alberta schools. Because the content was science there was a belief that such texts were context-free and acceptable for young Albertans.[17]

Expo 67, Hodgetts' *What Culture? What Heritage?*, the Royal Commission on Bilingualism and Biculturalism, and the Symons Report directed the attention of Canadians to their own country, its peoples, problems and potential.[18] One result was an increase in French as a language of instruction. In Alberta, a multicultural emphasis was adopted, more representative of Alberta's diverse peoples. The Worth Commission of 1972 recommended more Canadian content, and the province made the decision to produce the Alberta Resources Kits focusing on Alberta rather than Canada-wide content. This display of regionalism, long-standing political membership in the Empire and Commonwealth and public awareness of the proximity of the United States have resulted in continuing debate over the role of Alberta's schools in producing good Canadians.

Progressive Education

Another continuing debate has been between traditional and progressive educational ideas and practices. The introduction after the turn of the century of kindergartens, manual training, domestic science, school gardening, and physical education was the result of the first attempt to move schools away from an emphasis on books, facts, memorization and unrelated and irrelevant material to a focus which taught the whole child using objective methods and familiar content. These courses were also an attempt to use the schools as a vehicle for social reform. Educational reformers throughout North America emphasized learning by doing, focusing on the interests of the learner and developing a child-centred curriculum. In Canada, some aspects of the New Education, as it was called, became a part of most schools' curricula, remaining however on the periphery and having no impact on the academic component, considered to be the central function of the school.[19]

Albertan educators through their continued contacts with American graduate schools were keenly interested in this child- and activity-centred philosophy of learning. Although the twenties were not a time of educational reform in Alberta, aspects of progressive education were discussed and in a few instances attempted. The Dalton Plan, conceived in the United States, promoted by the United Farm Women of Alberta and introduced in Alberta in an Edmonton school, featured individualized instruction. Another individualized instruction model, known as the Winnetka Technique, also from the United States, was discussed in Alberta but considered too expensive for adoption.[20]

The Junior Red Cross (JRC) with its Friday afternoon meetings was an example of progressive techniques influencing the curriculum without a formal endorsement of the new approach. The JRC focused on health and social activities. Activity-centred learning was evident in the posters, plays and debates that occurred, in the committees that were organized and in the application of health rules to the classroom itself. The whole child was being educated — the physical, moral, emotional and intellectual — as the children worked to improve their own health and that of other children. Learning to cooperate and depend upon one another were factors if the JRC was to be a successful enterprise. If a JRC worked as it should, then surely it was an example of progressive educational techniques.[21]

These forays of the twenties bore fruit in 1935 after the election of the Social Credit Government with William Aberhart, a high school teacher and principal, as premier and minister of education. With eleven teachers in the Socred caucus, the government did not hesitate to introduce reforms, specifically a reorganization of the school structure, the introduction of the enterprise, the formation of large school divisions and the acknowledgement of the Alberta Teachers' Association as the voice of all teachers.

The change from an eight-year elementary, four-year high school to a six-year elementary, three-year intermediate or junior high school and a three-year senior high school paved the way for progressive educational recommendations to be translated into the program of studies. The new elementary school curriculum was an activity program which integrated subject matter, offered opportunities for socialization and included group planning and decision-making. Known as the "enterprise," the activity program incorporated social studies, science and health as basic components, leaving the skill subjects — the three r's — outside the enterprise framework. Progressive education had come to the province.[22] Donalda Dickie, a member of the committee which recommended the new program, wrote *The Enterprise in Theory and Practice* which became the bible of the activity program in Canada.[23] Credit for this change in focus must go to Hubert C. Newland, supervisor of schools for Alberta, who had obtained a Ph.D. from the University of Chicago in 1932.[24]

The intermediate school was to serve both as a preparatory school for pupils proceeding to high school, and as a "finishing school" for others, enabling them to leave school with a sense of accomplishment. A core of instruction for all pupils and elective or exploratory subjects to cater to individual interests and aptitudes were proposed. The core was to include the fundamentals of oral and written English; a comprehensive view of the world through social studies; some knowledge of the rudiments of science; and the practical application of useful concepts in mathematics. The elective or optional courses were to be of three kinds: courses to develop cultural appreciation such as music, art, craftwork; exploratory courses to assess the personal resources of students, including courses in shop, home economics, typing, and commercial art; and pre-vocational courses especially adapted to the pupil who would not proceed beyond junior high.[25]

The new senior high school program was also quite radical. First, one diploma only was awarded regardless of the mixture of courses a student might take. Second, a credit program was introduced where one credit equalled thirty-five minutes of instruction time per week per school year and 100 credits were needed for graduation. A third change occurred in the required "core-elective area," where only English, social studies and physical education were required of all students, the other two-thirds of the program to be made up of electives. The elimination of provincial examinations at the Grade X and XI levels in favour of promotion by teacher recommendation was a fourth change. It was believed that this system would enable pupils of varying abilities and interests to obtain a diploma; that it would allow all sizes of high schools to offer some non-academic options; and that academic and non-academic subjects would become a part of every student's high school package. Since the adoption of this program in 1936 it has been up to the student to choose the courses that fit his/her own interests.[26]

The curricula changes had the potential to improve the school offerings throughout the province. Such improvement did not immediately occur, however. The elementary "enterprise" program required teachers who had the ability to integrate subject matter and to use resources other than the textbook. An effective junior high program needed teachers with a knowledge of the psychology of adolescence, with specialized teaching certificates and with backgrounds in diagnosis and guidance. It also required a school plant equipped with libraries, labs, shops, a gymnasium and an auditorium. For most schools in the province, these requirements were difficult to meet. Teachers had traditional normal school training and generally no university experience, resources were scarce and the school plant small and inadequate.[27]

At the senior high level despite the "new" single diploma, most schools concentrated on the academic subjects: tradition, the prestige of certain subjects, the vested interests of teachers, the entrance requirements of the university and of professional schools and the perceived disciplinary value of subjects like Latin worked together to resist change. As well, in a very depressed economy these traditional subjects required less in the way of space, resources and equipment than did some of the newer subjects. Understandably, some children and their parents sought financial security via the professions and white collar jobs, occupations that required academic courses, not technical and vocational ones. For these reasons the preeminent academic nature of the school persisted. Nevertheless, these revisions were by far the most radical educational changes in the country. Alberta became the acknowledged leader in reform and, via the enterprise, the front runner in the implementation of progressive education. Despite this, R. S. Patterson argues, the reform measures as a departmentally imposed revision, were not well understood or accepted by the populace.[28]

JRC activities, manual training and domestic science which in effect used progressive philosophy were accepted by the people. However, when this same philosphy was applied to the heart of the curriculum, the three r's, it did not receive the same approval. As criticism grew, the term progressive education was dropped. Progressive ideas, though, had had some impact. One effect was in the area of textbooks. New books, more colourful, child-oriented and illustrated were introduced. The readers in particular had a controlled vocabulary, introducing new words one at a time and in order of difficulty. The content changed from "old" world to "new" world interests, from materials dealing with the past to those concerned with the present; and from an emphasis on the world of the adult to that of the child.[29]

The denunciation of this new education by Hilda Neatby in *So Little For the Mind* in 1954 as anti-intellectual, anti-cultural and amoral caused a furor in educational circles.[30] In Alberta the Report of the Royal Commission on Education in 1959 (Cameron Report) indicated that standards were too low, matriculation preparation was inadequate and classes in some areas were deemed "frills." The Commission's recommendations put an emphasis on specified content, drill, examinations and mastery of information.[31] A curriculum geared to the interests of the learners, to flexibility, and to informality was thought to have weakened the academic and knowledge component of the program of studies. Neatby's criticisms and the launching of "Sputnik" by the U.S.S.R. appeared to have influenced the committee.

Despite Cameron's recommendations, the sixties and early seventies did not see an emphasis on traditional education. Non-graded classrooms, individualized progress, and integrated programs of study were introduced. Ideas which were first introduced in the thirties, and downplayed in the forties and fifties, became the educational watchwords of the sixties. The interest of the government in education, the public monies allocated to it and the expectation of what education could accomplish produced conflicting messages. On the one hand, public expenditure and public expectation put pressure on the school to be a panacea for all the ills of society, including what was perceived as a loss of traditional values; on the other hand, money for education meant that new ideas and practices could be attempted, ideas which advocated individuality and freedom, and which questioned traditional courses and methodology. In the middle were the high school youth caught between the society's growing secularization and emphasis on materialism as wealth and urbanization increased, and the voters' nostalgic yearning for the values which had brought Albertans through two world wars and a severe depression. Traditionalism and progressivism continued a seesaw battle for supremacy.

While the Worth Commission (1972) was collecting its findings on cradle-to-grave education and recommending diversity in courses, programs and schools, the social studies curriculum was undergoing a major revision. Since 1936 social studies had held a favoured place in the program of studies in Alberta with the belief that it would give young citizens an adequate understanding of the complex society in which they lived. [32] By 1970 that society had become complex indeed, and many were of the opinion that its institutions were crumbling. The unconventionality of the sixties, rebellion against authority and traditional values, the increasing rate of marital breakdown, use of drugs, alcohol consumption and rising crime statistics caused concern. A boom economy, a rapidly increasing population and a changing technology made the Alberta society of the seventies unstable. Some Albertans thought that the society could regain something of the proven traditions of established institutions through the school. This perennial faith in schooling and concurrent hope for the youth seem to have been more the burden of the social studies curriculum than of other subject areas. A value-oriented curriculum which would give students the means for making considered and consistent choices was introduced. The new social studies aimed at developing "valuing skills," at dealing with "what ought to be," at learning how to make decisions and at how to make the future world a more ideal place. Some criticized this program as wishy-washy, with the students able to decide for themselves between right and wrong. A course, originally devised as a means of reestablishing traditional values, appeared to many to be doing just the opposite.[33]

The pendulum was beginning to swing once more.[34] By the mid-seventies a "back to the basics" movement had developed. Businessmen complained that high school graduates could not spell, the public generally felt that the students' factual knowledge was weak, and universities, like Calgary, introduced an Effective Writing qualification. In the 1980s a secondary school review in Alberta advocated a prescribed core, specified content, provincial examinations in all courses, and specialized diplomas — recommendations reminiscent of earlier times and other reports.[35] The two philosophies, traditional and progressive, thus continued to exist in the system and to compete with one another.

Vocational/Technical Education

A third curriculum area that has undergone much change over the century has been that of vocational/technical education. From the beginning, schools in Canada were to be practical, and Goggin's educational philosophy emphasized utility over intellectual achievement. He wanted material stressed which would be "helpful in the transaction of business, the duties of citizenship, the care of the body and the formation of moral character."[36] As the society developed, this utilitarian philosophy became associated with specific courses: manual training to prepare boys to earn a living; domestic science to give girls training in their future roles as wife and mother; military drill and rifle training to provide good soldiers; and school gardens to help rural youngsters relate school to their environment. Courses in the field of commercial education were the first non-academic high school courses to be considered and included typing, shorthand, bookkeeping and accounting. By 1919 separate Commercial High Schools were in operation in Calgary, Edmonton and Lethbridge. The federal Agricultural Instruction Act of 1913 proved to be the impetus needed for this province to get into agricultural education. Expansion into the related area of technical education was delayed until after World War I and the passing of the Technical Education Act in 1919,. Edmonton opened a technical high school in 1919, and Calgary opened one in 1929. These schools were equipped with shops for woodwork, electricity, auto mechanics and metal work as well as sewing rooms and kitchens. Designed to cater to the increasingly broad range of students continuing on to high school but whose interests did not lead to the university, these schools suffered from a lack of prestige.[37] Although their courses may have been of interest to the average student, the stigma of attending deterred many students. The solution was the "composite" high school which offered all programs under the same roof. In 1935 Western Canada Composite in Calgary became the first school of this type in the province.[38]

This desire to cater to the more practically-oriented student also surfaced in the creation in 1923 of the multi-diploma for high school graduation. Because of the needs of the industrial sector, the wish to lower the drop-out level and and desire to attract more boys to the high school, diplomas in areas such as technical, agricultural, commercial and general in addition to the normal school and matriculation routes were seen as the answer.[39] The idea was not successful. Most students who went to high school took either the normal school entrance or the matriculation diploma because of the prestige associated with academics, because women and rural residents had few choices besides teaching, and because small high schools did not have the capacity to offer the other programs. Generally, the technical diploma students were not trained for the workplace; only the urban high schools had the resources to offer the agricultural program; and the general course, rumoured to be a watered-down version of the matriculation diploma, did not attract many students. These criticisms of the technical/vocational programs were not confined to Alberta, of course. Timothy Dunn makes the same point about British Columbia's ventures into these areas.[40] In 1935 only 181 of that year's 2,458 Alberta high school graduates were awarded other than a normal entrance or a matriculation diploma. Clearly, the multi-diploma system was not working, and the way was clear for the Social Credit government to introduce the one high school diploma.[41]

Depression, war and post-war reconstruction had their effect on non-academic courses and programs which required specially trained teachers, well equipped workshops and large school plants. By the 1950s despite an increased high school enrolment, a one-diploma program, regional and composite high schools and a philosophy that included education for the workplace, the academic program maintained its tight rein on the school system. The high schools generally failed in providing a technical/vocational program for a good portion of adolescents. For example, in an agricultural province agricultural courses were not available; students who enrolled in Grade X technical and vocational courses did not continue into more advanced courses in these areas; and a great many dropped out before qualifying for the diploma.[42] The

Cameron Commission in 1959 commented that only 6 percent of the students enrolled in high school proceeded to university and yet every local high school had to offer the matriculation package to the detriment of other programs. Although 110 subjects had been outlined and authorized by the department in academic, commercial, shop, home economics, cultural and general areas, choice for the student tended to be very limited by virtue of the size of the high school and the requirements of individual university faculties.

The Cameron Commission had specific recommendations concerning the school's role in manpower training. The industrial needs of the society and the trend to more students going on to high school resulted in recommendations that favoured specialization in practical courses such as fine arts, business education, and many vocational fields.[43] The federal government interest in relieving unemployment and expanding the economy produced the Technical and Vocational Training Assistance Act in 1960. Under this Act, extensive funds were available to provinces to upgrade facilities for technical and vocational training, a goal which coincidentally had been recommended by the Cameron Commission. Three decades after the high school revision of 1936, and only with the financial assistance of the federal government did the province really begin to provide a high school education for non-academically inclined students. The number of courses and fields expanded, composite high schools with large vocational components were built, and junior vocational schools became acceptable. Programs in as many as twenty-four fields, ranging from agricultural mechanics and data processing to forestry trades and radio and television repair were introduced. The schools began to reflect in courses and programs the many opportunities and possibilities of Albertan society.[44] They also reflected the reality of the workplace as many of these courses were gender specific.

A Choice of Futures, the educational commission chaired by Walter H. Worth which charted the course of "cradle-to-grave" education for the seventies and beyond, was published in 1972. It advocated a career-oriented approach, one that would make education relevant to the adult role in society. Career guidance and work experience became important aspects of the school curriculum, at least in theory.[45] In practice suitable work experience programs were hard to find, streaming resulted in the intellectually and socially less able students opting for these programs, and the opportunity to earn a salary while in school was the main attraction. Despite these results, work experience programs have been re-emphasized in the just-completed *Review of Secondary Programs* (1985). The Review recommended that: "work experience programs be provided which include knowledge of employment opportunities; practical knowledge of the working of the market economy and its dependence on productivity; awareness of the expectations of employers; and the development of career knowledge in addition to the emphasis on actual job experience." The report also recommended that specialized high school diplomas be offered in areas such as General, Academic, Vocational, Business Education and Fine Arts.[46]

The role of the school in manpower training, in providing an education for the practically-oriented student and in satisfying the demands of universities, business and labour, and the public has generally proven to be a difficult task. Although vocational/technical courses and programs have grown over the years and have become an accepted part of the educational system, they still lack prestige.

Conclusion

As one looks back over the present century, a distinct pattern emerges that links societal change and development in educational research to curriculum modification and diversification. This pattern of development suggests a number of themes which have been central to educational, including curricular, developments. First, over the course of eighty years the high school curriculum has changed from an academic, intellectual education for entrance to the universities and professions catering to a small proportion of the population, to a program which prepared students for the workforce, for living in a complex society, for entrance to colleges and technical schools as well as universities. It is now a program directed at a broad spectrum of youth in the society and includes education in areas that had previously been the preserve of other societal institutions, such as the family, the church, and the workplace.

A horizontal increase occurred as more members of the age group began to attend high school; a vertical increase was caused by students staying in school for longer periods of time; and a lateral expansion took place as the school was expected to provide broader opportunities for its pupils. The secondary school curriculum has undergone incremental change over the years as it has continually been expected to do more for larger proportions of the age group. More students, longer periods of time in school, and more varied programs are only some of the aspects of this incremental change. In addition, society was becoming more complex, presenting the high school with an increasingly difficult role. Pioneer society was simple. The school's duty was to teach the three r's and the values of the day: duty, courage, honesty, thrift and obedience. As the society became more complex and pluralistic, agreement on right and wrong began to erode, and no widespread concurrence could be found on the school's mandate. These concerns plus the knowledge explosion meant that the curriculum of the high school could no longer be the simple, academic program of the past.

A second theme has been that of the role of national and international developments. Both professional educators and the public have been influenced by ideas, changes, and concerns that occurred outside Alberta. Whether it was Ontario's academic, imperialistic curriculum in the early years, John Dewey's progressive philosophy of the thirties, the Russian Sputnik in 1957, or the federal government's concern over unemployment in the fifties and economic development in the sixties, the school has undergone change in connection with these events. Sometimes these changes were warranted by conditions in Alberta, but not always; for example, industrial and technical courses were introduced when the West was very much an agricultural area. On the other hand agriculture, a course which was not popular in other, more metropolitan jurisdictions, was also not successful in Alberta, an agricultural province. The conclusion is that curriculum is affected by events and developments outside the province as well as within and that the school system has the task of preparing students to be citizens of Canada and the world as well as of Alberta.

Although education is a provincial responsibility in Canada and each province protects that control assiduously, the federal government has nevertheless had an impact on the curriculum. Politicians used Section 91 of the British North America Act, which gave the federal government control over industry, trade, and commerce, to appoint a royal commission in 1910 to inquire into industrial training and technical education.[47] The result was more provincial attention in the areas of agricultural and technical programs and schools. Again, the federal interest in the economy in 1960 produced the *Vocational and Technical Training Assistance Act* which helped provide Alberta with the facilities and equipment needed to offer a high school education for the non-academically inclined student. The focus on bilingualism and biculturalism, the resulting royal commission and the 1971 national policy on multiculturalism affected the curriculum in the area of French language instruction across the country, and resulted in a multicultural focus in Alberta. The third theme, therefore, is that the federal government, although technically excluded from jurisdiction in education, nonetheless has wielded extensive influence.[48]

Fourth, local input and attitudes have been very important to both policy-making and implementation. That input sometimes tends to be contradictory, resistent and subversive. It is often naively expressed and yet a public educational system must respond to the needs/desires of the public. The "back to the basics movement" is a good example. How basic, how backward one might ask. Examination statistics and inspectors' reports from earlier years certainly complain about students' ability to write at a time when few students went on to high school. Today, when most students do so, should the school be expected to have all students competent in skills which a few years ago very few mastered? How do computers and computer-related learning fit this movement? Latin is not one of the advocated basics and yet it is argued that knowledge of Latin might help in working with computer and other languages. The number of Albertan students taking Latin in high school and university has shown a small, but significant increase in the last few years.

Connected with local input is the role of organizations outside the school, like the United Farm Women, or the Trades and Labor Congress, or the Right-to-Life Coalition. Each group may be very organized and vocal and yet only represent a small proportion of the public. A curriculum unduly influenced in this way may not meet the wishes of the majority of the population.

At the same time, these "outside the school" groups may have performed the service of a national office or a national system of education. Many of these organizations have a framework which links local and provincial units with a national body which coordinated activities. Lobbying of provincial departments of education by provincial locals of national organizations may have helped effect curricula change nationally. The WCTU and the temperance curriculum, women's institutes and domestic science, and Expo 67 and Canadian studies are examples of national lobbying affecting provincial curricula decisions. Cultural conflict, involving the use of drugs, or the place of religion in public schools, or sexual morality, becomes in reality curriculum conflict. Such issues are promulgated by national organizations through their local affiliates. The work of these organizations may help explain why certain curricula changes have occurred simultaneously across the country.[49]

Another theme that impinges on curriculum development and implementation is that educational reform is a slow process. It takes time for a new or radical idea to be accepted by the public and to be implemented at the local level. Social, political, economic, technological and educational conditions need to merge in order for a fundamental change to occur. A political party or the government in power may not give education high priority; depressed economic conditions may not allow needed reforms to be carried out; advances in technology may make equipment outdated and a program not viable; or the public may not be ready for school change. Any one of these factors may take precedence over what appears in theory at least to be a good pedagogical or educational idea.

The impact of technology on the curriculum must also be considered. The textbook is no longer the sole authority for knowledge that it once was. Technology has broadened both the way children learn and what they learn. Resource centres equipped with the latest audio-visual equipment, the use of curriculum kits and resource packages by the students and the development of educational television, coloured curriculum-making in the sixties. More recently, the advent of the computer and its promotion by the Department of Education for use in the schools has necessitated further curriculum innovation. In a society driven by technology, the man-machine interface is of critical concern and the school must prepare students to adapt to technology-driven change. It has been forecast over the years that in this kind of a society the textbook would become passé. Certainly the textbook no longer has the authority it once did, but at the same time it is still the centre around which other resources revolve. The re-introduction of provincial examinations suggests that far from being passé, the textbook will remain at the core, buffered and buffeted by changing technology.

The history of the curriculum describes a struggle over the question of "what knowledge is of most worth to whom." Such a description includes both a class-based and a gender-based distinction. Technical and vocational courses have been directed more to children of workers, with the academic program appealing to the white collar and professional class. Although knowledge is not gender-based, some courses and programs have been designated for one sex or the other, confining students to the accepted view of male/ female roles in the society. Alternating cycles of subject-centred vs. child-centred learning have occurred and can be associated with the changing political and social climate of the century. From the "classical knowledge for its own sake" proponents to "work-centred" reformers, to those who advocated individual child development, the curriculum has swung back and forth. It has been difficult for authorities to assess how much stability was maintained and how much change actually occurred throughout these cycles because they have been hampered by the inability to control or even to know what happens inside the classroom. Teachers tend to modify or interpret curricula direction and guides according to their own experience and education and the circumstances of their classroom. Although teachers have sometimes been accused of entrenchment in curriculum matters they may also act as filters where indiscriminate change is concerned. This suggests that policy formulation is only one step in the process of curriculum decision-making.[50] Over the years, certainly, policy implementation has not always followed policy formulation. Despite changes in educational theory and the development of courses and programs for a broader range of the school-age group over a longer period of time, the three r's and the academic component of the school have remained intact.

The program with the most prestige, the program that is the centre of most secondary schools, and the program that attracts the bright, upwardly mobile student and his/her parent is the matriculation program. This fact suggests that, despite pedagogical developments and social, political and economic changes, the school curriculum has exhibited a stubborn continuity within its academic core. Around that core and peripheral to it, the fluctuating demands of the society for more education for a broader proportion of the population have been more or less met by means of an organization that has not changed in fifty years.

Notes

I would like to acknowledge the help of the late Dr. George S. Tomkins (UBC) who commented on an earlier draft of this chapter.

[1]For an analysis of Goggin's attitudes and contributions see: Neil C. McDonald, "David J. Goggin: Promoter of National Schools" in David C. Jones *et al.*, eds., *Shaping the Schools of the Canadian West* (Calgary: Detselig, 1979), pp.14-28. See also Ernest Hodgson, "Purposes of Alberta's Schools" (Ph.D. thesis, University of Alberta, 1964) and Bernal E. Walker, "The High School Programme in Alberta During the Territorial period, 1889-1905," in Jones *et al.*, eds., *Shaping the Schools of the Canadian West*, pp. 211-221.

[2]Nancy M. Sheehan, "Character Training and the Cultural Heritage: An Historical Comparison of Canadian Elementary Readers," in George S. Tomkins, ed., *The Curriculum in Canada in Historical Perspective*, (Vancouver: CSSE, 1979), pp. 77-84.

[3]Howard Palmer, *Patterns of Prejudice: A History of Nativism in Alberta* (Toronto: McClelland and Stewart, 1982).

[4]*Annual Report of the Department of Education,* 1920, p. 152, hereafter *AR Education,* 1920, p. 152.

[5]*AR Education,* 191 pp. 219, 226.

[6]Carl Berger, *The Sense of Power: Studies in the Ideas of Canadian Imperialism* (Toronto: University of Toronto Press, 1970).

[7]Neil McDonald, "Canadian Nationalism and North-West Schools, 1884-1905," in Alf Chaiton and Neil McDonald, eds., *Canadian Schools and Canadian Identity* (Toronto: Gage, 1977), pp. 59-87. See also Nancy M. Sheehan, "The IODE, the Schools and World War I," *History of Education Review* 13 (1984): 29-44.

[8]Sheehan, "Character Training and the Cultural Heritage." See also the *Alexandra Readers,* five book series (Toronto: Macmillan, 1908, reprinted through 1921).

[9]Robert M. Stamp, *School Days: A Century of Memories* (Calgary: McClelland and Stewart West, 1975).

[10]A. R. M. Lower, *Canadians in the Making* (Toronto: Longmans, 1958), pp. 349-353.

[11]*Canadian Readers,* five volume series (Toronto: Gage, 1922, reprinted through 1933).

[12]See *Edmonton Journal,* June 25, 1932; *Calgary Herald,* June 16, 1932; and *The Albertan,* June 16, 1932.

[13]Sheehan, "The IODE, the Schools and World War I," pp. 40, 41.

[14]See *The Red Cross Junior,* e.g. Vol. III, Mar. 1924.

[15]A. B. Hodgetts, *What Culture? What Heritage?: A Study of Civic Education in Canada* (Toronto: OISE, 1968).

[16]Robert M. Stamp, "Canadian Education and the National Identity," *Journal of Educational Thought* 5 (Dec. 1971): 133-141.

[17]See Paul Collins, "Canadian Studies: Something Old, Something New," in Hugh A. Stevenson and J. Donald Wilson, eds., *Precepts, Policy and Process: Perspectives on Contemporary Canadian Education* (London: Alexander Blake Assoc., 1977), pp. 231-246.

[18]*Report of the Royal Commission on Bilingualism and Biculturalism ,* (Ottawa, 1967); and Commission on Canadian Studies, *To Know Ourselves,* Vols. I and II (Ottawa, 1976). This report is commonly known as the Symons Report.

[19]The standard work on educational reform in the United States is Lawrence Cremin, *The Transformation of the School: Progressivism in American Education 1876-1957* (New York: Vintage Books, 1961).

[20]Robert S. Patterson, "Progressive Education: Impetus to Educational Change in Alberta and Saskatchewan," in Howard Palmer and Donald Smith, eds., *The New Provinces: Alberta and Saskatchewan, 1905-1980* (Vancouver: Tantalus Research Ltd., 1973), pp. 173-198.

[21]Nancy M. Sheehan, "The Junior Red Cross Movement in Saskatchewan, 1919-1929: Rural Improvement through the Schools," in David C. Jones and Ian MacPherson, eds., *Building Beyond the Homestead: Rural History on the Prairies* (Calgary: University of Calgary Press, 1985), pp. 66-86.

[22]J. Donald Wilson *et al.,* eds., *Canadian Education: A History* (Scarborough: Prentice-Hall, 1970), pp. 374-79; Robert S. Patterson, "The Establishment of Pro-

gressive Education in Alberta," (Ph.D. thesis, Michigan State University, 1968) and "Progressive Education: Impetus to Educational Change in Alberta and Saskatchewan." See also, Cy Groves, "What's Going On In Our Schools?" in Stamp, *School Days: A Century of Memories*, p. 116.

[23]Donalda Dickie, *The Enterprise in Theory and Practice* (Toronto: W. J. Gage & Co. Ltd., 1940).

[24]For an assessment of Newland see Robert S. Patterson, "Hubert Newland: Theorist of Progressive Education," in Robert S. Patterson *et al.*, eds., *Profiles of Canadian Education* (Toronto: Heath, 1974), pp. 289-307.

[25]*AR Education*, 1937, pp. 17-21; *Programme of Studies for the Intermediate School, Grades VII, VIII and IX, 1935* (Edmonton, 1935); *Programme of Studies for the Intermediate School, 1940* (Edmonton, 1940).

[26]John W. Chalmers, *Schools of the Foothills Province* (Toronto: University of Toronto Press, 1967), pp. 195-99; and H.T. Coutts and B.E. Walker, *G. Fred: The Story of G. Fred McNally* (Don Mills: J.M. Dent & Sons, 1964), p. 66.

[27]In 1939 1,269 one-room schools in Alberta were offering instruction in Grades IX, X and XI. *AR Education*, 1939, p. 62. The same report outlines a four-year schedule of courses for one teacher high schools offering Grades X, XI and XII.

[28]Robert S. Patterson, "Progressive Education," pp. 193-94.

[29]Sheehan, "Character Training and the Cultural Heritage," p. 82.

[30]Hilda Neatby, *So Little for the Mind* (Toronto: Clarke-Irwin, 1953).

[31]*Report of the Royal Commission on Education* (Edmonton: King's Printer, 1959). This is popularly known as the Cameron Commission. See also *Senior High School Handbook* (Edmonton: King's Printer, 1959).

[32]Alberta, *Programme of Studies for the High School*, Bulletin II (Edmonton: King's Printer, 1946).

[33]Nicholas Tkach, *Alberta Catholic Schools . . . A Social History* (Edmonton: Faculty of Education Publication Service, 1983) pp. 290-93.

[34]For a discussion of changing societal conditions and impact on the school see *A System in Conflict: A Report to the Minister of Labour by the Fact Finding Commission*, (Edmonton 1980). This is popularly known as the Kratzmann Report and followed the strike in 1980 by the teachers of the Calgary Board of Education.

[35]Alberta, *Review of Secondary Programs: Report of the Minister's Advisory Committee: Foundation for the Future* (Edmonton, 1985).

[36]McDonald, "David Goggin: Promoter of National Schools," p. 24.

[37]*AR Education*, 1920, p. 132 and *AR Education*, 1929, p. 117.

[38]Stamp, *School Days: A Century of Memories*, p. 36.

[39]In 1906 the percentage of students in grades above eight was 2.41; in 1916 it was 5.8 and in 1928 it was 11.44. *AR Education*, 1930, p. 14. The high school revision committee chaired by G. Fred McNally, supervisor of schools, was fifteen strong with representatives from women's organizations, boards of trade, labour, educational stakeholder groups and practising educators. *AR Education*, 1921, p. 28.

[40]Timothy A. Dunn, "Teaching the Meaning of Work: Vocational Education in British Columbia, 1900-1929," in Jones *et al.*, eds., *Shaping the Schools of the Canadian West*, pp. 236-256.

[41]Year after year the annual reports comment on the preponderance of the matriculation and normal school programs and include statistics on the diplomas awarded.

AR Education, 1935, p. 26. See also B. E. Walker, "Public Secondary Education in Alberta: Organization and Curriculum, 1889-1951" (Ph.D. thesis, Stanford University, 1955), p. 149.

[42]Chalmers, *Schools of the Foothills Province*, pp. 214-16 and Walker, "Public Secondary Education in Alberta," pp. 262-265.

[43]See *Report of the Royal Commission on Education*, pp. 13-21.

[44]Jo Anne Knobbe, "The Inception of the Junior Academic Vocational Program in Calgary Public Schools" (M.A. thesis, University of Calgary, 1978); John Chalmers, *Schools of the Foothills Province*, pp. 216-18; *Senior High School Handbook* (Edmonton, 1962); and *Program of Studies for the High School* (Edmonton, 1965). By 1980 courses in forty-two non-academic fields were offered. *AR Education*, 1979-80.

[45]Alberta "A Choice of Futures," *Report of the Commission on Educational Planning* (Edmonton, 1972), pp. 179-82.

[46]Alberta, *Review of Secondary Programs*, pp. 7, 8, 18 and 20.

[47]*Report of the Royal Commission on Industrial Training and Technical Education* (Ottawa 1913).

[48]*Report of the Royal Commission on Bilingualism and Biculturalism, Book II Education* (Ottawa, 1968); Manoly R. Lupul, "Multiculturalism and Canadian National Identity: The Alberta Experience," in Chaiton and McDonald, eds., *Canadian Schools and Canadian Identity*, pp. 165-75 , and *AR Education*, 1969, pp. 41-42.

[49]See for example Nancy M. Sheehan, "National Pressure Groups and Provincial Curriculum Policy: Temperance in Nova Scotia's Schools 1880-1930," *Canadian Journal of Education* 9 (1984): 73-88.

[50]See George S. Tomkins, "Towards a History of Curriculum Development in Canada," in G. S. Tomkins, ed., *The Curriculum in Canada in Historical Perspective*, pp. 1-17 and "Stability and Change in the Canadian Curriculum," in J. Donald Wilson, ed., *Canadian Education in the 1980s* (Calgary: Detselig, 1981), pp. 135-158.

4

Confronting "Modern" Problems Through Play: The Beginning of Physical Education in Manitoba's Public Schools, 1900-1915

Morris Mott

At present, the physical education program in Manitoba's public schools has two purposes. One is to "foster the development" of "habits" and "leisure-time activities" which can be practised and enjoyed "throughout life." The second is to "contribute to . . . present levels of health and fitness."[1] In Manitoba as in other provinces, the first objective was really only identified, or at least articulated, after World War II. Its presence reflects the assumption, held by educators and others for nearly forty years now, that youngsters need to be prepared for the vast amounts of "free" time they can expect to have as adults, and in particular must be exposed to constructive, or at least harmless, leisure activities. The second objective was not so recently introduced in Manitoba. In fact, it was dissatisfaction with "present levels of health and fitness" among school-aged boys and girls that led to the establishment of physical education in the province.

This took place between about 1900 and 1915, when hundreds of individuals involved in education in Manitoba, and thousands of members of the general public, rather suddenly became aware that too many of the children around them were physically unhealthy. They assumed that this state of affairs would inevitably cause — perhaps it already reflected — mental and moral weaknesses. They realized, as public school Inspector Charles K. Newcombe put it, that the education system paid "scant attention . . . to the needs of the physical organism," and concluded that it was "defective" for that reason.[2] As a result, far more than previously, teachers attempted to educate their pupils physically. In doing so they tried to utilize what was often referred to as the "play instinct," hoping to bring it, to use the words of Inspector E.E. Best, "under control as an educative force."[3]

Historical developments never occur "out of the blue," of course, and prior to the turn of the century certain Manitoban educators had taken some interest in the physical development and activities of students. From the 1870s on, many of them had certainly become familiar with the athleticist ideals emanating from the British public schools, and in particular with Thomas Hughes' articulation of those ideals in his extremely popular novel *Tom Brown's Schooldays*. This had been true especially of several teachers and administrators at Winnipeg's three private Protestant denominational colleges, St. John's (Anglican), Manitoba (Presbyterian), and Wesley (Methodist), where a real attempt to put the ideals into practice had occurred. The college newspapers

57

had constantly reminded students of the importance of activities on the playing field and in the gymnasium; reasonably impressive facilities for games and formal exercises had been provided; leagues and teams for a number of sports had been set up.[4] In the publicly supported schools too, the physical well-being of pupils had not been completely ignored, although less emphasis had been placed upon it, primarily because these pupils were normally younger than those at denominational colleges and were seldom if ever housed in residence. Still, several teachers had encouraged participation in "manly" games. One who did so was Nellie Mooney, later Nellie McClung, the famous woman's suffrage leader. She had accepted her first position at a rural school near Manitou in 1889, and had tried to get her students to play football at recess and noon hour, largely because she had read *Tom Brown's Schooldays* and believed that through games like football youngsters acquired valuable qualities and learned important lessons.[5] Moreover, in the city of Winnipeg, from the 1880s forward a few teachers had conducted classes in "military drill," and beginning in 1895 the Winnipeg school board had hired a Major T.S. Billman to visit specific schools, evidently about once every two weeks, to run students through calisthenics and military exercises.[6] In the late nineteenth century, then, "physical education" had not been completely unknown.

After 1900, however, there was much, much more of it, and individuals involved in education were conscious of its purposes and importance to a degree they had never been before. These facts are made clear by several developments. In 1902, for the first time, some prospective teachers — in this case all who wanted to earn "second class" permanent certificates — were required to learn how to conduct "physical training" classes.[7] In 1903 the Department of Education published new plans and specifications for rural schools, in which trustees were told that "sufficient room should . . . be left at the rear of the building for a good large play ground, and nothing should be done to diminish this all-important breathing space."[8] In Winnipeg's schools, after about 1904 the amount of attention given to formal drill increased dramatically.[9] In 1905 the Brandon school board, and shortly thereafter for a short time the Portage la Prairie board, followed Winnipeg's lead and hired special physical training instructors to conduct classes in schools in those cities.[10] Beginning around 1909 the annual field day, in which children from various schools in a district competed against one another in track and field events, in ball games, and in "parade" or competitive drill, became an institution, especially in rural centres.[11] In 1911 Manitoban authorities made arrangements to receive money from the Strathcona Trust, set up two years earlier by Sir F.W. Borden, minister of militia and defence, and Lord Strathcona, long known to Manitobans as Donald A. Smith of the Hudson's Bay Company and the Canadian Pacific Railway syndicate. This fund was designed to stimulate physical and military training in public schools, and it succeeded in doing so in Manitoba as in other provinces.[12] From 1911 on, a textbook containing an outline of appropriate physical exercises was made available to all teachers, and they were told that they must use it daily; *every* new teacher was now required to receive instruction at normal school on how to conduct "physical training"; teachers previously certified were now encouraged to take special summer courses offered so they could "upgrade" themselves; and, in schools where the teacher was not qualified to instruct in physical education, members of the militia often came to conduct classes.[13]

All these eventualities revealed a new commitment to physical education. Even more notable is that large numbers of teachers acted on the recommendations they received time and time again to the effect that they should get out on the playground at recess, at noon hour and after school, to organize and supervise games and other activities for their pupils.[14] Only one indication that they followed these exhortations is that dozens of new sports teams and leagues were formed between 1900 and 1915 for inter-school and intra-mural competition. In Winnipeg, for example, in 1900 and 1901 respectively, a Schools Football (Soccer) League and a Schools Lacrosse League were set up by teachers and principals; by 1914 each of them arranged games for perhaps one thousand boys of eleven to sixteen years of age.[15] In Neepawa in 1914 a six-team schools lacrosse league existed, and by then school teams or leagues had been formed, especially for football (soccer), lacrosse and hockey, in a number of centres around the province.[16] Not all teachers became enthusiastic supporters of games and sports, of course. However, their willingness to organize these activities reveals that many if not most of them agreed with Inspector Best's opinion that knowing "the how and why of the playground" was more important than they had assumed.[17]

There were several reasons why Manitoban educators and the general public became aware of the value of physical education, and anxious to incorporate it into the curriculum in the early twentieth century. One was that they were generally in favour of the notion, becoming more and more widely held throughout the western world, that schools should offer more than primarily academic training to normal children. They were adjusting to the ideas associated with "new education," and in this period they began to provide "special" education for the handicapped or others with particular needs, and to offer "manual training," "vocational training" and "domestic science" as well as "physical training." In short, physical education emerged in part because, as Keith Wilson has noted, "the aims and scope" of education were being broadened.[18]

Its implementation and the emphasis it received, however, owed more to Manitobans' new appreciation of the importance of play. By the first decade of the twentieth century many of them were familiar with opinions associated with G. Stanley Hall, Joseph Lee, J.J. Kelso and other child psychologists and child savers. Educators and others in the province seemed convinced that, as Dominick Cavallo has written in reference to turn-of-the-century American play organizers, "children's play was too important to be left to children."[19] Unorganized, unsupervised play was too often "aimless racing and yelling" that encouraged bullying and a wide variety of undesirable forms of behaviour.[20] Play activities should be structured and watched over by a responsible adult, though not to the extent that the youngsters' spontaneity was completely eliminated or their fun ruined. If activities were organized and supervised properly, especially by someone familiar with the capabilities of young people at various "stages" of growth, then children at play would unconsciously learn very important lessons at the age when they were best able to learn them, indeed when they *had* to learn them if they were to develop normally.[21] Moreover, when a teacher was the responsible adult in charge, there was an added benefit: he or she would really get to know each of the students, and be better prepared to deal with individual personalites in the classroom.[22]

By far the most important reason for the new emphasis on physical education, however, was that after 1900 Manitobans suddenly realized they were confronted with many of the problems associated with "modern civilization." These problems had been already spotted and to some extent dealt with, partly by broadening school curricula and harnessing play, in other parts of the English-speaking world. This was why Manitobans were able quickly to advance solutions to modern difficulties once they recognized them.

The modern problem that received the most attention was declining health. In Manitoba in the early twentieth century, as in other parts of the English-speaking world in the nineteenth, technological innovations, industrialization and rapid population growth all represented, on balance, "progress." But there were some bothersome developments associated with it. For one thing, the physical demands of virtually every occupation diminished.[23] For another, the growing population became more and more concentrated in urban centres. Manitoba's population grew 117 percent between 1901 and 1916, from 255,211 to 553,860, but during the same period the number of people living in communities of 1,000 or more grew from 70,436 to 241,014, or 242 percent.[24] Winnipeg's population grew from 42,340 to 163,000, or 285 percent, and in Winnipeg as in other large "modern" cities the health problems were both widespread and visible. The many poorly-heated, poorly-ventilated, overcrowded houses, with inadequate water supply and with very inferior facilities for waste disposal created appalling infant mortality and death-by-disease rates.[25] No wonder the *Western School Journal,* a periodical published for and by Manitoba educators, evidently took seriously a New York medical doctor who wrote that it had been "authoritatively reported that a family in the city dies out in three generations unless crossed by country blood."[26]

The problem of deteriorating physical health would not have seemed so significant had not Manitobans assumed that it would inevitably lead to mental and moral degeneration. In fact sometimes they seemed to argue that physical regression *revealed* moral decay that had already reached an advanced stage, thus echoing the opinion of Charles Kingsley, the famous English "Muscular Christian" clergyman and novelist, who once said that "souls secrete their bodies, as snails do shells."[27] Most Manitobans would not have gone quite that far. They assumed, however, that the healthy body was in some way associated with and accompanied by the healthy mind and the healthy soul.[28] It therefore seemed of a pattern to them that, at the same time as the overall physical health of the population seemed to be falling, the rates of juvenile delinquency, prostitution and violent crime seemed to be rising. Also increasing, in This Age of the Great Barbeque, was the appeal of those false gods, Mammon and Pleasure. In fact, it was the depraved and ultimately unwise desire for money and excitement that made it so difficult to keep young men and women on the farm or in the small village; despite all the evidence that showed how wicked and unhealthy life in the big city was, young people kept moving there.[29] The absence of fitness went hand-in-hand with irrational, immoral behaviour.

Therefore, educators who arranged for periods of formal exercises and supervised games and sports believed they would thereby foster the development of strong, efficient bodies, but they also assumed they would evoke much more than that. They would elicit a particularly commendable sort of calm courage because many of the ball games and other activities rewarded determination and physical bravery while penalizing recklessness and fierceness. Educators might contribute to sexual purity because at least in males, according to pre-Freudian assumptions, strength and vitality and especially endurance (which team games like hockey and lacrosse tested to a greater extent then than they do now) could not be present if semen were wasted.[30] Teachers would inculcate discipline, which was viewed by many as synonymous with "control of the body by the will," and which was regarded as the main benefit to be derived from periods of formal calisthenics and drill. They would help children learn how to win and lose in the proper spirit, so that they would become neither falsely proud in victory not enraged and disgusted in defeat, but instead reflective and therefore capable of learning something from what they had done rightly or wrongly. Teachers would create respect for rules, laws and legitimate authority. They would surely nourish an awareness that success depended upon perseverance, planning and skill. They would instill a sense of loyalty to the group, the essence of patriotism. They would help develop skills and attributes needed to cooperate effectively with others, thereby providing useful training for citizenship. They would stimulate wholesome amusements among rural young people, making it less likely that youths would head for the city in search of good times. Teachers would help form alert minds capable of making decisions rapidly and accurately. By organizing and supervising the right exercises, games and sports for children at the appropriate stages in their lives, educators would, to adopt the word they so often used themselves, develop "character."[31]

Not the least important point educators and others considered when they advocated physical education was that, as D.S. Woods (a prominent teacher who later became the first dean of the Faculty of Education at the University of Manitoba) put it in 1913, play "leads to the heart of the foreign child as readily as [to that of] the British-born."[32] Between the turn of the century and the beginning of World War I the number of Manitobans of "foreign" origin expanded much more rapidly than did the population as a whole. As already mentioned, between 1901 and 1916 the population of the province more than doubled to over half a million people. However, during the same fifteen years the number of Jews in the province jumped from about 2,000 to nearly 16,500, and the total number of Austrians, Bukovinians, Galicians, Hungarians, Ruthenians, Poles, Russians and Ukrainians rose from just under 25,000 to over 100,000.[33] More than a few members of the host British-Protestant culture group felt that allowing central and eastern Europeans into the West in such large numbers was a mistake. One who did so was the Methodist clergyman Rev. Wellington Bridgman, who believed these "foreigners" were "criminally inclined" by nature and should be left "at home" so there would be more room for "sturdy, trustworthy" immigrants of British stock.[34] Most British-Protestants were not exclusionists like Bridgman. Nevertheless, they assumed that immigrants from continental Europe were products of backward civilizations — some of them "a thousand years behind" the British-Canadian one, according to the agrarian leader G.F. Chipman — and they believed that no more serious modern problem confronted the majority of Manitobans than how to assimilate the newcomers.[35] Among the important agencies for Canadianizing at least the children of immigrants were, as Woods' comment would suggest, structured play activities, especially games, and still more especially team ball games.

Though they did not spell out the point, educators and other Manitobans of the early twentieth century were aware that games are *designed* activities, structured so as to reward, and therefore evoke, certain perceptions and forms of behaviour. They demanded a shared awareness and appreciation of different roles, rules, customs and actions.[36] When "foreign" youngsters played a "Canadian" game with a number of "Canadian" children they were, for the time being at least, obligated to think and act like Canadians. It was all but unanimously assumed that the perceptions, values and attributes acquired in games were transferable to, and valuable in, "real-life" situations. This is why immigrant youngsters who attended schools such as W.J. Sisler's Strathcona School in Winnipeg's North End, or who lived in the Presbyterian Boys' Home in Teulon and attended the local public high school, were virtually forced to play soccer and baseball.[37] By entering into these "Canadian" games they were compelled, at least for the duration of the contest but probably for longer, to see the world in a "Canadian" way, and to appreciate "Canadian" skills and qualities.[38]

That the establishment of physical education was motivated by the perceived necessity to respond to modern problems is revealed in particular in the encouragement given to girls to engage in formal exercises and games. In the very late Victorian and the Edwardian eras in Manitoba as in the rest of the English-speaking world, many people of "British" origin, or of what was imprecisely referred to as the "Anglo-Saxon" race, became troubled by perceived racial degeneration. A low birth rate and the evident negative consequences of living in large urban centres seemed to suggest that the British peoples might not have the physical, mental and moral qualities needed to carry out their mission to civilize the world. Suddenly, bringing forth healthier babies became a priority. Therefore the health of prospective mothers became of immense concern.[39]

Their health would benefit, so educators now believed, if they participated in exercises and games which called for grace, co-ordination and judgement but which were at least vigorous enough that deep breaths were required and a sweat appeared. Assumptions carried forward from the nineteenth century still dictated that females should not engage in activities in which significant degrees of strength or endurance were demanded, or in which there was body contact, or in which a highly competitive personality was rewarded. It was still accepted too that special care had to be taken to make sure that, when performing exercises or participating in a game, young ladies were not placed in embarrassing positions, and that they did not over-exert themselves and harm their reproductive capacities.[40] But by the early twentieth century the time was past when, as happened in 1883, a Winnipeg clergyman could seriously suggest that one of the eventual consequences of allowing boys and girls to play together was prostitution! The time was also past when, as happened through the early 1890s, school girls tested themselves in "silence" matches, the objective of which was to keep quiet for as long as possible; and no longer, for games requiring vigour, did girls chose boys to compete for them by "proxy."[41]

Females now took part in many of the track and field events, especially the standing long jump, the shorter dashes, and the softball or volleyball throwing-for-distance competitions.[42] They now took part in formal drill. Sometimes they did so in segregated classes, especially in large schools like those in Winnipeg, for which a separate girls' physical training instructor was hired in 1912. More often they did so with the boys, in which case they performed most of the exercises the young males did, but were expected to emphasize grace rather than power.[43] They now played baseball, hockey and the relatively new game of basketball which was, among them, for the time being primarily a summer outdoor sport. When playing these and other ball games they still wore remarkably inefficient clothing that made it all but impossible for them to run "too" hard for "too" long. In basketball there were even special girls' rules observed which made it still more unlikely that they would overtax their bodies; these rules might require six-a-side rather than five, or confine individual players to certain parts of the court.[44] Nevertheless, the young ladies were now far more active, in a wider variety of sports, than they had been a generation earlier and they were praised for being so. In 1913 a writer in the *Winnipeg Telegram,* probably a male, said that the old fears about the negative consequences of vigorous exercises for women had been simply unfounded. "There can be no doubt," he said, that when "reasonably conducted" they were "just as excellent for girls as for boys."[45]

Among young males or young females, then, play could be employed to inculcate attributes that seemed required and generally lacking in the modern age. The school was not the only institution through which this could be done, of course. In fact, educators as well as other influential people made sure that it was not.

Among the other institutions now utilized as never before to develop character through play were the churches. In the early twentieth century the major Protestant denominations as well as other churches began to facilitate and arrange exercise classes, team ball games, tennis, swimming, skating, and track and field, especially for teenagers. The Christian churches in Minnedosa formed an Inter-church Amateur Athletic Association in 1910.[46] In other towns similar organizations were established during the pre-war years, and in Winnipeg by 1914 churches sponsored so many teams, leagues and events that it was all but impossible to keep track of them all.[47] In Winnipeg and, to a lesser extent, in Brandon, the municipal governments provided funds to sponsor recreation. In these two cities organized, supervised playgrounds emerged between 1908 and 1913. Through the co-operation of school boards, these were normally set up on school grounds during the summer vacation months, and they were viewed as indispensable in the formation of character. In Winnipeg, besides the playgrounds, publicly funded, supervised skating rinks and swimming pools were inaugurated, to mention only those public faciltes established primarily for minors.[48] In Brandon and Winnipeg there were also very active local branches of the Y.M.C.A. Their officers, like officers of branches throughout the world, were now more committed than ever to developing the "whole" man, and in particular to instilling the best qualities of a Hercules, as well as of a Socrates and a Jesus. These officers set up impressive new facilities in both cities which were especially suited for indoor exercise classes and sports; thus they became more capable of meeting their goal than they had been previously.[49]

Another institution which used play activities to develop character was the Boy Scouts. Troops were formed in a number of centres in the half-dozen years after 1909. Their leaders employed track and field, basketball, baseball, hockey, soccer and lacrosse "to make of boys honorable, truthful, upright, punctual, honest, neat and tidy men of good morals."[50] In Winnipeg, for "neglected" young fellows such as newsboys, shoe-shine boys and others who learned about life "on the street" rather than in respectable homes, churches and schools, there were still further organizations founded such as the Winnipeg Boys' Club, through which concerned adults attempted to make working lads into "clean, strong, healthy, upright" Canadians, largely by arranging recreational activities for them.[51] The schools were not the only places where play was marshalled to meet modern problems. However, they were the places where this seemed capable of being done most effectively if only because, despite the absence of compulsory attendance laws, so many children spent so much time in them.[52]

It was in the early twentieth century, then, that Manitoban educators and Manitobans in general began to appreciate the importance of physical education. Play activities, they realized, could be deployed to instill a wide variety of praiseworthy attributes called for by modern conditions. Their efforts to utilize play met with some problems, of course. For example, those among them who especially appreciated precision and discipline tried to emphasize military drill. They discovered that among the general public there was a good deal of opposition to the encouragement of militarism. This meant that they could not insist on the use of "guns," which were for the most part broom handles anyway, and they usually agreed to compromise by having pupils do calisthenics in "military fashion," which is to say on command and in unison.[53] Another problem was that the children themselves often found the formal exercises boring. They approached games and sports much more enthusiastically; in the inter-war years in Manitoba as elsewhere, these latter activities would receive more emphasis in "phys. ed" partly for that reason.[54]

The difficulties of using play effectively were especially acute in rural one-room schools which, even as late as 1914, were attended by between one-third and one-half of Manitoba's school children.[55] At recesses, at noon hours, and after school, teachers in these institutions often found it next to impossible to supervise recreational activities, because they had to use these times to prepare lessons, mark assignments, and help children who had been absent recently or who were simply a bit "slow" to catch up in their reading, writing and 'rithmetic.[56] Moreover, even if they had the time, one-room school teachers had neither the facilities nor the equipment to arrange activities in which children of both sexes and all ages could joyfully engage, and from which all could benefit.

One-room schools, like all other schools in the province, were built and maintained at the expense of local taxpayers. Almost never did they possess a gymnasium or auditorium of the kind the larger schools were acquiring. In one-room schools, at least in winter, formal exercises had to be done in unused space in the basement if there was one, or in rows between the desks. The playground around the building was likely to be large, but often unsuited for some of the recommended activities because the outdoor toilets, the well, or the school barn might be in the way, or because the ground was not level, or was muddy, or was covered with trees or gopher holes.[57] The rural pupils rarely brought the lightweight, spiked athletic shoes, the tube skates, the colourful uniforms, or the recently manufactured bats, balls, gloves and sticks which, in the early twentieth century, were making such sports as track and field, soccer, baseball, lacrosse and hockey much more kinaesthetically and aesthetically satisfying. They normally played with their regular, slippery leather-soled boots, their everyday, cumbersome pants, sweaters and coats, their homemade, unreliable, inefficient balls, mitts and sticks, and their skate blades that snapped onto, or screwed into normal shoes, and which had an infuriating tendency to fall off. Of course, the lack of equipment and facilities could also represent obstacles to the utilization of play in the cities and large towns. But in urban centres greater tax revenues were available for each school, and frequently individuals or men's sports clubs donated equipment, so that the problems did not exist to the same degree.[58]

The first systematic efforts to capitalize on the power of play may not have been as successful as desired. Still, a great deal was accomplished in physical education in the first decade and a half of the twentieth century. In these years most Manitoban educators became aware of the subject's importance and, to adopt Neil Sutherland's words, they were able to "draw the plans for and rough in many of the dimensions of" this new part of the curriculum.[59]

Notes

[1]*K-12 Physical Education Curriculum Guide* (Winnipeg: Government of Manitoba, 1981), p. 3.

[2]*Manitoba Department of Education Annual Report,* 1906, p. 54.

[3]*Department of Education Annual Report,* 1910, p. 54. See also Geo. J. Fisher, M.D., "Physical Training in the Public Schools," *Western School Journal,* II (Jan. 1907): 3; D.S. Woods, "Playground Activities," *Western School Journal,* VIII (Apr. 1913): 135.

[4]See Morris Kenneth Mott, "Manly Sports and Manitobans, Settlement Days to World War One" (Ph.D. thesis, Queen's University, 1980), pp. 115-117.

[5]Nellie L. McClung, *Clearing in the West, My Own Story* (Toronto: Thomas Allen Ltd., 1935), p. 272.

[6]J.B. Wallis, "Military Drill in the Winnipeg Schools: An Historical Sketch," *Western School Journal,* I (Nov. 1906): 7-8; *Annual Report of the School Trustees of Protestant School District of Winnipeg No. 1,* 1888, p. 14; *Annual Report of the Trustees of the Winnipeg Public School District No. 1,* 1894, pp. 10-11.

[7]David Alexander Downie, "A History of Physical Education in the Public Schools of Manitoba" (M.Ed. thesis, University of Manitoba, 1961), pp. 63-64.

[8]S.A. Bedford, *Plans and Specifications for Rural Schools, Approved by the Advisory Board. Suggestions for the Planning and Decoration of School Grounds* (Winnipeg: Government of Manitoba, 1903), p. 21. Thanks to Mr. R.R. Rostecki for this reference.

[9]Richard Collier Green, "The History of School Cadets in the City of Winnipeg" (M.Ed. thesis, University of Manitoba, 1950), pp. 32-34, 37-39; *Manitoba Free Press,* hereafter *MFP,* July 4, 1908, sports section, p. 4.

[10]*Department of Education Annual Report,* 1905, in Manitoba: *Sessional Papers,* no. 7, 1906, p. 385; *Annual Report,* 1906, in Manitoba: *Sessional Papers,* no. 6, 1907, p. 353; *Annual Report,* 1911, p. 40; *Annual Report,* 1912-13, p. 50.

[11]*MFP,* Oct. 14, 1913, p. 6; *Minnedosa Tribune,* June 6, 1912, p. 2, June 5, 1913, p. 2, May 28, 1914, p. 2, June 11, 1914, p. 2; *Brandon Sun,* Oct. 27, 1910, part 1, pp. 2, 6; *Souris Plaindealer,* Sept. 29, 1910, p. 1; *Killarney Guide,* June 15, 1911, p. 1; *Dauphin Press,* Oct. 19, 1911, p. 7; Boissevain History Committee, *Beckoning Hills Revisited. Ours is a Goodly Heritage, Morton-Boissevain, 1881-1981* (Boissevain: Boissevain History Committee, 1981), p. 152; Lundar and District Historical Society, *Wagons to Wings, History of Lundar and Districts, 1872-1980* (Lundar: Lundar and District Historical Society, 1980?), pp. 40, 48.

[12]See James L. Gear, "Factors Influencing the Development of Government Sponsored Physical Fitness Programmes in Canada from 1850 to 1972," *Canadian*

Journal of History of Sport and Physical Education, IV (Dec. 1973): 11-14; Lorne W. Sawula, "Notes on the Strathcona Trust," *Canadian Journal of History of Sport and Physical Education,* V (May 1974): 56-61; L. Donald Morrow, "Selected Topics in the History of Physical Education in Ontario: From Dr. Egerton Ryerson to the Strathcona Trust 1844-1939" (Ph.D. thesis, University of Alberta, 1975), chapter 4; L. Goodwin, "A History of Physical Education in Alberta," in *Proceedings of the First Canadian Symposium on the History of Sport and Physical Education, University of Alberta, May 13-16, 1970* (Ottawa: Government of Canada, 1970), pp. 381-382; Robert F. Osborne, "Origins of Physical Education in British Columbia," in *Proceedings, First Canadian Symposium,* pp. 367-371; John MacDiarmid, "The Strathcona Trust — Its Influence on Physical Education," in *Proceedings, First Canadian Symposium,* pp. 397-409.

[13]Downie, "Physical Education in Manitoba," pp. 66, 75; N.A., "New System of Physical Drill," *Western School Journal,* VI (Oct. 1911): 300-301; J.S. Duncan, "The Cadet Instructor's Course," *Western School Journal,* VI (Oct. 1911): 278-280; *Department of Education Annual Report,* 1911, in Manitoba, *Sessional Papers,* no. 12, 1913, p. 617.

[14]N.a., "Physical Culture," *Educational Journal of Western Canada,* II (Dec. 1902): 571; Catherine M. Condon, "The Teacher as a Director of Play," *Western School Journal,* I (Dec. 1906): 19-20; H.R. Hadcock, "The Need of Physical Training," *Western School Journal,* II (Feb. 1907): 37-38; Woods, "Playground Activities," pp. 135-138; *Department of Education Annual Report,* 1911, pp. 98-99, 114-115; *Annual Report,* 1912-13, p. 83; *Annual Report,* 1915, pp. 96, 99, 111.

[15]*MFP,* Sept. 20, 1900, p. 5, Apr. 13, 1901, p. 5, Apr. 16, 1901, p. 5, July 11, 1908, sports section, p. 3, Oct. 10, 1913, p. 7, Apr. 4, 1914, p. 8; *Annual Report of the School Trustees of the School district of Winnipeg No. 1,* 1907, pp. 18-19.

[16]*Neepawa Press,* May 29, 1914, p. 1; *Brandon Times,* Nov. 6, 1902, p. 9, Nov. 2, 1905, p. 6; *Boissevain Recorder,* Jan. 22, 1914, p. 4.

[17]*Department of Education Annual Report,* 1911, in Manitoba: *Sessional Papers,* no. 12, 1913, pp. 655, 657.

[18]Keith Wilson, "The Development of Education in Manitoba" (Ph.D. thesis, Michigan State University, 1967), chapter 6, especially pp. 300-308.

[19]Dominick Cavallo, *Muscles and Morals: Organized Playgrounds and Urban Reform, 1880-1920* (Philadelphia: University of Pennsylvania Press, 1981), p. 25.

[20]N.a., "Value of Games for Children," *Western School Journal,* IV (June 1909): 203; Condon, "The Teacher as a Director of Play," pp. 19-20; Woods, "Playground Activities," p. 136; *MFP,* May 22, 1909, sports section p. 3.

[21]*Winnipeg Saturday Post,* June 14, 1913, p. 5; H.R. Hadcock, "Winnipeg Playgrounds, 1910," *Western School Journal,* V (Sept. 1910): 228; Emma G. Olmstead, "Play in Relation to Age and Sex," reprint from *Primary Education,* in *Western School Journal,* IV (Feb. 1909): 65-66; Major Joseph McLaren, "Physical Training with Special Application to Rural Schools," *Western School Journal,* IX (May 1914): 103; n.a., "Play," *Western School Journal,* VII Jan. 1913): 33.

[22]Condon, "The Teacher as a Director of Play," pp. 19-20; Woods, "Playground Activities," p. 136; n.a., "Physical Culture," p. 571; W.G. Pearce, "The Effect of the General Conduct on the Pupils of the Teacher's Presence on the Playground," *Western School Journal,* XII (May 1917): 208-209; H. Lambert Williams, "The Teacher on the Playground," *Western School Journal,* XII (May 1917): 209-210.

[23]*MFP,* Nov. 7, 1908, sports section, p. 1.

[24]*The Census of Canada,* 1931, vol. II, p. 87; *The Census of the Prairie Provinces,* 1916, p. 2; Alan Artibise, *Winnipeg An Illustrated History* (Toronto: James Lorimer and Company, 1977), p. 200.

[25]Some information on this is contained in Alan Artibise, *Winnipeg: a social history of urban growth 1874-1914* (Montreal: McGill-Queen's University Press, 1975, chapter 13.

[26]Fisher, "Physical Training in the Public Schools," p. 3.

[27]Robert Bernard Martin, *The Dust of Combat, A Life of Charles Kingsley* (London: Faber and Faber Ltd., 1959), p. 235; *MFP,* Nov. 7, 1908, sports section, p. 1; A.E. Garland, M.D., "Why the City Man Needs Gymnasium Exercise," *Western Sportsman,* II (Dec. 1906): 318.

[28]W.G. Cates, "The Relationship of Athletics to College Life," *Western Sportsman,* II (Oct. 1906): 283-284; J.M. McCutcheon, "The Relation of Physical Education to Moral Development," *Western School Journal,* XV (Sept. 1920): 291, McLaren, "Physical Training," p. 97; "Play," p. 32; *MFP,* Feb. 17, 1908, p. 5, Sept. 25, 1909, sports section, p. 1. On the mind, body, soul relationship, there is very interesting material in Bruce Haley, *The Healthy Body and Victorian Culture* (Cambridge, Mass.: Harvard University Press, 1978), chapters 1 and 2, in Donald J. Mrozek, *Sport and American Mentality, 1880-1910* (Knoxville: University of Tennessee Press, 1983), chapters 2 and 7, and in James C. Whorton, *Crusaders for Fitness: The History of American Health Reformers* (Princeton, N.J.: Princeton University Press, 1982), chapter 9.

[29]*Brandon Times,* May 11, 1905, p. 1; n.a., "City Life Problems,"*Grain Growers' Guide,* Apr. 8, 1914, p. 5; J.S. Woodsworth, "Some City Problems, III — The Solidarity of Modern Society," *Grain Growers' Guide,* May 6, 1914, p. 7; Nellie L. McClung, "Why Boys and Girls Leave the Farm," *The Nor'-West Farmer,* Sept. 5, 1913, p. 1106. On this theme in the entire Western Canadian context, see David C. Jones, "'There is Some Power About the Land' — The Western Agrarian Press and Country Life Ideology," *Journal of Canadian Studies,* XVII (Autumn 1982): 96-108.

[30]See Bryan Strong, "Ideas of the Early Sex Education Movement in America," *History of Education Quarterly,* XII (Summer 1972): 129-132; Michael Bliss, "'Pure Books on Avoided Subjects': Pre-Freudian Sexual Ideas in Canada," in Michiel Horn and Ronald Sabourin, eds., *Studies in Canadian Social History* (Toronto: McClelland and Stewart Ltd., 1974), pp. 334-339; *MFP,* June 8, 1875, p. 3.

[31]*MFP,* Feb. 15, 1904, p. 7, Nov. 14, 1908, sports section, p. 1, Nov. 21, 1908, sports section, p. 1, Aug. 31, 1911, p. 7; *Annual Report of the Trustees of the School District of Winnipeg No. 1,* 1900, pp. 18, 35; *Department of Education Annual Report,* 1910, p. 54; *Annual Report,* 1914, in Manitoba: *Sessional Papers,* no. 3, 1915, p. 313; "'Toba 03-04,'", p. 12, Manitoba College File, MG 10 B23, Public Archives of Manitoba; H.R. Hadcock, "Athletics and Sport in the West," *Western Sportsman,* II (Oct, 1906): 281-282; Professor Joliffe, "On Sport," *Vox Wesleyana,* XII (Nov. 1908): 25-26; "Value of Athletics," reprint from *Medical Record in Western School Journal,* I (June 1906): 19; n.a., "It is Character that Counts," *Western School Journal,* III (Mar. 1908): 98-99; "Playgrounds" *Western School Journal,* IV (June 1909): 209-210; Dr. Mary Crawford, "Physical Training in Public Schools," *Western School Journal,* VII (May 1912): 176-178; n.a., "Play," pp. 32-33; Woods, "Playground Activities," p. 136; McLaren, "Physical Training," pp. 96-103; *Neepawa Press,* Mar. 27, 1914, p. 1.

[32]Woods, "Playground Activities," p. 137.

[33]*Census of the Prairie Provinces,* 1916, p. 142; *Census of Canada,* 1931, vol. 1, pp. 717-718.

[34]Rev. W. Bridgman, "The Immigrant Problem As It Affects Canadian Methodism," *Vox Wesleyana,* XII (Nov. 1907): 63-66. Bridgman had more scathing remarks to make about the "foreigners" in his *Breaking Prairie Sod,* published in 1918. See Mott, "The Foreign Peril: Nativism in Winnipeg, 1916-1923" (M.A. thesis, University of Manitoba, 1970), pp. 11-13.

[35]G.F. Chipman, "Winnipeg: The Melting Pot," *Canadian Magazine,* XXXIII (1909): 413; *Neepawa Register,* June 27, 1912, p. 4; J.S. Woodsworth, *Strangers Within Our Gates or Coming Canadians* (Toronto: Methodist Mission Rooms, 1909), especially chapters 9-11.

[36]W.J. Sisler, *Peaceful Invasion* (Winnipeg: W.J. Sisler, 1944), chapter 5, especially p. 47; *MFP,* May 22, 1909, sports section, p. 3, Aug. 31, 1909, p. 7. On this theme in general, see Cavallo, *Muscles and Morals,* pp. 43-46, 96-106.

[37]Sisler, *Peaceful Invasion,* pp. 35-40; Peter Humeniuk. *Hardships and Progress of Ukrainian Pioneers. Memoirs from Stuartburn Colony and other Points* (Steinbach, Man.: Peter Humeniuk, 1977), p. 123; Orest T. Martynowich, "Village Radicals and Peasant Immigrants: The Social Roots of Factionalism among Ukrainian Immigrants in Canada, 1896-1918" (M.A. thesis, University of Manitoba, 1978), pp. 184-190.

[38]Soccer and baseball were not peculiarly Canadian games, of course. However, they and the other team ball games had evolved among, and were most popular among, the English-speaking peoples of the world with whom British Manitobans identified.

[39]*MFP,* Nov. 7, 1908, sports section, p. 1; "Diary of a Trip to Europe, July and August 1910," entry for July 31, Sisler Papers, Box 5, file 56, MG 14 C28, Public Archives of Manitoba; "Athletics," *Vox Wesleyana,* XII (Mar. 1908): 107; Geoffrey Harphan, "Time Running Out: The Edwardian Sense of Cultural Degeneration," *Clio,* V (Spring 1976); 283-286; Stephanie Lee Twin, "Jock and Jill: Aspects of Women's Sports History in America, 1870-1940" (Ph.D. thesis, Rutgers University, 1978), pp. 115-127; Anna Davin, "Imperialism and Motherhood," *History Workshop Journal,* V (Spring 1978); 9-22; Heather Rielly, "Attitudes to Women and Sport in Eastern Ontario, 1867-1885," in *Proceedings, 5th Canadian Symposium on the History of Sport and Physical Education, University of Toronto, August 26-29, 1982* (Toronto: University of Toronto School of Physical and Health Education, 1982), p. 385.

[40]*MFP,* July 11, 1899, p. 3; McLaren, "Physical Training," 99; n.a., "Ladies Column," *Northwestern Sportsman,* I (Apr. 8, 1896): 10; *Dauphin Press,* Oct. 28, 1909, p. 6; H.R. Hadcock, "Physical Training," *Western School Journal,* II (Apr. 1907): 116; Mrozek, *Sport and American Mentality,* chapter 5; Patricia A. Vertinsky, "The Effect of Changing Attitudes Toward Sexual Morality Upon the Promotion of Physical Education for Women in Nineteenth Century America," *Canadian Journal of History of Sport and Physical Education,* VII (Dec. 1976): 26-38; Helen Lenskyj, "Moral Physiology in Physical Education and Sport for Girls in Ontario," *Proceeding, 5th Canadian Symposium,* pp. 140-148; Isobel E. Disney, "College Athletics for Women," *Vox Wesleyana,* VI (July 1902): 153.

[41]*Winnipeg Times,* Apr. 9, 1883, p. 8; n.a., "Sports," *St. John's College Magazine,* IV (Apr. 1888): 189; *MFP,* Oct. 30, 1893, p. 5.

[42]*MFP,* Aug 31, 1909, p. 7, Oct. 14, 1913, p. 6; *Minnedosa Tribune* June 5, 1913, p. 2, May 28, 1914, p. 2.

[43]Sisler, *Peaceful Invasion*, p. 61; *Annual Report of the Winnipeg School Board*, 1912, pp. 18-19; Hadcock, "Physical Training," p. 116; Crawford, "Physical Training in Public Schools," p. 177.

[44]*MFP*, Oct. 10, 1902, p. 5, Nov. 4, 1905, p. 5, Oct. 14, 1913, p. 6; *Brandon Times*, Feb. 6, 1908, p. 9; *Brandon Sun*, Feb. 20, 1908, p. 5; Women's Institutes of Arrow River and Miniota, *Bridging the Years, 1879-1967*, (Arrow River: Women's Institutes of Arrow River and Miniota, 1970), pp. 94, 201; Beulah History Committee, *Minnewashta Memories, 1879-1970* (Beulah: Beulah Women's Institute, 1970), pp. 98-99; *History of Blanshard Municipality, 1884-1959* (n.p.; Blanshard Municipality, n.d.), p. 151; Darlingford Historical Book Committee, *The Darlingford Saga, 1870-1970* (Darlingford: Darlingford Historical Book Committee, 1970), p. 366; Marian W. Abra, ed., *A View of the Birdtail: A History of the Municipality of Birtle, the Town of Birtie and the Villages of Foxwarren and Scolsgirth, 1878-1974,* (Birtle: History Committee of Birtle Municipality, 1974) pp. 205-206; Anne M. Collier, *A Rear View Mirror, A History of Austin and Surrounding Districts* (Austin: Anne M. Collier, 1967), p. 130; Binscarth History Committee, *Binscarth Memories* (Binscarth: Binscarth History Committee, 1984), p. 62; Reta Shore, ed., *Ten Dollars and a Dream: Parkhill-Cheval:* (n.p. Parkhill-Cheval Community Club, 1977?) p. 363. Many of the local histories contain photographs illustrating athletic attire for girls.

[45]*Winnipeg Telegram*, Apr. 12, 1913, section 3, p. 2. See also, *Grandview Exponent*, May 29, 1903, p. 5; *Dauphin Press*, Oct. 28, 1909, p. 6; Disney, "College Athletics for Women," p. 153.

[46]*Minnedosa Tribune*, Dec. 8, 1910, p. 2.

[47]D.C. Coleman, "The Church and Wild Olive," *Western Sportsman*, II (Sept. 1906): 246-247; *Dauphin Press*, Feb. 4, 1915, p. 1; *Souris Plaindealer*, Apr. 1, 1914, p. 1; *Brandon Sun*, Aug. 19, 1909, part 2, p. 3, Jan. 8, 1914, part 2, p. 1; *North West Review*, July 16, 1910, p. 9; *MFP*, Dec. 17, 1910, p. 33, Apr. 25, 1914, pp. 19-20.

[48]Mott, "Manly Sports," pp. 204-206; *MFP*, Nov. 14, 1908, sports section, p. 1, Nov. 21, 1908, sports section, p. 1, Apr. 6, 1909, p. 6; *Brandon Sun* Feb. 20, 1913, part 1, p. 1.

[49]Murray G. Ross, *The Y.M.C.A. in Canada. The Chronicle of a Century* (Toronto: The Ryerson Press, 1951), pp. 169, 186-192; *MFP*, Jan. 18, 1901, pp. 6-7, June 12, 1909, sports section, pp. 1-2, Feb. 14, 1914, sports section, pp. 1, 4; *Brandon Times*, Apr. 11, 1907, p. 7; *Brandon Sun*, June 22, 1957, section A, p. 9.

[50]Col. C.W. Rowley, "Greetings from the Boy Scouts," *Western School Journal*, XI (May 1916): 185. See also, *Hartney Star*, June 29, 1911, p. 1; *Minnedosa Tribune*, Aug. 8, 1912, p. 3; *Gladstone Age*, Feb. 19, 1914, p. 1; *Dauphin Press*, Feb. 20, 1913, p. 1, May 7, 1914, p. 4.

[51]"Fifth Annual Report of the Winnipeg Boys' Club," 1909, p. 8, Winnipeg Boys' Club Collection, MG 10 B15, Public Archives of Manitoba; *MFP*, Jan. 18, 1908, p. 6, Sept. 27, 1909, p. 6, Feb. 13, 1914, p. 7, Apr. 17, 1914, p. 7.

[52]J.W. Bengough, "A Practical Suggestion," *Educational Journal of Western Canada*, I (Nov. 1899): 197.

[53]J.B. Wallis, "The Advantages of Military Drill," *Western School Journal*, I (Nov. 1906): 11-12; *MFP*, June 24, 1905, p. 7, July 4, 1908, sports section, p. 4; Frank Belton, "Military Drill in Ungraded Schools," *Educational Journal of Western Canada*, II (June-July 1900): 439-440; McLaren, "Physical Training," p. 99; n.a., "Physical Culture," *Western School Journal*, VIII (Jan. 1913): 34; J.W. Chafe, *An Apple for the Teacher: A Centennial History of the Winnipeg School Division* (Winnipeg: Win-

nipeg School Division No. 1, 1967), pp. 79-80; Sisler *Peaceful Invasion,* pp. 61-62; *Winnipeg Free Press,* May 7, 1974, section C, p. 2; Green, "School Cadets in Winnipeg," pp. 33-37.

[54]Hadcock, "Physical Training," p. 117; n.a., "How To Make Men," *Educational Journal of Western Canada* I (Mar. 1899); 27; Morrow, "Physical Education in Ontario," pp. 235-236, 255, 257-258; Helen Margaret Eckert, "The Development of Organized Recreation and Physical Education in Alberta" (M.Ed. thesis, University of Alberta 1953), pp. 123-126; Downie, "Physical Education in Manitoba," pp. 56-57.

[55]N.a., "The Convention," *Western School Journal,* IX (May 1914): 82.

[56]*Department of Education Annual Report,* 1911, p. 40, *Annual Report* 1913-14, p. 131; McLaren, "Physical Training," p. 100.

[57]Some excellent photographs of one-room schools, and sometimes the landscapes around them, can be found in Emmy Preston, ed., *Pioneers of Grandview and District* (Grandview: Pioneer Book Committee, 1976), pp. 14-17; Grosse Isle Women's Institute, *The Grosse Isle Story* (Grosse Isle: Grosse Isle Women's Institute, 1977?), pp. 90-91; Douglas History Book club, *Echoes of a Century: Douglas Manitoba Centennial, 1882-1982* (n.p. Douglas History Book Club, 1982), pp. 49-63; Deloraine History Book Committee, *Deloraine Scans a Century. A History of Deloraine and District, 1880-1980* (Deloraine: Deloraine History Book Committee, 1980), pp. 123-147; Ivan J. Saunders, *A Survey of Manitoba School Architecture to 1930* (Ottawa: Parks Canada Research Bulletin, 1984), especially pp. 18-25.

[58]Some information on, and pictures of, equipment in rural and urban schools can be found in *MFP,* July 8, 1908; Kenneth Osborne, *Daniel McIntyre Collegiate Institute: A History* (Winnipeg: Collegiate Institute Alumni, 1973?), p. 17; Sisler, *Peaceful Invasion,* pp. 36-40, 49; Connie Davidson, ed., *Gnawing at the Past* (Lyleton: Lyleton Women's Institute, 1969), p. 26; Domain Women's Institute, *Down Memory Lane: A History of the Domain Community, 1876-1967* (Domain: Domain Women's Institute, 1967?), p. 183. Some instructive photographs can also be seen in PAM, Still Images Section, W.J. Sisler Collection, Foote Collection, Oak Lake — Schools Collection, and in Western Canada Pictorial Index, University of Winnipeg, indexed under "Schools — Lifestyle — Parks."

[59]Neil Sutherland, *Children in English Canadian Society: Framing the Twentieth Century Consensus* (Toronto: University of Toronto Press, 1976), p. 241.

Teachers

5

Teaching the Teachers: Establishment and Early Years of the B.C. Provincial Normal Schools*

John Calam

I

In the fall of 1908, William Burns, principal of the Vancouver Provincial Normal School since January 1901,[1] laid the cornerstone of a fine new building. By 1909, a three-storey, fourteen-room, permanent normal school had risen above the commemorative stone and was in full use. Burns had "every reason to be satisfied."[2] The Vancouver Normal School was, by the standards of his day, a splendid building rising from the mud — a bit of old Oxford set down in Fairview, according to the *Province*.[3] Nor was Burns without resources, especially faculty. He, J. D. Buchanan and David Blair collectively offered psychology, management, literature, history of education; reading, language, arithmetic, geography, history; drawing, stencilling, modelling — a curriculum substantially enriched beyond its 1901 origins. As of 1907, Ivy Abercrombie taught nature study. John Kyle, ex-superintendent of drawing in the Vancouver schools, replaced Blair upon Blair's retirement in 1910, and for a brief period, Harry Dunnell also taught drawing. In 1911, E.H. Murphy, former principal of Vancouver Model School, took charge of practice teaching and under provisions of the Strathcona Trust, Q.M.S.I. Patterson, RCR, taught physical drill.[4] Enrolment increased. During 1910-1911, 120 registered for the preliminary session and 160 for the advanced.[5] Students came not just from Vancouver, New Westminster and Victoria but from other Island, Fraser Valley and inland communities as well. Contrary, moreover, to the *Times'* charges of class discrimination, family backgrounds of these students, whether Island or Mainland, urban or rural, proved broadly representative of a working class. Indeed, while the well-to-do did not send their daughters and sons in any numbers to the Vancouver Normal School, Cumberland, Ladysmith and Nanaimo miners, Chilliwack, Langley and Hatzic farmers, Victoria warehousemen, grocers and carpenters did.[6]

In those early years at Vancouver, Burns confronted problems not unusual for an institution such as the one he ran, outlining them in various reports and other public statements. Promotion, illness, resignation, retirement and demise

---

*This chapter, with alterations, is reprinted from *BC Studies*, 61 (Spring, 1984): 30-63, with permission.

necessitated staff shuffles. City facilities for practice teaching in ungraded classrooms of the sort most normal school graduates would encounter in rural B.C. during their novitiates were unavailable.[7] Candidates lacking full entrance standing continued to arrive despite regulations, and overcrowding became a matter of growing concern. Nevertheless, Burns publicly acknowledged what he considered notable gains. A new gymnasium provided better space for Swedish drill and first aid. A literary society, an athletic club and after-hour games furnished mental as well as physical recreation, together with a chance at learning how to organize social and athletic events — skills highly relevant to future teachers.[8] With the cooperation of the Vancouver board, practice teaching became "the chief test of a student's worth as a teacher."[9] Meantime, normal school instructors delivered addresses and papers at teacher institutes around the province,[10] and appear to have been well received.

Although Burns' public observations on the new normal school were largely positive, private correspondence revealed something of the pressures caused by institutional development without local precedent, and of the uncertainty over B.C.'s emerging civil service and bureaucratic style. It also showed Burns struggling to discover and apply a philosophy of teacher education consistent with what he took to be the educational purpose of the public elementary school in British Columbia.

Burns' administrative reach seemed total. His letter book reflected a range of anxieties from vandalism, accounts and recruiting to general public relations and more specific articulation with the Vancouver schools and the public education system as a whole. The superintendent and his inspectors, ministers and their deputies, merchants, faculty, parents, engineers, contractors, architects, telephone and transport executives alike received his missives. The "architectural gem" itself at first consumed much of Burns' administrative time, what with his attempts to hold builders and suppliers to contractual agreements and generally to protect the elegant new normal school from the sea of mud surrounding it. He obtained what he required by seeking verbal commitments from the highest ministerial authority and resolutely following up through the offices of lower-echelon functionaries; he also justified several instances of serious budgetary overruns.[11] As principal he stood very much *in loco parentis* with normal school students. His letters indicate he believed the younger women under his supervision to be especially impressionable. Accordingly, he corresponded with parents concerning their welfare, with Superintendent of Education Alexander Robinson about morality, and with students themselves regarding boarding arrangements and general comportment. All things to all, people he appeared "wrapped up"[12] in the institution he directed.

Among Burns' many letters were also to be found the makings of a philosophy of teacher preparation resting on an image of good teachers and belief in the normal school's capacity to produce them. Good teachers knew their facts. To their pupils they could put productive, connected, logically consecutive questions. They were clear. They knew how to enliven a lesson. Good teachers avoided colloquial speech. They could spell. They could write legibly on a blackboard. They avoided digressions. They encouraged children to answer. Above all, they prepared their lessons, made their pupils work and kept good order.[13] Training to these specifications called for collaboration with the best available model teachers capable of inspiring teachers.[14]

Connected with this vision of what good teaching entailed was Burns' conception of good normal school instructors. In Burns' time, they would be predominantly men. They would have demonstrated superior ability in the public system, B.C. or elsewhere. Often they would have had experience as principal or inspector. Their lectures would be related to other subjects on the curriculum.[15] Their lessons would aim at helping future rural teachers. Normal school instructors would be professionally resourceful with respect to development and modification of their year-to-year teaching assignments.[16] In short, they would be general practitioners, not specialists, practical rather than theoretical, able to show how, eager to supervise practice teaching.

While Burns wrestled with administrative and educational challenges, provincial and city inspectors continued to monitor the quality of teacher the normal school was producing. For the most part, they welcomed these novices. That many were British Columbians impressed some. Their willingness to work hard and ability to organize and handle their classes pleased others, and their "thorough instruction" and "excellent training" in drawing, art and physical education substantially offset their inexperience. The best of them knew the school curriculum, came prepared to teach it, set high standards, roused interest and were sympathetic to the rural school. By definition, of course, not all could be the best. Some seemed just to have slipped through, as inept in subjects like nature study as they were insensitive to a higher order of educational aim such as "strengthening and developing the child." Bearing in mind that the normal school launched hundreds of teachers into provincial classrooms, what inspectors wrote about these less-able normal school graduates betrayed some slippage between Burns' ideals and certain field realities.[17]

Many who held normal school diplomas, the inspectors reported, could not properly manage a classroom. Neatness, order and the "courteous conduct of the pupils" lacked due care. Legibility, spelling and punctuation received inadequate stress. Timetables were ignored, work was unsystematic, careless and unreviewed, and proper ventilation was disregarded. Management defects included faulty questioning, unrestrained calling out, too much teaching, too little seat work and an "absolute lack of method" in teaching history and composition. Classification of pupils for instruction left much to be desired. In the ungraded rural school, many teachers foundered hopelessly, revealing a serious training gap. Nobody questioned the fundamental concepts underlying normal school training and the educational and social benefits it promised. In the matter of detail, however, inspectors envisaged room for improvement.[18]

In 1914, there was added to this official appraisal a statement outlining the quintessential teacher. She would be diligent yet lively, alert to inattention, quick to question, her "finger upon the mental pulse of each student." This teacher would demand neat, concise writing, clear thinking and careful recapitulation, pacing the work steadily throughout the year and keeping accurate records of student progress. Under her encouragement, children would develop their imaginations, growing at length to enjoy their compositions, and appreciate — even love — the literary selections to be read. She would help children speak and draw well. But the key attribute of this teacher would be her ability and desire to see to the "true work of the school — the development of character.[19] So wrote Inspector Donald L. MacLaurin. It was soon to be his turn to try to realize for the public good the ideal teacher he so eloquently described.

II

Unlike William Burns, Donald Leslie MacLaurin was appointed not just to a post but to a permanent building as well. That a second normal school was a provincial necessity had of late attracted little direct challenge. Indeed, since quite early in his tenure at the new Vancouver teacher training school, Burns had become uneasy over high enrolment. In time the government responded,[20] and had by 1915 completed in Victoria a superlative facility the size and sophistication of which, compared with its Vancouver counterpart, immediately attracted Burns' attention.

By late November 1914, Victorians waited impatiently for news of a principal's appointment. D.L. MacLaurin got preferment. Teacher, principal and inspector, he enjoyed respect among students and colleagues alike and, following a full career, was described as a man whose knowledge of B.C., combined with teaching skill and executive ability, enabled him to direct the training "of many of our most valuable teachers."[21] Like Burns at Vancouver, MacLaurin shared with his staff the broad range of subjects and activities required by the Education Department. MacLaurin himself cut a remarkably wide swath — English literature, composition and grammar, junior and intermediate grade language, primary and advanced reading, practice and principles of school law, psychology and history of education. Transferred from Vancouver, First Assistant David M. Robinson handled primary and advanced arithmetic, intermediate and senior grade history and geography, and class management. Drawing master and technical instructor Harry Dunnell (also ex-Vancouver Normal School) taught drawing and writing during the first session, later adding manual training, including modelling and woodwork, as tools and supplies became available in the autumn of 1915.

Since it functioned under regulations common to Island and Mainland institutions, MacLaurin's Normal School in many respects matched Burns'. Students at the two provincial normal schools met common admission, examination, diploma and certification requirements. Their successes prompted similar annual press coverage, and accounts of their work appeared in the superintendent's yearly reports on the public schools of B.C. Nevertheless, several differences from the start distinguished the Victoria from the Vancouver enterprise. Although the more accommodating building, Victoria Normal School consistently recruited fewer students, in the order of 45 to 237, January to May 1915,[22] and 252 to 396, 1924-1925.[23] Victoria catered to all but Lower Fraser Valley and greater Vancouver candidates, these generally attending William Burns' normal school.[24] Victoria taught household science and manual training, subjects not available in Vancouver. Burns resented this curricular inequality and voiced his displeasure time after time,[25] particularly since Victoria's offerings in these disciplines could not possibly satisfy provincial demands, as was demonstrated by substantial registration in them each year at the Victoria Summer School for Teachers, operative since 1914. Concerning practice teaching arrangements, too, differences emerged. The two normal schools had classrooms at their disposal under the jurisdiction of their respective municipal school boards. In addition, though, the Victoria Normal School housed its own two-room model school. Though it came nowhere near meeting all MacLaurin's practice teaching requirements, it enabled colleagues and student teachers, on the spot, and at relative leisure, to discuss the many problems of practical work. A clear advantage in this respect, in MacLaurin's opinion it could not, however, offset yet another institutional difference detrimental to his efforts — the fact that the Vancouver school board allowed "extra remuneration"[26] for service as a critic teacher, whereas the Victoria school board did not.

It was in matters such as the Victoria Normal School's relations with those professional teachers who helped student teachers plan, deliver and review practice lessons that MacLaurin's persistent administrative style showed most favourably. He informed Superintendent Robinson that a modest outlay for honoraria would achieve parity with Vancouver's policy and encourage Victoria teachers to furnish assistance beyond the "farcical" minimum of one practice lesson per week. He also persuaded Inspector E.B. Paul to approach the Victoria board on the subject, but as of early 1917 nothing had resulted.[27] A little later he advised Robinson that after cooperating two and a half years, one city principal — J.A. Cunningham of Boys' Central — had withdrawn support of the practice teaching program because of the burden of extra work for which his staff received no tangible recognition. The urgency of the difficulty, MacLaurin urged Robinson, was surely worthy of the education minister's immediate attention.[28] Within three months Robinson had the matter in hand. The Victoria board was to establish the George Jay School as a model school whose "thoroughly competent" staff would receive for their participation an extra $60 each per year, the Education Department paying half. Victoria Inspector Paul likewise agreed to the further use for practice teaching of North Ward and Bank Street Schools[29] and invited MacLaurin to help select assisting teachers. By such tenacity, MacLaurin achieved three important goals: equivalence with procedure in Vancouver; the trust of practising teachers; and a voice in their selection as mentors for student teachers.

No less tenacious was Alexander Robinson, major engineer of that most important event, the establishment of B.C.'s first provincial normal school. Himself an ex-teacher and sometime principal of Vancouver's first high school, for twenty years he drove the Education Department tight-reined. Prodigious correspondence[30] over his signature as superintendent revealed a civil servant with a rational sense of his professional, if not his political, environment, and a profound loyalty to the cause of public education. He addressed premiers and ministers, deputies and their assistants, inspectors and principals, as well as a vast array of teachers, parents, students, board secretaries, contractors — anybody, in fact, who wrote him about anything, or to whom, unprompted, he was inclined to issue instructions. Ever-present throughout this voluminous communication was concern for the affairs of the normal schools he helped create and the efforts of the two men, Burns and MacLaurin, to direct them.

Though the Education Department's senior civil servant, Robinson remained a stickler for detail. He appeared ill-disposed toward minor slip-ups,[31] and waste (especially during wartime shortages) he refused to countenance,[32] not merely because of unnecessary costs but also because procedural principles were being ignored.[33] Responsible to his minister for well-run classrooms in B.C., he in turn kept meticulous watch over who and how many entered each normal school. He dealt with interminable exceptions to regulations in judgment of applicants who had passed matriculation exams at Columbia College in New Westminster but had not yet taken junior grade tests; mature students with non-professional studies outstanding; students who had passed third-year commercial exams; those who had taught successfully in rural districts but held no provincial certification; those who had advanced course (junior grade) exams yet to sit; who were only sixteen but wise beyond their age; those who missed much work during the influenza epidemic of 1918-1919; or returned veterans with missing limbs.[34] In fact, despite his request that Burns interpret conditions of admission "as liberally as possible," Robinson decided on many perplexing admissions cases himself.

Eventually, though, the administrative press of so many individual rulings proved too heavy even for Robinson. Regarding admissions, he filed Burns' proposal to send advanced students to Vancouver and preliminary candidates to Victoria, pending further discussion on this politically sensitive subject with Education Minister J.D. MacLean. Ultimately, the minister decided that beyond the standing arrangement whereby Vancouver Normal School admitted greater Vancouver and Lower Fraser Valley trainees and Victoria Normal School enrolled the rest, Burns and his staff should "ascertain what students have no particular reason for attending the Normal School at Vancouver,"[35] and instruct them to go instead to Victoria, exceptions to be treated on their merits.

Subsequent correspondence showed the social and political problems besetting anyone attempting to implement such vague instructions to the satisfaction of a superintendent still prone to take personal action in certain trying cases. In the B.C. interior, some students and their parents were in no way indifferent to which normal school best served their purposes. In Kelowna, for example, one group of acquaintances went ahead with house arrangements[36] in Vancouver so that their children could attend the Vancouver Normal School according to published regulations. Robinson told Burns to refuse them admission at Vancouver on the grounds of defiance.[37] Yet shortly afterwards, he himself wrote to a Kelowna mother assuring her that Burns would "no doubt . . . allow" her daughter to live in Vancouver with an aunt while attending normal school there.[38] These apparent inconsistencies hinged on fine distinctions between living with relatives as opposed to boarding with friends or making "house arrangements." At crisis point, Robinson ordered Burns "not to be guided by any political aspect. . . " Swamped with appeals, Burns found it difficult to identify and reject every "political" argument for special treatment since many such appeals were shrouded in seemingly legitimate compassionate terms. Relentlessly, Robinson pressed him to state "at once" the reasons in each case that had induced him to admit "upper country" applicants, hounding Burns until his retirement to carry out to the letter the terms of the minister's understanding. Robinson, meantime, continued to handle certain constitutional subtleties himself. The St. Joseph's Convent authorities at Nelson, he wrote to Burns in 1918,

> have been in communication with the office and I have informed them that since they have no branch of their institution in Victoria this Department would have no objection to allowing the pupils of their school to attend the Normal School in Vancouver on the distinct understanding that while in Vancouver they must remain in the house and under the charge of the Sisters of St. Joseph's Convent in Vancouver.[39]

Beyond these administrative complications surrounding admissions policy, during the Great War and early post-war period, the provincial normal schools became well-known as teacher training centres to which, for one reason or another, thousands of British Columbians could relate. Their senior personnel served on the Provincial Board of Examiners, setting as well as reading high school entrance examinations, or organizing and supervising these tests at various provincial localities. Some normal school staff carried out incidental inspectoral work and, under Robinson's direction, MacLaurin at one time investigated educational affairs at Victoria High School. Normal school staff also provided model timetables for inclusion in the *Manual of School Law,* addressed institutes, conventions and public meetings, and upon request wrote newspaper articles on various aspects of public education. Though constantly occupied with heavy administrative responsibilities, Burns and MacLaurin tried to keep alive their vision of good teachers. In aid of producing them, the pace in and about their training centres continued brisk. Newspapers made much of graduation news. Near-graduates were eager to secure jobs and clamoured for vacancy listings. Conversely, board secretaries asked Robinson to help them find new teachers, especially for isolated rural schools. MLAs themselves took recruitment initiatives; on behalf of Mr. Yorston of Cariboo, Robinson asked MacLaurin if he had a "young woman graduating in a few days" and a good disciplinarian, "since the former teacher was virtually run out by some of the older boys." Amid these accounts and exchanges regarding their students' futures, principals and faculties pursued their surrogate parental roles, dealing with complaints over perceived injustices such as failure to grant diplomas, too-severe grading or disciplinary dismissal from class. In politically delicate cases, Robinson himself arbitrated, sometimes summoning staff to his Victoria office for explanations, but in general supporting his principals, though demanding of them convincing clarifications and reasons whenever public trust was at issue.[40]

During these early years, too, Burns and MacLaurin eyed one another with a view to equal treatment for colleagues and students. Burns continued to urge the establishment at Vancouver of domestic science and manual training facilities to match Victoria's. MacLaurin asked that Victoria employ a stenographer-librarian like Vancouver's, that his assistant master's salary be made equivalent to Burns', and that, for consistency's sake, Victoria's drawing master, technical instructor, domestic science mistress, model school principal and model school teacher all receive salary raises. With their principal's support, staff at either normal school were eligible for subsidies aimed at professional development through attendance at Berkeley, Columbia, Stanford, Chicago, UBC and other centres of higher education in order that they might "keep in touch with the most advanced and approved methods of instruction, as well as with modern techniques in Education."[41]

In August 1920, after twenty years as principal at Vancouver, William Burns retired. Toward the end of his career, he had joined MacLaurin in pushing for certain reforms, in particular complete non-professional standing as a condition for normal school admission and practice teaching arrangements for future high school teachers. With Burns' successor, D.M. Robinson, MacLaurin continued to press for further improvement, apparently to some avail. By 1920, junior grade standing became minimal for applicants. By 1921, as a means of more effective staff deployment, preliminary and advanced courses were conducted during alternate sessions. As of 1922, all but university graduates were required to finish nine months of continuous training in order to graduate. Under new arrangements in 1923, a normal school standing of "fair" earned an interim certificate only, valid for just two years. The same year, King Edward High School started to provide practice facilities, and future high school teachers began a split training program of fifteen weeks at Vancouver Normal School and fifteen weeks at the University of British Columbia. Also announced in 1923 was junior matriculation as the preferred admissions standard.[42]

By 1925 the normal schools had become vital parts of a burgeoning education system. In 1901, the year of that "most important event," as Superintendent Robinson had termed the Vancouver Normal School's opening, the government cost of teacher education was $1,944.30, including Blair's salary of $750. By 1925, two dozen staff including engineers, gardeners and janitors drew salaries amounting to over $51,000 which, added to other teacher education costs, reached more than $75,000,[43] about 4 percent of total expenditures for B.C. education. Though enrolment had peaked somewhat earlier, during 1924-1925, 548 candidates sought diplomas at the two training institutions, each trainee teaching about thirty-five practice lessons, thanks to the co-operation in Victoria of the North Ward, Oaklands and George Jay Schools and in Vancouver of the Vancouver Model, Cecil Rhodes and Lord Tennyson Elementary Schools (practice), and the Lord Roberts, Dawson, Central, Strathcona, Mount Pleasant and Simon Fraser Elementary Schools (observation).[44] Citizens, moreover, appeared proud of their provincial normal schools, whose surroundings as of 1925 had achieved horticultural maturity, rendering the buildings themselves popular civic attractions. Newspaper editors wrote of new instructional plans, explained the advent of fees, announced raised standards, congratulated students for their splendid showing, quoted Education Minister MacLean on good teacher education and its connection with the dignity of labour and the value to the state of developing character in children, and told of enrolment nearly doubled, teacher supply strongly augmented and entrance requirements perceptibly tightened.[45]

To this optimism of the press was added confidence from within the education system itself. D.M. Robinson and MacLaurin each wrote of instructors thoroughly trained and experienced, school teachers co-operative in all respects, normal school students willing to work, model schools offering cheerful assistance, good morale all round, and weeding out of those who did not measure up.[46] In this last respect, Vancouver appeared to rule more severely. In 1924-1925, D.M. Robinson reported that of 396 candidates, 34 withdrew, 5 discontinued, 33 failed and 61 earned interim diplomas only, compared with MacLaurin's account of 174 trainees among whom 8 discontinued, 6 failed and 64 obtained interim status.[47] Whether or not aware of these double standards, those who survived their training wrote affectionately of their time at normal school. They owed much to his example, some said of D.M. Robinson, "for if you had trod less loftily we might never have had to look so high."[48] To MacLaurin, others declared, they owed "much of whatever success has been ours during our brief association with this institution."[49] Principals reciprocated. D.M. Robinson congratulated students for "most satisfactory work and a splendid spirit."[50] And MacLaurin concluded it was "the unanimous opinion of the Faculty" that candidates were, "with few exceptions, admirably adapted to the work of teaching."[51] From the field, inspectors added their appraisal. The more sanguine among them thought new teachers had received at the normal schools "excellent preparation for their life-work," were fully capable of creditable efforts, appeared intimately knowledgeable of both subject and method, and were preferred by the average school district. Such criticism as did arise ranged from the mistakes of inexperience, and the need for more thorough courses in English, management and school curriculum, to one charge that just a few normal school graduates were immature and irresponsible.[52] On the whole, though, inspectors seemed well disposed toward qualified neophytes teaching in their districts.

Though more indicative of their own enthusiasm for the "new education" abroad in North America than of their particular reaction to products of the normal schools, occasional inspectors reminded beginning and veteran teacher alike to keep up with the literature and with changing times. Their suggested reading lists attained impressive proportions, as did their fervour for mental measurement, standard tests, silent reading, psychology, sociology, history, philosophy, the project method, child study and socialized recitation. To help place this sort of reading within professional reach, they urged that district libraries be developed and school principals give inexperienced teachers "a training-in-service by directing their reading and study to the literature of the new education, and by demonstrations and periodical consultations. . ."[53] In short, when they wrote of normal school graduates as such, by the mid-1920s B.C. inspectors described teachers who *did* well or who *could* do well, given broader, more intense attention in terms of what the two normal schools were already doing. And when they told of the efforts of normal school graduates, observers like Inspector H.H. MacKenzie and his colleague J.T. Pollock wrote eloquently of the "new education," not as a function of the normal schools' curriculum but rather as "training-in-service" and summer school. Though closely interested in teacher training, as of 1925 B.C. inspectors had left the overall reputation of the provincial normal schools largely unchallenged. Such confrontation would be left to two prominent Canadian educational administrators who would soon prove singularly forthright at taking radical issue with the performance of British Columbia's normal schools.

III

In his 1924 annual report to Education Minister J.D. MacLean, Superintendent S.J. Willis spoke of a "request made to your Department by many public bodies" for a public education stock-taking in the province.[54] One such request had come in 1922 from the B.C. Teachers' Federation, a proposal later endorsed by both the Provincial Trustees' Association and the Provincial Parent-Teacher Association. At the 1924 BCTF annual convention, Willis announced the department's decision to act.[55] Principal commissioners were to be Dr. J. Harold Putman and Dr. George M. Weir. At the time of their appointment, Putman was Ottawa's top school inspector. Formerly a normal school instructor in English and psychology, he held a doctorate in pedagogy, was active in the Dominion Education Association[56] and was a leading figure in Canada's version of the child study movement. On the eve of their educational survey, his associate Weir (D.Paed.) was *the* Professor of Education at UBC's recently-established Department of Education, coming there from Saskatchewan, where he had served successively as teacher, inspector and normal school principal. Also an enthusiast for the "new education,"[57] future B.C. Education Minister G.M. Weir joined J.H. Putman in generating the most quickly executed, most comprehensive and exacting report on education the province had witnessed. Assisting them were experts on general education, finance, testing, administration and statistics.[58]

Under their terms of reference,[59] Putman and Weir listened to and/or accepted in writing "resolutions, opinions, and conclusions,"[60] from a remarkable if not complete spectrum of the B.C. public.[61] They also made over 150 visits to B.C. schools and spent ten days inspecting the two normal schools.[62] These visits, complemented by 215 conferences (some lasting six hours) held in city and rural municipalities and rural districts, laid the basis for a critique of the B.C. teacher, *circa* 1924, severe beyond public expression on the subject up to that point. This was how the commissioners summed up their findings:

> Too many unmarried teachers; the immaturity of the teachers, especially in rural schools; lack of vision and professional pride; deficient academic and professional qualifications; unwillingness to take additional professional training beyond the legal minimum; lack of experience; inability adequately to profit from experience; tendency to change schools too frequently; lack of special preparation for teaching in ungraded schools; lack of sympathy with, and appreciation of, problems of rural life; dogmatism; lack of personality.[63]

This dismal rendering prefaced a preliminary consideration of an ideal normal school. Instead of learning tricks at it, the commissioners said, beginners ought to leave in possession of a philosophy of education as a guide to classroom practice. Instructors should deal with principles of educational psychology, not dictate notes on "tricks of the trade." For it was the job of the normal school "to make" the teacher in the sense that method was "largely individual" and would fall into place once more general education was attended to. Looked at this way, normal schools became "strategic centres" deserving tangible support. They taught "rural sociology, applied educational psychology . . . and rural administrative problems. . . ." They also provided practice teaching for rural, ungraded school conditions, not just as a means of rehearsing the minor and manipulative functions of one-room school management, but rather as preparation on a sound theoretical basis for that "interaction of mind upon mind" which every child, urban or rural, deserves as a right. In sum, the ideal normal school had seven emphases: child study; ethics or social psychology; methods and curriculum; practice teaching; liberal education; social sensitivity; and physical health. Overall, it was a "laboratory for child study — a place for the observation of child growth."[64]

Against this glittering image, B.C.'s normal schools paled by comparison. A few minimal reforms aside, said Putman and Weir, the normal schools' inexcusable aberration was their conception of teaching as a trade dependent on definite methods; thus definite instruction in these definite methods became their preoccupation. But, Putman and Weir contended, teaching *wasn't* a trade — it was a science. And since only this premise could justify any normal school's existence, British Columbia's normal schools should fall into line with it insofar as it affected their organization and administration, curriculum, ways of imparting knowledge, course duration and practice teaching.

On the first count — organization and administration — Putman and Weir took a most careful look at staff recruitment, qualifications and deployment. They assessed the best instructors as really satisfactory, the next best as fairly good under careful direction, and the balance "lacking in the scholarship and professional training necessary for normal school work," in all very faint praise indeed. Unfortunately, they continued, meagre budgets hampered quality staff recruitment. School principals, for instance, considered themselves financially better off staying put. Accordingly, the normal schools had been appointing in their place poorly qualified instructors willing to accept reduced, even minimal remuneration. One adverse consequence was that intramural discussions assumed administrative rather than intellectual patterns. Another was that those too young or too old or too specialized had dropped out of touch with the "actual school problems of the Province." Yet another was that for want of pedagogical ingenuity, many normal school teachers were addicted to dictating notes instead of having their students read educational texts.[65]

The second area of criticism — curriculum — the commissioners introduced by outlining the 1921 syllabus and then enumerating its manifold shortcomings. In brief, the normal schools' program called for the school course of studies, methods, psychology, management and history of education, in addition to observation and practice teaching. Their curricular faults were assessed as including a lack of tests and measurements, inadequate texts, neglected educational psychology and rural sociology, vague, anachronistic and poorly scheduled educational history, understocked libraries, and students too immature in any event to benefit from what little intellectual stimulation such a lean curriculum might possibly produce.[66]

Closely linked with curriculum was the third subject of concern — knowledge transmission by indiscriminate use of lectures. Not that the commissioners denied the rightful place of the lecture for introducing or summarizing a topic or series of discussions. For several reasons, though, they deemed lecturing inappropriate as the unique teaching device. For one thing, few who delivered lectures actually excelled in the art. For another, lectures denied students an active part in an intellectual transaction. Then, too, student teachers themselves nurtured on the lecture method would probably inadvisedly adopt it as their own way of teaching in the public school classrooms of B.C. More threatening than all of these reasons was the fact that lectures stressed subject matter, whereas the ideal normal school, that "laboratory for child study," necessarily placed its emphasis on the child.[67]

A fourth subject of disapproval — length of the teacher training program — followed. In this section, Putman and Weir reacted to the 1924 B.C. Normal School Instructors' Association resolution that the pre-service teacher training term be substantially extended. The Association had based its resolution on three contentions: that there was never sufficient time for practice teaching; that some candidates graduated too young; and that with longer preparation, students could better assimilate relevant subject matter and relate it more closely to method. Responding negatively to this more-of-the-same route to improvement, the investigators said they believed additional subject matter ought to be taught in the high schools and that brilliant younger students should be encouraged to complete senior matriculation before entering normal school, thereby avoiding under-age graduation. With respect to a two-year course, as an alternative, they proposed tightening the institutional rigging; that is, reorganizing "to do more efficient work in the one year now devoted to professional training" before seriously considering a second year. They approved, however, of a short extension from thirty-six to forty weeks, provided the month thus gained was used for practice teaching and "experimental education."[68]

A fifth matter — practice teaching — also came in for censure. Instead of being a laboratory where a candidate's "theories and . . . mettle" were "put to the proof," said the commissioners, the practice classroom often became the site of an artificial, stage-set "performance" during which children, confused by the presence of two teachers, one of them a student herself, tried to cope with a set lesson, the success or failure of which depended upon imponderables. These lessons were often as short as twenty minutes and not necessarily related in a sequence to the other lessons. Accordingly, they precluded experience in that continuity necessary to developing good classroom management, a subject supposedly central to the normal school curriculum, but actually lacking systematic application. Practice teaching, moreover, called for specially qualified teachers and excellent schools. But, the commissioners observed, participating boards, especially in Vancouver, did not always seek normal school approval of their critic teachers, nor did teachers themselves seek these training assignments in any numbers or with particular enthusiasm.[69]

Earlier in their report, Putman and Weir had emphasized that their remarks on the normal schools were not intended as "a sweeping indictment."[70] Yet the sheer scope and intensity of their argument, plus the number, complexity and sensibility of their recommendations, stunned not a few. In his 1925 annual report Superintendent S.J. Willis acknowledged only briefly the suggestions which, if carried out, he thought would improve teacher training.[71] Reaching, it seemed, for even a fragment of optimism in the commissioners' survey, the *Province* declared that there had been "some praise" but composed its headline to the effect that the normal schools had lost their case for proficiency.[72] In a lengthy editorial the *Colonist* reminded its readers how difficult it was to keep educational institutions in phase with discernible social change and, musing "we get the kind of educational institutions we deserve," invited the Department of Education and the general public to sample the "food for thought" the educational survey had prepared.[73] In response, Vancouver Normal School instructors and their Victoria colleagues called on Education Minister J.D. MacLean, later conferring privately at the Strathcona Hotel. What they discussed at either meeting they were for the moment unwilling to share with the press.[74] In the wake of the Putman-Weir assessment, however, there could have emerged few easy solutions for the problems they might have addressed. The proof is that over half a century later similar problems continued to haunt British Columbia teacher educators who in many respects worked under far more favourable conditions.

IV

What had gone wrong? How was it that B.C.'s provincial normal schools, since 1901 respected components of the public education system, should in 1925, with apparent suddenness, become the targets of such fundamental discredit? Why had the "most important event" — establishment of the first normal school at Vancouver — not led to better things? Were the normal schools really that badly off, or was there something amiss with the survey itself? Did it reflect a province at odds with its teacher education facilities and programs, or simply the predetermined opinions of two dynamic, articulate progressives?

Had an unbridgeable gap developed, for instance, between the Putman-Weir blueprint for thoroughly professional teacher education and the powerful social, political and economic motives driving certain normal school promoters towards goals somehow abstracted from any educational function? To be sure, politicians, editors, civic officials, local suppliers, boarding house proprietors, property developers, architects, contractors, realtors and tourist planners were caught up in promotional activities that had little to do with the educational workings of the normal schools they so ardently supported. No doubt they gave those who ran, used or benefited from the normal schools the impression that all was well. Indeed, they had good reason to do so. The normal schools, after all, constituted impressive monuments to the West's ability to match the East when it came to constructing important public buildings. They inspired civic pride. They stood, moreover, as evidence of equal treatment at a time when so many Island-Mainland, Victoria-Vancouver, Coast-Upper Country rivalries persisted. In the legislature, too, questions arose not about what was taught at the normal schools, how and by whom, but about what they cost or the propriety of disbursements to those constructing and maintaining them. In the press as well, journalists explored their indirect importance, not as educational institutions in their own right, but as pawns in the larger game of locating a provincial university. Or they covered occasions such as closing ceremonies featuring sentimental exchanges among normal school teachers, graduating students and official guests, and wrote effusively of how splendidly the teacher training centres were doing. Little wonder that where quality of instruction or recency of educational theory were concerned, the more general politics of early B.C. teacher education proved hugely distractive.

Alternatively, did the graceful normal school buildings themselves subdue, if not extinguish, the impulse to relate critically their inner life to the day-to-day problems of B.C. provincial schools, let alone to research findings at prominent American graduate schools of education? For in their day, B.C.'s normal schools were no ordinary buildings. At Vancouver an arched entrance, mock battlements, square corners trimmed with New Zealand white stone, and a complex roof line, together with sturdy towers and chimneys, signalled an educational enterprise of considerable importance. So did the interior rooms and furnishings, particularly the assembly hall with its sloping floor, double aisles, raised platform, stained glass windows and delicate, bowed balcony.[75] At Victoria, too, a structure of elegance, symmetry and pleasing horizontal reach, complete with impressive clock tower, graced Mount Tolmie. Inside, a superb assembly hall likewise set a serious tone. In this spacious facility the plaster busts of Shakespeare, Goethe, Virgil and Homer viewed with empty-eyed serenity an arched platform facing a classical curved balcony. Midway, a high window decorated with B.C.'s coat-of-arms in vivid stained glass cast a mellow light upon those gathered within.[76] Certainly, the supposition that what went on in places such as these two magnificent training schools must have been educationally sound — even excellent — is natural enough.

Or could it be argued that the Putman-Weir critique of B.C. teacher education startled so many because provincial inspectors as a group had up to 1925 rarely confronted the normal schools with any searching challenges? In their most congratulatory moods during this period, inspectors had instead reported consistently that rural boards liked to hire teachers trained at the normal schools. They wrote, also, of individual successes as normal school graduates took with them into the field new subjects such as domestic science, physical education, manual training and commercial studies. Admittedly, inspectors were not always so sanguine, and in their grimmer frames of mind they lamented the scandal of a few incompetents who had somehow run the gauntlet of normal school requirements to the educational detriment of children now under their inept charge. Yet to most inspectors, even these fugitives seemed to indicate not that the normal schools were seriously out of touch with educational innovation so much as that these institutions should afford more "attention" to important components of a long-established program. Indeed, the inspectors' point of view was clearly valued in teacher training circles. By 1925 there had been or yet remained on the normal school staffs at least seven ex-inspectors of schools or services.[77] During their tenure, those of their inspector colleagues in the field who occasionally flirted with the ideals of the "new education" did not ask the normal schools to teach these beliefs, recommending instead systematic in-service training for teachers, which inspectors and their principals would conduct, as the most promising ameliorating factor in the education of British Columbia children.

Again, was it that the normal schools administratively engulfed the educational reformers — Superintendent Robinson and Principals Burns and MacLaurin — most directly responsible for their advent and early management? It would be reasonable to expect that their pre-appointment statements in favour of normal schools, plus their direct understanding of education in the field, would have laid the foundation for up-to-date teacher training institutions. Nor, as their subsequent reports, public statements and correspondence revealed, were they unaware of a developing need for longer terms, stiffer admission requirements, expanded curricula, increased practice, augmented libraries, preparation for rural teaching and improved building facilities — all concerns reflected in the Putman-Weir recommendations.[78] Yet at the time of the educational survey, the normal schools seemed, after all, little changed from their initial policies and routines, and perhaps only modestly altered with respect to program. Somehow the day-to-day preoccupation with getting paper off desks — invoices, vouchers, incidental reports, records, requisitions, testimonials, complaints, assessments, contracts, inquiries — together with certain seasonal events such as sessional openings, ceremonial closures, examinations and annual reports, stood in the way of long-range, more sustained exchanges over aims or ideals or learning or childhood. Ironically, this administrative busyness perhaps isolated the normal schools. Having heralded an educational panacea — normal schools — which their government had seen fit to inaugurate and leave to their collective professional care, three educational leaders apparently discovered they had little time to explore essentially educational issues. In office, they were swallowed up in the bureaucratic particulars of institutional life. Though Putman and Weir did not conceive of the problem in quite this way, it is not unlikely that administrative imperatives reduced the level of intellectual activity at the normal schools.

Looked at yet another way, could it have been that up to 1925, B.C.'s normal schools were justifiably confident that through their respective efforts over these years, their teacher candidates were actually satisfied with the training they received? As in the case of one who paid homage to Mac-Laurin's lectures with their "clearcut notes on arithmetic and class management,"[79] yearbook esprit de corps must be tempered with the caution its sense of occasion demands. And, of course, not all were so kindly in their praise. On the other hand, future teachers continued to arrive by the hundreds seeking certification through attendance at Vancouver or Victoria normal schools. One might assume that either they were indeed content with their instruction or, in the credentialist society they inhabited, willing to take in their stride whatever curriculum, organization, length of study, practice teaching arrangements or mode of instruction at the time obtained. Further, were not their parents satisfied to leave educational matters to the professional discretion of instructional staffs — delighted, in short, that their daughters or sons should qualify, regardless of how, for a respected means of self-support in uncertain times?

Finally, is it possible that dramatic differences separating the normal schools' generally good reputation from the Putman-Weir account of their ineptitudes were functions not of the schools' actual shortcomings in 1925 but of the commissioners' own visitation schedule and overall progressive outlook while carrying it out? Concerning schedules, Rogers[80] has reminded us that Putman and Weir called on the normal schools only in September 1924, "when the year had barely started" and their staffs were occupied with settling hundreds of beginning students into courses and routines "totally new to them." Understandably, here was an occasion for "explicit instruction with strong direction." But it was scarcely representative of teaching methods pursued throughout the year. As for educational outlook, normal school pioneers Robinson, Burns and MacLaurin had been educational general practitioners entering teacher education from posts in public school systems. They held no advanced degrees. From the start, they, their staffs, and immediate successors served educationally conservative teacher training institutions stressing the supremacy of practice teaching. Conversely, Putman and Weir arrived on the scene in possession of earned doctorates in pedagogy, their enthusiasm for child study, measurement, psychology and advanced studies for normal school personnel reflecting both the substance and level of their own academic achievements and educational leadership roles. As their 1925 *Survey of the School System* clearly shows, what they were looking for in a normal school was a "laboratory for child study." That they did not find one in British Columbia is hardly surprising. As official critics, though, it was their task to criticize. They did so in generous measure.

Notes

I am much indebted to my colleagues J. Donald Wilson, Neil J. Sutherland, the late George M. Tomkins, William A. Bruneau and Jorgen Dahlie who in so many ways helped write this study.

[1] For a review of events leading up to this occasion see John Calam, "Teaching the Teachers," *BC Studies*, 61 (Spring 1984): 30-38.

[2] "Provincial Normal School, Report of the Principal," hereafter PNSRP, *Annual Report of the Public Schools of the Province of British Columbia*, hereafter ARPS, 1910, A40.

[3] *Province*, Sept. 26, 1908, p. 26.

[4] This arrangement therefore placed one aspect of the normal school's program under the supervision of the Canadian Army.

[5] PNSRP, ARPS, 1911, p. A44.

[6] Home addresses for a sample of students who attended Vancouver Normal School, Jan. 9, 1911 to June 16, 1911, were noted in a ledger entitled *Vancouver Normal School, January, 1911 - June, 1938*, currently located in the vault of the Division of Teacher Services, Ministry of Education, Province of British Columbia. I am indebted to Dr. Bruce Andrews, formerly Director of Teacher Services, for his re-discovery of these and related materials. Home owner occupations were noted in Henderson's *Vancouver City and Suburban Directory, 1905-1906* (Victoria, B.C.: Henderson Publishing Company, 1906), and *Victoria City Directory Including Vancouver Island, 1914* (Victoria, B.C.: Trecillus Thompson, Ltd., 1914).

[7] PNSRP, ARPS, 1912, p. A52.

[8] PNSRP, ARPS, 1913, p. A60.

[9]Ibid.

[10]See H.H. MacKenzie, *Report,* hereafter R, ARPS, 1913, p. A45; J.B. DeLong, R, ARPS, 1914, p. A49.

[11]Burns to Thomson Stationery Co., Vancouver, Sept. 20, 1909, *Vancouver Normal School Letter Book, 1908-1915,* hereafter VNSL, p. 39, B.C. Provincial Archives, Victoria, B.C.; Burns to Dr. F.C. MacTavish, Vancouver, Mar. 27, 1911, VNSL, p. 120-21; Burns to H.E. Young, Minister of Education, Vancouver, n.d., 1910, VNSL, p. 53; Vancouver, Aug. 12, 1910, VNSL, p. 77; Burns to Thomas Taylor, Minister of Works, Vancouver, Nov. 15, 1910, VNSL, p. 100; Vancouver, Jan. 8, 1915, VNSL, pp. 216-17; Burns to W. Allison, Auditor-General, Vancouver, Oct. 19, 1904, VNSL, p. 205; Burns to A. Robinson, Superintendent of Education, Vancouver, Nov. 26, 1908, VNSL, pp. 7-8; Burns to Robinson, Vancouver, Nov. 27, 1908, VNSL, pp. 9-11; Burns to F.C. Gamble, Deputy Minister of Works, Vancouver, Sept. 18, 1909, VNSL, pp. 37-38; Burns to W.F. Gardiner, Vancouver, Nov. 17, 1909, VNSL, p. 41; Burns, partial note, VNSL, p. 56; Burns to A. Robinson, Vancouver, June 17, 1910, UNSL, p. 59; Burns to A. Robinson, Vancouver, Aug. 11, 1910, VNSL, p. 74; Burns to F.C. Gamble, Vancouver, Sept. 26, 1910, VNSL, p. 84; Burns to Gamble, Vancouver, Oct. 4, 1910, VNSL, p. 87; Burns to Gamble, Vancouver, Oct. 12, 1910, VNSL, p. 91; Burns to A. Robinson, Vancouver, Mar. 10, 1911, VNSL, p. 117; Burns to J.E. Griffith, Deputy Minister of Public Works, Vancouver, Feb. 2, 1915, VNSL, p. 221; Burns to Taylor, Vancouver, Jan. 8, 1915, VNSL, pp. 216-17.

[12]Burns to M. McTaggart, Vancouver, Sept. 9, 1910, VNSL, pp. 80-81; Burns to W.H. Dandy, Vancouver, Nov. 13 1914; VNSL, p. 206; Burns to Mr. McCorkell, Vancouver, Apr.11, 1914., VNSL, p. 201; Burns to General Manager, B.C. Electric Railway Co., Vancouver, Nov. 12, 1912, VNSL, pp. 159-60; Burns to A. Robinson, Vancouver, Mar. 17, 1915, VNSL, p. 223; Burns to A. Robinson, Vancouver, Aug. 20, 1910, VNSL, p. 78; Burns, letters to Miss Annie Kenyon, Miss Dockrill, M. Robertson, Vancouver, Aug. 22, 1910, VNSL, p. 79.

[13]This reconstruction is extrapolated from recorded criticism of a teacher candidate referred to in Burns to A. Robinson, Vancouver, Apr. 28, 1909, VNSL, pp. 18-20. It squares fairly well with the Langdon and Bagley models of method and management.

[14]See Burns to C.R. Evans, Principal, Cecil Rhodes School, Vancouver, Mar. 12, 1914, VNSL, p. 198; Burns to W.P. Argue, City Superintendent of Schools, Vancouver, Jan. 19, 1911, VNSL, pp. 114-15.

[15]Burns to A. Robinson, Vancouver, June 8, 1909, VNSL, pp. 22-25.

[16]This last view is reflected in Burns to Miss Abercrombie, Vancouver, Jan. 2, 1911, VNSL, p. 106.

[17]Thomas Leith, R, ARPS, 1911, p. A33; D.L. MacLaurin, R, ARPS, 1911, p. A37; Albert Sullivan, R, ARPS, 1912, p. A36; W.P. Argue, R, ARPS, p. A40; John B. DeLong, R, ARPS, 1913, p.A32; G.H. Gower, R, ARPS, p. A40; H.H. MacKenzie, R, ARPS, 1913, p. A45; Leslie J. Bruce, R, ARPS, 1913, p. A48; John Martin, R, ARPS, 1914, p. A54; Bruce, R, ARPS, 1914, p. A57; H.P. Hope, R, ARPS, 1915, p. A41; Martin, R, ARPS, 1916, p. A36; W.N. Winsby, R, ARPS, 1912, p. A39; MacKenzie, R, ARPS, 1914, p. A51; Leith, R, ARPS, 1911, p. A33.

[18]MacLaurin, R, ARPS, 1911, p. A37; MacLaurin, R, ARPS, 1912, p. A33; J.T. Pollock, R, ARPS, 1912, A36; Winsby, R, ARPS, 1912, p. A39; DeLong, R, ARPS, 1913, p. A32; MacKenzie, R, ARPS, 1914, p. A51; Sullivan, R, ARPS, 1911, p. A34; Pollock, R, ARPS, 1913, p. A42; Sullivan, R, ARPS, 1912, p. A37.

[19]MacLaurin, R, ARPS, 1914, p. A31.

[20]See Province of British Columbia, *Journals of the Legislative Assembly,* hereafter JLA, Session 1914, vol. XLIII, p. 94. Cost entailed was a preliminary sum of $332,382 and a supplement of $64,000. See JLA, Session 1915, XLIV, p. 15. Compare with $54,000 initial and $15,000 supplementary grants for the Vancouver Provincial Normal School, see JLA, Session 1909, vol. XXXVIII, p. 69; ibid., Session 1910, vol. XXXIX, p. 76.

[21]Dr. F.T. Fairey, Superintendent of Education, cited in Henry C. Gilliland, *Notes on MacLaurin,* p. 2, "Provincial Normal School Principal's Office," University of Victoria Archives, Box 80-56.

[22]Compare MacLaurin, PNSRP, ARPS, 1915, p. A54 with Burns, PNSRP, ARPS, 1915, p. A53.

[23]See PNSRP, ARPS, 1925, pp. M49, M50.

[24]ARPS, 1915, P. A54; 1916, p. A52; 1917, p. A53. This essential division of registrants proved a source of constant anxiety for Burns, whose job it was to dissuade, later forbid up-country students to attend the Vancouver Normal School.

[25]Examples include Burns, PNSRP, ARPS, 1918, p. D48; Burns, PNSRP, ARPS, 1920, p. C46.

[26]MacLaurin, PNSRP, ARPS, 1916, p. A52.

[27]MacLaurin to A. Robinson, Victoria, Sept. 18, 1915, University of Victoria Archives, hereafter UVA, Box 80-56; A. Robinson to MacLaurin, Victoria, Sept. 20, 1915, UVA, Box 80-56; MacLaurin to E.B. Paul, Victoria, Jan. 18, 1917, UVA, Box 80-56; W.S.C. Pope, Secretary of the Board, to MacLaurin, Victoria, Jan. 31, 1917, UVA, Box 80-56.

[28] MacLaurin to A. Robinson, Victoria, Dec. 31, 1917, UVA, Box 80-56.

[29]A. Robinson to MacLaurin, Victoria, Mar. 19, 1918, UVA, Box 80-56; Edward B. Paul to A. Robinson, Victoria, Mar. 14, 1918, UVA, Box 80-56; MacLaurin to A. Robinson, Victoria, Mar. 20, 1918, UVA, Box 80-56; A. Robinson to MacLaurin, Victoria, Mar. 22, 1918, UVA, Box 80-56; Paul to MacLaurin, Victoria, Mar. 23, 1918, UVA, Box 80-56.

[30]See Superintendent of Education, *Letterbooks,* hereafter SEL, B.C. Provincial Archives. These are fairly complete for outgoing letters, 1873 to 1919 and constitute a splendid resource for B.C. social and educational history. For the period in question, *circa* 1915-1919, vols. 138-91 number close to 53,000 pages of letters touching on every aspect of B.C. public education.

[31]See, for example, A. Robinson to Burns, Victoria, Nov. 1, 1917, SEL, vol. 168, p. 8987.

[32]A. Robinson to MacLaurin, Victoria, Dec. 7, 1917, SEL, vol. 168, p. 10010; A. Robinson to Burns, Victoria, Feb. 27, 1917, SEL, vol. 161, p. 1570; A. Robinson to Burns, Victoria, Dec. 19, 1917, SEL, vol. 170, p. 10339.

[33]A. Robinson to Burns, Victoria, May 20, 1918, SEL, vol. 173, p. 3435; A. Robinson to Burns, Victoria, Apr. 12, 1919, SEL, vol. 183, p. 2757; A. Robinson to Burns, Victoria, Nov. 2, 1915, SEL, vol. 147, p. 10121; A. Robinson to Burns, Victoria, Apr. 20, 1917, SEL, vol. 162, p. 2917; A. Robinson to Burns, Victoria, Oct. 3, 1917, SEL, vol. 167, p. 8193; A. Robinson to Burns, Victoria, Oct. 11, 1918, SEL, vol. 178, p. 8113.

[34]A. Robinson to Burns, Victoria, June 1, 1915, SEL, vol. 142, p. 4101; A. Robinson to Burns, Victoria, June 21, 1915, SEL, vol. 142, p. 4857; A. Robinson to Burns,

Victoria, Aug. 5, 1915, SEL, vol. 144; p. 6260; A. Robinson to Burns, Victoria, Aug. 10, 1915, SEL, vol. 144, p. 6431; A. Robinson to Burns, Victoria, Aug.28, 1917, SEL, vol. 165, p. 6913; A. Robinson to MacLaurin, Victoria, Aug. 23, 1918, SEL, vol. 176, p. 6515; A. Robinson to Burns, Victoria, Jan. 17, 1918, SEL, vol. 170, p. 448; A. Robinson to Burns, Victoria, Nov. 27, 1918,SEL, vol. 179, p. 9307; A. Robinson to Burns, Victoria, Oct. 7, 1919, SEL, vol. 189, p. 8856; H.H. MacKenzie, R, ARPS, p. D29; A. Robinson to Burns, Victoria, June 1, 1915, SEL, vol. 142, p. 4102.

[35]A. Robinson to Burns, Victoria, Feb. 1, 1915, SEL, vol. 138, p. 818; A. Robinson to Burns, Victoria, Dec. 6, 1916, SEL, vol. 159, p. 10272.

[36]A. Robinson to Burns, Victoria, July 24, 1917, SEL, vol. 165, p. 5608.

[37]Ibid.

[38]A. Robinson to Mrs. J.E. Reekie, Victoria, Aug. 10, 1917, SEL, vol. 165, p. 6253.

[39]A. Robinson to Burns, Victoria, Aug. 15, 1917, SEL, vol. 165, p. 6425; A. Robinson to Burns, Victoria, Aug. 16, 1917, SEL, vol. 165, p. 6456; A. Robinson to Burns, Victoria, Jan. 16, 1918, SEL, vol. 170, p. 407; A. Robinson to Burns, Victoria, Jan. 21, 1918, SEL, vol. 170, p. 532; A. Robinson to Burns, Victoria, Jan. 25, 1918, SEL, vol. 170, p. 721; A. Robinson to Burns, Victoria, Feb. 1, 1919, SEL, vol. 181, p. 968; A. Robinson to Burns, Victoria, Sept. 2, 1919, SEL, vol. 187, p. 7251; A. Robinson to Burns, Victoria, Aug. 8, 1918, SEL, vol. 176, p. 5945.

[40]This section is compressed from a great deal of correspondence. Comments refer only to items within the sentences of which the comments form a part. A. Robinson to MacLaurin, Victoria, Nov. 5, 1917, SEL, vol. 168, p. 9102; A. Robinson to D.M. Robinson, Victoria, Nov. 5, 1917, SEL, vol. 168, p. 9105; A. Robinson to MacLaurin, Victoria, Aug. 9, 1919, SEL, vol. 186, p. 6249. In 1915, A. Robinson appointed Burns presiding examiner, Abbotsford and Chilliwack Centre. "That you will accept this appointment," he wrote, "has been taken for granted." See A. Robinson to Burns, Victoria, June 8, 1915, SEL, vol. 142, p. 4435. A. Robinson to E.H. Murphy, Victoria, Apr. 21, 1915, SEL, vol. 141, p. 3058; A. Robinson to MacLaurin, Victoria, June 11, 1916, SEL, vol. 153, p. 4249; Minutes, Council of Public Instruction, Box 1. Robinson requested through his principals that either Miss E.M. Coney (Vancouver) or Miss Ida Morris (Victoria) provide an article entitled "The Future of Music in the Schools." Miss Coney obliged. See A. Robinson to Burns and MacLaurin, Victoria, Sept. 13, 1918, SEL, vol. 177, pp. 7154, 7155; A. Robinson to Burns, Victoria, Sept. 18, 1918, SEL, vol. 177, p. 7404; A. Robinson to Burns, Victoria, Nov. 11, 1915, SEL, vol. 147, p. 10412. Reference to teaching vacancy listings are made in A. Robinson to E.H. Murphy, Victoria, Jan. 11. 1915, SEL, vol. 138, p. 237; A. Robinson to Burns, Victoria, Dec. 4, 1916, SEL, vol. 158, p. 10156; A. Robinson to Burns, Victoria, Dec. 12, 1917, SEL, vol. 168, p. 10168; A. Robinson to Burns, Victoria, Nov. 25, 1919, SEL, vol. 190, p. 10321. Examples of schools in need of teachers were the Giscombe School on the "Fraser River Grand Trunk Pacific, East of Prince George," and the Blue River School. See A. Robinson to Burns and MacLaurin, Victoria, May 3, 1917, SEL, vol. 163, pp. 3247, 3250; A. Robinson to Burns, Victoria Sept. 8, 1917, SEL, vol. 167, p. 7255. The Giscombe authorities specified a man to teach. Robinson replied it was "almost impossible to secure a male teacher at present owing to the large number who have gone to the front." See A. Robinson to Leo Bower, Secretary, School District, Giscombe, B.C., Victoria, May 3, 1917, SEL, vol. 163, p. 3258; A. Robinson to MacLaurin, Victoria, Feb. 3, 1919, SEL, vol. 181, p. 856; A. Robinson to Burns, Victoria, Aug. 24, 1915, SEL, vol. 145, p. 7997; A. Robin-

son to J.D. MacLean, Minister of Education, Victoria, Feb. 20, 1917, SEL, vol. 161, p. 1386; A. Robinson to Burns, Victoria, Sept. 27, 1917, SEL, vol. 167, p. 7988; A. Robinson to MacLaurin, Victoria, Oct. 30, 1919, SEL, vol. 190, p. 9546; A. Robinson to MacLaurin, Victoria, Oct. 17, 1919, SEL, vol. 189, p.9031.

[41]See A. Robinson to Burns, Victoria, Oct. 23, 1917, SEL, vol. 168, p. 8752; A. Robinson to A.E. Foreman, Public Works Engineer, Victoria, Feb. 5, 1919, SEL, vol. 181, p. 936; A. Robinson to J.D. MacLean, Victoria, Jan. 27. 1919, SEL, vol. 181, p. 517. Memoranda, resolutions, etc. (some undated) pertinent to the department's support of the professional development of its personnel may be found in the B.C. Provincial Archives, Council of Public Instruction, Box 1.

[42]See D.M. Robinson, PNSRP, ARPS, 1921, p. F44. Note that while J.B. DeLong, Inspector of High Schools, conceded the advantages to pupil teachers of practice teaching at the high school level, he observed that the plan interfered with the progress of the high school pupils themselves, see J.B. DeLong, R, ARPS, 1924, p. T36. References to sundry adjustments of normal school requirements occur sporadically in much correspondence. For consolidated information, see for instance ARPS, 1918, pp. D48, D49; ARPS, 1919, p. A45; ARPS, 1920, pp. C45, C47; ARPS, 1921, pp. F44, F45, F46; ARPS, 1922, pp. C11, C48, C49; ARPS 1923, pp. F11, F12, F48; ARPS, 1924, p. T36.

[43]ARPS, 1924, p. T29; D.M. Robinson, PNSRP, ARPS, 1921, p. F44; D.M. Robinson, PNSRP, 1922, p. C48. Note the reduction from sixty practice lessons reported by MacLaurin in 1916, PNSRP, ARPS, 1916, P. A53.

[44]MacLaurin, PNSRP, ARPS, 1924, p. T70; D.M. Robinson, PNSRP, ARPS, 1925, p. M49.

[45]*Province,* Apr. 11, 1925, p. 26; *Times,* Nov. 21, 1922, p. 7; ibid., July 23, 1923, p. 9; *Colonist,* July 26, 1923, p. 5; *Times,* Jan. 23, 1925, p. 9; *Colonist,* Oct. 21, 1923, p. 5; *Times,* May 30, 1924, p. 7; ibid., May 29, 1925, p. 9; *Colonist,* Sept. 8, 1922, p. 5; ibid., May 29, 1923, p. 29; ibid., Jan. 24, 1925, p. 4.

[46]For details of these intramural perspectives, see ARPS, 1923, pp. F47, F48, ibid., 1924, pp. T69, T70; ibid., 1925, pp. M49-M51.

[47]See D.M. Robinson, PNSRP, ARPS, 1925, p. M49; MacLaurin, PNSRP, ARPS, 1925, pp. M50-M51.

[48]P.N.S. Class 1927-28, Provincial Normal School, Vancouver, B.C., *Annual, 1927-1928,* p. 7.

[49]*The Normal School Annual (Victoria), 1923-1924,* p. 8.

[50]D.M. Robinson, PNSRP, ARPS, 1924, p. T69.

[51]MacLaurin, PNSRP, ARPS, 1921, p. F45.

[52]See the following reports from inspectors, ARPS, 1915, p. A41; ARPS, 1916, pp. A29, A36; ARPS, 1917, pp. A24, A35.; ARPS, 1918, pp. D23, D25, D33; ARPS, 1920, p. C26; ARPS, 1921, pp. F17, F21, F23, F27, F28, F34; ARPS, 1922, pp. C22, C26, C27, C28, C32, C40; ARPS, 1923, pp. F27, F28, F29, F30, F35, F39; ARPS, 1924, pp. T41, T50; ARPS, 1925, pp. M31, M35.

[53]For instance, MacKenzie, R, ARPS, 1923, F28.

[54]See S.J. Willis, ARPS, 1924, p. T10.

[55]J.H. Putman and G.M. Weir, *Survey of the School System* (Victoria, B.C.: King's Printer, 1925), p. V.

⁵⁶In 1917, A. Robinson had supplied him with a statement of "the conditions of education affairs in B.C." See A. Robinson to J.H. Putman, Victoria, June 6, 1917, SEL, vol. 163, p. 4029.

⁵⁷Despite such enthusiasm, others have argued that though the survey which Weir helped produce was a "condemnation of traditional concepts and practices," it was nonetheless "essentially a conservative document" in that it did not seek to achieve through improved schools "a new, better, or radically changed society." See Jean Mann, "G.M. Weir and H.B. King: Progressive Education or Education for the Progressive State?" in J. Donald Wilson and David Jones, eds., *Schooling and Society in Twentieth Century British Columbia* (Calgary, Alberta: Detselig Enterprises Ltd., 1980, p. 93.

⁵⁸Putman and Weir, *Survey. . . .* p. V. The experts were Mr. J.L. Paton, sometime High Master, Manchester Grammar School; Professors H.F. Angus and S.E. Beckett, UBC; Professor Peter Sandiford, University of Toronto; Professor F.C. Ayer, University of Washington; and Mr. A.W. Cocks.

⁵⁹Ibid., pp. 2-3.

⁶⁰Ibid., p. 1.

⁶¹Ibid., pp. 1-2. Included were "school boards; boards of trade; councils of city and rural municipalities; trade and labour councils; associated property owners; ratepayers' associations; local councils of women; university clubs; Canadian Clubs; Chapters of the IODE, Rotary, Kiwanis, Gyro, and Lions Clubs; librarians' associations; Native Sons of Canada; Native Sons of British Columbia; boy scouts' associations; ministerial associations; child welfare associations; and representatives of other organizations."

⁶²Ibid., p. 7.

⁶³Ibid., p. 174.

⁶⁴Ibid., pp. 174, 175, 189, 194.

⁶⁵Ibid., pp. 202, 204.

⁶⁶Ibid., pp. 207-14, *passim.*

⁶⁷Ibid., pp. 215-17, *passim.*

⁶⁸Ibid., pp. 217-19, *passim.*

⁶⁹Ibid., pp. 219-22, *passim.*

⁷⁰Ibid., p. 217.

⁷¹See ARPS, 1925, p. M10.

⁷²*Province,* Oct. 14, 1925, p. 30.

⁷³*Colonist,* Nov. 10, 1925, p. 4.

⁷⁴Ibid., Nov. 8, 1925, pp. 1-2.

⁷⁵For striking photographs, see ARPS, 1910, *passim.* For plans, see Pearce and Hope, Architects, April 1908, *Blueprints,* Provincial Normal School, Sheets 1, 2 and 3. Originals in Vancouver City Archives.

⁷⁶*Provincial Normal School, Victoria. Specifications.* B.C. Provincial Archives.

⁷⁷Burns, MacLaurin, H.H. MacKenzie, A. Anstey, A.R. Lord (from Apr. 1925), H. Dunnell (Manual Training), and V.L. Denton.

⁷⁸As A.W. Rogers notes, many of the Putman and Weir recommendations had been subjects of concern to normal school personnel in the years leading up to the

1925 survey. See his "Riding Out the Storm: The Normal Schools and the Putman and Weir Survey of the School System," unpublished manuscript, UBC, 1982, p. 4.

[79]*The Normal School Annual (Victoria), 1925-1926,* p. 9.

[80]Rogers, "Riding Out the Storm," pp. 4-5.

6

Voices From the Past: The Personal and Professional Struggle of Rural School Teachers

Robert S. Patterson

Under the heading, "The Schoolmarm" the editors of the February, 1930 *ATA Magazine* paid tribute to the female rural schoolteacher by highlighting on the magazine's cover the following words from Walt Mason, their "own Canadian rhymster,"

> The teacher in the country school, expounding lesson, sum and rule, and teaching children how to rise to heights where lasting honor lies, deserves a fat and handsome wage, for she's a triumph of this age.
>
> No better work than hers is done beneath the good old shining sun; she builds the future of the state; she guides the youths who will be great; she gives the childish spirit wings, and points the way to noble things.
>
> And we, who do all things so well, and of our "institooshuns" yell, reward the teacher with a roll that brings a shudder to her soul. We have our coin done up in crates, and gladly hand it to the skates who fuss around in politics and fool us with their time-worn tricks.
>
> In Blankville one common jay will loaf a week, and draw more pay than some tired teacher, toiling near, will ever see in half a year. If I were running this old land, I'd have a lot of statesmen canned; politicians and folks like those, would have to work for board and clothes; I'd put the lid on scores of snaps, and pour into the teachers' laps the wealth that now away is sinned, for words and wiggle-jaws and wind.[1]

Despite the existence of such praise, bestowed sometimes begrudgingly by their contemporaries and often more lavishly by later nostalgic commentators, these teachers — their thoughts, feelings, behaviour and challenges — remain relatively unknown contributors to prairie social life and growth. In part this has resulted from the judgment that the lives of teachers and activities in school are not significant enough to warrant attention. These individuals, mainly women, engaged in a low-status and low-profile occupation, are a part of a larger group who, because of lesser visibility due to role, occupation or status, have not received, until recent years, the attention of historians.[2] Their lives may not be epic, yet the student of history cannot overlook the fact that each life is a tiny capillary, a vein or artery contributing to the strong heartbeat of the collective experience. The unique, "lived" experience is a vital part of our history which we need to acknowledge, uncover and understand. Vera Lysenko recognized the importance of such a history when through the eyes of a teacher in her novel *Westerly Wild* the following observation was made:

"'I sometimes think the prairie provinces were built up by the labours of pioneer teachers,' Julie would think on such a morning. As she recalled all those hopeful young Normal School graduates going out to teach in the bush country of Manitoba or the Dust Bowl of Saskatchewan, some of them mere slips of girls stranded alone in bachelor shacks in communities of alien people, she wondered that so many had survived at all, and had stuck it out, alongside the people, through droughts, frosts, hail and snowstorms. 'Nobody has written their story, really,' she thought. 'Not the way it was.'"[3]

Such a story is difficult to tell because of the innumerable participants and conditions, but if it is to be told as it really was, the personal experiences of the participants must be utilized.

The subject of this chapter, the concerns of a novice, often female, rural schoolteacher, has been selected so as to provide insight into the personal trials and struggles of rural schoolteachers in western Canada and, also, to add to our understanding of a continuing, important professional issue. The transition from student to teacher or of shifting from the realm of teacher preparation to professional responsibility may be both dramatic and traumatic. Contemporary scholars, studying the phenomenon of profession-entry, refer to it as "reality shock." While the label and the interest may be relatively new, the experience is not. Just as conditions in our modern schools and the characteristics of beginning teachers cause some to forfeit their idealism, alter their behaviour, attitude and personality or even leave the profession, so, too, in our pioneer era did the reality of the prairie classroom and the qualities of teachers precipitate similar personal adjustments. Veenman has observed that "little is known about the cognitive and affective processes that characterize the transition into teaching."[4] This is as true, if not more so, for teachers beginning their careers fifty to seventy-five years ago as it is for their counterparts in our day. What follows is an attempt to reveal some of the reflections of pioneer prairie schoolteachers on what they encountered as young, inexperienced mentors in the period 1914 to 1939 on the Canadian Prairies.

The story of their solitary persistence in the face of adversity, helps us to appreciate why the establishment of a teachers' organization was so essential to teacher well-being and the improvement of schooling. Help was needed in order to change conditions which demanded far too much from individuals trying to provide schooling in rural western Canada and which were too entrenched for isolated individuals to change on a permanent basis.

The source material for this chapter, primarily accounts of retired schoolteachers acquired through questionnaires and interviews at the close of their careers, is problematic. Intervening years have dimmed, distorted or destroyed significant information. Even where memory is intact, privacy and personal discretion have limited the disclosures which have been made public. Therefore, in some instances the reader must fill in the blanks with conjecture and inference; these teachers, in describing their experiences, do not always state how they were affected by them. Nevertheless, the attempt to gain an empathetic appreciation of their experiences, even in the face of such limitations, remains important in enriching our knowledge of the past.

An effort could be made to derive from the hundreds of questionnaire responses and interview transcriptions a variety of historical topics including the ethnic and socio-economic origins of western Canadian teachers, their reasons for choosing teaching as a career, the nature of their teacher preparation programs, their employment opportunities, instructional problems, working conditions and community and professional help. As interesting as these observations might be, they are not the substance of this chapter. Teaching conditions, experiences, and responsibilities are highlighted, and the reader is invited to seek an understanding of how individual teachers reacted and managed their situations.

In the main, prairie schoolteachers in the period between the two world wars were female and of rural origin. Although women were numerically dominant in the profession, outnumbering men three to one, their ability and professional worth were undervalued, generally, in comparison to their male peers. Normal school officials noted declines in male recruitment, commenting that such trends did not "promise well for material from which to recruit our force of instructors, inspectors and supervisors."[5] Few, if any, seemed sensitive to the demeaning message being conveyed to the female teacher candidates. It was obvious men were preferred for leadership roles and often for classroom responsibility. Some women, like Nellie W., were not prepared to accept such biased selection procedures without a fight. Recalling her experience with the normal school principal who attempted to screen her out of the teacher preparation program on such irrelevant criteria as size and appearance, she notes how her resistance helped overcome the evident prejudice of his decision. The principal, Dr. Coffin, called her into his office at the end of the first week and informed her there were too many normal school students. She was among the group being asked to drop out of the program. The reasons given for her inclusion were that she was only seeking a second-class certificate, she couldn't pay her fees or purchase books, and she looked too young to discipline the children. The principal also wanted fewer female students in order to avoid combining men and women students in one class. Her account of the incident, as follows, reveals her willingness to stand up for her rights:

> "What I said, I can't recall exactly, but I do remember that I told him:
> 1. My mother had died when I was a baby and I had helped with the family cooking and washing ever since. (No hired help in our farm home.)
> 2. I always stood first in all my classes and had won the Governor-General's Medal on my High School entrance.
> 3. I had helped the country teacher with all the little grades in my spare time.

4. We had driven four miles to school (3 little girls) and had taken the neighbour children, too — weather, no matter.

5. In High School we delivered 3 - 100 pound cans of milk each morning before we went to classes.

6. I had always dreamed of being a teacher, and would probably become the best one of the four hundred applicants. (I came 3rd.)

He grinned at my 5-foot 1 inch height and 110 pounds of self-confidence and said, "I believe you have the stuff from which a teacher is made. I have changed my mind. You may stay."[6]

Although the ranks of the teaching profession would have been virtually empty without female teachers, these young women learned, subtly and not so subtly, that their value to society in the role of teacher was not great. In some communities, their value was depreciated because the residents attached little importance to schooling. In other cases, they learned that their worth was measured by their eligibility for marriage or by their lower financial demands in salary and living accommodation. Whatever the source and nature of the indignity experienced through such messages directed at these young women, they largely went unchallenged and were accepted as conditions of the time.

There were those, albeit a limited number, who were critical of the unfair treatment of women and who were willing to pay a price for challenging bastions of male dominance. Edith M. tells of her decision, while attending the Calgary Normal School, to nominate and campaign for a female student as president of their student organization. This was a first. Heretofore, women candidates had not been allowed. Her action, confronting such a traditional practice, undoubtedly came at great personal cost, due to the worry, fear and conflict associated with the undertaking. As campaign manager, she led the parade through the men's common room, an area absolutely out-of-bounds to women. The principal, understandably, was shocked. Immediately, he summoned the candidate and the campaign manager to his office to censure their behaviour. The intimidation tactic did not daunt these upstarts. Aware that expulsion might result, the campaign manager accepted responsibility for organizing the parade and years later acknowledged that "he thought he could scare me to death, but I didn't back down."[7] As a result of the determination of these forceful, courageous young women, the administration was faced with difficult decisions. The principal who had agreed to the candidacy, in part on the belief that a woman could not win an election, eventually had to accept the first female student president in his school.

Confrontations precipitated by women students or by women teachers to assert their rights were not commonplace, and the differential treatment afforded males and females worked to the disadvantage of women throughout the period. Not until membership in professional organizations for teachers became law in the late 1930s was the inequity addressed and, then, rather slowly.

The disadvantages associated with being young and female as either a normal school student or a teacher in an isolated rural community were not limited to differential status or unequal opportunity. Novelists dealing with prairie life in the 1920s and 1930s commonly present the schoolteacher as a young female more interested in marriage than in professional responsibility. Typical is the picture presented by Arthur Storey in *Prairie Harvest:*

> Miss Mill was far from being an inspiration to the children. Like most of the young women who came to teach at Melness during and after the war, she had no real interest in the boys and girls or in education. Her teaching license she regarded merely as an admission ticket to a community in which there might be an eligible male. When she found one she married and left the school. Had she not found one within the year, she would have moved on to another school to continue her quest. So it was with Miss Crabb and Miss McIntosh and others who followed in quick succession.[8]

Even in the normal schools, the instructors reinforced this view of the women students by joking about preparing teachers who would become wives of farmers. Self-esteem as a professional, as a teacher with much to offer a community through its young people, must have been difficult to build when so many shared the view that women entered teaching to find a marriage partner.

Prospective suitors in a community unabashedly evidenced their interest in the teacher, contributing to the belief that marriage, rather than teaching, was the preferred object of her existence. According to a male teacher, observing the attention shown the new teachers in the district adjacent to his, "it was the custom that when the young teacher arrived all the eligible young men, as soon as was convenient, sometimes within the first day or two, would turn up at the school and introduce themselves."[9] Credibility is afforded this observation by an amusing anecdote told by Mary G. One day her students informed her that the inspector's car was approaching the school. When the driver knocked on the school door and was admitted by the teacher, he agreed to have her proceed with her teaching until recess when they would talk. The intervening twenty minutes of "The Ugly Duckling" passed quickly and then, at recess, the teacher discovered that the inspector "was an insurance salesman who had seen me at the last country dance and he had come to ask me for a date."[10]

There were other ways in which the rights of women teachers were denied or violated by the male members of society. Some men used positions of trust to take advantage of these teachers. Evidently, one normal school physical training instructor, enamoured with one of his class members, attempted to use another unwilling classmate to promote jealous feelings. He singled out an injured female student for his highly personal attention in the presence of the whole class. Considerable embarrassment, hurt and indignation resulted from the student's unwilling participation in this charade. She noted that:

Our physical training teacher had a "crush" on one of the girls in our class. By misfortune I had injured my right wrist. My wrist had been wrapped (with surgical tape and tongue depressors for splints) to prevent the cartilage from popping out. Two days later out P.T. instructor called me out of line and examined my wrist, while the class was instructed to circle the gym. Each time his student friend came by he teased her by "lovingly" stroking my hand, or embracing me, expressing his regrets at my suffering. Each time I tried to withdraw my injured wrist he held me closer just to see his friend's face turn red.[11]

Her position of vulnerability did not deter Florence M. from taking appropriate action. "I reported this to the principal, because he had hurt my wrist as well as my feeling of propriety."[12] Her concluding observation, "we lost our P.T. instructor,"[13] indicates that senior officials in the school were not prepared to tolerate such conduct.

Gaining a position of responsibility as a teacher did not free women from the demeaning and inappropriate behaviour of some men in the school district. Bessie M. remembers that at her boarding house, one shared periodically by threshing or railroad crews, the men (sometimes under the influence of liquor) caused considerable concern because it was difficult to "get them to keep their hands off."[14] School board officials occasionally manifested similar behaviour. Teachers were expected to attend the dances and parties of the community. Some were told by their hiring authorities "where to stay and which boy friends were acceptable."[15] One teacher reports how she "had to watch the chairman of the school board because he would get quite liquored up and he would start out to dance with the schoolteacher."[16] All night she was forced to be on guard in order to stay unavailable and out of reach until the dance concluded. She was a fair match for her drunken employer as she observed, "I never did dance with him."[17]

Some of the eligible bachelors were not above trading favours for the attention of the schoolmarm. Billie, the forty-two-year-old unmarried son of the landlady, offered the boarders a ride to school on his stoneboat in the cold weather. He informed Mairi B., during her ride, that the previous teacher had put her arms around him in order to be secure during the bumpy ride. Unlike her predecessor, Mairi ignored the invitation, observing that "never again was I offered a ride to school."[18]

Several observations emerge from these examples about what it meant to be a female teacher in prairie Canada after World War I. Many were confronted with conflicting signals about their place and responsibility in the community. People expected competence and virtue in their teachers. Yet, at the same time, these qualities were undermined or compromised. By failing to build the teacher's professional worth and contribution, by refusing to endorse the equal rights of women and men teachers and by minimizing the abilities of the large female membership, society ensured that large numbers of teachers would see the role as little more than a stepping stone to marriage or some other occupation.

Winning acceptance and respect in a community was difficult not only because one was young, inexperienced, female and single, but because teachers, whether male or female, frequently were viewed as outsiders in the community. Differences in ethnic or socio-economic background were used in some instances as excuses for treating the teacher as an intruder. In other cases the values represented by the teacher made parents and community members uncomfortable. Obvious differences in perspective and standard heightened the awareness of family or community practices and values which were not congruent with those of the teacher. It was risky, therefore, for teachers to seek living and employment conditions which further set them apart from others in the school district. To argue for better accommodation or remuneration, in the eyes of many, was a way teachers had of conveying that they were somehow superior to the rest of the community.

Teachers were required to endure considerable hardship and isolation in their teaching situations in order to maintain employment. This necessitated not only abiding physical deprivation or inconvenience, but also considerable emotional strength. While many were from rural homes, in the main, teachers were not familiar with the situations they encountered and endured. Living accommodations varied remarkably in standard. The query of one teacher aptly captures the challenge faced by those not raised on the farm — "Can you imagine a city girl being faced with green trees for kindling wood, coal buried under snow, janitorial duties or wrestling with a potbelly stove?"[19] In retrospect she could say little more than, "Ah well, I lived through it."[20]

In their living quarters, teachers were routinely plagued by mice, bed bugs, lice, the cold, the damp, poor food, primitiveness, lack of privacy, hostile neighbours and loneliness. Jean D. observed about her residence:

> The physical conditions during the first year were primitive. The main part of the house was made of logs which were swarming with bed bugs. My room was a lean-to made of lumber. In order to keep the bugs from invading my privacy, everything moveable in my room was taken outside and washed with coal-oil; this was a weekly occurrence. As my bedding-mattress, pillows and quilts were stuffed with raw wool from the local sheep (a smell I have always hated) I did not smell exactly like Chanel No. 5.[21]

Another teacher slept with the mother and child in one bedroom while a male boarder slept with the husband in the other bedroom. In her second boarding place Lenore S. found the temperature occasionally dropped below zero in her room during the night.[22] There were districts where no one wanted the teacher as a boarder. In one such area a family was willing to provide room and board in their mud house. The roof was thatched with straw and the walls were made of mud and straw. The house was one long building, first the kitchen and living room, then the bedroom for mother, father and three children, next the teacher's bedroom, and on the other side of her room was the barn attached to the house.[23] Some were fortunate to have the privacy of a teacherage, but like the boarding house, the quality of these varied considerably. Water stored in barrels froze and spilled over the floor.[24] Some living quarters were little more than a lean-to built on the school. One teacherage had a felt roof that absorbed water and sagged with the weight of water from melting snow. Poking a hole in the felt alleviated the threat of the roof collapsing, but it created the problem of running water.[25] Not only were these facilities primitive; they were also "lonely and scary."[26] That teachers endured such stressful conditions is a strong testimonial to their qualities of character.

Social conditions faced by some teachers added greatly to the demands of their assignment. Margaret G. acknowledged that in one home she had to abide "much quarreling and lying and violence."[27] The threat of a mentally unstable landlady hung over the head of Bessie M. When finally the landlady poured red ink on her clothes, she decided it was time to move.[28] Personal sacrifices of teachers were only part of their ordeal. The struggles of children facing abuse, malnutrition or deprivation affected the outlook of their teachers. Teacher Alfred H. was so offended by the conditions experienced by his students during the Depression that he decided to enter politics under the Social Credit banner in an effort to alleviate their pain.[29] The sense of futility or frustration experienced by teachers who faced the suffering of their students is captured by Vera Lysenko as she had her teacher Julie think out loud about one of her students:

> What is a teacher to do, when she sees a promising pupil like Katie slipping away from her, because her environment is too much for her to handle? What are those few moments I can give her each day? With fifty-five pupils, I have about six minutes daily with each. That's hardly enough to counteract the effects of a lifetime of abuse.[30]

Having to face children daily who were hungry and cold was a serious concern of teachers. "There were families who were really poor . . ., they didn't have anything really. I felt sorry for the children. I know the children were hungry."[31] Some little ones were inadequately clothed for the weather conditions they faced in winter. When a serious storm developed one day in Eva's school, sensing the children's lack of proper apparel she recalls, "I remember taking our school curtains and tearing them in strips and wrapping the children's limbs."[32] Not all teachers dealt successfully with life-threatening situations, particularly those associated with winter storms. Children like those recalled by Hector T. died in a blizzard, getting lost between the outhouse and the school.[33] Teachers willingly shared their beds, their food, their shelter in order to protect their students.

While there was much to do to keep busy as a beginning teacher facing large classes and multi-grades, and while there were trying physical conditions to endure, even more oppressive were hours of fear and loneliness with which rural teachers contended, not always successfully.[34] Some of the isolation and loneliness was overcome through association with families in the school district. Others longed for such an opportunity. "I was never taken anywhere with the farm family. They would spend Sunday with friends leaving me at home. Once I asked to go to town fifteen miles away. They didn't have room."[35] Young Bessie M. felt a similar loneliness, her unhappiness compounded by her unsuitable accommodation. She wished her parents would come get her and take her home. Yet she knew "it wasn't possible because my parents were poor and they couldn't do it. They didn't even have a car. They never came to see me in the three years that I was there which was only about fifty-five miles from my home. They never came to see me once in those three years that I was there."[36]

Beginning teachers armed with their normal school education and their Grade XI or XII schooling experienced endless challenges in their one-room classrooms. Whatever their struggles in their personal lives due to prevailing views about women or teaching and due to conditions of hardship and loneliness, the situation within the classroom was even more demanding. Foremost in importance was the concern of orchestrating instruction for twenty to thirty youngsters, even fifty to sixty at times, in numerous grades, sometimes including high school. The numbers of students, separate preparations and courses of instruction were enough of a professional challenge to the beginner to demand seemingly endless hours of work. "Handling grades one through nine was very, very difficult for me. I used to work until twelve o'clock at night preparing lessons and I would get up at five o'clock in the morning preparing lessons. . . . Many of the exercises that we did, I had to write on the board. So I would get up in the morning and fill the boards with exercises for these students and do the same thing after school and sometimes I would have to spend my noon hour putting questions on the board for the students to do."[37]

Survival and success as a teacher required more than hard work and management skills. Teachers were tested in a variety of ways. Forer, writing about a rural schoolteacher, noted that Miss Langois

> had survived that stench of urine poured into the school stove; she had laughed off rumours of an illicit affair with a student, she had conquered the midwinter cold of broken windows and stolen fuel-oil, and she had extinguished one serious attempt to burn down the schoolhouse. She had lived with nights of catcalls and peeping boys; she had confiscated real pistols, dynamite caps, kitchen knives, and obscene drawings.[38]

Some of the escapades were nothing more than harmless pranks. Ivan N. recalls coming to school one morning and discovering a bunch of chickens mysteriously locked in the school.[39] Hyacinthe B. had to contend with dead mice in her desk[40] and Moline W. with a freshly butchered pig's tail.[41] The contest for control between students and teachers was not always won by the teacher. Rifle shells exploding in the stove were enough to cause Miss Langois' predecessor to seek employment elsewhere. Some of the student pranksters engaged in dangerous sport on occasion. The school building was a favourite target. Ivan N. tells of his experience with an arson attempt on the schoolhouse.

> I don't know why it happened but some boys set the school on fire. They got up into the attic somehow and there was no doubt at all that the fire was set because there were rags and kerosene. Fortunately, a young man who lived in the neighbourhood was coming home rather late at night and saw this school on fire. I suppose the boys who set the fire didn't like school or didn't like me.[42]

Discipline was a concern of many teachers. One inspector readily acknowledged he "believed in hiring big people as teachers"[43] as one way of ensuring teacher dominance in the classroom. The older, bigger boys were not always willing to submit to the direction of their teachers. Davis K. tells of his gaining the upper hand over an unruly boy by physical means. When the boy defied him, Davis K. "just hauled off and gave him a slap on the side of his face and kicked his feet from under him."[44] He then stretched him over a register under a window and strapped him. There was no room for a teacher who could not keep order.

Similarly, there was no place for a teacher who could not deal with a wide variety of unpredictable crises and responsibilities. While practicing with the children for the Christmas concert, Mable M. was frightened by the behaviour of a student experiencing an epileptic seizure, something she had never seen let alone treated before.[45] She recalled a short talk on the subject given at normal school which enabled her to help the lad. Medical expertise was required of teachers for a variety of reasons. In normal school Florence M. was taught not to leave a dislocated finger or toe unattended or it would swell. When one of her students presented his dislocated toe to her for treatment, she remembered the instruction to reset it. Not knowing whether it was broken or dislocated, she experienced considerable relief when her pulling resulted in the toe being restored to its proper fit.[46] The absence of qualified medical personnel in rural areas meant that rural residents ran the risk of poor or non-existent treatment or long-distance travel under adverse conditions to see a doctor. Gertrude N., while boarding with an elderly gentleman and his daughter, had to care for the old man when he had a stroke. Even though they were over one hundred miles from a major city, the teacher decided to drive the girl and her father to the city, in a Model T truck. She knew that if she did not venture out, risky as the long drive was for two young women, the elderly man would die.[47]

Just as teachers faced social isolation and loneliness they also encountered professional isolation and neglect. There was no readily-available source of professional help for the teacher of the rural one-room school. The inspector was often the sole professional contact for the fledgling teacher.

Unfortunately, their services often left much to be desired. They seldom visited one school more than once a year, nor stayed long enough during their visit to offer much constructive assistance. According to Cloe D. not one ever said, "Can I help you?"[48] When they were asked for assistance by those brave or needy enough to make the request, their responses were not always helpful. One teacher noted, "When the new Course of Study arrived, I wrote to my inspector and said, "Why don't you come out and give me some instructions. I haven't a clue how to do this and I can't afford to go to summer school.""[49] He wrote right back to say, "Neither have I. But do it anyway for this year, and next year I will get you a grant to go to summer school."[50] Olive M.'s first school was like that of many of her fellow rural prairie schoolteachers.

> There were fifty-one children to grade seven. The people, I soon discovered, were all Eastern European — Ukrainian, Russian, Romanian and Galician. It was a badly built school. Light could be seen under the windows. The desks were the double seat variety and there were not enough of them. The little ones had to sit three in a desk. . . . Worst of all, there was a shortage of textbooks and no library at all.
>
> Language was the real and worst problem. . . . It had never dawned on me that there were places in Alberta where English was not spoken. From grade three up English was spoken, but the beginners were my Waterloo. I did not know how to handle the situation. Now I know, I failed at it.[51]

Where was her professional help? Sadly she acknowledges, "The inspector did not come at all. I felt these schools should have been given special attention, that we should have had more assistance, supplies and backing. Nobody seemed to care."[52]

Changes in the curriculum, especially changes as pronounced as the Enterprise introduced in Alberta and Saskatchewan in 1936 and 1939 respectively, heightened teachers' awareness of their professional isolation and the inadequacies of their preparation and their support system. One teacher recalls that the enterprise system was introduced in her third year of teaching. "The inspector was firm in his opinion that the enterprise system must be taught, but did not give much idea as to what and how."[53] Many practicing teachers openly admitted, as did Nettie S., that when the new curriculum was introduced, "I wasn't prepared at all."[54] According to her "no one could tell you what to do, inspectors least of all."[55] She went so far as to ask the deputy minister, Dr. G.F. McNally, what to do. When she expressed her lack of understanding, he observed, "To tell you the truth Nettie, I don't know much about it either."[56]

It is not surprising that one Alberta inspector, W.R. Hay, commented that he had "found the quality of instruction given by teachers in the rural schools rather mediocre."[57] Prior to World War II little had been done to alter significantly the conditions of teaching in rural, western Canada. The personal accounts and recollections of the teachers of the period suggest that the rural school experience, the beginning assignment for nearly all normal school graduates, was physically, emotionally, and professionally demanding, so much so that many of these young people lived lives of quiet, lonely, desperation as they tried to provide a limited level of educational service to their students. Their willingness to endure these conditions at considerable personal discomfort and sacrifice has led to the establishment of a professional support system which enables modern beginning teachers to function at much higher levels of professional competence and personal fulfilment.

Notes

[1] Walt Mason, "The Schoolmarm," *The ATA Magazine* (Feb. 1930): cover.

[2] In Canada this growing interest in teaching as a focus of historical research is reflected in such publications as Elizabeth Graham, "Schoolmarms and Early Teaching in Ontario," in *Women at Work* (Toronto: Canadian Women's Educational Press, 1974), Alison Prentice, "The Feminization of Teaching" in S.M. Trofimenkoff and A. Prentice, eds., *The Neglected Majority: Essays in Canadian Women's History* (Toronto, McClelland and Stewart Ltd., 1977), John Charyk, *The Little White Schoolhouse* (Saskatoon, Prairie Books, 1968), *Those Bittersweet Schooldays* (Saskatoon Prairie Books, 1977), *Syrup Pails and Gopher Tails* (Saskatoon Prairie Books, 1983) and Robert S. Patterson "History of Teacher Education in Alberta" in D.C. Jones, N.M. Sheehan, R.M. Stamp, eds., *Shaping the Schools of the Canadian West,* (Calgary: Detselig Enterprises Ltd., 1979).

[3] Vera Lysenko, *Westerly Wild* (Toronto: Ryerson Press, 1956), p. 173.

[4] Simon Veenman, "Perceived Problems of Beginning Teachers," *Review of Educational Research* (Summer, 1984): 168.

[5] Alberta Government, Department of Education, *Annual Report of the Department of Education* (Edmonton: King's Printer, 1917), p. 20.

[6] Project Yesteryear Questionnaire No. 47, R.S. Patterson file, University of Alberta, p. 1, hereafter PYQ.

[7] Interview No. 24, R.S. Patterson file, University of Alberta, p. 4, hereafter Interview.

[8] Arthur Storey, *Prairie Harvest* (Toronto: Ryerson Press, 1959), p. 104.

[9] Interview No. 32, p. 19.

[10] PYQ No. 661, p. 5.

[11] Normal School Questionnaire No. 78, R.S. Patterson file, University of Alberta, p. 3, hereafter NSQ.

[12] Ibid.

[13] Ibid.

[14] Interview No. 45, p. 10.

[15] PYQ No. 225, p. 4.

[16] Interview No. 41, p. 9.

[17] Ibid.

[18] NSQ No. 95, p. 6.

[19] PYQ No. 268b., p. 3.

[20] Ibid.

[21] PYQ No. 487, p. 3.

[22]Interview No. 25, p. 7.
[23]Interview No. 45, p. 3.
[24]Interview No. 8, p. 7.
[25]Ibid.
[26]PYQ No. 151, p. 3.
[27]PYQ No. 661, p. 3.
[28]Interview No. 45, p. 10.
[29]Interview No. 1, p. 2.
[30]Lysenko, *Westerly Wild,* pp. 124-125.
[31]Interview No. 25, p. 9.
[32]Interview No. 26, p. 10.
[33]Interview No. 8, p. 1.
[34]PYQ No. 151, p. 3.
[35]PYQ No. 197e, p. 3.
[36]Interview No. 25, p. 8.
[37]Interview No. 21, p. 21.
[38]Mort Forer, *The Humback* (Toronto: McClelland & Stuart, 1969), p. 186.
[39]Interview No. 29, p. 9.
[40]Interview No. 27, p. 12.
[41]Interview No. 34, p. 4.
[42]Interview No. 29, p. 26.
[43]Interview No. 33, p. 9.
[44]Ibid.
[45]NSQ No. 95, p. 6.
[46]NSQ No. 78, p. 5.
[47]Interview No. 50, p. 13.
[48]PYQ No. 124C, p. 13.
[49]Ibid., p. 15.
[50]Ibid.
[51]NSQ No. 2844, p. 4.
[52]Ibid., p. 6.
[53]PYQ No. 625, p. 5.
[54]PYQ No. 5, p. 5.
[55]Ibid.
[56]Ibid.
[57]Alberta Government, Department of Education, *Annual Report of the Department of Education,* (Edmonton: King's Printer, 1931), pp. 51-52.

7

Ten Forgotten Years:
The Saskatchewan Teachers' Federation and
The Legacy of the Depression

John E. Lyons

There are two periods in Saskatchewan's educational history which have attracted the attention of historians. J.T.M. Anderson, whose 1929 election victory ended twenty-four years of Liberal rule in the province, was premier during one of these periods. Anderson headed the Department of Education as well as the government, and the changes he introduced into the province's school system have been studied in some detail.[1] The other era which has come increasingly to the fore is that of the first socialist government in North America. T.C. Douglas' Cooperative Commonwealth Federation (CCF), which took power in 1944, has also attracted wide attention.[2] The important changes which took place both in the public school system[3] and in the field of adult education[4] under the new regime have been carefully analyzed.

The decade between these two governments, however, has been largely ignored by educational historians because it lacked the major changes associated with these other periods. This decade saw the laying of a groundwork for the educational changes which took place after the 1944 election. The legacy of these years continued long after the people involved had disappeared from the scene.

James Thomas Milton Anderson, a former teacher, had served as the Director of Education among the New Canadians before taking over the leadership of the Saskatchewan Conservative Party. The vitriolic election campaign of 1929, in which the Orange Lodge and the Ku Klux Klan threw their support behind him,[5] saw Anderson draw support from minority parties to form a government. Over the objections of the Liberal opposition, Anderson instituted amendments to the School Act, restricting the educational rights of Catholics, French-Canadians, and non-British immigrant groups.[6] Anderson's drive to use the schools as an agency of assimilation was soon overshadowed by an even more relentless leveler, the Great Depression.

For the rest of the continent the Depression is best symbolized by the stock market crash of 1929 and soup kitchens for the unemployed, but for Saskatchewan, it was the "dirty thirties." Not only did the province have to contend with unemployment and the disappearance of markets for its agricultural products, it was struck by a series of natural disasters. Farmers, who made up the lifeblood of the economy, reeled from one problem to another. The opening sentences of the 1935 *Annual Report* of the Saskatchewan Department of Education give a sense of what the province faced.

The Spring of 1935 opened with every prospect of a good crop. However, as the season advanced, drought and grasshoppers were destructive in some parts of the province, while rust affected a large portion of the remaining crop area. The season as a whole proved to be one of the most disappointing in the history of the province. Under the circumstances, the problem of financing the schools became even more difficult than in the preceding year.[7]

The Depression's impact on the public schools is graphically illustrated in the record of school taxes collected. In 1929, they amounted to more than $11 million; but by 1937 this had dropped to less than $4.5 million. Not until 1943 did these tax revenues grow to pre-Depression levels.[8] Since property taxes were established according to fixed land valuation, this decline in revenue meant either that the mill rate was being cut or that people were not paying these taxes — if not both. Whatever the reason, school revenues were reduced. The provincial government, whose revenue had also fallen, instead of compensating for this loss of taxes, reduced the province's per diem grant to school boards from $1.50 to $1.00 per teacher in 1932.

Teachers' salaries plummeted by 50 percent or more. Salaries were individually negotiated, and one inspector, after analyzing the salaries of his rural teachers, decided that salaries bore no relationship to the wealth of the district, the qualifications or experience of the teacher, or the number of grades or pupils taught.[9] Female teachers in rural areas holding first-class certificates earned an average of $1,142 in 1930, but six years later this had dropped to $407.[10] Teachers in some districts were lucky to get the $200 annual grant.

Saskatchewan teachers at the outbreak of the Depression lacked any effective means of protecting themselves from such abuses. None of the existing educational organizations represented all or even most teachers, and none of them had the statutory right to represent teachers in bargaining or to defend their rights. Using the Depression as an excuse, individual school boards often took advantage of this lack of organization to play teachers off against each other in order to drive wages down. As revenues fell, some boards took to paying teachers in whole or in part by means of promissory notes. By 1934 these notes were estimated to amount to $600,000,[11] and two years later the total was over $1 million.[12] James R. MacKay, the first president of the Saskatchewan Teachers' Federation, complained that

> . . . the tragedy of it is that the teachers who hold the notes are the ones who were engaged for the lowest salaries, and these notes are not negotiable or negotiable only at tremendous discount, to people who do not scruple to make profit out of human misery. Instances are not lacking where teachers' notes have been taken at 40% and 50% discount and used to pay taxes in the same municipality at par value.[13]

Under the circumstances it is not surprising that the teachers decided to form a single association. In the fall of 1933, members of the Saskatchewan Teachers' Alliance and the Rural Teachers' Association arranged for a joint meeting of their two executives to discuss a merger. Inviting the Saskatchewan Education Association to join with them, they formed the Saskatchewan Teachers' Federation. This new organization set out to achieve a statutory salary schedule, security of tenure, revisions to superannuation legislation, and the formation of larger units of school administration.[14]

The executive of the new body immediately approached Premier Anderson for action on salaries. They argued that under the Minimum Wage Act waitresses were guaranteed $574.80 per year (plus tips) and that teachers should be covered by similar guarantees.[15] Although the delegation even claimed that there was a case of one school board paying their teacher $100 less than the annual per diem grant, Anderson declined to implement changes. He declared himself in favour of a minimum salary but claimed that this would be dealt with at the next session of the legislature.[16] Anderson was not anxious to make commitments to the teachers for fear of offending the electorate which he knew he had to face in less than six months' time.

In certain areas, however, the new organization was mobilizing itself into a potentially important force.[17] This growing body decided to take advantage of the upcoming election to send a questionnaire to the leaders of the Liberal, Conservative, and Farmer-Labor parties and to publish their replies. Although the responses were all rather similar, Anderson, as premier, was tied to current policy and lacked the flexibility of his two rivals. Whatever the impact of the teachers, the Liberals under former premier James G. Gardiner won a landslide victory, leaving Anderson's Conservatives without a seat in the legislature.

Although the fledgling Teachers' Federation was not a major force in the 1934 election, its strength was increasing. By November of that year, 65 percent of all of the province's teachers belonged.[18] It had become a large enough body that it could make its voice heard by the new government. When the STF executive met with the new minister of education, James Wilfred Estey, he told them that the government was committed to larger school units, increased school grants, improved rural high schools, a minimum salary and a salary schedule, security of tenure, a board of reference to hear teacher-trustee disputes, compulsory STF membership, and government consultation with the federation in the framing of educational legislation.[19]

The government, however, could not afford to launch initiatives which would cost more money; it was hard pressed to pay for programs already in place. Consequently, the educational legislation passed by the legislature in early 1935 did not involve increased government expenditure. The first of these changes, an amendment to the School Act, required school boards to state the salary being offered when advertising for a teacher. Prior to this, trustees had expected teachers to bid for positions — a situation which had encouraged underbidding and an annual reduction in salaries. Another amendment fixed June and December as the only times that teachers' contracts could be terminated. It also established procedures for a board of reference to which teachers could take disputes over such things as unfair dismissal. These moves halted the practice of dismissing a teacher so that the position could be bid on in order to reduce the salary. A new section added to the School Act made it clear that teachers would be entitled to 1/200 of the annual salary for each day taught. If the school was open for fewer than 200 days due to board action, the teacher was still to receive full salary. This placed the responsibility for providing both schooling and the teacher's salary squarely on the shoulders of the trustees.[20]

The new government did recognize that something had to be done to assist destitute school districts. The number of special grants to school districts to enable them to pay teachers' salaries jumped dramatically in 1935.

Table 1

Special Grants[21]

Year	Number of Districts	Total Granted
1932-33	2	$ 200.00
1933-34	12	$ 500.00
1934-35	659	$93,061.70

The most important change made by Gardiner's government, however, was an act respecting the teaching profession, The Teachers' Federation Act. This statute, which came into force on February 21, 1935, made membership in the Saskatchewan Teachers' Federation compulsory for all teachers in the province's public schools.[22] The first legislation of its kind in the country, it was hailed by teachers' organizations across the Dominion as an important landmark.[23] Although the organization was poor (membership fees were only 1/10 of 1 percent of current contract), the STF's 8,447 members provided the potential for tremendous influence in the province.

The bill, which had been drafted after consultation with the STF executive, had originally been intended to grant the federation the power to discipline members. The executive, however, decided that the incorporation of disciplinary provisions should best be left until the federation formulated and approved a code of ethics. The premier promised that when this was done, the STF could then establish a discipline committee which could control the professional matters of teachers.[24]

Although the legislation did not give the STF complete jurisdiction over the profession, teachers were slowly achieving more professional control. As of June 1935, teachers in the larger high schools and collegiates were permitted to grant students standing in one or more Grade XI subjects without their having to write departmental examinations. At the same time, departmental examinations for normal school graduation were abolished and, in 1938, exemptions were permitted at the Grade XII level as well.[25]

This general tendency to grant teachers more autonomy in matters of examination and promotion was not appreciated by everyone. One inspector reported that many teachers, unused to accepting professional responsibility, were apprehensive about this system and expressed a desire for the return of departmental exams.[26] At least one official, concerned about the maintenance of standards at the normal schools, declared, "Though this new plan be in keeping with modern trends in progressive educational systems, I seriously doubt if it has resulted in a better teacher-in-training attitude towards what makes for success in the normal school and in the teaching profession."[27]

Despite such concerns, the academic qualifications of teachers were gradually increasing. Third-class teaching certificates had been phased out during the 1920s, and as of 1936 all students wishing to enter Saskatchewan normal schools were required to have completed Grade XII. In order to phase out all second-class certificates, teachers holding such credentials were given until 1942 to complete their Grade XII, thus qualifying for first-class certification. In 1936, the province instituted a new permanent certificate — a superior first-class — issued to first-class certificate holders who had successfully completed five university courses.

Teachers had no financial incentive to upgrade their certificates, however. Salaries were individually negotiated, and the differences in pay between second-class, first-class, and superior first-class, certificate holders were very small. In fact, the average salary of female teachers holding second class certificates in 1938 was higher than that of those holding first-class credentials.[28] One teacher summed up the frustration felt by many of his colleagues:

> Fifty cents per day! Then the Department of Education intensifies the sore by sending forth the decree that teachers must improve their standing. You are ordered to sacrifice clothing, comforts, and necessities, you are robbed of your summer vacation, you are urged and dragged and driven, in order, we are told, to bring the province "into line" with the standard of other provinces. It seems that a more appropriate action would be first to bring the impoverished rural school into line with the standard of a civilized country. The improvement of standing is a very nice thing under reasonable circumstances, although I am not any too sure that academic standing is at all synonymous with pedagogical ability.[29]

Not everyone agreed with this view. One writer claimed that increased academic standards would reduce the teacher surplus, increase teacher efficiency, raise teacher status, and give teachers more influence.[30] Many teachers obviously agreed with this view because throughout the depths of the Depression they continued in large numbers to attend summer school to upgrade their certificates.

The federation had hoped that, with the election of a new government, it would obtain a statutory salary schedule. It realized, however, that improvements in salary would be possible only if the province would assume a larger share of educational costs and establish a uniform educational tax across the province. Disappointed by its failure to achieve this, the STF started a campaign in support of larger units of school administration as an intermediate goal.

The larger unit of school administration was not a new idea. Prior to the First World War, the Saskatchewan legislature made provision for the establishment of consolidated school districts.[31] Although some districts took advantage of this legislation, poor roads, a pioneer population without a tradition of schooling, and the lack of province-wide truancy laws led to the formation of no more than a handful of consolidated districts. By the 1930s, however, the province was beyond the pioneer stage, and there were new educational needs to be met.

The federation campaign to gain support for larger school units was intended to improve not only teacher status but also high school education in rural areas. Because there were few jobs for young people, many of them opted to stay in school. Although Saskatchewan's population dropped steadily between 1929 and 1945, a trend clearly reflected in the total number of pupils in the province, high school enrolment climbed steadily until the outbreak of World War II.

In 1930 Anderson's government had amended the School Act, requiring all school boards to offer instruction to the end of Grade X unless they received a special exemption.[33] Teachers with second and even third-class certificates were now being expected to teach up to ten separate grades each day. By 1934 there were 11,882 high school students enrolled in one-room schools, placing an unbearable burden on these teachers.[34] Many of those enrolled in high school grades in one-room rural schools were using correspondence courses which the teachers then corrected. This attempt at providing a high school education for rural Saskatchewan was almost unanimously condemned by school inspectors.[35] The quality of high school education in rural Saskatchewan cried out for reform.

Many of the school inspectors agreed with the STF in its desire to achieve larger units; they knew only too well the problems of the small rural school districts. Most had been members of the Saskatchewan Education Association, one of the constituent bodies from which the STF had been formed, and throughout the federation's formative period they continued to cooperate closely with the new body. Sympathetic inspectors and other departmental officials lent encouragement to the teachers' aspirations. Even the Director of School Organization was critical of the existence of 5,123 school districts whose assessed valuation varied from under $50,000 to over $500,000.[36]

Table 2
School Enrolment[32]

Year	Schools Under the School Act*	Change	Total High School*	Change
1930	220,352	+4,380	24,451	?
1931	221,556	+1,204	28,292	+3,842
1932	219,484	−2,072	35,131	+6,839
1933	215,695	−3,379	34,912	− 219
1934	214,076	−1,619	35,137	+ 225
1935	210,945	−3,131	35,758	+ 621
1936	206,694	−4,251	35,877	+ 119
1937	204,871	−1,823	36,077	+ 200
1938	200,345	−4,526	36,735	+ 658
1939	195,430	−4,915	37,778	+1,043
1940	194,256	−1,174	37,620	− 158
1941	190,752	−3,504	36,617	− 3
1942	186,765	−3,987	36,480	− 137
1943	176,875	−9,890	33,724	−2,656
1944	170,396	−6,479	32,511	−1,213
1945	165,673	−4,723	32,722	+ 211

*Because of the way in which enrolment was reported, there may be an overlap between these two columns — making the contrast even more marked.

The campaign for larger units was occurring not only in Saskatchewan. The Minister of Education in Alberta had been proposing such a system since 1928,[37] and the British Columbia government had imposed a large unit in the Peace River region in 1934.[38] The STF *Bulletin* provided a steady flow of information to Saskatchewan teachers about developments in these neighbouring provinces. After 1935, when the new Social Credit government in Alberta implemented a province-wide system of larger units, the *Bulletin* sang its praises.

While most teachers and inspectors were easily convinced, the trustees were another matter. Although prior to World War I the Saskatchewan School Trustees' Association had given almost unanimous consent to consolidated schools, the 1935 SSTA conference defeated a resolution urging the government to set up a commission to study larger school units.[39] A school inspector who attended that meeting blamed William Francis Goulden, the SSTA president, and a group of trustees for going on an anti-teacher binge. He lamented that "the part that was disturbing . . . was the almost unholy glee which some of the trustees took in rebuffing the legitimate desires of the teaching profession."[40]

While some trustees simply may have been opposed to teachers, others had real reservations about larger units. They believed that local control was important in education and that the local trustee's intimate knowledge of the district led to improved schooling. They knew from experience that local schools encouraged popular involvement including much free labour which would, they claimed, disappear in larger units. While rural trustees were afraid that in any centralized system urbanites would control the education of their children, urban residents saw nothing for their electors in such a plan except for higher taxes. Pupil conveyance was seen as an expensive innovation which would only lead to an increased dropout rate. Trustees also feared, with increased salaries for secretary treasurers, the evolution of a new class of expensive civil servants. A survey of SSTA members in March 1936 found that only seventy-four local boards favoured the larger units while 645 opposed them. A survey two years later of the secretary-treasurers of the larger units in Alberta seemed to show just what many Saskatchewan trustees feared: the taxes had increased and local involvement waned in the new larger areas.[41]

Not all the opposition to larger school units was altruistic, however. A study of the rural schools in two Saskatchewan municipalities uncovered some other reasons. School district secretaries who opposed larger units did so mainly because they were satisfied with the status quo, they feared a loss of their control over the teachers, and they feared the loss of their own jobs.[42] STF president Lorne F. Titus, launching the federation's third year, told the province's teachers:

> It has been estimated and I think conservatively estimated, that over $500,000 per year is being paid to secretaries in school districts in Saskatchewan. If the province were divided into 100 large units and a secretary appointed for each at $1000 a year (and efficient full time rural secretaries could be secured for that sum today) a saving of $400,000 would be effected, an amount that would be twice what would be needed to provide an efficient supervisor for each district.[43]

This was effective propaganda among teachers who were earning, on the average, considerably less than $1,000 per year. Titus added:

> How is the plan to be instituted? "Ay, there's the rub." How convince 15,000 or more trustees and 5,000 secretaries that they must turn over their control and, in the case of the secretaries, their jobs, to someone else?[44]

Despite trustee apprehensions about larger units, the deepening educational crisis led SSTA representatives to meet with an STF delegation in the spring of 1936. The meeting resulted in a joint call for a government commission to study the educational problems facing the province.[45] The government, now under Premier William J. Patterson, refused the request.

Conditions had reached the critical stage. The government was forced to cancel tax arrears in some areas to prevent the wholesale eviction of the populations of entire districts. While this provided assistance to the ratepayers, it left these districts without the wherewithal to pay the promissory notes which the teachers had accepted. Another joint teacher-trustee delegation called on the government to impose a two-percent sales tax to support education.[46] The province, desperate for a means to pay the cost of schooling, agreed and implemented this new Education Tax in August 1937.

Using these funds, the province restored the per diem grants to $1.50 in 1937.[47] According to the STF, however, it was often debenture holders, not the teachers, who were the beneficiaries of this largess. The federation urged the government to pay the grant directly to the teachers because in spite of the minister of education's ". . .faith that most of the boards would pass the increase on to the teachers. . .", this happened in only 16 percent of the cases.[48]

Despite such problems, a measure of cooperation was developing between the STF and other educational bodies in the province. Increasingly, the province's teachers, inspectors, trustees, normal school instructors, and departmental officials were seeing themselves as part of an educational team. This did not mean, however, that the STF was soft-pedalling its drive for larger school units. Titus stated in his 1937 presidential address:

> It has been said publicly in this province that the teachers' leaders cannot open their mouths without talking about larger units of administration. In so far as utterances on educational matters are concerned, I plead guilty of the charge. A reorganization into larger units of administration is the crying need of the time. We cannot hope to make educational progress as long as the present small unit board exists.[49]

In spite of the teachers' strong stand on the abolition of the small school district, from 1936 onwards an increasing measure of cooperation emerged between the STF and the SSTA, with a corresponding increase in trustee support for the larger unit concept.

The larger unit was not the only thing for which the STF was striving, however. After adopting a professional code of ethics, the federation called on the government to fulfill its promise made three years earlier. It requested "That the Act Respecting the Teaching Profession be so amended as to provide for disciplinary powers based on the code of Teaching Ethics."[50] This would have been a truly revolutionary change: it would have given teachers professional status by allowing and requiring them, through their professional organization, to control their own members. The Liberal administration of 1938 was not the same one which had taken power in 1934, however. Premier Gardiner, a former teacher himself, had headed the government which had passed the Teachers' Federation Act. He had, in November 1935, gone to Ottawa to join Prime Minister Mackenzie King's federal cabinet, and power was now held by William J. Patterson, a cautious individual whose party was going to the polls in a few months. Rather than acceding to the teachers' request, he replied:

> The Department of Education must assume the responsibility for the issue and cancellation of Teachers' Certificates, and therefore the responsibility for the academic qualifications and other requirements for each of these certificates. It is our opinion that disciplinary power should rest with the body charged with these responsibilities.[51]

Although this set back the STF's professional aspirations, it did not dampen its desire for educational reform in the province. The STF continued to hold the plight of its members in the public spotlight in the hope of getting some redress. Titus rejected any suggestion that teachers' complaints were not serious:

> . . .I have never exaggerated conditions. It would be impossible for me to do so. When I read letters written our office by teachers trying to teach while enduring actual privation my heart bleeds and I grow angry at any show of apathy. When a teacher writes that his only suit of underwear is three years old, that his infant child is without clothing, that himself and family had only twenty-seven dollars in three months to provide food and clothing, and that he asked for relief and was refused because he was in receipt of a salary, I feel that I am lacking in the bowels of compassion if I do not cry out the existence of these conditions from the very housetops. Let people accuse me of exaggeration if they will, but I reiterate that this case is only one of many.[52]

Conditions actually seemed to be getting worse in the late 1930s. The establishment of community pastures under the federal Prairie Farm Rehabilitation Act affected a number of school districts. In 1938 alone, 192 districts had to be "disorganized" or have their boundaries readjusted because of this Act.[53] This gave a new thrust to the larger unit argument. Faced with a continuing barrage of criticism from all sides, Patterson's government finally gave in to demands for an educational study.

In the summer of 1938, the government established a special committee to study school administration. Headed by Chief Justice (and former premier) William Melville Martin, the committee included a representative of the Department of Education, a trustee, and a teacher. The STF brief to the committee urged reform at all levels of the educational system but stressed the importance of larger units. The committee praised the brief and even utilized its information about the educational conditions in other countries in its interim report.[54]

Having won over most teachers and a number of trustees, the federation now set out to work on public opinion. The STF printed ten thousand copies of a pamphlet extolling the virtues of larger units and sent them to teachers across the province to distribute to ratepayers.[55] Teachers were urged

> . . .to see that the ratepayers in your district are made acquainted with the advantages of the larger unit of administration and to urge, as far as possible, ratepayers favouring the experiment to attend the annual meeting and to explain the policy to their fellow ratepayers.[56]

Individual teachers and STF locals repeated these requests wherever the committee met.

Martin's committee polled those attending the annual school district ratepayers' meetings in 1939 and found public opinion overwhelmingly opposed to larger units. Although the committee toured Alberta's larger units and reported extensively on them, the final report rejected the idea of legislating larger units, fearing that such a move would shatter the harmony of rural schools. Although it recommended a form of larger unit, it did not suggest a system of provincial equalization grants as a means of overcoming inequalities. Poor districts were only being allowed, as it were, to share their misery. The committee did, however, recommend that three experimental larger units be established by the government to test the viability of the concept.[57]

Following on the heels of the Martin Committee Report, the minister of education introduced the School Division Bill into the legislature. Like the earlier Consolidated Schools Act, this legislation was permissive: it allowed the government to form a larger unit if the ratepayers petitioned for it and voted in favour of it. The new division board could then levy uniform taxes, provide high school instruction, and pay for the transportation of children.[58] This arrangement would work best where town or village districts would be included in the division. These districts, however, were reluctant to see their taxes increase simply to transport rural children into their schools. Wealthy rural districts were similarly unwilling to throw in their lot with their poorer neighbours. Under the circumstances, it is not surprising that no school divisions were formed.

The government also moved on the question of teachers' salaries in 1940. This was not, however, entirely spontaneous. The federation had long attempted to achieve a legislated minimum salary and a salary schedule. Failing that, in the fall of 1939 the STF asked all teachers in the province to sign a pledge committing themselves to accept no less than $700 for the following year.[59] Rather than face the chance of a showdown with the teachers, the government imposed a $700 minimum salary. While this temporarily diffused teachers' demands, it did nothing to assist school boards to raise the funds to pay these salaries, and, in some areas of the province, non-payment of salaries and promissory notes continued to be a problem.

In 1941, two new figures appeared on Saskatchewan's educational stage: Woodrow Lloyd, a twenty-seven-year-old principal, took over the presidency of the STF and Hubert Staines, a former teacher, became the minister of education. Teachers' hopes that Staines would be sympathetic to their cause were soon shattered. The outbreak of war and rising prosperity in the rest of the country had led to a flight of teachers from the province. In the fall of 1941, faced by a teacher shortage, Staines allowed ninety-four normal school students to take over schools which could not find teachers.[60] Although these "normalites" returned to their studies in January, their places were taken by others only slightly better trained. The STF condemned this policy, blaming poor pay for the loss of qualified teachers to other provinces. The government launched special summer schools and winter schools (during Saskatchewan's then-common two month winter vacation) to upgrade or reinstate lapsed certificates, but this still did not meet the demand for teachers. The normal schools were therefore required to restructure their programs to include four twelve-week quarters and a system of rotating "normalite" teachers working on interim certificates. This system put 479 such "teachers" into Saskatchewan schools in 1942-43; 1,451 in 1943-44; and 1,950 in 1944-45.[61] Moreover, the standards for admission into normal school were also compromised. In 1942, for the first time in six years, students without a completed Grade XII were admitted into normal school.[62]

The teachers were angered by these moves. Despite improved economic conditions, salaries were being depressed by waves of unqualified teachers. Not only did the STF blame the government for creating a teacher shortage by tolerating poor teaching conditions, it felt the government had broken faith with the federation by failing to consult it before these decisions were made. Instead of dealing with these concerns, Staines called on teachers to cooperate: "Saskatchewan teachers must carry on, overlook lowering of teaching standards because of the shortage of teachers, overlook low salaries, and give their services to the teaching of democratic principles."[63] The federation, still feeling that teachers had not been treated democratically by the government's failure to grant disciplinary powers, was no longer willing to accept praise and promises in lieu of action. It called for the creation of a certification committee, representing all aspects of the province's education, to assist the government in long-range educational planning.[64] While the government did establish a Representative Advisory Committee on the Certification of Teachers in 1943,[65] the committee was only advisory; power remained in government hands. Moreover, requests for action on salary and disciplinary powers were ignored.

If this were not enough of a blow, in the summer of 1943 the federal government took steps to solve the problem of teacher shortages: an Order-in-Council prevented teachers leaving their positions.[66] Bound into a system not dissimilar to medieval serfdom, teachers began turning to political action. Advertisements for the CCF began appearing on the pages of the STF *Bulletin*.[67] The Saskatchewan Co-operative Wheat Producers (the Wheat Pool) also began to advertise in the *Bulletin*, calling for farmer-teacher solidarity, and the federation joined with the Wheat Pool to promote hospitalization and medicare.[68] By October 1943, the CCF was soliciting memberships through the pages of the *Bulletin*.[69]

When the June 1944 provincial election was called, all three parties advertised in the *Bulletin* and all were allowed space to outline their educational policies. It was evident, however, that the CCF was making a strong play for the teachers' votes. Thirteen teachers or former teachers were running for the socialists, including Woodrow Lloyd, the federation president.

The CCF victory resulted in cabinet posts for Lloyd; John Sturdy, a former STF secretary; and Clarence Fines, a former president of the STF Regina local. Lloyd, the new minister of education, immediately announced plans for larger school units[70] and for a minimum salary of $1,200.[71] The Department also raised the standards of admission to normal schools to a completed Grade XII and insisted further on a 60 percent grade in English.[72] In early 1945, the Department, the STF, and the SSTA worked out a salary schedule for rural and village schools. The invitation given to the new STF president, Ethel M. Coppinger, to attend the opening of the legislature,[73] while not of practical importance, symbolized the new partnership in Saskatchewan education.

On the surface, 1934-44 would appear to have been a decade in which little happened. Salaries were worse in 1944 than they had been in 1929; more than five thousand school districts still existed, and the teaching profession was again being flooded by poorly-qualified teachers with temporary certificates. The changes which had occurred, however, were significant. The 1935 Teachers' Federation Act required membership in the STF as a condition of employment in the province's public schools. The first such Act in the English-speaking world, it set the stage for Saskatchewan teachers to launch their struggle towards professional status. Although not able to achieve full disciplinary power, the federation now represented over eight thousand teachers. Because of this power base, the federation was able to speak with some authority on Saskatchewan education.

The STF chose the route of cooperation rather than confrontation in dealing with other educational agencies in the province. In its infancy it drew on the good will and hard work of school inspectors and other departmental officials. The inspectors were especially supportive of the federation's aims and urged the teachers under their jurisdiction to become involved in all aspects of the new organization's work. Despite some early suspicion on the part of school boards, many of the trustees were also won over, and, by the end of the Depression, a widespread educational network had been developed in the province.

These cooperative links had a positive impact on public opinion as well. The spirit of independence which was the hallmark of the prairie pioneer had been reinforced by the small school districts. The residents of rural Saskatchewan, many of whom had suffered at the hands of remote bureaucrats and industrialists, were very suspicious of centralization. Only the steady flow of reasoned, persuasive propaganda by the Teachers' Federation laid the groundwork for the implementation of larger school units in the post-1944 period.

The struggle that the STF had to undergo in order to achieve its objectives had other effects. The provincial government's resistance to the consideration of any meaningful change strengthened the resolve of many of the federation leaders. The stubborn refusal of Patterson and Staines to deal with teacher grievances created a spirit amongst federation members which was translated into political action. The militancy of teachers across the province contributed to the CCF victory, including the election of a number of teacher MLAs to the government benches. The link between the new administration and many of the STF leaders facilitated educational reforms following the 1944 election. Without the preceding decade of struggle, with its steady expansion of educational awareness and organizational development, many of these reforms would have been impossible.

Notes

[1]See Keith A. McLeod, "Politics, Schools, and the French Language, 1881-1931," in N. Ward and D. Spafford, eds., *Politics in Saskatchewan* (Don Mills: Longmans, 1968), pp. 124-150; Raymond Huel, "French Language Education in Saskatchewan," in S. M. Trofimenkoff, ed., *The Twenties in Western Canada* (Ottawa: National Museum of Man, 1972), pp. 230-242.

[2]See especially Seymour Martin Lipset, *Agrarian Socialism*, (New York: Doubleday, 1968).

[3]See Ormond Knight McKague, "Socialist Education in Saskatchewan, 1942-1948: A Study in Ideology and Bureaucracy," (Ph.D. thesis, University of Oregon, 1981); McKague, "The Saskatchewan CCF: Education, Policy and the Rejection of Socialism, 1942-1948," *Journal of Educational Thought*, XIV (Aug. 1980): 138-159.

[4]Ormond McKague, "Big Tempest, Small Teapot," a paper presented to the annual conference of the Society for Educational Biography, Chicago, Illinois, May 1984; Michael Robert Welton, "To Be and Build the Glorious World: The Educational Thought and Practice of Watson Thomson, 1899-1946," (Ph.D. thesis, University of British Columbia, 1983); John E. Lyons, "Folks, Phantasy, and Flower Power: Saskatchewan Flirtation with Grassroots Adult Education," a paper presented to the annual Alberta Universities Educational Foundations Conference, Edmonton, Apr. 1984.

[5]See Patrick Kyba, "Ballots and Burning Crosses — The Election of 1929," in Ward and Spafford, eds., *Politics in Saskatchewan*, pp. 104-123; W. Calderwood, "The Rise and Fall of the Ku Klux Klan in Saskatchewan," (M.A. thesis, University of Saskatchewan, Regina, 1968); W. Calderwood, "Pulpit, Press and Political Reactions to the Ku Klux Klan in Saskatchewan," in Trofimenkoff, ed., *The Twenties in*

Western Canada, pp. 191-229; Peter A. Russel, "The Saskatchewan Conservatives, Separate Schools and the 1929 Election," *Prairie Forum*, VIII (Fall, 1983): 211-223; Anthony Appleblat, "The School Question in the 1929 Saskatchewan Provincial Election," *Canadian Catholic Historical Association Study Sessions*, 43 (1976): 75-90.

6Huel, "French Language Education;" Huel, "The Anderson Amendments and the Secularization of Saskatchewan Public Schools," *Canadian Catholic Historical Association Study Sessions*, 44 (1977): 61-76; Huel, "The Anderson Amendments: A Half Century Later," *Canadian Catholic Historical Association Study Sessions*, 47 (1980): 5-21.

7Saskatchewan Department of Education, *Annual Report*, 1935, (Regina: King's Printer), p. 8, hereafter *Annual Report*.

8Figures are taken from *Annual Reports* for the years indicated.

9 *Annual Report*, 1939, p. 31.

10*Annual Report*, 1930, p. 50; *Annual Report*, 1936, p. 25.

11C.E. Little, "The Crisis in School Finance," *STF Bulletin*, I (Nov., 1934): n.p.

12J.R. MacKay, "Presidential Address," *STF Bulletin*, 111 (Jan., 1936): 8.

13Ibid.

14*A Message To Our Educators* [Became *Saskatchewan Teachers' Federation Bulletin* and was considered to be Volume I, Number 1], (Feb., 1934): n.p.

15*Monthly Bulletin of the Saskatchewan Teachers' Federation* I (Mar., 1934): n.p. The average annual salary of a female teacher in rural Saskatchewan at this time was $442 (rather ironically, this was $10 less than her counterpart with a second-class certificate) *Annual Report*, 1935, p. 34.

16Ibid.

17By May 1934, for example, 119 of the 124 teachers in Moose Jaw and 134 of the 174 in Kamsack belonged to the STF. This membership was very spotty, however; only 2 of the 151 teachers in Meyronne and 3 of the 151 in the Watrous region belonged. *STF Bulletin*, I (May, 1934): n.p.

18*STF Bulletin*, I (Nov., 1934): n.p.

19*STF Bulletin*, I (Oct., 1934), n.p.

20Saskatchewan. *Statutes of the Province of Saskatchewan, 1934-35*. An Act to Amend the School Act. 25 George V, 1934-35, chap. 49, 1935, pp. 372-379. (Regina: T.H. McConica, King's Printer, 1935).

21*STF Bulletin*, III (Mar., 1936): 7.

22Saskatchewan. *Statutes of the Province of Saskatchewan, 1934-35*. An Act respecting the Teaching Profession. 25 George V, 1934-35, pp. 393-400. (Regina: T.H. McConica, King's Printer, 1935).

23*STF Bulletin*, II (May, 1935): 2.

24*STF Bulletin*, II (Mar., 1935): 2.

25*Annual Report*, 1934, p. 10; 1937, p. 30; 1936, p. 9.

26*Annual Report*, 1934, p. 42.

27J.A. McLeod, Principal of Regina Normal School, *Annual Report*, 1934, p. 37.

28Rural female — first class $481, second class $485. Urban female — first class $770, second class $794.

29E.G. Fielding, "The Scuttling of Public Education in Saskatchewan," *STF Bulletin*, III (Nov., 1936): 19.

[30]W. G. Manning, "How to Get the Larger Unit," *STF Bulletin*, III (Sept., 1936): 15-18.

[31]Saskatchewan. *Statutes of the Province of Saskatchewan, 1912-13.* An Act to amend The School Act. 3 George V, 1912-13, chap. 35, 1913, pp. 166-172.

[32]Statistics taken from *Annual Reports* of years indicated. Note that because some high school students were enrolled under the School Act (not the High School Act, The Collegiate Institute Act, or the Vocational School Act) there is some overlap between the columns. Because the number of high school students was increasing steadily and the elementary school enrolment was declining, the contrast is even greater than it appears on the table.

[33]Saskatchewan. *Statutes of the Province of Saskatchewan, 1929.* An Act to amend The School Act (No. 2). 20 George V, 1929, chap. 46, 1930, pp. 193-197.

[34] *STF Bulletin*, III (Apr., 1936): 4.

[35]*Annual Report*, 1934, pp. 41-42.

[36]N.L. Reid, "Equalization of School Costs," *STF Bulletin*, III (Nov., 1936): 2-8.

[37]L.J. (Roy) Wilson, "Perren Baker and Alberta's School District Reorganization," *Canadian Journal of Education*, II:3 (1977): 25-36.

[38]Alan H. Child, "A Little Tempest: Public Reaction to the Formation of a Large Educational Unit in the Peace River District of British Columbia," *B.C. Studies*, 16 (Winter, 1972-73): 57-70.

[39]*STF Bulletin*, III (Mar., 1936): 3.

[40]Alex Cameron, "The Trustee's Convention," *STF Bulletin*, III (Mar., 1936): 12-13.

[41]*The School Trustee* VI (Feb., 1936): 12; IX (Sept., 1938): 18; VII (May, 1937): 38; VIII (Sept., 1937):27; VII (May, 1937): 13; VIII (Sept., 1937): 22; VI (Feb., 1936): 12; IX (Sept., 1938): 21; VII (May, 1937): 6; X (Sept., 1939): 17.

[42]F.R. Bolton, "Reports of a Survey of 28 Rural Schools on Municipalities of Mariposa and Progress," *STF Bulletin*, II (Nov., 1935): 10-12.

[43]Lorne F. Titus, "President's Message," *STF Bulletin*, III (Jan., 1936): 9.

[44]Ibid.

[45]*STF Bulletin*, III (June, 1936): 5-6.

[46]*STF Bulletin*, III (Nov., 1936): 13.

[47]*Annual Report*, 1936, p. 8.

[48]Lorne F. Titus, "Presidential Address," *STF Bulletin*, V (Feb., 1938): 5.

[49]Lorne F. Titus, "Presidential Address," *STF Bulletin*, IV (Jan., 1937): 10.

[50]*STF Bulletin*, V (Feb., 1938): 11.

[51]"Pre-Election Questionnaire," *STF Bulletin*, V (Feb., 1938): 7.

[52]Lorne F. Titus, "Presidential Address," *STF Bulletin*, V (Feb., 1938): 7.

[53]*Annual Report*, 1938, p. 25.

[54]*Interim Report of the Committee on School Administration to the Minister of Education for Saskatchewan*, (Regina: King's Printer, Feb., 1939), pp. 6, 20.

[55]"The Larger Unit," *STF Bulletin*, V (Sept., 1939): 13.

[56]"Central Office Information," *STF Bulletin*, V (Dec., 1938): 13.

[57]*Report of the Committee on School Administration to the Minister of Education for Saskatchewan*, (Regina: King's Printer, 1939).

[58]Saskatchewan. *Statutes of the Province of Saskatchewan, 1940.* An Act to provide for School Divisions 4 George VI, 1940, chap. 76, 1940, pp. 229-252.

[59]*STF Bulletin*, V (Sept., 1939): 4-6.

[60]*Annual Report*, 1941, p. 9.

[61]*Annual Report*, 1942-43, p. 10; 1943-44, p. 10; 1944-45, p. 13.

[62]*Annual Report*, 1942-43, p. 33.

[63]Quoted in *STF Bulletin*, VII (Dec., 1941): 3.

[64]*STF Bulletin*, IX (Feb., 1943): 53.

[65]*Annual Report*, 1943-44, p. 10.

[66]*Canadian War Orders and Regulations Vol. 2, 1943*, PC 4862, Order in Council Amending the National Selective Service Civilian Regulations — persons to be retained in the teaching profession, June 1943 (Ottawa: King's Printer, 1943), pp. 729-731.

[67]The earliest of these advertisements appeared in the *STF Bulletin*, , VIII (Apr., 1942): 37.

[68]E. R. Powell, "Organize for State Medicine," *STF Bulletin*, XI (Feb., 1943): 45; J. H. Cumming, "The Tragic Toll of Unorganized Medical Services," *STF Bulletin*, IX (Apr., 1943): 51-53.

[69]*STF Bulletin*, IX (Oct., 1943): 19.

[70]*STF Bulletin*, X (Sept., 1944): 18.

[71]*Annual Report*, 1943-44, p. 9.

[72]*Annual Report*, 1944-45, p. 46.

[73]*STF Bulletin*, X (Dec., 1944): 27.

Ethnicity, Women, Class

8

Indian Industrial Schools in Western Canada

E. Brian Titley

The name "industrial school" conjures up images of bleak, factory-like institutions in which neglected or delinquent children were trained by brutal regimen for the menial roles they were destined to play in the system of production. The growing body of sentimental discourses on the plight of "waifs and strays" in the Canadian past has given some attention to these institutions. It has failed to mention, however, that the majority of industrial schools were created for a category of children quite different from the urchins and "street arabs" of Victorian cities: native Indians. That an institution ostensibly designed to reform those with a predeliction for crime should be chosen as the premier form of schooling for Indian children is, of course, curious. It is an analogy that will be returned to later, when the rise and fall of these schools has been documented.

The policy of educating Indians in European ways in British North America sprang from the misguided humanitarianism of the early nineteenth century, which was connected intimately with a revival of missionary zeal among both Catholics and Protestants. It was assumed that primitive cultures which came into contact with those that were more advanced were doomed unless they adopted the behaviours and values of the latter. As settlement advanced in Upper Canada in the 1820s and 1830s, the civil and religious authorities came to view the plight of the original inhabitants with increasing concern. The Indians were becoming marginal economically, and a program of education that fostered both Christianity and civilization in its European form seemed necessary to prevent them from becoming an indigent pauper class and a burden to the public purse.[1]

By the 1840s the manual labour residential school had emerged as the favoured institution for the promotion of assimilation. It had been developed in the United States in 1804 by Gideon Blackburn, a Presbyterian missionary to the Cherokees. It apportioned equal time to work and study, offering a combination of skills which would make its graduates economically self-sufficient.[2] In a report of May 1847 to the assistant superintendent general of Indian Affairs, Egerton Ryerson (superintendent of education in Canada West) proposed a number of these institutions for Indians in that colony and suggested that they be called industrial schools. State-financed but managed by religious bodies, they were to provide "a plain English education adapted to the working farmer and mechanic." The mechanical aspect of the curriculum was to be confined only to the repair and maintenance of agricultural implements. Ryerson believed that instruction in trades for Indians would be an extravagant waste of public funds. They were better suited to becoming "working farmers and agricultural labourers."[3]

The Mount Elgin Institute at Muncey Town, established by the Methodists, and the Mohawk Institute at Brantford, created under the auspices of the Anglican New England Company, were the first experiments in Canada West with this type of school.[4] Anglican missionary E. F. Wilson's Shingwauk Home at Sault Ste. Marie and the Jesuits' Wikwemikong School on Manitoulin Island were later examples.[5] Although the results were initially disappointing, no serious re-evaluation of policy took place. In the post-Confederation era the system was expanded to Western Canada in a more elaborate form.

Because of both its peculiar objectives and the division of powers worked out at Confederation, education for Indians was administered in a manner different from that for other Canadians. The British North America Act declared education a provincial responsibility. Consequently, most children attended schools that functioned under provincial departments of education and locally-elected school boards. At the same time, the Act gave to the federal government the responsibility of legislating for Indians and lands reserved for Indians. It meant that Indian children were to attend schools established under the auspices of the federal Department of Indian Affairs. And the segregation inherent in this provision was further reinforced by clauses in the western treaties committing the federal government to the support of schools and teachers on reserves.

In fulfilling the obligations incurred under the BNA Act and subsequent treaties, Indian Affairs tended to rely very much on the cooperation of the major Christian churches. The Roman Catholic, Anglican, Methodist and Presbyterian churches had all been involved in educational and missionary work among the natives of the West prior to 1870. Federal officials quickly realized that building on existing ecclesiastical institutions would be much more economical than creating a separate educational infrastructure. They also believed that the dedication and moral suasion of missionaries would be vital elements in the venture's success. And, the tradition of church-state cooperation in such endeavours had been well-established in central Canada for several decades. As a result, the system of Indian schooling that emerged in the West tended to be financed substantially by the federal government but managed and manned by ecclesiastics or their nominees.

Three categories of Indian schools appeared: day, boarding and industrial. Day schools enrolled the vast majority of children. But they suffered from irregularity of attendance and the inability to find and maintain competent teachers. Neither church nor state officials put much faith in the schools' ability to sever the children from their ancestral culture.

Like day schools, boarding schools were located on or near reserves. But they offered the advantage of residence, which ensured some isolation of the children from home influences. Regular attendance was another advantage.

These schools were the property of the missionary organizations that built them. Operating costs were subsidized by an annual per capita grant of $60 by the Department of Indian Affairs.

Industrial schools were first established on the Prairies in the 1880s as showpiece institutions in Indian education. They owed much to the examples of the Mount Elgin and Mohawk Institutes, but American influences were also paramount. In fact in January 1879, Nicholas Flood Davin, an Irish-born poet, lawyer and journalist who later served as Conservative M.P. for Assiniboia West, was sent by Ottawa to investigate and to prepare a report on the system of Indian industrial schools operating in the United States.[6] These schools were the principal feature of the policy of "aggressive civiliza-tion" which had been inaugurated by President Ulysses S. Grant in 1869. Davin discovered that they were administered either directly by the Indian agencies or through contracts with church bodies. In the latter instances, per capita grants ranging from $100 to $125 were paid by the Bureau of Indian Affairs. In addition to the academic program, boys were instructed in cattle raising and agriculture and in such trades as carpentry, blacksmithing and shoemaking; girls were instructed in household skills.

Davin was evidently impressed by what he saw south of the border. He visited Winnipeg and consulted with officials of both church and state regard-ing the possibility of a similar system of schooling in the Canadian West. His report, which was submitted in April 1879 to Lawrence Vankoughnet, deputy superintendent general of Indian Affairs, proposed the establishment of four industrial schools initially. The schools ought to be denominational, as the influence of Christianity was vital. In Davin's opinion, the first step in civiliz-ing the native population was "to take away their simple Indian mythology." And the active involvement of the churches would ensure a teaching body of superior moral calibre — men and women fired by zeal and dedication.[7]

Davin's report was not acted upon immediately. Ottawa was determined to reduce the cost of the proposed scheme by employing the services of mis-sionaries and by allowing for competition between missionaries. Complex negotiations with the churches were therefore necessary before the schools could be established.[8] The somewhat leisurely pace of these deliberations masked the seriousness of the crisis facing the prairie Indians at the time. Most of them had signed treaties with the federal government during the 1870s, but were finding the transition to reserve life and agriculture difficult. The disappearance of the buffalo in 1878 created a new sense of urgency as far as education was concerned. The need to make the Indians self-supporting became all the more pressing. John A. Macdonald's national policy, which involved completing the transcontinental railway and settling the West with farmers, also underlined the necessity of "civilizing" the Indians and incor-porating them into the new economic system.

The supplementary estimates for 1883-84 allocated $44,000 for the establishment of industrial schools in the West.[9] There were to be three schools initially: at Qu'Appelle and High River under Roman Catholic management, and at Battleford under the Anglican church. Their location a distance from reserves and close to centres of white settlement was deliberate, and it reflected their *raison d'être*: isolating the young Indians from the influence of their parents and the traditional culture and immersing them in a program of "civilization."

Arrangements were worked out between the Department of Indian Affairs and the various church authorities that took on the task of management. The department provided the land — usually on lease from the Interior Department — and the fencing. It also constructed the building and equipped it with such materials as desks and books. Repairs, however, were a joint responsibility, the department supplying the materials and management the labour. Operating costs, such as teachers' salaries, food, clothing and heating, were to come from a grant paid by the department to management. School principals were appointed on the recommendation of the local ecclesiastical authorities.

While some thought was given to distributing the operating grant on a per capita basis (the prevailing practice in Ontario and in the United States), it was not done so initially. In its enthusiasm for the scheme, the department agreed to pay for all costs incurred. This proved to be an expensive *modus operandi*, and it was much preferred by the churches. Nonetheless, management was obliged to maintain exact accounts at all times. And even though the schools were to be showpiece institutions, measures of "the strictest economy" were encouraged.[10] They were to be open to inspection by department officials upon demand.

When the schools opened in the autumn of 1884, they were immediately confronted with a problem that would continue to plague them throughout much of their chequered existence: securing an adequate number of suitable students. This difficulty was most acute in the case of the High River Industrial School, which was sometimes called Dunbow or St. Joseph's. The Indians of the Blackfoot Confederacy were intensely suspicious of this cultural Trojan horse that had been thrust into their midst. Only a personal appeal by Father Albert Lacombe, the legendary missionary who had been appointed principal of the school, to Chief Crowfoot secured a number of Blackfoot youths. The boys who arrived were reported to be "too big and too well acquainted with the Indian fashion" to remain.[11] By March 1885, Lacombe admitted that he had not been able to make the boys like the place. Most of them had either left on their own initiative or had been expelled.[12] When the North-West Rebellion broke out shortly afterwards, the school came virtually to a standstill. Lacombe left for Calgary, and most of the remaining students were taken home by their parents.

The "black-robed voyageur" continued as principal until the following year but spent little time at the school. He evidently found the job distasteful and was bitter at his failure. In a long letter to Indian Commissioner Edgar Dewdney,[13] who was also lieutenant governor of the North-West Territories, the intensity of his frustration was made clear. Lacombe complained that the boys he had received had been independent and proud and had refused to have their hair cut. He had been hesitant to impose obedience or to inflict punishment lest they run away. In future, the school should accept only those under eight years of age. Lacombe was aware, however, that parents would not part with younger children, and he proposed that they be pressured into cooperating "by threatening and deprivation of rations." Bribery should also be employed. He suggested rewarding parents "who behave well in giving their children," and in the case of a child who was intelligent, "buy him if necessary." He also proposed that agents and the police should have the responsibility of forcing runaways to return to the school.[14] These draconian measures were never adopted by the department with the rigid prescriptiveness that Lacombe advocated, but elements of them did appear over the years in operating the system.

Battleford Industrial School also had an inauspicious beginning. It was located in that part of the North-West which was the scene of battles and skirmishes during the rebellion of 1885. During the disturbances the principal, the Rev. T. Clarke, abandoned the school for the safety of Winnipeg. He returned after the triumph of General Middleton to find the building in shambles. Temporary quarters had to be found to carry on the enterprise while renovations were underway. The renovations included expanded accommodation in anticipation of a larger number of students, including girls. Clarke struggled along in temporary quarters over the winter of 1885-86 with an enrolment that fluctuated between nine and seventeen students. Possession was taken of the repaired building in October 1886, and the future began to look brighter. By January 1887, there were thirty-two boys and twelve girls in attendance. Clarke credited the efforts of Assistant Indian Commissioner Hayter Reed with allaying the fears and prejudices of parents regarding the institutions.[15]

The Qu'Appelle school experienced some growing pains but quickly became the most successful of the institutions. Commissioner Dewdney attributed this state of affairs to the "business-like manner" of the principal, Father J. Hugonnard.[16] It is true that recruitment of students posed an initial problem. And the rebellion aggravated this difficulty as parents feared that the government would turn their children into soldiers who would make war on each other. But a vigorous public relations campaign by Hugonnard on the reserves broke down some of the opposition to the school. He even allowed parents to visit the school in order to allay their suspicions.[17]

By the end of the decade the schools had overcome many of their initial difficulties. Even High River, under a new principal, Father E. Claude, seemed to be doing well. A number of Cree students had been recruited, and they were proving more compliant than the stubborn Blackfoot. The schools were winning the admiration of politicians and newspapermen as beacons of civilization, and plans were afoot to expand the good work both on the Prairies and in British Columbia. The expansion of the system appears to have been inspired at least in part by the North-West Rebellion. An intensive course in civilization for all young Indians would prevent the recurrence of the rebellious spirit.[18]

J. A. Macrae, appointed inspector of Protestant schools for Manitoba, Keewatin and the North-West Territories in October 1887, emerged as one of the principal advocates of the industrial schools on the Prairies. He spent some time prior to his appointment observing operations at the Mohawk Institute and reported extensively on the matter to Commissioner Dewdney in December 1886. Macrae stressed the necessity of removing Indian children from parental influences and advised that new industrial schools, like existing ones, be located in centres of white settlement. Not only would this sever familial connections, but it would surround the children with the wonders of white civilization. And it would have the further advantage that Indians would be less likely to cause trouble if their children were under the direct control of the state. He also proposed that day and boarding schools become "stepping stones" to industrial schools. When parents saw their children well cared for in the former institutions, they would raise no objection to having them sent to the latter ones. If industrial schools became the pinnacles of the new system, students would only have to stay in them for three years.[19]

Macrae's proposal to turn industrial schools into institutions of advanced study for teenagers found support among leading department officials and was advocated on several occasions in subsequent years. But it proved impossible to put into effect. As the number of boarding and industrial schools expanded in the 1890s, competition for pupils between schools and denominations increased with such intensity that it precluded the possibility of cooperation.

Indian Commissioner Hayter Reed was another vociferous champion of industrial schools. Reed was a former military officer who joined the department in 1881 as Indian agent at Battleford. He was promoted to assistant Indian commissioner in 1883; to commissioner in 1888; and to deputy superintendent of Indian Affairs in 1893.[20] In 1889 he visited the Mohawk and Mount Elgin institutions and also spent some time at Carlisle Industrial School in Pennsylvania. He disapproved of the Mohawk Institute practice of allocating two-thirds of the school day to the academic program. The half-day system in vogue at Carlisle was preferable. As he explained, "Unless it is intended to train children to earn their bread by brain-work rather than by manual labour, at least half of their day should be devoted to acquiring skill in the latter." He advocated hiring Indian students out to settlers at intervals in order to provide practical experience in civilization.[21] This idea was adopted at some of the schools in the 1890s with limited success.

The Wakashada Home at Elkhorn, Manitoba — an offspring of E. F. Wilson's Shingwauk Home and part of his grand design for a missionary empire — became an industrial school in cooperation with Indian Affairs in 1888, with the missionary's son, Archibald E. Wilson, as principal. It was the first of the post-rebellion industrial schools. During the next four years most of those destined for the prairie region were opened. One of the new schools was under Presbyterian management — that at Regina. The Methodists were placed in charge of two — at Red Deer and at Brandon. Rupert's Land Industrial School (also known as St. Paul's) at Middlechurch, Manitoba and Calgary Industrial School were contracted out to the Church of England. The one new Roman Catholic school was at St. Boniface.

The system was extended to British Columbia around the same time. Four of the new schools were Roman Catholic: Kamloops, Kootenay, Kuper Island and Williams Lake. Two were placed under Church of England management: Alert Bay and Metlakahtla. And there was one Methodist school — the Coqualeetza Home. The British Columbia industrial schools tended to be smaller than their prairie counterparts, and they were generally located in Indian communities.

The department's annual report for 1891 gave the following statistics: 1,045 pupils were enrolled in nineteen industrial schools; 307 in eighteen boarding schools; and 6,202 in day schools. There were 13,420 Indian children of school age in the country at the time.[22] The expansion of the industrial school system had been accompanied by a growth in the number of boarding schools as well. In fact J. A. Macrae observed that there was little difference between the two types of school except that the industrial institutions were more demanding on the public purse.[23]

Macrae had touched upon an issue that was to be of growing concern to the department during the following three decades: the cost of operating the industrial schools. This was the subject of a lengthy memorandum by Duncan Campbell Scott to the acting deputy superintendent general in June 1892. Scott was later to become well known as a literary figure and was to serve as deputy superintendent between 1913 and 1932.[24] At the time, he was chief clerk of the department and was already displaying that obsession with economy that would become the hallmark of his incumbency as department head. A small number of the industrial schools had operated since their inception on a per capita grant basis, and Scott observed that they were less of a drain on the government's coffers. The schools for which the department bore all expenses were costing "too much money." Unnecessary supplies were ordered, and unnecessary employees engaged.

Scott pointed out that in the previous year the operating cost per pupil at Qu'Appelle had been $134.67. The figure for High River was $185.55 and for Battleford $145.45. In his opinion these costs were far too high and the difference between schools was too great. He saw no reason why all schools could not get along on a $100 per capita grant. If all schools were paid the same, it would counteract the accusation of favouritism that was sometimes levelled against the department. It would also encourage school workshops to produce goods that could be sold profitably and school gardens to produce more food. More time would thereby be spent in work than at the desk. Such a shift in emphasis made sense to Scott, not just because of the savings that would ensue, but also because he believed that "instruction from books, a fact which is commonly called an 'education,' is almost wasted on an Indian child of Manitoba and the North-West Territories."[25]

Scott's initiative resulted in an order-in-council being handed down in October 1892 declaring that all industrial schools would be placed on the per capita system effective July 1, 1893. Grants were to vary from school to school and were to range from $100 to $140.[26]

This new arrangement was designed to reduce government expenditure and to force the churches either to make greater economies or to contribute more of their own resources to the enterprise. Ecclesiastical reaction was predictably unenthusiastic. The Presbyterian Synod accepted the per capita system in principle but complained that $120 was inadequate to run the Regina school. After some hesitation the churchmen agreed to try it out on an experimental basis for a year.[27]

Archbishop Taché of St. Boniface had similar concerns. He felt that $115 for Qu'Appelle would not be sufficient unless enrolment could be maintained at two hundred pupils. Father Albert Lacombe received letters from the principals of Catholic industrial schools who doubted that they could get by on the proposed grants. Deficits were anticipated, and Lacombe asked Hayter Reed what the department would do in such instances. Reed, who had been promoted to deputy superintendent general in 1893, was only partly reassuring. He said that it "was expected that schools would employ officials at less wages and buy the necessary supplies at cheaper rates" and thereby avoid losses. The department would continue to examine individual situations and would revise the grants if necessary. Lacombe appeared to be satisfied with this and promised that the utmost economy would be used. But he warned that the students needed good food and "good men to teach them."[28]

The Anglican church proved most intractable. Four of its schools — Rupert's Land, Calgary, Elkhorn and Metlakahtla — found it impossible to survive on the per capita system and were taken over by the department.[29] Ottawa paid all the bills and regarded the schools as non-denominational. The church, however, continued to regard them as components of its missionary apparatus.

In December 1896, Calgary Industrial School opened its doors to twenty pupils. It was the last of the species, for no more were to be created. By then the department had imposed the per capita system on most of the schools, confident that this would minimize public expenditure on the enterprise while ensuring that the schools were run with the maximum efficiency and economy. The rapid increase in educational costs since the beginning of the decade was obviously a matter of concern within Indian Affairs, and the question of accountability continued to be raised. In fact Deputy Superintendent Reed reported in 1894 that he had created a Schools Branch to supervise more carefully the educational work of the department in order "to ensure a proper return for the large outlay of funds."[30]

In spite of the obsession with cost-cutting, the mid-1890s were the heyday of the industrial schools. Results were admittedly slow in coming, but those who looked hard enough could find some cause for optimism. A. W. Vowell, superintendent of Indian Affairs for British Columbia, noted in 1895 that former industrial school pupils were working in stores as clerks and bookkeepers. And in some villages, stores were operated by the Indians themselves.[31] A. E. Forget, assistant Indian commissioner for the prairie region, reported that seventeen prizes had been won by exhibits from industrial schools at the Territorial Fair in Regina in the summer of 1894.[32] And Reed himself confidently asserted:

> Experience has proved that the industrial and boarding schools are productive of the best results in Indian education. . . . It is in their success that the solution of the Indian problem lies.[33]

A number of observations must be made about the internal operations of the schools. The industrial school environment was one in which Indian children were forcibly initiated into the social and occupational patterns of white life. Punctuality and obedience — so vital for effective functioning in the capitalist economic system — were instilled in a relentless program of behaviour modification which involved the ringing of bells to indicate time periods and the liberal infliction of corporal punishment. The sense of order thereby imparted was deemed essential for the offspring of nomads.

The imposition of a military form of discipline was a key element in effecting change. The uniforms worn by the boys strongly indicated that the regimen of the boot camp prevailed, but it was also frankly admitted by the managers. In the words of Father E. Claude, principal of the High River school: "The system of discipline is a military one and is strictly carried out, no breach of the regulations remaining unpunished. . . ."[34] And when Martin Benson, head of the department's Schools Branch, visited the Mohawk Institute in 1895, he observed that the boys were organized into military units and were drilled with wooden muskets. The school was regulated like a "piece of machinery," and the principal, Rev. R. Ashton, boasted that he could "train the Indian child to work whether he [liked] work or not."[35] The creation of marching brass bands in several of the schools in the 1890s gave further impetus to their military ambience. An anticipated result of this incessant regimentation was the adoption by the inmates of the white concept of time. As Edgar Dewdney explained: "The importance to the Indian child of such instruction cannot be overestimated, as innate to him, inherited from his parents, is an utter disregard of time, and ignorance of its value."[36] Cutting the children's hair and dressing them in white clothes created the illusion that cultural transformation had taken place. This often surprised and delighted visitors to the schools, especially if these apprentices in civilization could muster a few verses of "God Save the Queen." But school principals, while proud of such superficialities, demanded more fundamental evidence of change from their charges. Most critical from their point of view was the abandonment of the use of Indian languages in favour of English. The task was not easy, and there were frequent expressions of frustration at the tenacity with which the children clung to their ancestral tongues. At the Shingwauk Home, E. F. Wilson developed an elaborate system of rewards and punishments to encourage the use of English.[37] At Wikwemikong, those who spoke "Indian" were denied the privilege of playing shuffle-board.[38] Obviously, the tactics varied from place to place. And they were often brutal. At Battleford, boys who spoke Cree were beaten, while girls had their hair cut off.[39]

Children who stayed in the schools for a few years undoubtedly acquired some working knowledge of English. The slow decline of Indian languages in the more settled areas of the country was thereby accelerated. It is ironic that French-Canadian priests, themselves members of a beleaguered minority, should participate in this process of anglicization. There is no evidence that they showed any more sympathy for the Indians' right to cultural integrity than their Anglo-Protestant counterparts.[40]

The inmates of industrial schools not only learned English, but were inducted into the totality of English-Canadian culture. Civic and religious holidays were celebrated with appropriate fanfare, for example. Christmas and Easter, concepts completely alien to the Indian experience, were major occasions. Even when it came to recreation, it was white customs that prevailed. Brass bands have already been mentioned. They served not just to instill a form of military precision, but to introduce students to new forms of music. When A. W. Vowell visited Kuper Island Industrial School in 1891, he discovered that the older Indians in the community were opposed to the school's band as they feared that it would do away with their own music. Vowell admitted to Lawrence Vankoughnet,[41] who served as deputy superintendent of Indian Affairs between 1874 and 1893, that this was precisely the intention. "Modern standards of music would," he asserted, "do away with the potlatch practice and the barbarous dances and so-called music that accompanied them."[42] Cricket, baseball, soccer, marbles and skittles were other forms of recreation that were encouraged in the schools. After a visit to the Battleford school in 1889, J. A. Macrae observed that the games played there were "thoroughly and distinctly white." Boys played at boxing, cricket and football "with great interest and truly Anglo-Saxon vigour. . . . From all their recreation Indianism is excluded."[43]

"Indianism" was also excluded from the academic program, although not completely. The Indian department had its own program of studies which was followed in day, boarding and industrial schools across the country. It was modelled on the Ontario curriculum and made few concessions to the background of the children for whom it was designed. In fact Hayter Reed admitted in 1890 that teachers were finding the readers inappropriate as their subject matter was "beyond the experience of Indians."[44] Nothing appears to have been done about this. It is true that in Standard 3 students learned "Stories of Indians of Canada and their civilization," but it is difficult to say how this subject was approached. In Standards 5 and 6 a number of Indian topics were also listed under "Ethics." These included "Citizenship of Indians," "Indian and White Life," "Evils of Indian Civilization" and "Enfranchisement."[45]

Perhaps the most significant feature of the academic program was that it was offered in industrial schools for half of the day only. Given that Indian children arrived in school with little or no knowledge of English and found the transition to the routine of the institution difficult, it was improbable that they could complete the requirements of a particular standard or grade in one year. Few mastered the entire academic program.

Practical instruction in trades and agriculture for the boys and in domestic skills for the girls took precedence over the academic program. This was in accordance with the economic role envisaged for the Indians by both church and state. Of the trades taught to the boys, carpentry was by far the most important. It was offered at virtually all of the industrial schools during the 1890s. Shoemaking and repair was also widely taught. Tailors, blacksmiths, bakers, harness makers, printers and tinsmiths offered instruction in some of the schools, but this tended to be exceptional. Training in agriculture and/or gardening was even more important than trades instruction and was almost universally provided. Girls learned sewing, knitting, laundry, cooking, gardening and poultry care — skills deemed essential for the establishment of civilized households.

Practical training of this sort gave the children skills they would find useful in adulthood, but it also introduced them to the rhythm of steady work — something that was lacking in the Indian character, or so the authorities believed. And the skills acquired proved valuable to the institutions themselves. School farms and gardens attempted to produce all the food required by staff and students, but rarely succeeded in doing so. Those with carpentry and blacksmithing skills could do much of the repairs to buildings and equipment. Those who had learned shoemaking and sewing could make and repair the students' supply of shoes and clothing.[46] In this way operating costs could be kept down, and this economy became particularly vital after the per capita grant system was imposed.

It seems that the Indians, the intended beneficiaries of the industrial schools, failed to share the enthusiasm of church and state for the experiment. In fact, one of the foremost problems with the system was the persistence of Indian hostility. Most parents adamantly refused to part with their children, even when threatened with a withdrawal of rations. Those who complied with the wishes of officialdom frequently regretted the decision. They soon came to miss their children, and in the early years of the experiment parents often were seen camping on the school grounds. This annoyed the principals, who felt it was a source of distraction for their apprentices in civilization. Moreover, the loneliness of the parents frequently became unbearable, and they demanded the return of their children. To officials such as Edgar Dewdney, these sentiments were both unreasonable and inexplicable:

> As was first premised, no little difficulty is met with in prevailing upon
> Indians to part with their children; and even after the latter have been cared
> for in the kindest manner, some parents, prompted by unaccountable freaks
> of the most childish nature, demand a return of their children to their own
> shanties to suffer from cold and hunger.[47]

The policy of holidays for the students was certainly a legitimate cause
of parental concern. In the early years the department tended to discourage
any leave as it involved the expense of transportation over long distances, and
it brought the young Indians into contact with "undesirable influences" at
home. When parents realized that with no holidays and the distant location
of the schools, they might not see their children for several years, they were
naturally reluctant to part with them.[48] And Father Hugonnard admitted
that some Indians feared that at the completion of the school program their
children might never return to the reserve.[49] They were conscious, of course,
of the deliberate policy of cultural transformation which was the *raison d'être*
of the entire experiment.[50]

Reports of the mistreatment of children in industrial schools served to
intensify Indian hostility. In September 1886, the *Montreal Gazette* contended that parents were opposed to sending their children to Battleford
Industrial School because of the physical abuse one boy, "Charlie No. 20"
had received there. Indian Affairs denied the allegation, but it was not an
isolated occurrence.[51]

In 1893, when the committee of the Anglican church responsible for the
Rupert's Land school complained of the persistent low enrolment, Commissioner Reed felt obliged to point out that the institution had a reputation for
harshness:

> I have been particularly impressed when visiting the institution with the
> depressed bearing of the pupils, who seem to lack the cheerful demeanour
> and alacrity of friendly response met with in kindred institutions.

Reed went on to state that the local agent had reported in August 1891 that
the school's problems were largely due to the severe thrashings administered
to its pupils. Some parents had removed their children as a result. The agent
had described the beatings as "a remnant of the dark ages." And a recent
report had commented unfavourably on the hard labour inflicted on both boys
and girls of a tender age.[52]

The sordid reputation of Rupert's Land Industrial School did not diminish with time. In March 1899, Commissioner David Laird was obliged to
investigate complaints laid by the chief and councillors of St. Peter's Reserve
against J. H. Fairlie, principal of the school. The Reverend Fairlie, an Anglican clergyman, admitted to feeding bad butter to the children and to entering
the dormitories at night to kiss some of the girls. He was also accused of

administering harsh punishment to the students. Some young girls (eight or nine years old) showed marks on their bodies several weeks after being strapped.[53] Fairlie was dismissed as a result of the investigation.

The whiff of scandal also plagued the reputation of Kamloops Industrial School. In the spring of 1892, it was discovered that a number of teenage boys from the local reserve were in the habit of sneaking in a school window at night and enjoying a sexual frolic in the girls' dormitory. Three of them were caught and charged under the Vagrancy Act. One boy received a sentence of six months' hard labour while his two companions received one month each. Parents were appalled and began to withdraw their children from the school. When the agent paid a visit in May, he discovered only thirteen in attendance. The scandal was only part of the problem, he reported. Parents were also opposed to the manner in which the principal forced the students to work hard clearing land around the school. They preferred that their children learn useful trades when not engaged in their lessons.[54]

Problems with brutality and hard labour were compounded in the eyes of Indian parents by an unacceptably high rate of death and disease in the schools. While the schools could not be held entirely responsible for Indian ill-health and mortality, they frequently contributed to these difficulties. Students with contagious diseases were often enrolled merely to secure the per capita grant. Within the institutions, poor ventilation, inadequate diet and little medical attention combined to create the prime conditions for epidemics.[55] For example, when Commissioner Reed visited Battleford Industrial School in 1891, he found a general lack of cleanliness. Slops had not been taken out, and there were foul smells in the toilet rooms. The hospital rooms were also in an unacceptable state, and sick students were not receiving adequate attention.[56] Indian Affairs bore some responsibility for such conditions as its budgetary allocation for medical services was ridiculously low.

As the schools struggled on in the face of parental hostility, their sponsors were forced to give some thought to a rather fundamental consideration: what would become of the graduates? Hayter Reed raised this question in his report for 1888. Should the graduates be sprinkled about among the white population or returned to their reserves? In the event of the latter option, would they act as civilizing agents for their fellow Indians or merely relapse into barbarism?[57] By the following year he had evidently concluded that a return to the reserve would be disastrous. The best solution, he believed, was the creation of special farming colonies of suitable graduates. He also favoured the idea of hiring out students to local settlers for certain periods. This would give them practical experience in wage labour and prepare them for the transition from school to work.[58]

Hiring students to settlers, or the "outing system," as it was known, was promoted by Reed and some of the school principals during the 1890s. Qu'Appelle, the largest of the institutions, also had the largest number of participants. Boys were hired out to farmers, usually during harvest time. They received wages ranging from $5 to $20 per month. Girls were employed as domestic servants and earned from $2 to $10 per month.[59] These rates of pay were comparable to those paid to other farm labourers and servants at the time. The earnings were saved on their behalf by the school so that they would have a small sum with which to start their adult lives upon leaving. Some parents objected to the outing system as another scheme to get cheap labour out of their children.[60] The total number of students participating in the system was never significant, and it did little to incorporate young Indians into white society.

Reed's idea of a farming colony composed of industrial school graduates was experimented with in the first decade of the new century. The well-known File Hills colony was established near Balcarres, Saskatchewan, in 1902 by Indian Agent W. M. Graham. It was reported to be a great success and was frequently cited as an example of what could be accomplished with the Indians under careful management.[61] Yet it was an isolated case and involved but few who had experienced an industrial school education.

By 1896 the initial enthusiasm for industrial schools had run its course. Laurier's Liberals, who had been highly critical of government spending while in opposition, came to power that year. The new minister of the Interior and superintendent general of Indian Affairs was Clifford Sifton, who was determined to reduce the cost to the public of Indian administration. Education was the major item in the department's budget, and Sifton soon announced that it had reached what in his opinion was "a high water mark" and that it was time for retrenchment. Moreover, he felt that industrial school education was probably a waste of time as the Indian did not have "the physical, mental or moral get-up" of the white man, and could never compete with him on equal terms.[62]

Sifton's sentiments were shared by his new deputy superintendent, James A. Smart, who, in his annual report for 1897, provided figures that showed the relative costs of educating children in day, boarding and industrial schools. Smart believed that this was evidence of the need for "extreme caution with regard to further expansion."[63]

Indian Affairs Annual Report 1897

TYPE OF SCHOOL	NUMBER OF SCHOOLS	ENROL-MENT	ATTEND.	GRANT	COST PER PUPIL BASED ON ATTEND.
Day	232	6877	3110	$ 25,804	$ 8.29
Boarding	31	874	697	68,504	98.28
Indust.	22	1877	1550	212,645	137.19

The imposition of the per capita system had evidently not solved the problem of rising costs. But it succeeded in aggravating the difficulties already facing the industrial schools. It resulted in intense rivalry between denominations and schools for the bodies of young Indians. Principals were obliged to spend considerable time scouring the countryside for potential recruits.

The financial constraints placed on the schools by the per capita system resulted in less attention to trades instruction, which tended to be expensive. For example, in 1898 there were 262 boys learning a variety of trades in industrial schools. By 1908 the number had fallen to 185, and the same variety of trades was no longer offered.

Department disillusionment with the industrial schools was compounded by the bleak results they were producing. A memorandum from the head of the Schools Branch, Martin Benson, in 1902 clearly illustrates this:

> Returns from the industrial schools show that up to the 30 June last there had been 2752 pupils admitted and of these 1700 had been discharged. Of the latter number 506 are known to be dead; 249 lost sight of; 139 in bad health; 86 transferred to other schools; 121 turned out badly and 599 said to be doing well.[64]

The schools were increasingly seen as cumbersome, expensive, non-productive and prone to scandal. They had become the white elephants of Indian education by the first decade of the new century. Their inability to compete with the boarding schools, whose fortunes were in the ascendant, hastened their demise. Boarding schools, it will be recalled, were located on reserves, and for that reason were much preferred by Indian parents. They were in receipt of per capita grants of $72 by the turn of the century, and this relative cheapness was endearing them to the department. In 1891 the number of boarding schools was a mere eighteen and 307 students were enrolled; by 1911 the number of schools had risen to fifty-five and enrolment was at 2,335. In the latter year the number of industrial schools had fallen to nineteen and 1,569 students were enrolled.[65] In other words, between 1891 and 1911 boarding schools were growing steadily and surpassed their industrial counterparts in both the number of institutions and students enrolled.

Competition with boarding schools tended to aggravate the plight of the industrial schools. Managerial bodies facing enrolment declines were caught in a dizzy spiral of falling per capita grants and rising deficits. And deficits became one of the major weapons in the hands of the department when it wished to close particular schools. Fire could also be helpful.

In January 1906, the much-maligned Rupert's Land Industrial School burned to the ground. The department estimated that it would cost $40,000 to rebuild. There was little enthusiasm in any quarter for the resurrection of the institution, and in April 1907, it was decided that the verdict of the flames should prevail. In the same year the department also decided to close the St. Boniface and Calgary institutions. Metlakahtla met its end in two phases: the girls' school ceased to operate in 1907, and in the following year the same fate befell the boys' section. Department officials were of the opinion that Metlakahtla had been a "complete failure" as an industrial school.[66] Only thirteen boys were in attendance at the end.

Regina Industrial School was the next to go. It had experienced a decline in enrolment from 106 students in 1900 to seventy-two in 1904. In January of the latter year its deficit stood at over $9,000, prompting an investigation by the department. Managerial incompetence was singled out as the major cause of the financial difficulties, and Indian Affairs decided to close the school. But vigorous agitation by Presbyterian church authorities, who wished to preserve their only industrial school, secured a stay of execution until 1910.[67]

By December 1912, the Battleford school had accumulated a deficit of over $5,000 and thereby drew the wrath of the cost-conscious department. It was closed in May 1914.[68] Elkhorn followed suit in 1918; Red Deer in 1919; and High River in 1922.[69] Most of the schools that were shut down were in poor physical condition, and it would have required a major investment to put them in a state of proper repair. The department was generally not disposed to make such an investment, especially during the Great War when its parliamentary appropriation was reduced. Closures usually involved complex negotiations with the churches who were generally reluctant to lose any component of their missionary enterprises. It was sometimes necessary for the department to offer additional funds for day or boarding schools as compensation for the loss of industrial schools.

Phasing out the most inefficient of the industrial schools owed much to the initiative of that penny-pinching master of the account books, Duncan Campbell Scott. Scott became chief clerk and accountant in the department in 1893 and was promoted to superintendent of education in 1909 and deputy superintendent general in 1913. He played a major role in the re-evaluation of education policy that took place within the department during the first decade of the twentieth century.

One consequence of this rethinking was a new faith in day schools — the least expensive of the three types of school in operation. Games were introduced to make the curriculum more appealing, and free meals were offered the students as an additional enticement to attendance. Teachers' salaries were increased to attract more competent individuals to the job. An amendment to the Indian Act providing for compulsory school attendance in 1920 complemented these incentives.

Boarding schools were also placed on a sounder financial footing. New arrangements were worked out between Scott and representatives of the Anglican, Methodist, Presbyterian and Roman Catholic churches during a conference in Ottawa in November 1910. Scott agreed to raise the per capita grants for boarding schools to between $100 and $125 provided certain conditions regarding ventilation, sanitation and health care were met. The sudden concern with such matters was prompted by devastating reports by Dr. P. H. Bryce on death and disease in Indian boarding and industrial schools that had appeared in 1907 and 1909, much to the embarrassment of the department.[70]

The new grant structure and the increasing willingness of the department to contribute to the capital costs of boarding schools soon blurred the distinction between those institutions and their industrial counterparts. In fact the "industrial" component of industrial schools had never been a great success, and most had attempted to impart little beyond carpentry and farming skills to their male charges. It meant that the curricular differences between the two types of school had not been significant either. In recognition of this new reality, the terms "boarding" and "industrial" were phased out of administrative terminology and were replaced by the all-encompassing "residential" by 1923. The industrial schools, as a distinct category within Indian education parlance, were gone.

It was observed at the outset that industrial schools also existed at this time for non-Indians. They were reformatory institutions in which young offenders were incarcerated for periods ranging from two to five years. "Incorrigible" children could also be placed therein by their parents. These schools were remarkably similar to those of the Indian variety in their programs of instruction.[71] Academic studies occupied about half the day and the remainder was devoted to the acquisition of skill in trades and agriculture. The Victoria Industrial School at Mimico, Ontario (opened in 1887), for example, provided instruction in carpentry, printing, tailoring shoemaking and farming. And some of the schools operated a "boarding out" system in which the inmates were apprenticed to farmers or artisans.[72]

Middle-class Canadians were passing judgment on the family background of delinquent children in placing them in industrial schools. The lower-class family was failing in its perceived responsibility, and it was imperative to intervene in order to break that cycle of crime, poverty, depravity and disorder. The superior environment of the industrial school would save the children from their parents' folly. Indian and non-Indian industrial schools, therefore, were also similar in their *raison d'être*. Missionaries and bureaucrats viewed Indians with the same mixture of contempt and fear that was apparent in the middle-class attitude towards the poor. Native people were perceived as a deviant, indigent class incapable of raising their children in an acceptable manner. Direct intervention in the process was therefore necessary. A new generation of Indians would be brought up in the confines of a specially-created institution and would join society when safely purged of their parental legacy.

But the Indian industrial schools were a failure. They never became the crucibles of white civilization that their founders envisaged. Even in their heyday they did not enroll more than 10 percent of Indian children of school age. And of those who did attend, few stayed long enough to have their lives transformed in the intended manner. In the Shingwauk Home, for example, the average period of attendance was less than 2.5 years.[73] Some schools had a higher retention rate, but not significantly so.[74] Most of those who survived the ordeal returned to their reserves. Few made the transition to white society. Prejudice against Indians integrating into white society was probably greater than missionaries or government officials would admit, and this hardly encouraged the process.

Nonetheless, many who experienced an industrial school education probably acquired some skills that proved useful when readjusting to life on the reserves. Knowledge of carpentry and farming, for instance, could be beneficial. Literacy and a familiarity with English could also be put to use, if not always in the intended manner. In fact it is conceivable that the industrial schools sowed the seed of pan-Indian consciousness by bringing native people of diverse backgrounds together for the first time. A sense of common identity and purpose may have thereby been formed. Organized opposition to the assimilationist policies of the government appeared during the first three decades of the twentieth century, and industrial school graduates were frequently to the fore in such movements. It seems that the schools had inadvertently created the nucleus of a new Indian leadership — articulate, familiar with the white man's methods, and able to manipulate for the sake of their own people the political and legal system of the dominant society. It was an ironic legacy of a system of schooling that had been intentionally designed to obliterate Indian culture.

Notes

[1] L.F.S. Upton, "The Origins of Canadian Indian Policy," *Journal of Canadian Studies*, VIII (Nov. 1973):51.

[2] J.W. Grant, *Moon of Wintertime: Missionaries and the Indians of Canada in Encounter Since 1534* (Toronto: University of Toronto Press, 1984), p. 86.

[3] Walter J. Wasylow, "History of Battleford Industrial School for Indians" (M.Ed. thesis, University of Saskatchewan, 1972), pp. 306-308.

[4] R.M. Connelly, "Missionaries and Indian Education," in L. G. P. Waller, ed., *The Education of Indian Children in Canada* (Toronto: Ryerson Press, 1965), p. 14.

[5] For a critical analysis of the Shingwauk Home, see David A. Nock, "The Social Effects of Missionary Education: A Victorian Case Study," in R. W. Nelson and D.A. Nock, eds., *Reading, Writing, and Riches: Education and the Socio-economic Order in North America* (Kitchener: Between the Lines, 1978), pp. 233-250.

[6] For a full biographical study of Davin see C.B. Koester, *Mr. Davin, M.P.* (Saskatoon: Western Producer Prairie Books, 1980).

[7] Nicholas Flood Davin, "Report on Industrial Schools," 1879, Records of the Department of Indian Affairs, RG 10, vol. 3674, f 11422, Public Archives of Canada, hereafter PAC.

[8] Jacqueline Kennedy, "Qu'Appelle Industrial School: White 'Rites' for the Indians of the Old North-West" (M.A. thesis, Carleton University, 1970), pp. 42-43.

[9]Lawrence Vankoughnet to Sir John A. Macdonald, May 17, 1883, RG 10, vol. 3674 f 11422, PAC.

[10]Commissioner E. Dewdney to Rev. T. Clarke, principal, Battleford Industrial School, July 31, 1883, RG 10, vol. 3674, f 11422, PAC.

[11]"Journal Quotidien," Nov. 5, 1884, Documents Oblates, Dunbow, Bôite 1, Provincial Archives of Alberta, hereafter PAA.

[12]Father A. Lacombe to E. Dewdney, Mar. 24, 1885, Documents Oblates, Dunbow, Bôite 1, "Lettres du père A. Lacombe," PAA.

[13]Dewdney's career in the North-West is critically examined in John L. Tobias, "Canada's Subjugation of the Plains Cree, 1870-1885," *Canadian Historical Review*, LXIV (December 1983), pp. 519-548.

[14]Father A. Lacombe to E. Dewdney, June 12, 1885. Documents Oblates, Dunbow, Bôite 1, "Lettres du père A. Lacombe," PAA.

[15]W.J. Wasylow, "Battleford Industrial School," pp. 70-79.

[16]*Report of the Department of Indian Affairs for the Year ended December 31, 1885*, p. 142.

[17]J. Kennedy, "Qu'Appelle Industrial School," pp. 77-81.

[18]Ibid., p. 87.

[19]J.A. Macrae to E. Dewdney, Dec. 18, 1886, RG 10, vol. 3647, f 8128, PAC.

[20]See "biographical note," Hayter Reed Papers, MG 29, E106, PAC.

[21]J. Kennedy, "Qu'Appelle Industrial School," p. 91.

[22]*Report of the Department of Indian Affairs for the Year ended December 31, 1891*, p. xv.

[23]Ibid., p. 97.

[24]E.K. Brown, "Duncan Campbell Scott: A Memoir," in E.K. Brown, *Responses and Evaluations: Essays on Canada* (Toronto: McClelland and Stewart: 1977) provides a succinct account of Scott's literary career.

[25]D.C. Scott to Acting Deputy Superintendent General, June 28, 1892, RG 10, vol. 3879, f 91,883, PAC.

[26]Order in council 2810, Oct. 22, 1892, RG 10, vol. 3879, f 91,883, PAC.

[27]Rev. Andrew B. Baird to the Indian Commissioner, May 13, 1893, and A.E. Forget to the Deputy Superintendent General, July 24, 1893, RG 10, vol. 3879 f 91,883, PAC.

[28]Father A. Lacombe to Hayter Reed, Nov. 20, 1893; Reed to Lacombe, Nov. 30; and Lacombe to Reed, Dec. 7, RG 10, vol. 3879, f 91,883, PAC.

[29]See, for example, General Committee of Rupert's Land Indian Industrial School to Superintendent General T.M. Daly, May 8, 1893; and Hayter Reed to the Bishop of Rupert's Land, May 31, 1893, RG 10, vol. 3879, f 91,883, PAC.

[30]*Report of the Department of Indian Affairs for the Year ended June 30, 1894*, p. xxi.

[31]*Report of the Department of Indian Affairs for the Year ended June 30, 1895*, p. 183.

[32]Ibid., p. 196.

[33]J. Kennedy, "Qu'Appelle Industrial School," p. 150.

[34]*Report of the Department of Indian Affairs for the Year ended Dec. 31, 1887*, p. 127.

[35]M. Benson, "Report on the Mohawk Institute and Six Nations Boarding Schools," Aug. 30, 1895, RG 10, vol. 2006, f 7825-1A, PAC.

[36]*Report of the Department of Indian Affairs for the Year ended Dec. 31, 1889*, p. xi.

[37]D.A. Nock, "Social Effects of Missionary Education," pp. 238-239.

[38]*Report of the Department of Indian Affairs for the Year ended June 30, 1894*, p. 21.

[39]W.J. Wasylow, "Battleford Industrial School," pp. 444-483.

[40]J.W. Grant, *Moon of Wintertime*, p. 184.

[41]For an analysis of Vankoughnet's career, see Douglas Leighton, "A Victorian Civil Servant at Work: Lawrence Vankoughnet and the Canadian Indian Department, 1874-1893," in Ian A.L. Getty and Antoine S. Lussier, eds., *As Long as the Sun Shines and Water Flows* (Vancouver: University of British Columbia Press, 1983), pp. 104-119.

[42]A.W. Vowell to L. Vankoughnet, Feb. 7, 1891, RG 10, vol. 3850, f 75,536, PAC.

[43]W.J. Wasylow, "Battleford Industrial School," pp. 90-91.

[44]*Report of the Department of Indian Affairs for the Year ended Dec. 31, 1890*, p. 138.

[45]*Report of the Department of Indian Affairs for the Year ended Dec. 31, 1890*, p. 138.

[46]W.J. Wasylow, "Battleford Industrial School," pp. 85-86.

[47]*Report of the Department of Indian Affairs for the Year ended Dec. 31,1884*, p. 161.

[48]A.J. McLeod (principal, Regina Industrial School) to Commissioner David Laird, June 10, 1899, RG 10, vol. 3926, f 116,836-1, PAC.

[49]Report of the Department of Indian Affairs for the Year ended Dec. 31, 1887, p. 130.

[50]The best discussion of Indian resistance to cultural change is found in Jacqueline Gresko, "White 'Rites' and Indian 'Rites': Indian Education and Native Responses in the West, 1870-1910," in A.W. Rasporich, ed., *Western Canada: Past and Present* (Calgary: McClelland and Stewart West, 1975), pp. 163-181.

[51]Newspaper clipping, *Montreal Gazette*, Sept. 15, 1886, RG 10, vol. 3767, f 33,170, PAC.

[52]Hayter Reed to the Bishop of Rupert's Land, May 31, 1893, RG 10, vol. 3930, f 117,377-1A, PAC.

[53]Report by David Laird, Mar. 19, 1899, RG 10, vol. 3558, f 64, pt. 39, PAC.

[54]J.W. Mackay (Indian agent, Kamloops-Okanagan) to A.W. Vowell, Apr. 11 and May 29, 1892, RG 10, vol. 3918, f 116,659-1, PAC.

[55]J. Kennedy, "Qu'Appelle Industrial School," p. 159.

[56]W.J. Wasylow, "Battleford Industrial School," pp. 99-100.

[57]*Report of the Department of Indian Affairs for the Year ended Dec. 31, 1888*, p. 131.

[58]*Report of the Department of Indian Affairs for the Year ended Dec. 31, 1889*, p. 169.

[59]*Report of the Department of Indian Affairs for the Year ended June 30, 1895*, pp. XXIV-V.

[60]*Report of the Department of Indian Affairs for the Year ended December 31, 1882*, pp. 87-88.

[61]E. Brian Titley, "W.M. Graham, Indian Agent Extraordinaire," *Prairie Forum*, VIII (1983): 26-28.

[62]D.J. Hall, "Clifford Sifton and Canadian Indian Administration, 1896-1905," *Prairie Forum*, II (1977): 133-134.

[63]*Report of the Department of Indian Affairs for the Year ended Dec. 31, 1897*, p. xxvii.

[64]M. Benson to J.D. McLean, Mar. 24, 1902, RG 10, vol. 3964 f 149, 874, PAC.

[65]Tabular information in annual reports of the Department of Indian Affairs.

[66]M. Benson to the Deputy Superintendent, Jan. 14, 1908, RG 10, vol, 3937, f 120, 048-1, PAC.

[67]The correspondence relating to Regina Industrial School is found in RG 10, vol. 3927, f 166, 836-1C, PAC.

[68]W.J. Wasylow, "Battleford Industrial School," pp. 263-266.

[69]Jules Le Chevalier, "St. Joseph's Indian Industrial School at Dunbow," Documents Oblates, Bôite 1, item 22, PAA.

[70]For a more detailed account of the changes introduced by Scott, see E. Brian Titley, "Duncan Campbell Scott and Indian Educational Policy" in J. Donald Wilson, ed., *An Imperfect Past: Education and Society in Canadian History* (Vancouver: C.S.C.I., 1984), pp. 141-153.

[71]While on his way to visit the Mohawk Institute in 1895, Martin Benson dropped in to see the Alexandria Industrial School for girls and the Victoria Industrial School for boys and noted the similarities between these reformatories and the Indian school. Martin Benson, "Report on this Mohawk Institute and Six Nation's Boarding Schools," Aug. 30, 1895, RG 10, vol. 2006, f 7825-1A, PAC.

[72]Neil Sutherland, *Children in English Canadian Society: Framing the Twentieth Century Consensus* (Toronto: University of Toronto Press, 1976), pp. 99-110.

[73]D.A. Nock, "Social Effects of Missionary Education," p. 245.

[74]James Redford, "Attendance at Indian Residential Schools in British Columbia, 1890-1920," *B.C. Studies* 44, (Winter 1979-1980): 52-53.

9

The Schooling Experience
of Ukrainians in Manitoba, 1896-1916

Stella M. Hryniuk and *Neil G. McDonald*

The schooling of the immigrant child in western Canada has usually been interpreted from the perspective of the assimilationists, whether bureaucrat, inspector, or teacher.[1] Rarely has it been examined from the viewpoint of the immigrants themselves. Moreover, consideration has seldom been given to their educational experiences in their native lands or the aspirations they held for their children. This chapter describes and interprets the Ukrainian schooling experience in Manitoba during the first twenty years of Ukrainian settlement in this province, mainly from the immigrants' perspective.

Ukrainians are a Slavic people who inhabit extensive territories in Eastern and East-Central Europe. At the time of their mass migration to western Canada at the end of the nineteenth and beginning of the twentieth centuries, their lands were divided between the Austro-Hungarian Monarchy and the Russian Empire. The total number of Ukrainians at that time was around twenty million, of whom about four million lived in Austria-Hungary. The Ukrainians who came to Canada were from two Austrian provinces, Galicia and Bukovyna.[2]

Although they formed a majority of the population in eastern Galicia and in Bukovyna, in neither province did the Ukrainians enjoy much political influence. Mostly they were peasant agriculturalists working small land-holdings of 1-5 hectares; many of them also worked for large landowners, especially at seeding and harvest time. Productivity was low, but significant improvements were evident in the last two decades of the nineteenth century: crop yields increased, as did the number and quality of the animals that were raised. The Ukrainians lived mainly in the small towns and villages of the two provinces, going out daily to work their intensively cultivated plots. Villages could be clusters of houses of two or three hundred inhabitants or larger conglomerations of two thousand people or more.[3]

From the 1880s onwards, the Ukrainian rural population began to free itself from the influence of Polish and Rumanian landlords. They participated in movements for promoting popular education and producer and consumer co-operatives, and they strove to acquire greater control of local government. Ukrainians in Galicia were Ukrainian-rite Catholics, while those in Bukovyna belonged predominantly to the Ukrainian Orthodox church. Village priests, particularly in Galicia, played a leading role in furthering popular enlightenment and economic improvements in the countryside, though schoolteachers and a handful of lawyers and doctors also played a part.[4]

At the provincial level, school authorities in Galicia were controlled by the politically-dominant Polish element, those in Bukovyna by Germans and Rumanians. School curricula were set by the Austrian (federal) government, but it was the province that determined the language or languages of instruction. Until the 1870s there had been very few village schools in eastern Galicia and Bukovyna, and their rural populations were almost entirely illiterate. Compulsory education was then introduced by law, but it was a long time before it could become a reality.[5]

The building of a school was the responsibility of a local school district. Over the years Ukrainian villagers organized themselves, and taxed themselves in order to construct and maintain schools, and frequently provided manual labour and materials. Transfer payments from local school taxes also contributed toward teachers' salaries and pensions, though these were in fact paid by the next highest level of educational authority, the county education councils. The latter might on occasion also provide loans or subsidies for local education purposes. During the 1880s and 1890s many new schools were built in the villages. In the Southern Podillia region of eastern Galicia, from which a great number of Manitoba's early Ukrainian immigrants came, the number of elementary schools in Borshchiv county (seventy-five small towns and villages, population about 100,000) rose from 27 in 1880 to 57 in 1900, and the number of those in Chortkiv county (44 small towns and villages, population about 67,000) increased from 23 to 39 in the same two decades. Moreover, by 1900 many of the schools were no longer one-room schools.[6]

School attendance also rose quite dramatically, though it is clear that not every child attended, or attended for the period prescribed by law. By 1900, however, an ample majority of the children of school age were attending school.[7] In first and second grades they learned reading and writing, arithmetic, and singing; religious instruction was also given, not by the teachers but by priests. The teaching of a second language was introduced in grade two. In grades three and four the natural sciences, geography and history, drawing and geometry, and domestic science for girls and physical education for boys were added. By 1900 a few more technical or practical subjects had also entered the curriculum: physics and chemistry in the towns, horticulture and agriculture in the villages. Despite systematic attempts by the provincial authorities to ensure that villagers should not receive an education "above their station in life," some village children — usually encouraged by their priests and/or teachers — went on to higher education.[8]

With the increased emphasis on schooling, there was also a significant increase in the literacy rate. Literacy rates, here expressed as a percentage of the *total* population, varied from one county to another, depending on local circumstances. In Borshchiv county, in 1880, only 8.4 percent of the male population and only 4.8 percent of the female population could read; in nearby Terebovlia county the percentages were 20 and 11.9 respectively. By 1900 there had been considerable improvements: 20.8 percent of males and 13.4 percent of females in Borshchiv county were now literate, while in Terebovlia county the percentages were now 45.2 and 33.1 respectively.[9] It is interesting to note that Paul Wood, immigration agent in Dauphin, Manitoba, estimated in 1900 that,

> . . . fully 35 percent of the male adult Galicians can read and write in their own language, and many of these can also read and write Polish. Of the children who were attending school any length at home in the old country before leaving for Canada, nearly all can read and write.[10]

Wood's reference to "their own language" (i.e. Ukrainian) and to Polish is instructive. Bilingual schooling was not at all unusual for Ukrainian villagers. Their children attended schools in which Ukrainian was generally the language of instruction in the first grade. In Galicia, Polish was added in the second grade, and normally as a second language of instruction.[11] For villagers living in mixed-language areas, the learning and use of two languages was part of their daily experience.

The Ukrainian immigrants to Manitoba, therefore, came from regions in which there had been recent and significant improvements, including those in the realm of public education. Important also was the work of voluntary societies which published simple reading materials and to which the reading clubs that were established in many villages were loosely affiliated. A tradition of schooling had been painstakingly established over the years, and many villagers were proud of their schools and what they had accomplished: as the village of Kolodribka reported in 1890, "we have educated people now."[12]

It has been estimated that about 100,000 Ukrainians migrated to Canada between 1896 and 1914. With natural increase, there were probably about 128,000 people of Ukrainian origin in Canada in 1911 and around 220,000 in 1921, mostly in the three prairie provinces. It appears that over one-third lived in Manitoba.[13] Their initial arrival, however, followed one of the most unsettling social and political periods in the post-Confederation era. The immediate cause of the friction was located in Manitoba and became known as the Manitoba School Question. This issue preoccupied Canadian political life from 1890 to 1897, and the negotiated compromise solution, however unanticipated, directly influenced the schooling experience of the early Ukrainian immigrants.

Although Manitoba came into Confederation in 1870 as a bilingual province and with a dual (Catholic and Protestant) school system, these arrangements were not to last.[14] Within twenty years, under the impact of a population growth that altered the early French/English balance, the fledgling province began to reflect the social and cultural image of its new majority — Anglophone, Protestant, and largely Ontario-born.

Consequently in 1890, a Liberal government, led by Premier Thomas Greenway, abolished the official use of the French language and the dual system of denominational schools. This heavy-handed legislation resulted in a long campaign of litigation and political agitation. The dispute engaged French and English, Catholic and Protestant, Quebec and Ontario, and Conservative and Liberal in a national debate that challenged the very basis of Confederation. So serious was the controversy that it became a major issue of the federal election of 1896, and was a significant factor in the defeat of the governing Conservative party. In 1897 a newly-elected Liberal government, under Wilfrid Laurier, negotiated a compromise that led to an amendment to the Manitoba Public Schools Act of 1890. It read:

> When 10 of the pupils in any school speaks the French language or any language other than English as their native language, the teaching of such pupils shall be conducted in French or such other language, and English upon the bilingual system.[15]

The wording in this clause that allowed pupils to be taught in "any language other than English" was an attempt to avoid charges from Ontario that the French language had been made equal to English.[16] In Manitoba, however, the practical application of the legislation gave great comfort to the new immigrants. They soon realized that the amended School Act was permissive and allowed their children to be schooled partially in their own language. This "loophole" in the act helped solve two of the most pressing and closely-related schooling problems that worried Ukrainian parents. There was the real concern first about linguistic assimilation; and second, about the supply of Ukrainian/English-speaking teachers. Although parents acknowledged the need for their children to learn English, they were not willing to let this happen at the risk of losing their first language. The obvious solution was a reliable supply of certified bilingual teachers. As the first organizer of Ukrainian schools, John Baderski, observed, the new settlers did not wish "to go to the expense of building a school if they must afterwards see the school stand idle for want of a teacher."[17] Moreover, from a practical perspective it was important that bilingual teachers be found because the immigrant children could not speak English.[18]

Interestingly, the anxiety of the immigrant parents neatly complemented that of other Manitobans who worried about the possible social costs arising from this heavy influx of culturally distinct peoples. The latter group regularly expressed two distinct but related concerns, namely assimilation and illiteracy. To many among the latter group the best answer was a more selective immigration policy; to others, the public school could become an effective solution. Arguments for the two positions often found public expression. For example, in 1901, W. Sanford Evans, a recent Ontario-born arrival and newly-appointed editor of the *Winnipeg Telegram,* wrote in reference to "Slavonic immigrants":

> Those whose ignorance is impenetrable, whose customs are repulsive, whose civilization is primitive, and whose character and morals are justly

condemned are surely not the class of immigrants which the country's paid immigration agents should seek to attract. Better by far to keep our land for children, and for the children's children of Canadians, than to fill up the country with the scum of Europe.[19]

Another less strident but equally concerned voice was represented by prominent clergy in the province, especially among those Presbyterians, Catholics and Anglicans who helped organize the Galician Education Committee.[20] Their view was perhaps best expressed by the Presbyterian Reverend Thomas Hart, a professor at Manitoba College. In an article on schools in Manitoba, he wrote:

> The education problem of Manitoba is both difficult and important . . . when we consider that . . . almost one third of the whole population is of other than British origin we can easily see that the task of unifying these diverse races, and making them intelligent citizens, English in speech, Canadian in sentiment, and British in loyalty to the empire, is one of no ordinary magnitude.[21]

The appraisal of the situation by Hart, his implied resignation to the task, and the "other language" clause in the School Act combined with the expressed wishes of the Ukrainians to modify the school experience of some children in those first years of settlement. These factors, however, did not always ensure satisfactory relationships with the school system.

The Ukrainians were lured to Canada by cheap land and the opportunity to create a better life, politically and materially, than appeared possible in Galicia and Bukovyna. They settled for the most part in areas still undeveloped — in the Dauphin, Riding Mountain, and Stuartburn areas, the Interlake, and the Cook's Creek-Brokenhead region.[22] Initially, the energies of the settlers were almost entirely taken up with clearing the land, planting their first crops, and erecting a dwelling. Males often left their homesteads to work for wages elsewhere, leaving much of the farm work to their wives and children.

The pattern of life on the homesteads with their widely-dispersed houses was very different from that of the villages of the homeland with their clusters of houses and better means of communication. Some settlers, misled by statements about Canada's excellent schools, appear to have expected to find schools in the rural areas to which they came.[23] Occasionally, this was indeed the case, as in Winnipeg and for some settlers in the Stuartburn area,[24] but in such instances the Ukrainian children at times encountered discrimination which led parents to keep their children at home.[25]

The schooling experience of Ukrainians in Winnipeg differed from that elsewhere in the province. According to the census data, there were 3,599 Ukrainians in Winnipeg's metropolitan area in 1911 and 7,001 in 1921;[26] these figures were probably understated. The Ukrainians lived mainly in the city's north end, and the children attended schools such as Strathcona, Aberdeen, Lord Selkirk, Norquay and Somerset. Daniel McIntyre, the long-term, influential superintendent of Winnipeg's public schools, was an adamant advocate of a unitary school system and of unilingual English instruction.[27] Although obligated by law to provide bilingual instruction when there was sufficient demand, McIntyre and the school board ignored petitions from Ukrainians for its introduction into the division's schools.[28] Notwithstanding the school board's failure to live up to its obligations, some Ukrainians looked back with appreciation to the education they received at Strathcona school where W.J. Sisler, another outspoken opponent of bilingual education, was principal.[29]

The Ukrainian press of Winnipeg regularly paid attention to educational matters. It encouraged the attendance of children at school and of adults at evening classes (some of which were organized by the city council and others by Ukrainian associations), and it stressed the importance of learning both English and a trade.[30] How many of Winnipeg's children of Ukrainian extraction attended school regularly cannot be established; clearly quite a number did not.[31]

It is scarcely surprising that the Ukrainian community in Manitoba, as most other communities, was factious. In the winter of 1915-16, for example, one grouping ultimately set up its own socialist Sunday schools "to counter the influence of the capitalistic schools on our young generation."[32] But the absence of bilingual elementary education in Winnipeg's schools seems to have been accepted by the Ukrainian community with a fair amount of equanimity. Evening and Sunday schools served to some extent to educate children in their mother tongue. One private bilingual elementary school was established, however, in 1905: St. Nicholas School, run by the Sisters Servants of Mary Immaculate (a Ukrainian-rite Catholic religious order). Numbers quickly increased from fifty students in 1905 to 160 in 1906 and even more in subsequent years; when health inspectors wanted to close the school, the Roman Catholic Archbishop of St. Boniface raised money for the building of a new one.[33]

The experiences of Ukrainian settlers and their children in the rural areas of Manitoba were very different. Predominantly, they came into empty lands. Where there were already some settlements, as in in the Stuartburn area, they tried to work within the established school system at least for a time, but by 1915 they had set up a large number of school districts.[34] In some instances, the Ukrainian settlers took over some already-existing school districts, but in most cases it was they who formed the district and built the schools. In January 1916, two months before the Manitoba Legislature voted to repeal the section of the Public Schools Act that permitted the bilingual schools, Charles K. Newcombe, superintendent of schools, reported on the state of these schools: "One hundred and eleven districts operate Ruthenian, or Polish, bilingual schools, employing 114 teachers, with an enrolment of 6,513 pupils and an average attendance of 3,884."[35]

Interest in schooling, therefore, was evident from the outset, and by and large the settlers were well aware of the advantages that education and a knowledge of English would provide for their children. Thus, A.L. Young reported from the Stuartburn area in 1901: "The Galician settlers take an active interest in all school meetings and are evidently quite alive to the necessity of giving their children all the advantages of a good school education."[36]

There were instances when Ukrainian settlers organized informal classes for their children or where parents taught their children to read and write in Ukrainian.[37] Quite early, however, some of the settlers, following normal Manitoba practice, were able to organize their own school districts. The first public school district established by Ukrainians in Manitoba appears to have been the "Galicia" district in the Interlake in 1898.[38] The Presbyterian and Roman Catholic churches helped establish a handful of early Ukrainian schools: Trembowla, Kosiw, Willow Creek and St. John Cantius.[39] The immigration agent in Sifton was for a time authorized by his superiors to teach the Ukrainian children there, and lessons were held in a makeshift schoolhouse — the station of the Lake Manitoba Railway & Canal company.[40]

Some Ukrainian areas organized their own schools without any outside help. As early as 1901-02, for example, schools appeared at Mink River, Ukraina, Lukowce, Wolodimir, Kolomyja and Olha.[41] Among the early immigrants were three qualified teachers who taught school in Manitoba: Ivan Negrych, Ivan Bodrug, and Vasyl Cichocky. The last-named, at least initially, taught only in Ukrainian.[42] Other teachers were unilingually English, and settlers' children who had acquired some English acted on occasion as interpreters for those who had not learned English. Occasionally, an English settler's child learned Ukrainian and could also act as translator. And "Eaton's catalogue was also very useful" as a tool in the classroom.[43] Some schools, for the first two or three years, were held in private homes until a schoolhouse was built.

By no means could all the Ukrainian settlers during the first decade of the century afford to tax themselves sufficiently to support a school. Most of them had come to Canada with relatively little capital. Inspector E.H. Walker noted in 1905 that:

> Not one of the six Galician districts in Rossburn Municipality has a school. This failure is explained partly by the fact that they have been in the country such a comparatively short time that they do not feel able to support schools.[44]

The school at McMillan — "The building was a shabby job, cold and drafty, with rough seats and an oil-drum heater" — cost around $500 to build.[45] Later, schools cost more: $850 for Budka school, $1,355 for that at Malonton. The potential tax base was reduced where adjacent lands were owned by non-resident speculators, who were exempt from paying taxes. "This state of affairs is not only a hardship and a grave injustice to the settlers, wrote Inspector Best, but also a formidable hindrance to education work."[46]

Frequent alterations of district boundaries, caused by changes in land ownership, for example, from private to public and vice versa, also affected the potential funding base.[47] Established municipalities were at times most unsympathetic to the educational needs of the new settlers' children and refused to help them. In consequence, the Ukrainians formed their own municipalities, as in the case of Stuartburn:

> When they applied to Franklin council for financial help to build schools, they were turned down. Franklin said they were too new a community to receive financial assistance. Their only option was to break away from Franklin and form their own municipality. And thus the Stuartburn municipality came to be formed.[48]

As the settlers became better established, more schools were founded. In 1903 the Department of Education appointed a School Organizer and Inspector for Schools Among the Galicians, and although the appointee, John Baderski, was not much liked among Ukrainians on account of his pro-Polish sympathies, he, and later Theodore Stefanyk and Paul Gigeychuk, did help settlers organize school districts.[49] Also helpful in this respect were articles in the Ukrainian language press explaining how settlers might approach the task of establishing school districts.[50] Undoubtedly, there were also Ukrainian settlers who were not much interested in education.

In his 1904 report, Baderski noted that school attendance in Ukrainian areas had improved under bilingual teachers. He recommended that there be established a "special preparatory school" for bilingual teachers, and in February 1905, the Manitoba government opened the Ruthenian Training School in Winnipeg to prepare Ukrainian/English and Polish/English teachers. It was so successful that in 1907 it was divided into two sections and the Ukrainian section was moved to Brandon, where it functioned until the abolition of bilingual education in Manitoba in 1916.[51] Some prospective teachers took a three-year course there, others attended for shorter periods. "Some knew much English; others very little." It is difficult to establish their competence as teachers, though it is clear that some came to be greatly respected.[52]

Once there was a steady supply of bilingual teachers, the number of school districts began to rise quickly. Ukrainians became school trustees in greater numbers, formed school districts, and undertook the responsibility of building and maintaining schoolhouses and sometimes teachers' residences too. Due to their lack of knowledge of the English language, the Ukrainians kept school district records at times in various combinations of Ukrainian, Polish and English, but a steady and lively interest in their schools is revealed in the minutes of meetings and the ledgers.[53] Not atypically, in Lukowce school district in 1904, the parents did carpentry, hauled lumber and repaired the chimney for a minimal fee, and later maintained the school building and grounds and the school equipment.[54]

The rate of establishment of schools varied from one settlement to another, but public schooling clearly became a regular feature in the Ukrainian settlements of Manitoba. As of the middle of 1915, the official list of "Ruthenian" schools kept by the Department of Education, contains the names of ninety-one school districts that offered bilingual instruction in English and Ukrainian,[55] a handful of which also offered instruction in Polish. In addition, there were school districts in areas of mixed settlements, for example around Beausejour, where Poles and Ukrainians, and sometimes Germans too, could not agree on what language other than English should be used, and decided that the Ruthenian-English teacher should teach only in English.[56] Often, extraordinary efforts were made to provide schooling opportunities for the children. Thus, Inspector Best, reporting on the Gimli district, wrote in 1913:

> On the completion of the new schools at McMillan, Komarno, Kreuzberg, Malonton and Rembrandt, there will be more than twenty schools in this settlement erected within the last few years, a fact that speaks well for the enterprise and self-sacrificing spirit of these people. . . . The efforts of these Northern colonies can be better appreciated when it is known that to obtain the most meagre education for their children they tax themselves sometimes as high as forty mills on the dollar; they pay higher salaries than most places and provide accommodation that would put to shame many of our old and wealthy districts.[57]

Likewise, Inspector Fallis wrote as follows about one new school district in what had been just a short time before the virgin lands south of Riding Mountain:

> In the Galician settlement north east of Erickson, the new district of Round Lake has been formed. The anxiety of these people to have a school is shown by the fact that the district comprises only eight sections, of which only about six and one-half sections are assessed at a valuation of about fifteen thousand dollars and not over twelve hundred acres of land are cultivated in the district. I venture to say that many of our Canadian people might hesitate before assuming the responsibility of operating a school under such conditions and yet these people have called for tender for the erection of a new school, to be completed as soon as possible.[58]

Clearly, education for their children was important for many of the settlers. In the early days of settlement, some parents even taught their own children at home, "Of course, when we did not go to school, my father taught us at home. However, he did not know English so he taught my brother and sister other languages: Ukrainian, German and Polish."[59]

Some parents, even though illiterate themselves, gave every encouragement to their children to learn. F.T. Hawryluk, who had completed grade three in Galicia and was later a teacher in the Gimli area, recalled that he had to study on his own for two or three years before a school was opened in his neighbourhood. He said: "My father, though he himself was illiterate, always encouraged me to study and would carefully observe me as I wrote and listened attentively as I read." [60]

Some parents were indifferent to schooling: W. Kostiuk's father did not mind his going to school when he was not needed for farm work.[61] Others were no doubt hostile, afraid perhaps that their children would be alienated from them in the strange Canadian environment if they acquired an education and a knowledge of English. Like Kostiuk, they also felt themselves in need of all the family's work potential.[62] Some, however, clearly went to great lengths to ensure that their children got education, even when it entailed a financial sacrifice. One example was that of a child whose parents were themselves illiterate, but sent him to attend grades three to eight in Dauphin. There he boarded with a family who were paid for his keep in produce and in money.[63] Often, great physical exertion and discomfort were experienced. One mother recalled that:

> We belonged to Senkiw School District, but were on the other side of the Roseau River. In spring when the children were small, they could not cross the river — there was no bridge, so I had to go with them. I would hitch up my skirt and carry them across on my back. I also had to meet them again in the evening — but the children had to get an education.[64]

While the desire for education for their children can be well documented, it is not always clear why this should have been so. In some instances, one may assume that respect for schooling, inculcated in the homeland, was carried over into the new land: attendance at school had thus become part of everyday life. Many settlers had migrated primarily to secure a better life for their children,[65] and no doubt recognized that education was one way towards achieving that better life. One person interviewed recalled that his parents wanted him to learn agriculture, reading and writing, and the English language, so that he should be able to communicate and to get work.[66] A striving for greater security for their children thus appears to have been a motivating factor. So too, it seems, was a concern that their children might be able to avoid the hardships which the parents had faced, possibly in Galicia and Bukovyna, but probably more so during the initial years in Manitoba; as one son was told: "Go to school, learn, so you don't have to work hard like us."[67]

Newspaper articles and letters to editors noted other reasons for education: public schooling was the first step towards the training of teachers, government officials, lawyers, doctors and priests.[68] Education would put Ukrainians "on an equal footing with other nationalities";[69] it was the road to success and everybody would then live together in harmony;[70] arithmetic was important so that "everyone should know the income and expense from his husbandry."[71]

The Ukrainian settlers also knew that ability in English was vital for their children — "One cannot exist in Canada without English."[72] This necessary knowledge could normally be best provided by the schools. But parents also wanted their children to retain their knowledge of Ukrainian and of their Ukrainian culture; here too the fear of their children becoming culturally separated from them played a major part.[73] Bilingual education thus seemed best to answer their needs. The children would grow up literate in both languages; learn what was useful to them in their Canadian context, and yet not forget their Ukrainian heritage. Furthermore, attendance was likely to be better at schools in which children had no difficulty communicating with their teacher and vice versa,[74] and it was thought that children learned more when they received instruction in Ukrainian as well as in English.[75] Moreover, bilingual education was a right. As *Kanadyiskyi Farmer* stated in 1909:

> We need to know the English language but we have the right to learn the Ruthenian language in schools. We should see to it that in all Ruthenian colonies school should be taught in both languages. . . . Because our people pay for the schools and teachers, we should have Ruthenian instruction too.[76]

Settlers, and children too, wrote to the newspapers about their satisfaction with bilingual schools and bilingual teachers.[77] Initially, however, they were in very short supply, and even later there were never enough. Salaries were sometimes low, and teachers' accommodation was often not satisfactory. Isolation and poor communications were other impediments.[78] Even officially bilingual schools, on occasion, had to hire unilingual English teachers.[79] At times, too, parents and school trustees did not appear to some members of the Manitoba-Ukrainian community to be concerned sufficiently about the need for a bilingual teacher.[80] The number of advertisements for bilingual teachers in the Ukrainian language press in Manitoba, however, plainly shows the general demand.[81] The clearest evidence of the desire for bilingual teaching was provided by the united opposition among Ukrainians of all political persuasions to the abolition of the bilingual system in 1916.[82]

Bilingual teachers, and sometimes unilingual English-speaking ones, were highly respected in their communities.[83] They not only taught the children but also promoted choral and musical groups, drama clubs, and organized evening classes to provide opportunities to those who had grown up before schools had been organized in outlying districts.[84]

The Ukrainian language press, the Ukrainian Teachers' Association, and individuals also called for the introduction in Manitoba of compulsory education, to which they were accustomed in their original homeland.[85] The Ukrainian socialist press also called for compulsory education,[86] while at the same time demanding a different type of education. It was this faction of the community which railed most insistently against the shortcomings of the school curriculum. They objected, for example, to the monarchist, imperialist and capitalist content of the stories used in the children's primers.[87] Other Ukrainians merely asked that Ukrainian books be used even if they had to be obtained from the homeland.[88] Bilingual readers were eventually published for Manitoba schools in 1913, but their usage was not altogether favoured by the school inspectors.[89]

Some Ukrainians resented portions of the curriculum because they believed that the children were deliberately being anglicized.[90] Others thought it very proper that the children should be taught knowledge appropriate to living in one of the Dominions of the British Empire, including Anglo-Saxon principles of democracy.[91] Ukrainian language primers were evidently used by bilingual teachers, often at the request or instruction of the school trustees.[92] Following the formal abolition of the bilingual system in 1916, a few continued to be used, though more secretively because communities risked the wrath of the school inspectors.[93]

School attendance was an ongoing problem, and one that was not resolved by the decreeing of compulsory education in Manitoba. In the early years of Ukrainian settlement in Manitoba, when many heads of families worked away from their homesteads for months at a time, children were especially needed for farm work.[94] Sometimes an individual was not suited for a teaching position and "antagonize[d] both parents and pupils."[95] Another inspector reported that, "In many cases when the teacher is not experienced and probably not too well educated and does not speak the Galician language, parents come to think that their children are not making progress and they take them from the school altogether."[96] In some instances the trustees were unable to hire teachers, and schools remained closed for months at a time.[97] Seasonal farm work also caused many parents to keep their children at home — the Kosiw School Register consistently showed low attendance in September[98] — and this problem was certainly not resolved by the introduction of compulsory education or by placing allegedly recalcitrant Ukrainian school districts under official trusteeship, as is evidenced by the report from Pine Ridge school which explained low attendance in September 1921, by reference to Jewish holidays and delayed work on the farms: "everybody seems busy digging potatoes just now."[99] The biggest obstacle to school attendance, however, was the distance that often had to be covered by small children, in all sorts of conditions and over various types of terrain. One vivid example from a memoir, not atypical, stated:

> The children walked as far as five miles to school. In the beginning the roads were very poor. Many used only trails, crossing creeks and grades made of young white poplar or willow covered with manure. If the winter were heavy, the grades would get so mucky in the spring that the children had to walk through the fields to get to school. For years those coming from the south had to cross a ravine gushing with water every spring. One of the bigger boys would have hip-waders and would take the young children across one by one. In the winter months most children came with a horse and buggy.[100]

It was not until more schools and better roads were constructed that the dream of schooling for all Ukrainian settlers' children could be realized.

Meanwhile some, to their regret, were unable to go to high school.[101] Quite a number did manage to go on to higher education, including university, and became teachers, lawyers and so on.[102] Others, with their grade school education, became the backbone of the communities in which they resided.[103]

The schooling experience of Ukrainians in Manitoba up to 1916 was in many ways not dissimilar to that of other non-English-speaking immigrant groups. They did not find in their new homeland an established school system in the rural areas, as many of them had expected. Some regressed from educational standards which they had achieved in Galicia and Bukovyna.[104] They had to contend with the bigotry of people like Sisler, who in an article published in 1906 wrote that Ukrainians were "inferior in every department both of mental and physical activity, excepting where only slow mechanical movements are required."[105] Although some of the school inspectors recognized both the difficulties they encountered and their achievements, city-bound administrators, politicians and editors knew and cared all too little about the long distances, bad roads and inadequate tax bases which the Ukrainian settlers and their children confronted in their quest for schooling.

Yet clearly there was this quest, and by 1916 an extensive network of "Ruthenian" schools covered the areas where the Ukrainian settlers lived. They had shown themselves to be seriously concerned about their children's education, and according to their means (and sometimes beyond) they had built schools and hired teachers, and thus provided for their children's elementary education. The children themselves were frequently recognized by their teachers to be intelligent and eager to learn, and they often made quite extraordinary efforts under the most difficult circumstances to attend the schools in their scattered settlements. Contemporary Anglo-Canadian literature, however, often portrayed these Ukrainian settlers and their children as ignorant and backward. The evidence suggests that this characterization was grossly unfair.

Notes

[1]See, for example: Alan F.J. Artibise, *Winnipeg: A Social History of Urban Growth, 1874-1914* (Montreal: McGill-Queen's University Press, 1975), pp. 195-206; Cornelius J. Jaenen, "Ruthenian Schools in Western Canada, 1897-1919", in David C. Jones, Nancy M. Sheehan, and Robert M. Stamp, eds., *Shaping the Schools of the Canadian West* (Calgary: Detselig, 1979), pp. 39-58; and J.E. Rea, "'My Main Line is the Kiddies . . . Make Them Good Christians and Good Canadians, Which is the Same Thing,'" in Wsevolod Isajiw, ed., *Identities: The Impact of Ethnicity on Canadian Society* (Toronto: Peter Martin Associates, 1977), pp. 3-11.

[2]Hence the earlier description of the Ukrainians as Galicians and Bukovynians.

[3]See S. M. Hryniuk, "Peasant Agriculture in East Galicia in the Late Nineteenth Century", *Slavonic and East European Review*, 63, (Apr. 1985): 328-243; also S.M. Hryniuk, "A Peasant Society in Transition: Ukrainian Peasants in Five East Galician Counties, 1880-1900," (Ph.D. thesis, University of Manitoba, 1984), pp. 47-49 and 52-54.

⁴Hryniuk, "A Peasant Society," esp. pp. 414-418.

⁵S.H. Badeni, "Schulpflicht und Schulbesuch in Oesterreich," *Statistische Monatschrift*, XXVI (1900): 281; A. Sirka, *The Nationality Question in Austrian Education: The Case of the Ukrainians 1867-1914* (Frankfurt: Lang, 1980), pp. 35-50; Hryniuk, "A Peasant Society," pp. 115-122.

⁶Hryniuk, "A Peasant Society," pp. 124-126, 131-133; Sirka, *The Nationality Question* pp. 76-78.

⁷Relevant data are in *Oesterreichische Statistik*, LXII, no. 2. Education was compulsory for children aged 7 to 12; those aged 13 to 15 were to attend "continuation classes" in the elementary school for four to six hours per week.

⁸Hryniuk, "A Peasant Society," pp. 122 and 133-135; on education in Bukovyna see V. Kubijovyc, ed., *Encyclopedia of Ukraine*, vol. I (Toronto: University of Toronto Press, 1984), p. 798.

⁹Hryniuk, "A Peasant Society," p. 153.

¹⁰Cited, from *Dauphin Weekly Herald*, in V.J. Kaye-Kysilevskyi, "The Descendants of the Boyars of Halych on the Prairies of the Canadian West," in A. Baran *et. al.*, eds., *The Jubilee Collection of the Ukrainian Free Academy of Sciences* (Winnipeg, 1976), p. 363.

¹¹In Bukovyna, the second language was normally German or Rumanian.

¹²*Batkivshchyna*, Mar. 28, 1890; Kolodribka's school was older than most, having been established in 1865.

¹³Kubijovyc, *Encyclopedia*, p. 821; Canadian census data are not reliable sources for the numbers of Ukrainians in Canada, see W. Darcovich, "The 'Statistical Compendium': An Overview of Trends," in W.R. Petryshyn, ed., *Changing Realities: Social Trends Among Ukrainian Canadians* (Edmonton: Canadian Institute of Ukrainian Studies, 1980), esp. p. 8.

¹⁴For a discussion of these developments in Manitoba, see W.L. Morton, *Manitoba: A History*, 2nd edition (Toronto: University of Toronto Press, 1967), pp. 199-250; also Gerald Friesen, *The Canadian Prairies: A History* (Toronto: University of Toronto Press, 1984), pp. 195-219 and pp. 242-273; and Cornelius Jaenen, "The Manitoba School Question: An Ethnic Interpretation," in Martin Kovacs, ed., *Ethnic Canadians: Culture and Education* (Regina, Canadian Plains Research Centre, 1978), pp. 317-331.

¹⁵*Canada: Sessional Papers*, Vol. XXXI, No. 13, 1897, p. 2, Clause 258.

¹⁶J.W. Dafoe, *Clifford Sifton in Relation to his Times* (Toronto: MacMillan company, 1931), p. 98.

¹⁷Manitoba, Department of Education, *Annual Report*, 1904, p. 351.

¹⁸See, for example, Peter Humeniuk, *Harships and Progress of Ukrainian Pioneers* (Winnipeg: Author, 1977), p. 103; and M.H. Marunchak, *The Ukrainian Canadians: A History* (Winnipeg; Ukrainian Free Academy of Sciences, 1982), p. 115-120.

¹⁹*Winnipeg Tribune*, May 13, 1901.

²⁰*Winnipeg Tribune*, Jan. 17, 1902; Marunchak, *The Ukrainian Canadians*, p. 116.

²¹Thomas Hart, "The Educational System of Manitoba," *Queen's Quarterly*, XII, (1905): 240.

²²P. Yuzyk, *The Ukrainians in Manitoba: A Social History* (Toronto: University of Toronto Press, 1953), pp. 33-35.

²³V.J. Kaye, *Early Ukrainian Settlers in Canada, 1895-1900* (Toronto: University of Toronto Press, 1964), pp. 15, 173; M. Ewanchuk, *Spruce, Swamp and Stone: A*

History of the Pioneer Ukrainian Settlements in the Gimli Area (Winnipeg: the author, 1977), p. 77; the CPR's propaganda as early as 1890 stated that "railways, schools, churches, and thriving towns are now scattered all over the country." (*Free Homes and Cheap Railway Land,* CPR pamphlet, n.d., p. 5).

[24]Ukrainian children "are bright, intelligent, and most anxious to acquire a knowledge of the English language. They are well behaved in school and easily managed," Public Archives of Manitoba (hereafter PAM), Department of Education, *Annual Report,* 1897, p. 35. See also Kaye, *Early Ukrainian Settlers,* p. 165.

[25]P. Humeniuk, as quoted in M. Ewanchuk, *Pioneer Profiles: Ukrainian Settlers in Manitoba* (Winnipeg: the author, 1981), p. 196; see also Ibid, p. 213; for a different, pleasant experience, see p. 26.

[26]L. Driedger, "The Urbanization of Ukrainians in Canada," in Petryshyn, ed., *Changing Realities,* p. 114.

[27]W.J. Wilson, "Daniel McIntyre and Education in Winnipeg," (M.Ed. thesis, University of Manitoba, 1978), esp. p. 142.

[28]*Kanadyiskyi Farmer,* May 24 and June 7 and 14, 1907; J. Pampallis, "An Analysis of the Winnipeg Public School System and the Social Forces that Shaped it, 1897-1920," (M.Ed. thesis, University of Manitoba, 1979), p. 76; O. Woycenko, *Litopys ukrainskoho zhyttia v Kanadi, I, 1874-1918* (Winnipeg: Trident Press, 1961), p. 16. Ukrainians, of course, were not the only immigrant group to have a request for bilingual instruction turned down: for example, a German petition was declined in 1899 (School District of Winnipeg No. 1, Board Minute Book 1897-1900, no. 4, p. 292).

[29]For Sisler's early views on Ukrainians see "The Immigrant Child," *The Western School Journal,* 1, (Apr. 1906): 3-6, and his 1912 address to the Council for Character Education, "The School and the Newer Citizens of Canada," (PAM, W.J. Sisler Papers, Box 66); for a later and more positive view see Sisler's letter of May 1, 1919, to R.L. Richardson, M.P.P (Ibid, box 5). We are indebted to Mrs. G. Russin for much of the above information.

[30]*Kanadyiskyi Farmer,* Oct. 11, 1906; Jan. 10, Apr. 26, Oct. 11 and 25, 1907; Feb. 12, June 11, Oct. 15 and 22, and Dec. 15, 1909, etc.; *Ukrainskyi holos,* Jan. 18 and 25, and Feb. 11, 1911, etc.

[31]According to Sisler's calculations, in April 1910, 19 out of Strathcona school's 618 students were "Galician or Ruthenian"; in 1915 the total was 147 out of 1254 (11.7 percent) (PAM, Sisler Papers, Box 6).

[32]*Robochyi narod,* Oct. 17, 1916, Jan. 26 and Sept. 26, 1917.

[33]F. Swyripa, "The Ukrainians and Private Education," in M.R. Lupul, ed., *A Heritage in Transition: Essays in the History of Ukrainians in Canada* (Toronto: McClelland and Stewart, 1982), p. 248; Marunchak, *The Ukrainian Canadians,* p. 152.

[34]A listing of the "Ruthenian" school districts with bilingual instruction together with dates of their establishment is given at the end of this chapter. The list goes to 1915: PAM, Department of Education, Inspectors' Reports, 1915, "Ruthenian Group." See also note 55.

[35]Manitoba, Department of Education, *Special Report on Bilingual Schools in Manitoba, 1915.*

[36]PAM, Department of Education Annual Reports, 1901.

[37]See for example, "Had Mother not taught me Ukrainian, I would have been illiterate," Ewanchuk, *Pioneer Profiles,* pp. 101 and 194.

[38]Ewanchuk, *Spruce, Swamp and Stone,* p. 79.

[39]Ibid.; Kaye, *Early Ukrainian Settlements,* pp. 220-222; Swyripa, "Ukrainians and Private Education," pp. 245-246. Later, the Roman Catholic church also funded for the Ukrainian Catholics a minor seminary in Sifton (1912-16), which subsequently became a school for girls.

[40]Kaye, *Early Ukrainian Settlements,* p. 223.

[41]On the founding of the schools at Kolomyja and Olha see Ewanchuk, *Pioneer Profiles,* pp. 27 and 49.

[42]Marunchak, *The Ukrainian Canadians,* p. 115; Ewanchuk, *Spruce, Swamp and Stone,* p. 78. On the other hand, Olha's first teacher, Mr. Drabyniasty, "followed the bilingual approach and taught using the Ukrainian and the English languages." (Ewanchuk, *Pioneer Profiles,* p. 49.)

[43]Ewanchuk, Pioneer Profiles, p. 27; Ewanchuk, *Spruce, Swamp and Stone,* p. 80; on Eaton's Catalogue see also *Canadian Heritage,* 11, (Feb./Mar., 1985): 21.

[44]Inspector E.H. Walker, PAM, Department of Education, *Annual Report,* 1905, p. 50. See also Inspector Young in same, 1906, p. 34.

[45]Ewanchuk, *Spruce, Swamp and Stone,* p. 80.

[46]Inspector E.E. Best, PAM, Department of Education, *Annual Report,* 1905, pp. 28-30.

[47]Inspector T.M. Maguire, PAM, Department of Education, *Annual Report,* 1897, pp. 31-32.

[48]M. Paximadis, *Look Who's Coming: The Wachna Story* (Oshawa: Maracle Press, n.d.), p. 32; see also Ewanchuk, *Spruce, Swamp and Stone,* pp. 81 and 142.

[49]PAM, Department of Education, *Annual Report,* 1903, esp. pp. 50-51; Marunchak, *The Ukrainian Canadians,* pp. 118 and 121; M.R. Lupul, "Ukrainian Language Education in Canada's Public Schools," in Lupul, M.R., ed., *A Heritage in Transition,* pp. 216-217. (We have made a conscious effort here to avoid a discussion of Manitoba party politics, but it has to be noted that all the Department's organizers of schools for Ukrainians and Poles were Conservative party activists.)

[50]*Kanadyiskyi farmer,* July 12, 1907, Feb. 14, 1908, July 13, 1910.

[51]PAM, Department of Education, *Annual Report,* 1904, p. 46; *Kanadyiskyi farmer,* July 12, 1907, Feb. 14, 1908, July 13, 1910.

[52]*Kanadyiskyi farmer,* July 12, 1907, Feb. 14, 1908, July 13, 1910.

[53]PAM, School district Records, Bradbury S.D. no. 1481, Record Book and Ledger; Budka S.D. no. 1717 Ledger; Kupczanko S.D. no. 1434 Record Book 1909-1921 and Ledger; Lukowce S.D. no. 1202 Record Book 1904-1919.

[54]PAM, Lukowce Record Book.

[55]PAM, Department of Education, Education Inspectors Report, 1915, "Ruthenian Group," lists 87 English-Ukrainian school districts, 4 school districts with English-Ukrainian-Polish instruction, and one each with English-Polish and English-Russian. Other authorities give different totals, e.g. 132 in 1914 (Marunchak, *Ukrainian Canadians,* p. 148), and 111 in 1915/16 (Marunchak, *Ukrainian Canadians,*, p. p. 148; and Lupul, "Ukrainian-Language Education", p. 218. For the dates of establishment of school districts see M.B. Perfect, "One Hundred Years in the History of the Rural Schools of Manitoba: Their Formation, Reorganization, and Dissolution (1871-1971)," (M.Ed. thesis, University of Manitoba, 1978), pp. 95-147.

[56]*Kanadyiskyi farmer,* Jan. 8, 1909; see also the recollections of probably the first graduate of the Ruthenian Training School of how he obtained his first job, in the

Beausejour area, W.A. Czumer, *Recollections About the Life of the First Ukrainian Settlers in Canada* (Edmonton: Canadian Institute of Ukrainian Studies, 1981), pp. 65-67.

[57]PAM, Department of Education, *Annual Report* 1912-13, p. 63.

[58]*Annual Report,* 1912-13, p. 78.

[59]Ewanchuk, *Pioneer Profiles,* p. 194.

[60]Ewanchuk, *Spruce, Swamp and Stone,* p. 85.

[61]Interview with Mr. W. Kostiuk, 1984 Oral History Project, Tapes 16/17.

[62]The family structure of the regions from which the Ukrainians came to Canada was in a transitional state at the turn of the century, moving from "extended" to "nuclear." However, the eldest son was still expected to look after his parents until their death; see O. Kravets, *Simeinyi pobut i zvychai ukrainskoho narodu* (Kiev, 1966), p. 19, and H. Muchin, "The Evolution of the Ukrainian Family and its Portrayal in Illya Kiriak's novel *Sons of the Soil,*" (M.A. thesis (in Ukrainian), University of Manitoba, 1978), esp. p. 6.

[63]Interview with Mr. J. Melosky, 1984 Oral History Project, Tapes 12/13/

[64]Ewanchuk, *Pioneer Profiles,* p. 70.

[65]This was an often-heard theme; see for example Kaye, *Early Ukrainian Settlers,* p. 165; Ewanchuk, *Pioneer Profiles,* pp. 58 and 191; and *Kanadyiskyi farmer,* Mar. 6, 1908.

[66]Interview with Mr. V. Chopek, 1984 Oral History Project, Tape 1.

[67]Interview with Mr. W. Kostiuk, 1984 Oral History Project, Tapes 16/17.

[68]*Kanadyiskyi farmer,* May 24, 1906, and May 21, 1909.

[69]*Kanadyiskyi farmer,* Jan. 24, 1907, also June 25, 1909.

[70]These sentiments were contained in an 88 line poem by H. Burak in *Kanadyiskyi farmer,* Mar. 5, 1909.

[71]*Kanadyiskyi farmer,* Jan. 10, 1908.

[72]*Kanadyiskyi farmer,* May 10, 1907.

[73]*Kanadyiskyi farmer,* Mar. 6, 1908 and Sept. 10, 1909.

[74]J. Baderski's report in PAM, Department of Education, *Annual Report,* 1905, p. 53.

[75]*Kanadyiskyi farmer,* July 12, 1907.

[76]*Kanadyiskyi farmer,* Jan. 29, 1909.

[77]*Kanadyiskyi farmer,* July 10, 1908, June 25, July 9, Oct. 1, and Nov. 19, 1909.

[78]PAM, Department of Education, *Annual Report,* 1906, p. 51, 1910, p. 67 and 1911, p. 41; *Kanadyiskyi farmer,* Nov. 15, 1907; *Ukrainskyi holos,* May 10, 1911.

[79]B. Bilash, "Bilingual Public Schools in Manitoba, 1897-1916," (M.Ed. thesis, University of Manitoba, 1960), pp. 66, 72. Interview with Mrs. K. Michalchyshyn, Mar. 8, 1985.

[80]Complaints from "Ukrainets," Sifton, *Kanadyiskyi farmer,* Dec. 29, 1909.

[81]*Kanadyiskyi farmer,* Jan. 18, 1906, Mar. 15 and 22, and Apr. 5, 1907, Jan. 17, Feb. 14 and 21, Mar. 6 and 13, 1908, etc.; *Ukrainskyi holos,* Jan. 4 and Feb. 15, 1911, etc. The trustees of Wheathill decided in 1914 that they wanted a certificated teacher who would "be moral, sober, Greek Catholic"; PAM, Wheat Hill S.D. no. 1650, Minute Book, Dec. 14, 1914.

[82]Lupul, "Ukrainian-Language education," p. 219-221; *Ukrainskyi holos,* Dec. 29, 1915, Jan. 112, 19, and 26, 1916, etc.

[83]Interviews with W. Kostiuk and J. Melosky, 1984 Oral History Project; Ewanchuk, *Pioneer Profiles*, pp. 192-194.

[84]Ewanchuk, *Pioneer Profiles*, p. 39; E. Preston, ed., *Pioneers of the Grandview and District* (Grandview: Pioneer Book Committee, 1976), p. 240. Marunchak, *Ukrainian Canadians*, p. 120, notes that some schools had libraries for the general public.

[85]*Kanadyiskyi farmer*, July 17, 1907, July 10, 1908, Jan. 8, 1909.

[86]*Robochyi narod* Oct. 23, 1912, and Feb. 26, 1913.

[87]*Robochyi narod*, Oct. 30, 1912.

[88]PAM, Department of Education, *Annual Report*, 1908, p. 108; *Kanadyiskyi farmer*, July 17, 1908; *Ukrainskyi holos*, Apr. 19, 1911 (which also reported that the Department of Education had forbidden the use of old-country books).

[89]Interview with Mr. P. Humeniuk, Aug. 11, 1983; see also Marunchak, *Ukrainian Canadians*, p. 144. The Manitoba Department of Education evidently ordered the withdrawal of bilingual primers, at least from some schools, before the ending of bilingualism in 1916, see PAM, RG 19 G1, Education Inspectors Report, 1915, reports by Inspector Peach on Borden school, Inspector Van Dusen on Lakedale school, and Inspector Jones on Franko school. For the introduction of the bilingual primers see *Ukrainskyi holos*, July 30, 1913.

[90]*Kanadyiskyi farmer*, Feb. 14, 1908; *Ukrainskyi holos*, Jan. 25 and Mar. 22, 1911.

[91]P. Gigejczuk in PAM, Department of Education, *Annual Report*, 1910; interview with W. Kostiuk; Marunchak, *Ukrainian Canadians*, p. 122.

[92]PAM, Education Inspectors Report, 1915, reports by Inspectors Peach on Borden school and by Inspector Poulain on Oukraina school.

[93]Interview with P. Humeniuk, Aug. 11, 1983.

[94]PAM, Department of Education, Annual Report, 1904, pp. 34 and 46.

[95]*Annual Report*, 1901, p. 34; Ewanchuk, *Pioneer Profiles*, p. 173.

[96]PAM, Department of Education, *Annual Report*, 1904, p. 46.

[97]*Annual Report*, 1910, p. 67, and 1911, p. 41.

[98]Dauphin-Ochre School Area No. 1 Archives, Dauphin, Kosiw School District no. 1245, School Register.

[99]PAM, Pine Ridge S.D. no. 608, unsigned letter of Oct. 4, 1921, to I. Stratton, official trustee of schools. On the placing of school districts under official trusteeship in 1916 and subsequently, and the resentment this caused in the Ukrainian areas of settlement see M. Ewanchuk, "Development of Education Among the Early Ukrainian Settlers in Manitoba: 1896-1924," in Baran *et. al*, eds., *Jubilee Collection*, pp. 399-400; and Ewanchuk, *Spruce, Swamp and Stone*, pp. 237-238.

[100]*Echoes — Oakburn, Manitoba, 1870-1970* (Oakburn: Centennial Committee, n.d.), p. 54. Poor communications were mentioned often by the school inspectors; see for example PAM, Department of Education Annual Reports, 1906, p. 62 and 1908, p. 108. See also Ewanchuk, *Pioneer Profiles*, p. 108, etc.

[101]Ibid, pp. 52, 58, 70, and 155.

[102]See, for example, ibid, pp. 52, 77, and 96, Ewanchuk, *Spruce, Swamp and Stone*, p. 81 and *passim*.

[103]Ewanchuk, *Pioneer Profiles, passim;* Marunchak, *Ukrainian Canadians*, pp. 223, 233-237, and *passim*.

[104]The Mennonites likewise did not find the schooling arrangements in Manitoba that they had been led to believe; see in particular the bitter remarks of G. Bryce,

"Yes, British Manitoba has been a better foster mother of ignorance than half-civilized Russia had been," cited in J.S. Ewart, ed., *The Manitoba School Question* (Winnipeg, n.p., 1894).

[105]W.J. Sisler, "The Immigrant Child," *Western School Journal,* I, (Apr. 1906): 5.

10

Education Among German Catholic Settlers
in Saskatchewan, 1903-1918: A Reinterpretation*

Clinton O. White

While much has been written on the various groups of people who settled western Canada, very little of it deals with German Roman Catholics. In addition, works on German Catholics, at least when they discuss schools and their use as vehicles to perpetuate the German language and Catholic religion, are generally incomplete, vague or inaccurate. My research on a large German-American, Catholic settlement in central Saskatchewan, St. Peter's Colony, has led to the conviction that extensive research into local development can clear up misconceptions and pave the way for more accurate generalizations about these people and what they did respecting primary education. This chapter is a step in that direction. The method used is as follows. First, comments of the three authors who have most recently dealt with the subject are summarized, and earlier works are analyzed briefly. Second, detailed accounts of some aspects of education that such researchers sought to describe, based on primary sources, are presented. Third, and quite briefly, documentary evidence is supplied, leaving little if any doubt that existing interpretations of German Catholics and their primary educational institutions require revision. The accounts I have constructed and the documentary evidence I have provided are based upon the records of over a hundred local schools, local English and German language newspapers, interviews, a priest's day books, a nun's diary and other resources generally left unexploited. The difference between what has been written and what can be written demonstrates the value of researching easily-accessible, but seldom-explored resources.

In a recent article entitled "German Settlements in Saskatchewan," as well as in his doctoral dissertation completed in 1972, Alan B. Anderson makes such highly questionable statements as the following about the school and language situation in St. Peter's Colony for the years preceding 1918: Benedictine monks, the colony's religious leaders, organized at least fifteen bilingual separate schools. Separate schools in the western part of the colony were of poor quality. Public schools were at times bilingual and Catholic, like separate schools. Teachers, whether religious or lay and regardless of the type of school they taught in, were in the majority of cases Catholic and if not German at least often fluent in German. Beginning in about 1918, this situation was rapidly altered. . . . Among other weaknesses in Anderson's

*This chapter, with minor changes, is reprinted from *Canadian Ethnic Studies*, XVI (1984): 78-95, with permission.

treatment of the subject is his failure to distinguish clearly between separate and private or parochial schools.[1]

Kurt Tischler also dealt with the topic recently both in an article entitled "The Efforts of Germans in Saskatchewan to Retain Their Language before 1914" and in his 1978 Master's thesis. While his works are among the best thus far to appear on the subject, they leave certain questions unanswered and can easily lead to incorrect conclusions. Among those which one might draw are the following: Prior to 1914, there were no disputes among Germans or between them and other residents of the colony or with the government as to the type of school to be established. We cannot know such things as when, where and how many private or separate schools existed in St. Peter's Colony. That being the case, it is highly improbable that we can learn who taught in such schools, what they taught, or when each school ceased to operate. Nonetheless, one is expected to believe that before World War I teachers in all three types of schools, public, private and separate, were generally Catholic and of German background.[2]

A third recent work touched on the subject only peripherally. But it is worth citing because it illustrates the kinds of comments to which a lack of accurate works on German Catholics and their schools can lead. In "Canadianization Through the Schools of the Prairie Provinces before World War I: The Attitudes and Aims of the English Speaking Majority," Marilyn J. Barber states:

> German Catholics coming from the United States who spoke English as well as German were able to establish private Roman Catholic bilingual schools in their Saskatchewan Colonies and escape the assimilating force of the public school without attracting attention of educational authorities or from the public until the First World War.[3]

This article would have us believe apparently that prior to at least 1915, no children of St. Peter's Colony German Catholics attended public or separate schools and that all teachers were bilingual in English and German. Moreover, no one in the province protested the situation. Such was scarcely the case.

Other writings on the subject of schools in St. Peter's Colony were all, with one exception, written earlier. Of these it can be said that they generally deal only briefly with the topic, contain inaccurate or misleading statements, are written from a critical or defensive standpoint, or fail to take into account the totality of the primary school situation.

The first two works to discuss the subject dealt with only part of the total school picture and with that portion as it existed in the colony in about 1915. In addition, the emotional state of the authors is evident in both accounts: one sought to attack private schools and the other to defend them.[4] Shortly thereafter, two other writers produced works on Saskatchewan schools. They have since been occasionally cited as authorities on education in German Catholic areas, but neither had anything specific to say on that matter.[5] At about the same time, a survey of education in the province was completed for the government. Its author dealt with the colony's schools in a single page; and while he described the private school situation as it existed in 1917 quite accurately, he failed to mention a very critical fact about the settlers — their American background.[6] Their experience in the United States and widespread knowledge of English certainly influenced their actions with respect to primary education. That writer's account of schools in St. Peter's Colony appears to have been the major, and perhaps the sole, source examined by a subsequent researcher when he wrote on the subject over forty years later.[7]

In the 1930s no less than five works made reference to the school system within St. Peter's. Two of these in particular merit examination by scholars interested in the subject. However, both are weak on the origin of schools and early educational developments in the colony. For example, one makes no mention of separate schools and the other conveys the impression that teachers in the colony were generally fluent in German.[8] The other three works, while reasonably accurate in content, touch upon the subject only briefly and are not primarily concerned with early developments.[9]

Between 1940 and 1970 only one other work not already mentioned appeared in print. It is useful in that it contains a number of references to specific schools: when they were established, where they were located, who taught in them, and so forth. And it was written by a person deeply involved with private schools from the beginning. However, it does not present an overview of primary education.[10]

To fulfill the purpose of this chapter, as good a place as any to begin a discussion of schools in St. Peter's Colony is with the Roman Catholic separate schools. Tischler suggested that their number could not be known. Anderson, on the other hand, said there were fifteen founded by Benedictines and operated on a bilingual basis. The truth of the matter is that there were only two, neither of which was bilingual and both of which were essentially established by laymen. One was set up at Humboldt in 1907 and the other at Watson in 1910. Let us examine the one at Humboldt first. But it should be stated at once that its birth cannot be adequately described without reference to certain private or public schools which preceded it.

The first school to serve German Catholics in the Humboldt district was a private school. In 1903, the year settlement got underway, Gottlieb Schaeffer opened a store about four miles west of what became Humboldt. At about the same time, the Benedictine Fathers chose that site for a mission named St. Bernard's.[11] In the summer of 1904, one of Schaeffer's daughters taught school there in a tent. Perhaps she opened a temporary school at the behest of Father Chrysostom Hoffman, who had charge of the mission.[12] However, about all that can be really said of it is that it was set up by German Catholics, was private, and apparently ran for only one term. Later in 1904, the railway passed through the district and Humboldt began to take shape. Schaeffer moved his store to the new community,[13] and St. Bernard's mission was soon abandoned.

By the summer of 1905 a school was needed in the Humboldt area, a number of children having had no schooling for two years. In July a group of rural residents, all Roman Catholics and probably all German, petitioned the government to set up a "Country Public School" which village children could also attend. Not long afterwards, village people, the majority Protestant but with Catholics involved in the leadership, petitioned for establishment of a public school in Humboldt. After some study, the government approved the second request. This brought objections from the first group, who protested that farmers could not afford the higher village school tax. Urban residents were prepared to compromise and delete part, but not all, of the rural area from their district; some farmers wanted to remain within it. But educational authorities, probably recognizing the urgent need for a school, advised all parties to proceed with the district as approved.[14] Up to this point one can detect no friction of a religious or ethnic nature among the different parties involved. But such tensions would soon arise and intensify.

The government having approved creation of the Humboldt Public School District, ratepayers could now vote on the matter. This they did, casting sixty affirmative and eight negative ballots. The opponents were apparently rural Germans.[15] Next came the election of school trustees. Three Protestants and four German Catholics were nominated. One suspects that there was an understanding that both Protestants and Catholics would be elected. But voting closely followed religious lines. Of the seventy-six persons taking part, only three did not vote uniformly for either three Protestant or three Catholic candidates. Since Protestant outnumbered Catholic ratepayers by approximately forty-two to thirty-eight, the result was an all-Protestant board.[16] Needless to say, Humboldt Catholics were upset and promptly dissociated themselves from the public school.

Four days after the election of trustees, some of the same German Catholics who had worked very hard to create the public school district petitioned the government for the establishment of a separate school.[17] The request was eventually granted, but before it was, just about everything that could go wrong went wrong.[18] This series of unfortunate developments meant that a school for Humboldt Catholic children, German as well as a few others, was not ready as quickly as originally expected. To deal with the situation as best he could, the local Benedictine priest, Father Rudolph Palm, ran a temporary Catholic private school for two to three months. Two former students state that it was conducted mainly in German.[19] Except for Miss Schaeffer's school, this appears to have been the only instance when German served as a language of instruction rather than merely a subject of study in a Humboldt school.[20]

The origin of the Watson Roman Catholic separate school was similar to, yet different from the one at Humboldt. At Watson in July 1905, a group of settlers, many of them German and a larger number Catholic, successfully petitioned the government to establish a public school. Some months later, they elected trustees, all Catholic and two of them also German.[21] Before a school was opened, however, a second group of people, mainly villagers, petitioned to have the district's boundaries changed. Membership in the two groups overlapped, but the second consisted mainly of non-German, Protestant businessmen.[22] Their request was granted. Consequently, in the spring of 1906 a meeting to approve the altered district was held, and new trustees were elected. In this election, two of the original trustees ran but were defeated.[23] The successful candidates included a German Catholic and two Protestants. The change of trustees produced a split within the community, but significantly not all Catholics were on one side and all Protestants on the other. Nor were all Germans and non-Germans arrayed against each other.

Two interpretations of the split exist. One appeared in the Benedictines' German-language newspaper, the *Bote*. Here a Watson correspondent alleged that Watson Protestant businessmen unlawfully succeeded in manipulating German settlers and electing a Protestant-dominated board. German Catholics, it was said, had not come to the colony to establish non-religious schools. And they were urged to stand up for their rights and demand a separate school as their co-religionists had done at Humboldt.[24] Such action, however, was legally impossible since Catholics constituted a majority of ratepayers.[25]

The second interpretation appears more reasonable. It was provided by the new trustees and signed by thirty-one ratepayers, including some German Catholics. It implied that the dispute was of the sour grapes variety. The letter stated that after the new election the unsuccessful candidates set about trying to block creation of the public school by refusing to sign certain papers. Those candidates also began calling for a separate school. "Had the election resulted in favour of the other three candidates nominated, these committeemen would then no doubt have been ready to sign the papers."[26] There was no reference in the document to differences of a religious or ethnic nature.

One of the most interesting aspects of the whole affair is a statement by the *Bote's* Watson correspondent about Watson Catholics, who formed the majority in the district and under the School Act could demand religious instruction in the public school between 3:30 and 4:00 p.m. He stated that they were willing to tolerate the fact that religious instruction would not be given in the school during school hours but rather would be permitted only twice a week in the school after classes ended.[27]

After the 1906 dispute simmered down, nothing seems to have been said of a separate school for over three years. Then late in 1909, Watson Catholics returned to the subject. Why the change since they do not appear to have complained about the public school during the interval?[28] The answer might be that having become a minority in the district and, consequently, legally entitled to a separate school, they simply decided to set one up.[29] They may also have been urged to do so by their religious leaders. But such an explanation may be entirely erroneous. The reason for their decision may lie wholly in local developments. To appreciate this possibility, one must be aware of two things: the nature of the Watson Catholic community and who headed the movement for a separate school.

Watson Catholics consisted not only of German-Americans but also of Irish and other elements.[30] And two of the three people taking the lead to create the separate school were of Canadian background.[31] With those two facts in mind, consider the following events. In December 1909, the Watson branch of the Loyal Orange Lodge was founded. Among its charter members was William Allnatt.[32] Two weeks later Watson Catholics completed their petition for a separate school. In March 1910, Mary Palmer, the public school teacher for the past two years, married William Allnatt.[33]

That the Allnatt-Palmer wedding was to take place was probably common knowledge in Watson at the time the Orange Lodge was founded. Forget about German-American Catholics, and simply ask yourself this. How would Canadian Catholics, Irish, German or others, view the prospect of their children being taught by the wife of a prominent local Orangeman? Recalling the activities of the Orange Order in the past twenty years, they would not relish it. And they would realize that Catholics could not by themselves change teachers since they did not control the school board.[34] The only means by which they could assure themselves an acceptable teacher was to establish a separate school.

Having examined the origins of the colony's separate schools, as well as public and private schools associated with them, one can draw a number of conclusions, some of which vary considerably from the stereotypes we often encounter. For example, German Catholics frequently did not set up bilingual schools. They were at times prepared to compromise on the matter of religious instruction. They did not always agree among themselves on the type of school to set up. At times they created temporary private schools which they dissolved when the schools had served their purpose. They evidently did not hesitate to create government-regulated public schools and were prepared to cooperate with Protestants in doing so. When they resorted to establishing separate schools, they may have been responding more to Protestant actions than to their own desires.[35] Other generalizations could also be drawn, but let us confine ourselves to a single additional one. That conclusion is one I drew in a 1978 article, namely, "that the types of primary educational facilities appearing in the colony were more the product of evolving circumstances than preconceived plans."[36] Subsequent research has obliged me to modify that conclusion only slightly.

What was said in that earlier article will not be repeated here except to summarize portions such as those which contradict statements made by authors cited earlier. Its theme was that a 1916 Anglo-Protestant attack on German Catholic private schools in St. Peter's colony was based heavily on misinformation. It discussed in some detail the origins of certain private schools, and in a more cursory fashion those of others.[37] The article also demonstrated that in more than one instance, German Catholics argued among themselves over schools. In St. Henry's Public School District, for example, a lengthy, bitter debate erupted over substituting a private for a public school. The school was first private, then public, then private again. It showed as well that at about the same time, German Catholics at Bruno quarrelled not only among themselves over schools, but also with Protestants and the government. After setting up a private school, they were forced by authorities to establish a public one too. According to Tischler and Barber, such clashes did not occur in the pre-war years.

Among other things dealt with in the article were the numbers of each type of school set up during the years before World War I. According to Barber, all schools were bilingual, Catholic and private. According to Tischler, we cannot know how many there were of certain types. Anderson's statements on the subject, by the way, are confusing to say the least. Numbers of schools are also worth examining since other writers at times make statements that are potentially misleading. Lehmann, for example, asserts that German Catholics set up "large numbers of private schools."[38] Before adjectives such as "large" or "many" are used, some work on quantification should be done. Table 1 represents such an attempt.

It should perhaps be noted, that when turning to numbers of schools, this chapter changes its approach. Rather than providing further case studies of a specific nature from which generalizations may be made, it deals with matters of a broader type and makes limited use of statistics. The change in procedure, when supplemented with other information, will provide an overall picture of primary education in the colony. It will also point out that there is a variety of relatively unexploited sources available to scholars who wish to generalize on this or similar subjects.

Table 1 admittedly has flaws and will be refined by future research. However, certain tentative conclusions may be drawn from it. While the first school erected by German Catholics was a private one — referred to by one of their number as a "temporary school"[39] — they established only approximately eighteen by 1915. Fully half of them appeared in a three-year period, 1906 through 1908. About 20 percent of all private schools ever set up operated for only brief intervals, and another 20 percent closed during the war years. That the remaining 60 percent disappeared during the decade 1923-1932 raises questions about Alan Anderson's assertion that the war had a profound effect upon them.

While German Catholics were establishing private schools, the table indicates that they were setting up even larger numbers of public schools. By 1907 they had more public than private schools in operation and by World War I, over three times as many: fifty to fourteen. In the early years, German Catholics appear to have had difficulty making their public schools work. The reasons for this relate to teachers, living accommodations and finances. And, may I add, those same difficulties explain, at least in part, the rapid increase in the number of private schools between 1906 and 1908. The table also shows that in thirty years, German settlers closed only one public school in favour of a private one and that they made very little use of the separate school.

Table 1
Schools in the German Catholic Portions of St. Peter's Colony, 1903-1933

Year	Private Schools			Public Schools			Separate Schools	
	Set up	Closed	Operating	Set up	Closed	Operating	Set Up	Operating
1903	1		1					
1904	2 (3)		3	9		2		
1905	1 (4)		4	7 (16)		2		
1906	2 (6)		6	9 (25)		4		
1907	4 (10)	1	9	1 (26)		13	1	1
1908	5 (15)	1	13	7 (33)	1	21		
1909		1	12	11 (44)		28		
1910	2 (17)		14	5 (49)		37	1	2
1911			14			41		
1912			14			42		
1913			14	4 (53)		43		
1914	1 (18)	1	14	5 (58)		50		
1915		2	12	4 (62)		55		
1916	1 (19)		13			58		
1917		1	12	3 (65)		59		
1918		1	11	1 (66)		61		
1919			11	1 (67)		63		
1920			11	1 (68)		63		
1921			11			64		
1922	1 (20)		12			65		
1923		1	11			65		
1924		1	10	1 (69)		66		
1925			10	1 (70)		66		
1926			10	2 (72)		66		
1927		1	9	1 (73)		69		
1928		3	6	2 (75)		71		
1929		1	5			72		
1930		3	2	1 (76)		73		
1931			2	1 (77)		75		
1932		2	0			75		
1933			0			77		

Note: the Private School column does not include a few very temporary ones such as that at Schaeffer's store. It also excludes a longer- lived one, St. Veronica, the existence of which I only recently confirmed. By 1933 there were in the confines of the colony approximately 115 public schools. The 77 included in the table are those where significant numbers of German Catholics resided.

Sources: Public, Separate and Private School files of D of E, A.S. Information on private schools was also obtained from such sources as newspapers, parish records, Father Chrysostom's day books, and interviews.

All three recent authors cited earlier err directly or by implication regarding what was taught in the various schools and by whom. Space does not permit a lengthy discussion of subjects taught, but a general impression can be supplied in a few words. Of the private schools, Abbot Bruno Doerfler[40] had this to say in 1916. The German Catholic ideal was that

> children should become true bilingualists in the best sense of the word. . . . In them [the private schools] everything was taught which is taught in the rural government schools. Furthermore, the pupils learnt an additional language. . . .[41]

The bulk of the evidence supports his claim. However, it should be added that children were also taught catechism and Bible History and that two or three schools northwest of Humboldt and another in the Bremen area may at times have tended more toward German than bilingual instruction.[42]

In the beginning, teachers in these schools were generally colonists, German-American males.[43] By 1906, females appeared and soon became an overwhelming majority.[44] Some of these women were Canadian[45] but most often were recruited in the United States;[46] some settled permanently in the colony, while others migrated annually from the U.S.[47] Approximately a decade after settlement began, children of the colonists began appearing as teachers in the private schools.[48] All these teachers seem to have been German and were no doubt fluent in German.[49]

We can assume that public schools generally followed the curriculum laid down by the Department of Education. Only scattered evidence to the contrary has so far turned up. And not only were their teachers certified by the department, but their students were examined periodically by departmental inspectors. Of course, catechism was often also taught. But were the children, as scholars have generally concluded, frequently instructed in both English and German? One approach to answering that question is to determine who their teachers were. Here are three examples going back as far as records appear to exist. St. Bernard's Public School, 1906-1918: James O'Brien, Harriet Murphy, Lawrence Boyle, James Jordan, May Ryan, William McGinn, V. LeVandier, Margaret Quinn, Michael Connors, Francis McGarry, Emmett Crough and Michael Pitzel. St. Benedict Public, 1908-1918: Alphonsus Lannan, Mrs. John Ryan, W. O'Meara, Mary O'Callaghan and Margery Bissett. St. James Public, 1909-1918: W.S. McLennan, Katherine Curtin, Rosalie Howell, Sara Scullin, Katie O'Byrn, Lena Gilhooly, Doris St. Ruth, Minnie Leslie, Anna Hinz and Elizabeth Hinz.[50]

One need not be an expert on names to recognize many of these as Irish, probably originating in eastern Canada or the British Isles. So far only a small start has been made in determining where they were born or where they obtained their first teaching certificates. Of the seven individuals in the above group about whom we have information, two possessed certificates from Prince Edward Island, one from Nova Scotia, one from Ontario, two from Ireland,

and one from Saskatchewan, that person having been born at Portage, Manitoba.[51] Research shows only three of the group to have been German: Pitzel who taught in 1918 and the Hinzs who taught from 1916 to 1918. Further evidence demonstrates that few, perhaps even none, of the others were fluent in German.

The three foregoing examples might be called vertical samples of teachers selected from a large number of school districts which contained German Catholic settlers. Let us examine what might be called a horizontal sample. In 1914, there were fifty public schools operating among St. Peter's Colony German Catholics. According to Anderson and Tischler, very often their teachers were German or fluent in German. But what are the facts? During 1914, fifty-eight people taught in forty-eight of these schools.[52] Only four are definitely known to have been German.[53] Many of the remaining fifty-four could have been participants in a St. Patrick's Day parade. Twenty-one were probably of Irish origin[54] and at least another five possibly also Irish.[55] The remainder appear to have been English or Scottish, except for about five who had either French or Scandinavian names.

From the beginning of St. Peter's Colony, then, the vast majority of public school teachers traced their roots to the British Isles. That the greater portion of them were probably Catholic can be demonstrated. But that any significant number of them were fluent in German is extremely doubtful. Consequently, we may conclude that with regard to perpetuating the German language prior to or during World War I, the public school had a negative rather than a positive effect in St. Peter's Colony. Moreover, examination of the list of teachers present refutes the belief expressed by Tischler and others that unilingual English-speaking teachers avoided non-English districts. This belief simply falls apart when applied to St. Peter's Colony.

Throughout this chapter, I have confined myself to pointing out and seeking to correct flaws in literature relating to the German Catholics of St. Peter's Colony. What has emerged is a more complex school situation than that portrayed in writings referred to at the beginning. Those accounts, to a greater or lesser degree, stressed uniformity, with Barber suggesting existence of a monolithic educational structure. I have shown the educational system to have been in essence pluralistic. Three types of schools were in use: two separate, a larger number private, but the vast majority public. These numbers suggest that while some children attended Catholic private schools, most attended state-regulated, public or separate institutions. The teachers in the schools differed. In private schools, they were mainly German-American Catholic lay people or their children. In the public and separate schools they were usually Canadians who had originated in the British Isles.

What children received in the way of primary education also varied. Soon after the colony was founded, they were, with few exceptions, evidently taught the curriculum established by provincial authorities. Most children also appear to have received religious instruction, but there were wide variations. A minority obtained a substantial amount, the majority anywhere from none to half an hour a day. Finally, bilingual instruction was not very common. While children in private schools received at least half their lessons in German, public school teachers with few exceptions were not fluent in that language. Is it any wonder that when critics attacked the colony's schools during the war years, Premier Scott spoke out in their defence?[56]

How does one account for the rise of the pluralistic system I have described? Certainly not by restricting research to wartime accounts by critics of German Catholics and their schools, nor by relying largely on those on the other side who spoke broadly on what they referred to as the ideals of the settlers. Rather, we must discover what was occurring from the beginning at the grass-roots level. When we direct our search there, a variety of reasons is soon uncovered, three of which particularly stand out. The first matter of importance is the circumstances in which German Catholics found themselves upon settling St. Peter's Colony and how they responded to those circumstances.

The colony was scarcely a year old when Benedictines began publishing their German-language newspaper. In the first issue, they pointed out that settlement had reached the stage at which schools could be considered. The writer explained existing school laws and discussed establishment of schools. He stated that most settlers had come to the colony so that their children might obtain a good religious upbringing, something best accomplished in parochial schools. However, he continued, the creation of such schools was impossible for three reasons: the sparse population in some districts, the inability of settlers to bear all costs, and a lack of teachers. Given these conditions, settlers would have no choice but to set up "temporary public schools." The government would bear part of the cost of such schools. In them, religious instruction could be given during the last half-hour of each day. And, while the language of instruction was English, German could also be taught. Finally, the writer stated, the government would be requested to place German on an equal footing with English, a change which would allow for bilingual education.[57]

About five months later, the *Bote* took up the teacher question. Public schools teachers would have to be obtained mainly from Ontario and the eastern provinces, and among them people who could give lessons in German were simply not to be found. Raising money to pay a certified teacher would be difficult. It would likewise be difficult to provide lodgings for teachers, because most settlers still lived in log cabins. In view of such circumstances, the best approach to obtaining schools "in the coming year" would be for settlers to set up private ones and hire their own teachers. The paper was of the opinion that in every district there lived settlers with enough knowledge to teach. Or at the very least, there were people in every district who could teach the important things, as well as German and the German Catechism. The government might grant such people temporary or emergency certificates.[58]

These two statements by the Benedictine Fathers in their newspaper help us understand subsequent developments with regard to schools. But they are particularly important in two ways. First, they amounted to the Benedictines' giving their blessing not only to private or parochial schools but to public schools, at least on a temporary basis. Second, taken together, they laid out an extremely difficult course for settlers to follow. Colonists were advised to set up temporary private schools, which would be succeeded by temporary public schools, which, teachers being available, could be converted at a later date to bilingual private or parochial schools. While the first two steps were easy, the third was not, and settlers accomplished it only once. The reasons for there being only one such reconversion, however, lay only partly in the difficulty. It also related to the settlers themselves. They did not take the step because many of them simply did not want to.

The second very important matter to note is that St. Peter's Colony German Catholics were not all of one mind when it came to teaching and using the German language.

The discussion of schools in the first issue of the *Bote* touched upon the question of how they should be named. It stated that German Mennonites and French-Canadian Catholics avoided English names and that German Catholics should do likewise. However, the colonists were different. "Unfortunately," said the *Bote,* "there are many people in our colony who, because of their long stay in the United States, have lost their German heart and spirit, those, who, when they speak with the English try to hide their German nationality."[59] Would these "many people" insist upon instruction in German in their schools? Would they seek hard and long for German speaking teachers? Would they be willing to finance bilingual private schools which after a time became more costly to operate than public schools? Would they do battle with the government to have German given the same status as English? That they would is highly unlikely.

The third important matter to note is that not only did the colony's German Catholics differ in their views about the importance of German, they also had different ideas as to how much religious instruction was required for a child to obtain a proper Catholic upbringing. Nowhere was this better illustrated than when Father Chrysostom led the losing battle to maintain St. Bruno's parochial school as Bruno's one and only school. By the way, there were at the time about three Protestant families in the area. In his day books and in a letter, he recorded the following statements:
First:

> Three years ago in Sept. [1906] against the wishes of the majority in this district but with the approval of the majority in the parish, I opened the parochial school here. . . .[60]

Second:

> Mr. Leinsen told me that not so very long ago some of my (?) friends were trying to get up a petition to have me removed.[61]

And third:

> Once there is a public school here it will mean no end of trouble for the pastor to keep certain parents from sending their children to it. Many parents do not understand that if a child's religious instruction should amount to anything, it must enter into the child's flesh and blood. It can do that only when all the text books are Catholic and the teacher is Catholic and the children are taught to pray.
>
> Now the public school in Sask. is just a little bit better than in the States. Here where the majority of the ratepayers demand it, catechism may be taught from half past three till four. . . . It's this half hour of religion that causes many to favour the public school and makes it difficult to maintain parochial schools.[62]

Father Chrysostom's comments not only attest to the division among German Catholics on the subject of religious instruction, they also do much to explain it. Coming from the United States where such instruction was not permitted in public schools to a jurisdiction where it was, and no doubt observing that children of other national groups passed through its public school system and grew up as Catholics, it was easy for many to believe that a half-hour of religious teaching must be enough. Such a belief was probably also promoted by the existence of established channels through which Catholic teachers might be obtained, and by the fact that the provincial government gave financial aid to public, but not to private schools.

It is evident that historians and others who have described primary education in St. Peter's Colony have almost uniformly failed to consider certain very important matters: the circumstances of settlement, the composition of the local teaching population, and the views of the settlers on the use of the German language and on religious instruction. Because of these factors, German Catholics set up very few separate, many times more public and a limited number of private schools, the latter numbering approximately one per parish and being established particularly when living accommodations were primitive and teachers hard to come by. For some of the same reasons, by World War I they had established fully three times as many unilingual as bilingual schools. And while there is no reason to doubt but that the majority of teachers in the colony were Catholic, it would be stretching the truth to say that more than a quarter of all schools could be classed as Catholic. All in all, St. Peter's colony German Catholics set up a pluralistic primary educational system which provided an education, in the vast majority of cases, little different from that available elsewhere in the province. That they generally ran their schools as well as or better than people of other ethnic backgrounds can also be demonstrated. However, a word of caution is in order. The findings presented in this chapter may hold true only for St. Peter's Colony. No other group of German Catholic settlers originated as exclusively in the United States or had on average lived there as long. These colonists consequently had a better knowledge of English and were, upon arrival in Canada, more familiar with North American educational institutions and practices than other German Catholic settlers.

Notes

[1] Martin L. Kovacs, ed., *Roots and Realities among Eastern and Central Europeans* (Edmonton: Central and East European Studies Assoc. of Canada, 1983), pp. 175-221; Anderson, "Assimilation in Bloc Settlements of North-Central Saskatchewan, A Comparative Study of Identity Change Among Seven Ethno-Religious Groups in a Canadian Prairie Province," (Ph.D. thesis, Univ. of Saskatchewan, 1972). Since I will not discuss Anderson's point about the quality of separate schools directly, I should point out here that there were none in the western part of the colony.

[2] Kurt Tischler, "The Efforts of Germans in Saskatchewan to Retain Their Language Before 1914," in *German Canadian Yearbook* (Toronto, 1981), IV, pp. 42-61. Tischler, ':The German Canadians in Saskatchewan with Particular Reference to the Language Problem 1900-1930," (M.A. thesis, Univ. of Saskatchewan, 1978).

[3] Marilyn J. Barber, "Canadianization Through the Schools of the Prairie Provinces before World War I: The Attitudes and Issues of the English Speaking Majority," in Martin L. Kovacs, ed., *Ethnic Canadians, Culture and Education* (Regina: Canadian Plains Research Centre, 1978), p. 284.

[4] Rev. E.H. Oliver, *The Country School in Non-English Speaking Communities in Saskatchewan* (Saskatoon: Saturday Press and Prairie Farm, n.d.), and Rev. Bruno Doerfler, *German Schools in the Humboldt District* (Muenster: n.p., 1916). The latter can be located in Parochial School Folder, St. Peter's Abbey Archives, Muenster, hereafter cited as SPAA.

[5] C.B. Sissons, *Bilingual Schools in Canada* (Toronto: J.M. Dent and Sons, 1917), and J.T.M. Anderson, *The Education of the New Canadian* (Toronto: J.M. Dent and Sons, 1918).

[6] Harold W. Foght, *A Survey of Education in the Province of Saskatchewan, Canada* (Regina: King's Printer, 1918).

[7] Morley P. Toombs, "The Control and Support of Public Education in Rupert's Land and the North-West Territories to 1905 and in Saskatchewan to 1960," (Ph.D. thesis, Univ. of Minnesota, 1960).

[8] Albert Moellmann, "The Germans in Canada: Occupational and Social Adjustments of German Immigrants in Canada," (M.A. thesis, McGill Univ., 1934), and Heinz Lehmann, *Das Deutschtum im Westkanada* (Berlin: Junker und Dunnhaupt Verlag, 1939), in translation to English by Gerhard P. Bassler, Memorial Univ. St. John, Nfld., Ch. X. (Copy located at the Canadian Plains Research Centre, Regina).

[9] Robert England, *The Colonization of Western Canada* (London: P.S. King and Sons Ltd., 1936); C.A. Dawson, *Group Settlement: Ethnic Communities in Western Canada* (Toronto: Macmillan Co., 1936), and C.A. Dawson and Eva R. Younge, *Pioneering in the Prairie Provinces: the Social Side of the Settlement Process* (Toronto: Macmillan Co., 1940).

[10]Rev. Peter Windschiegl, *Fifty Golden Years 1903-1953* (Muenster: St. Peter's Press, 1954).

[11]Humboldt Journal, *The Best of Humboldt* (Humboldt: Humboldt Publishing Co., 1982), p. 3.

[12]*St. Peters Bote* (Muenster), Sept. 10, 1919, see column "Fifteen Years Ago." Father Chrysostom appears to have been the most active Benedictine where establishing parochial schools was concerned. See his Day Books, SPAA.

[13]*The Best of Humboldt*, p. 4.

[14]See documents July 3, 1905 to Mar. 1, 1906, Department of Education, hereafter D of E, Public Schools, file No. 1529, Saskatchewan Archives Board, hereafter SAB.

[15]Poll book, Mar. 22, 1906, ibid.

[16]Minutes of First School Meeting, Mar. 22, 1906, ibid.

[17]F. Heidgerken to Commissioner of Education, Mar. 26, 1906, D of E, Roman Catholic Separate Schools hereafter RCSS, file No. 15, SAB.

[18]Documents got lost in the mail. Departmental officials overlooked a promise they had made to act on a certain matter by a specific date. For a time Catholics were refused permission to open their school in a building used as the Catholic Church, the department overlooking the fact that Protestants were using the Presbyterian Church. And a Protestant outbid Catholics for a piece of land upon which they planned to construct their school. See ibid., 1906-1907. Also see Calder Papers, p. 3197, SAB, and *St. Peters Bote*, Mar. 7, 1908, p. 8.

[19]Interviews with George Heidgerken and Mrs. Agnes Bauer (nee Flory), Humboldt, Apr. 29, 1978.

[20]German was of course used at least some of the time in the separate school during the last half-hour of the day when catechism was taught.

[21]Petition for Formation, July 31, 1905, and Minutes of First School Meeting and Poll Book, Nov. 15, 1905, D of E, Public Schools, 1604, SAB. Trustees elected were Thomas J. Robinson, Joseph Hufnagel and Frank Vossen Jr. Robinson was an Irish Catholic, with perhaps a touch of Scottish in his background. He was born at Prescott, Ontario, but moved to Manitoba where he married a Westburn, Manitoba girl, Anna Elizabeth Shannon, on Mar. 7, 1893. He moved from there to Watson in 1905. See Robinson obituary, *Watson Witness* (Watson), Dec. 23, 1932. Also interviews with Mr. and Mrs. Herb Vossen, Watson, and with J.A. (Bert) Robinson (son of Thomas), Saskatoon, Sept. 13, 1983. The other trustees were German American Catholics.

[22]Twelve individuals to Department of Education, Jan. 4, 1906, D of E, Public Schools, 1604, SAB.

[23]Multiple Individuals to Commissioner of Education, Apr. 28, 1906, ibid.

[24]*St. Peters Bote*, Apr. 5, 1906, p. 5.

[25]When the first steps were taken to set up the public school district, there were twenty-five Catholic and eleven Protestant ratepayers. See Petition for Formation, July 31, 1905, D of E, Public Schools, 1604, SAB.

[26]Multiple individuals to Commissioner of Education, Apr. 28, 1906, ibid.

[27]*St. Peters Bote*, Apr. 5, 1906. The sentence has been designed to convey as nearly as possibly precisely what was said. The German passage reads: "die Katholiken erklärt hatten, dass sie bereit seien zuzugeben, dass während der Schulstunden kein Religiousunterricht erteilt werde, sondern nur zweimal in der Woche der Priester

nach der Schule Religious; unterricht erteilen durfe." I am indebted to Veronica Garland, graduate student at the Univ. of Regina, for her assistance in researching and above all for translating items appearing in the *Bote,* 1904 through 1918.

[28]Examination of Department of Education records, the *Watson Witness,* the *Humboldt Journal* and the *St. Peters Bote* has so far turned up no criticism. Meanwhile, it is interesting to note that Watson Catholic children along with others went to school in the local Presbyterian church until the public school building was ready for use. Vossen interviews.

[29]Petition for Formation, Jan. 4, 1910, D of E, RCSS, 19. By late 1909 there were thirty-four Protestant and twenty-seven Catholic ratepayers.

[30]Included were such names as Peter Sullivan, Mayme Sheridan, J.H. Wilkes and Thomas J. Robinson. Minutes of First School Meeting and Poll Book, Mar. 11, 1910, ibid. Two years earlier it had been stated that most people in the area were from the U.S., some of German, Scandinavian and French origin. Others were from Ontario, Quebec and the British Isles. See *Watson Witness,* Sept. 13, 1907.

[31]The three people signing the Petition for Formation, Dec. 17, 1909, D of E, RCSS, 19, SAB, were Thomas J. Robinson, an Irish Catholic; John Bettin, a German American Catholic colonist; and J.C. (Jake) Guittard, a German Canadian Catholic. Guittard came to Watson from Ontario, perhaps from the vicinity of Nevstadt or Mildmay. In any case, one of his neices, a Merkle, was born at Nevstadt and married Frank Vossen Jr., an early settler at Watson. See obituary, *Watson Witness,* Sept. 4, 1916. On the other hand, his father died at Mildmay, Ontario in 1903. See his mother's obituary, ibid. Feb. 24, 1922. Such data suggests that he resided in Ontario for some time.

[32]*Watson Witness,* Dec. 3, 1909.

[33]Ibid., Apr. 1, 1910.

[34]Mrs. Allnatt reopened the public school in 1910 and taught for a short time. See ibid., Aug. 18, 1910.

[35]These conclusions should be treated as examples of generalizations which might be made following a partial examination of the six schools referred to. Examination of a larger sample would result in qualification of some of them. Approximately 140 schools of all types were set up in the colony between 1903 and 1932.

[36]Clinton O. White, "Language, Religion, Schools and Politics among German American, Roman Catholic Settlers in St. Peter's Colony, Saskatchewan, 1903-1916," *Study Sessions,* Canadian Catholic Historical Assoc., 45, 1978, p. 91.

[37]Those discussed in most detail are St. Bruno's at Bruno and St. Angela's in St. Henry's Public School District. Reference is also made to organizing St. Joseph's at Fulda, St. Boniface at Leofeld and St. Maurus at Dana. Dates when others were set up are provided, and who organized private schools and why they did so are discussed.

[38]*Das Deutschtum im Westkanada,* Bassler translation, Ch. X, p. 12.

[39]Joseph Hanacek to Deputy Commissioner of Education, July 19, 1904, D of E, Public Schools, 935, SAB.

[40]By 1916 the Vatican had designated St. Peter's Colony an abbacy. That year Father Bruno was Abbot, the spiritual leader of Catholics, within its confines.

[41]*German Schools in the Humboldt District.*

[42]St. Joseph's at Fulda, St. John's at Willmont and St. Mary's at Bremen.

[43]Of the four schools established by 1905 the individuals known to have taught in them are: St. Boniface, 1903, Peter Schwinghammer; St. Peter's, 1904 and 1905,

Father John Balfrey; St. Joseph's, 1904 and 1905, Henry Kalthoff; and St. Angela's, 1905, Mr. F.X. Strueby.

⁴⁴A selective survey of the *St. Peters Bote* for the years 1906 to 1918 shows females appearing in parochial schools in 1906: Clara Mayer and a Miss Röder. The numbers of males and females respectively identified for each of the remaining years were: 1907, three and four; 1908, five and four; 1909, two and five; 1910, four and six; 1911, three and five; 1912, one and five; 1913, zero and five; 1914, zero and three; 1915, zero and six; 1916, zero and six; 1917, zero and seven; 1918, two (including a priest in an emergency situation) and three. Not included in these figures are any Ursuline nuns who began teaching in private schools in 1913.

⁴⁵For example, Winnie Krammer, daughter of a Regina separate school principal.

⁴⁶The survey mentioned in note 44 revealed fifteen teachers with their places of origin shown: Emma Johanning, Laura Meyer and Celestine Meyer, Missouri; Constantia Wagner, John Görgen, Rosa Zimmeth, Caroline Deustermann, Katharina Diethelm, Julia Diethelm, Karl Warfenberg, Hilda Schwarz, Sofia Kranz and Anna Schwegmann, Minnesota; Agnes Litshauer and Mary Pastors, Wisconsin. Others appearing in the sample are known to the author as coming to the colony from the U.S. to teach.

⁴⁷At least three teachers appear to have returned annually to the U.S., the Diethelms to Victoria, Minn. and Pastors to West Bend, Wisc.

⁴⁸Agnes Kopp and Michael Pitzel in 1911, Pauline Pitzel in 1912, Agnes Flory in 1916, and Maria Michels and Cordula Hermle in 1917.

⁴⁹Numerous people who attended the parochial schools uniformly assured me that their teachers taught partly in German.

⁵⁰D of E, Public Schools, 1102, 1299 and 1433, SAB. The population of these three districts was heavily or almost exclusively German.

⁵¹P.E.I.: McGarry and McGinn; Nova Scotia: Bissett who when married was McCormick; Ontario: O'Meara; Ireland: Ryan and O'Callaghan; Saskatchewan: O'Reilly. See D of E, Teachers' Register Sheets, A.S. The reason only seven have been identified is that I have so far examined only records of teachers whose last names begin with the letters L, M, N, O, P and R.

⁵²See data for 1914 in D of E, Public Schools, 935, 1052, 1069, 1102, 1150, 1185, 1187, 1299, 1310, 1353, 1415, 1433, 1434, 1466, 1473, 1476, 1521, 1584, 1587, 1714, 1747, 1770, 1827, 1872, 1959, 1973, 2058, 2189, 2190, 2192, 2271, 2273, 2329, 2343, 2350, 2375, 2407, 2455, 2568, 2634, 2655, 2695, 2724, 3064, 3073, 3138, 3196, SAB. Two districts were not included, Humboldt and Watson, since they both had separate and public schools.

⁵³Hilda Schwarz, Clara Kopp, Leo Schumacher and Otto Becker.

⁵⁴Patrick Leacy, Mary O'Callaghan, Mary Keegan, Margaret Quinn, Austin McGuigan, Martin Reynolds, J.F. Doyle, Ellie Reynolds, Michael Hanratty, Lawrence Walsh, Mary Scullin, Ruby Sullivan, Margaret Sinnett, Michael Connors, Pearl Hanning, Margaret Walsh, Patrick Dowd, Mary O'Neill, Nora Reynolds, Alice McGeough and Christopher Kiernan.

⁵⁵Amy Chappel, Ed Crough, Mary Rowan, James Gaynor and Mary Maugan.

⁵⁶According to a report of a meeting with a Loyal Orange Lodge delegation, Jan. 21, 1916, Premier Walter Scott stated with respect to German Catholic schools: "At Muenster where most of these schools are, English is as well taught as in the public schools. The children going to these schools are children of German-American par-

entage. The parents speak English very well and their children are taught it. There is no serious problem with them." See Calder Papers, p. 2678.

[57]*St. Peters Bote*, Feb. 4, 1904, pp. 1-2. The German words for temporary public school were "die öffentliche Schule wenigstens vorläufig einzuföhren."

[58]Ibid., June 14, 1904, p. 2. The German expressions used for "in the coming year" and "private school" were respectively "dieses kommende Jahr" and "Privat-Schule."

[59]Ibid., Feb. 4, 1904.

[60]Chrysostom to Bertha, Oct. 9, 1909. Correspondence of P. Chrysostom with sister, SPAA.

[61]Father Chrysostom's Day Books, Nov. 2, 1909.

[62]Chrysostom to Bertha, Oct. 9, 1909.

11

The WCTU and Educational Strategies on the Canadian Prairie*

Nancy M. Sheehan

There has been increasing interest in the past several years in the history of temperance and prohibition in both Canada and the United States. Researchers of women's history, religious history and social history have viewed the temperance movement as a key element in understanding developments in each of these areas. One of the organizations central to the temperance movement, and one which has been given credit as a catalyst in organizing the "anti-drink" campaign, was the Woman's Christian Temperance Union. Until quite recently most of the studies related to the WCTU have been parts of much larger works on prohibition itself. Although this women's organization has been credited in these studies with an important role in the campaign, the essence of the WCTU, its philosophy, organization and methodology are lost in the ongoing rush to tell the story of the rise and fall of prohibition. Andrew Sinclair's *Prohibition: An Era of Excess,* Joseph Gusfield's *Symbolic Crusade: Status Politics and the American Temperance Movement,* and James Timberlake's *Prohibition and the Progressive Movement, 1900-1920* are examples of such work.[1] Norman H. Clark's *Deliver Us From Evil: An Interpretation of American Prohibition* shows the interest women took in the number of saloons and the problems associated with alcohol.[2] In *Retreat from Reform: The Prohibition Movement in the United States, 1890-1913,* James Blocker identifies prohibitionist leaders, both men and women, as "decent citizens."[3] What each of these works tells us is what women did for temperance.

Recent scholarship has zeroed in more directly on the WCTU itself and not only looks at the role of these women in temperance, but asks the question, What did temperance do for women? *Women and Temperance: The Quest for Power and Liberty* by Ruth Bordin is the most recent example of this approach. She labels the WCTU as "unquestionably the first mass movement of American women" and "one of the most powerful instruments of women's consciousness raising of all time."[4] Barbara Leslie Epstein's *Politics of Domesticity* and a work by Meredith Tax which includes WCTU women who became feminists are further efforts in this direction.[5]

---

*This chapter is reprinted from *History of Education Quarterly* (Spring 1984): 101-119, with permission.

In a Ph.D. thesis done at York University, Wendy Mitchinson compares four women's organizations in nineteenth-century Canada and concludes that the WCTU was the most radical of the four.[6] One subsequent article by Mitchinson looks at the WCTU as a feminist organization, and another at its internal organization, to which Mitchinson ascribes the success of the WCTU.[7] Marcia McGovern, in her work on the WCTU in Saskatchewan, shows the relationship between a regional union and the National Union and indicates that although the National Union established the organizational framework, leadership, policy, and departments of work, these were often circumscribed at the local level by indigenous concerns.[8]

Common to all the research on the WCTU is the conclusion that the underlying philosophy which allowed many women to become involved in temperance activities outside of the home was the belief that the innocent victims of the traffic in alcoholic beverages were women, children and family life. To save the children, to protect the home, and to fulfill their duties as wives and mothers, women came into the public sphere with the goal to rescue not only the children but the whole society. Their concern for the children, their frequent experience as public school teachers, their accepted role in the home as mothers of children, and their belief that successful strategy with the children would ensure a dry society for the future meant that "departments" within the WCTU which concentrated on children were very important. The Scientific Temperance Instruction, the public school arm of the WCTU, the Sunday School department, and three informal departments, the Little White Ribboners, the Loyal Temperance Legion, and the Young WCTU are examples. The WCTU clearly believed that education was a non-school, as well as a school matter and, to achieve success, strategies for both had to be devised.

This chapter looks at the educational work of one WCTU organization in order to ascertain the effectiveness of using both the public school system and informal educational arrangements to accomplish their goals. Specifically, the essay wants to go beyond the rhetoric of success common to the WCTU assessment of its own program, and look at the departments in action. The period is 1890-1930, and the WCTU chosen for this study is the North-West Territories WCTU, which became the Alberta-Saskatchewan WCTU when these provinces joined Canadian confederation in 1905.

I

A very active department in the National WCTU of the United States under Mrs. Mary Hunt was the department promoting Scientific Temperance Instruction (STI). In an article entitled "Scientific Temperance Instruction in Schools," Norton Mezvinsky has argued that the WCTU was successful in persuading Congress and the State legislatures to pass laws compelling some form of temperance instruction in the public schools. Strong STI legislation with stringent curricula and teaching requirements and penalties for non-enforcement was passed. Textbooks were rewritten according to Mrs.

Hunt's views that they "should teach that alcohol was a poison, should advocate total abstinence, and should avoid all references about the medical use of alcohol." By 1903 there were thirty-three "WCTU-endorsed" textbooks for use in the schools.[9]

James Timberlake in *Prohibition and the Progressive Movement, 1900-1920* argued:

> To what extent temperance instruction contributed to the success of the prohibition movement, it is impossible to say. But that it aided materially in creating dry sentiment can hardly be doubted, for it was during the Progressive Era that children indoctrinated in the scientific argument were inclined to credit it with being a major factor in bringing about national prohibition.[10]

A U.S. Commissioner of Education remarked that in the creation of a sentiment which resulted in local option, followed by state prohibition and culminating in national prohibition, a very important, if not major, part was played by the schools. "The instruction in physiology and hygiene with special reference to the effects of alcohol . . . has resulted first in clearer thinking, and second in better and stronger sentiment in regard to the sale and use of alcoholic drinks."[11] Joseph Gusfield in *Symbolic Crusade: Status Politics and the American Temperance Movement* concluded that there was much affinity among the schools, the WCTU, and the temperance movement.[12]

With the U.S. experience and reported success as a barometer and with Mrs. Hunt's energy and "plan of work" as a guide, the STI departments in the various Canadian provincial WCTUs approached school boards and departments of educaton. They also had some success. By the turn of the century most provinces had some form of temperance teaching in the schools. The North-West Territories, for example, had a compulsory course by 1896 for the public school grades, and the teachers were exposed to it in the model and normal schools where Nattress' text *Physiology and Temperance* was required. On the surface, then, it appears as though the STI in the Canadian WCTU was as successful as its American counterpart. Closer scrutiny, however, reveals that legislative directives did not guarantee a successful program at the classroom level. The North-West Territories (NWT) and Alberta programs are cases in point.

As mentioned earlier, the Territories program included a course of study, a textbook for the teacher, and model and normal school preparation. Despite this, indications suggest that it was not a priority. Inspector Perrett in 1900 said that the course of study was "being closely followed in all subjects except singing, drawing, and hygiene, in which branches there is too much incidental teaching."[13] A study of Standard V (Grade VIII) examinations in Hygiene and Temperance concluded that "the knowledge of the candidates as revealed in these answer papers is fair to good. The first four questions are answered well." The answers to questions five and six, which were the temperance questions, caused concerns.[14] One examiner said: "Temperance is evidently taught in intemperate language. An extreme view is held and vulgar method employed in describing the effects of alcohol and tobacco." Another examiner offered advice to the teacher: "Teachers should assuredly be much more careful than they are in the statements they make before their classes when teaching this branch."[15] In 1903 Inspector Bryan commented that "except in schools where pupils are being prepared for the school leaving examination, very little time is devoted to hygiene and temperance. Sometimes a place is assigned to these subjects in the teacher's timetable but as a rule the teaching is of a desultory nature."[16]

A look at both the normal school course of study and one of the recommended textbooks may help explain the problems that the temperance and hygiene course experienced. The Normal School Course of Study for 1898, 1900 and 1903 listed principles of hygiene as one of the topics under Art of Education for all classes of certificate.[17] However, no question on this subject appeared on any of the professional examinations. If the topic did not receive much attention at the normal school and was not tested for the teaching certificate, many teachers would not only not have had the background and methodology to handle the topic in the classroom, but also might not have felt that it was important enough to warrant much time and attention.

Besides the *Ontario Manual of Hygiene*, the other recommended text for teachers was *Ontario Public Physiology and Temperance* by William Nattress, authorized in Ontario in 1893. The "Introduction" told the reader that "One of the most destructive agents man has brought into use is alcohol . . . every tissue and every organ of the body is influenced by its use . . . that *perfect health* cannot be hoped for when alcohol is taken in even so small a quantity." Each chapter devoted to one aspect of the body — bones, muscles, digestion, circulation, respiration, the skin, the nervous system, etc. — concluded with the effects of alcohol on the particular bodily function under discussion. For example, in the chapter devoted to "The Bones," the last section intoned:

> It has often been observed that children of intemperate parents frequently fail to develop into manhood or womanhood. They may not be deformed, but their growth is arrested, and they remain small in body and infantile in character . . . Such are examples of a species of degeneracy, and are evidences of the visiting of the sins of the fathers upon the children, which may extend even into the third and fourth generations.

The chapter on "Circulation" ended with this statement: "Very often in chronic, though perhaps moderate, drinkers, the arteries, instead of being strong, elastic tubes, like new rubber hoses, become hardened and unyielding, and are liable to give way." The final point made in the chapter on "Digestion" was that "in some cases the liver reaches an enormous weight, fifteen, and even twenty to twenty-five, pounds being not uncommon."[18] The difficulty with these statements and others was that the lack of evidence cited might be a deterrent to adult acceptance of the facts learned at school. A second problem of the text could be the difficulty of the subject matter — beyond the comprehension level of the majority of elementary-age students.

Inadequately-trained teachers, poor reference books, a crowded time-table and a short school experience for the majority of youngsters meant that the temperance and hygiene course had little impact in the North-West Territories. In 1903 Inspector Bryan's comment above was the only mention made by inspectors on this subject. They omitted it either because they never saw the course taught or because they did not think it an important part of the curriculum. Then in 1903 the course of studies for the upper standards was revised and the number of examination subjects reduced. The Standard V examination in Hygiene and Temperance was dropped, even though the course itself remained compulsory.[19] The course had received little attention when it was an examination course; the loss of even this status made the course more impotent than ever.

When the provinces of Alberta and Saskatchewan were formed in 1905, they adopted intact the North-West Territories system of education, including the temperance program. Immediately the WCTU began petitioning both governments to upgrade the course. Through the early years of the century as prohibition sentiment was building, and even in 1916 when wartime prohibition was introduced, the departments of education made no move to change their offerings. Although the minister of education and other officials showed sympathy for the WCTU viewpoint,[20] and although they made assurances and promises of a curriculum change,[21] the letters, interviews, initiatives in sending texts for perusal,[22] and the cooperation received from other groups[23] seemed to have no positive effect on the curriculum. The departments of education claimed that they already had "temperance programmes" with a philosophy of inducing good habits rather than formal instruction on the subject.[24] The WCTU and the departments did not agree on the role of the school in temperance education, on the methodology, or the use of a textbook.

In 1922, however, a revised Elementary Curriculum was adopted in Alberta including a course in Elementary Science embracing nature study, geography, and physiology and hygiene for the first six grades, and geography, physiology and agriculture for grades VII and VIII. It was expected that forty minutes per week would be devoted to physiology and hygiene and that facts rather than habits would be emphasized. It stressed that "not only is physical education necessary, but a definite understanding of elementary anatomy, simple laws of health, and first aid, as well." In succeeding grades each of the body's systems, digestive, circulatory, respiratory, excretory and nervous, was to be studied with a view to understanding alcohol's effect upon each system. A review of these systems would take place in Grade 8 in preparation for a compulsory final exam.[25]

A WCTU resolution in 1925 read: "That the Provincial WCTU wish to express their appreciation to the Department of Education for the introduction of the Text-Book, *Physiology and Hygiene* by Ritchie and Caldwell."[26]

This text not only explored the effect of alcohol and tobacco on the systems of the body but also devoted paragraphs to such topics as: "What employers think of the use of alcohol"; "Alcohol and the Great War"; "What medical men think of the use of alcohol"; "Tobacco and scholarship"; and "The effect of a moderate use of tobacco."[27] Not only had the Alberta WCTU achieved a place for hygiene in the regular timetable and a compulsory examination, but they also saw accepted a WCTU-approved text. Success in this field at long last! However, a similar change did not occur in Saskatchewan.

A preliminary look at the actual implementation of the course in Alberta classrooms reveals that perhaps even that success was illusory. To have an effective program in the schools certain requirements should have been met. Teachers' timetables, inspectors' reports, examination schedules, and teacher training programs surely would give some attention to the program. The hygiene-temperance program of the twenties appears to have been neglected. Although the curriculum guide indicated forty minutes per week for temperance instruction, a perusal of individual teacher timetables shows that it was often ignored.[28] Reminiscences by a few teachers who taught in the twenties do not mention the course, although they do mention other "new" courses, e.g. school gardening, agriculture, manual training and physical education.[29] The course was also ignored by inspectors, who comment on just about every aspect of the school, from the grounds and physical condition of the school-house to the content and methodology of the individual courses of the curriculum.[30] It was not until 1927, five years after the 1922 curriculum change, that an instructor for health and hygiene was hired for the normal school at Calgary. The first nurse and hygiene instructor for the Edmonton Normal School was on staff January, 1929.[31]

Examinations also reveal the lack of importance the authorities gave to this topic, showing few questions devoted to alcohol and tobacco, and in some years none at all. For example, in 1924, the examination in Agriculture, Physiology and Hygiene, and Art had no temperance questions. The next year's examination, which awarded forty marks for agricultural questions, forty for art, and only twenty for physiology and hygiene, had a two-part question on alcohol worth four percent. The question asked the student to: "Write an account of the effects of drinking alcoholic liquors under the following headings:

a. the effect on the heart and blood vessels

b. the effect on the brain."[32]

Both students and teachers could be excused if preparation in this area was downplayed, if not ignored.

The program was also short-lived. By 1935 the *Programme of Studies* for Grade IX stated: "No programme in Health Education for adolescents can be complete without a treatment of the use of alcohol and tobacco. . . . Nevertheless, these topics do not easily lend themselves to school instruction. . . . It is the consensus of competent opinion that in teaching the hygiene of alcohol and tobacco, more is gained by the "method of indirection" than by a direct frontal attack on the subject."[33] This hardly was reflective of the WCTU's ideas about the course nor conducive to the use of the WCTU-approved textbook. It would seem that a course approved and adopted at the administrative level did not necessarily have an impact in the classroom. The temperance section of the physiology and hygiene course was "in name" only.

II

Sunday schools were also seen as vehicles for advancing and strengthening temperance sentiment. From the earliest days Sunday schools had been an impetus for temperance teaching. It was through a Sunday school in Ontario that Letitia Youmans, the founder of the Canadian WCTU, became interested in temperance, and it was at a Sunday school meeting in Chautauqua, New York, that the initial plans for the WCTU in the U.S. were formalized. When Mrs. Craig, the first organizer in the West, made her tour of NWT centres in 1904 she addressed a number of Sunday school gatherings.[34] Here was a captive audience, whose parents thought enough of their beliefs to educate their children in a church which, for the most part, espoused temperance principles.

The work in the Sunday schools pursued a number of tactics, and it indicated the close ties between the Protestant churches and the WCTU. In the beginning the quarterly temperance lesson was considered all that was needed for educational work in the Sunday schools. Using the Quarterly Temperance Lessons put out by the Ontario WCTU, the Sunday school teacher had lesson plans, materials, and suggestions for topics, special speakers, and a temperance program.[35] In 1912 thirty-five Sunday schools in Alberta observed Temperance Sunday, used the WCTU Temperance Quarterlies, and encouraged the students to sign pledges at the completion of the temperance lessons.[36] In Saskatchewan, although only twelve unions took up this work, twenty-one Sunday schools were active in temperance lessons.[37]

World Temperance Sunday was also a way of interesting Sunday school goers in this question. In conjunction with the Provincial Prohibition Association, the Alberta WCTU Sunday School department launched a campaign for the special observance of this Sunday, featuring pledge signing, leaflet distribution, and help for the Sunday school lesson on that day. In 1927, forty thousand copies of the temperance leaflet were distributed. The Sunday school superintendent had only praise for the cooperation received from the churches to mark the special observance of World Temperance Sunday.[38]

In the late twenties both the churches and the WCTU increased their Sunday school activity. Some schools appointed a temperance superintendent and increased the temperance program to once a month or once every two months.[39] The WCTU also increased its activity and in 1928 launched a "nation-wide educational competition" through the Sunday schools of all denominations. A series of lessons was prepared, suitable for all ages, and the

Northern Messenger, an interdenominational religious weekly published in Montreal, agreed to promote the content and publish the lessons. Prizes in the total amount of $3,000 were awarded the first year. The lessons, which consisted of the twelve chapters of Miss McCorkindale's book "Alcohol and Life" were published in twelve consecutive issues of the *Messenger*, and distributed through Sunday schools.[40] The students would study the material, answer the questions at home, and return them to the teacher. The examination was divided into "Junior Questions, for scholars 13 years old, or under" and "Senior Questions, to be answered by those of 14 to 17 inclusive." Each exam consisted of twenty-seven questions with varying marks assigned to such questions as:

> What is the difference between grape juice and fermented wine?
>
> What is the duty of the white corpuscles?
>
> Many people think alcohol is useful and beneficial. Why this popular belief?

The WCTU declared this type of competition a tremendous success, with papers received from fifty-eight cities and towns in Alberta.[41] Saskatchewan does not appear to have participated in this program although it appointed a Sunday School Temperance Superintendent every year.

The Canadian Girl and *The Canadian Boy*, papers published by the United Church of Canada, included six temperance lessons in their 1930 editions, running through October and November. The titles of the lessons,"Alcohol and the Human Body," "Alcohol and Well-Being," "Alcohol and Health," for example, were reminiscent of the WCTU material, as were the questions asked and the certificates awarded.[42]

Then in 1931 a "National Temperance Study Course for Sunday Schools" was initiated, sponsored by both the Religious Education Council of Canada and the Woman's Christian Temperance Union. The lessons appeared in the Sunday school papers for October 4 through November 11. They consisted of stories surrounding one theme. For example, "Beaten at the Start" extolled the virtues of temperance for the athlete. Examinations were given and the Sunday schools awarded Pass and Honour certificates and the WCTU prizes. This Study Course appeared to be a combination of the United Church material and the WCTU-*Messenger* contest. The churches and the WCTU had joined forces in the Sunday school.[43]

What is interesting about the Sunday school work was the timing. The WCTU had had a Sunday school department from its inception and it had promoted the quarterly temperance lesson with some, but by no means all Sunday schools participating. The churches held total abstinence views, and yet in the early years, the Sunday school did not always teach the temperance lessons. It was not until the late twenties that both groups, the WCTU and the churches, began to make a more concerted effort to include temperance teaching in Sunday school. Two possible reasons suggest themselves: the

WCTU finally realized that STI in the public schools was not going to do the job that they had hoped it would, and that the one other institution that did speak to a number of children was the church. At the same time, perhaps, the churches saw government control instituted, realized that alcohol was now readily available to all, and that its use was acceptable, and even sanctioned by government authority. It became more important than ever that the youth get proper training in temperance principles. The Sunday school program was the best vehicle at hand for this purpose.

III

The educational work of the WCTU was not confined to the public and Sunday schools. The women organized and ran youth groups: the Little White Ribboners (LWR) for babies and young children, the Loyal Temperance Legion (LTL) for children from seven years of age, and the Young WCTU (YWCTU) for the working girl. The women wanted to "educate and organize the boys and girls and young people so that a vast army of recruits may be in training to take up the work of the next generation. . . ."[44]

Little White Ribboners (LWR)

The purpose of the Little White Ribboners department was not only to obtain a pledge of abstinence for the little ones, but to "train up a race" who would not know the taste of alcohol. It was to bring before nursing mothers the fact that in taking alcoholic beverages themselves, they transmitted the alcohol into the child's system; to guard children until they were seven years of age; and to circulate literature dealing with scientific and medical temperance, health and hygiene among parents.[45] LWR reports quoted numerous authorities on the evil effects of alcohol on babies and young children:

> Liquor consumed by parents brings children into the world with enfeebled minds, tendency to idiocy, dullness and epilepsy, and with weakened bodies which early succumb to disease. (Report of a Chief Medical Officer to the Board of Education, England).
>
> Intemperance in husband or wife is a serious cause of excessive infant mortality (Sir A. Newsholme).
>
> Five times as many alcoholized infants die as those of sober mothers. (Lt. Col. Sir A. Pearce-Gould, M.D., KCVO).
>
> Even small quantities of alcohol taken habitually injure the unborn child. (Sir A. Simpson, M.D., F.M.S.E.)[46]

The LWR department operated by enrolling babies and children under seven years of age, for whom the mother made the following pledge: "I place my child's name among the Little White Ribboners promising not to give or allow him (or her) to take any Intoxicating Drink."[47] It distributed literature such as "Wise Words to Mothers and Fathers" in which the slogan "before birth it starves, after birth it stunts the child" was found.[48] It particularly hoped to break the custom of treating childish ailments with alcohol by influencing parents not to do it themselves, and not to allow a doctor to treat their child with alcoholic medication. Using figures supplied by the Massachusetts State Board of Health and the Colorado State Medical Society, Mrs. Craig, the first NWT president, warned of the alcoholic content found in patent medicines: Brown's Iron Tonic, 19.7 percent; Paine's Celery Compound, 21 percent; Lydia Pinkham's Vegetable Compound, 16.8 percent; Warner's Safe Tonic Bitters, 35 percent; and Parker's Tonic, 41.6 percent. Paregoric, commonly used for babies with colic and teething problems, was said to contain two grams of opium in each ounce.[49]

The Little White Ribboners department, although it tried to interest parents in their babies, and held entertainments where the young children learned to sing temperance songs and received some treat, was not the healthiest of departments. Workers were hard to find, departments were abandoned particularly after the vote for prohibition in 1915,[50] and "in the foreign sections in Canada [where] there are four babies born to every one of Anglo-Saxon parentage . . ." the department never got off the ground.[51] In most cases also, it was the problem of preaching to the converted. The membership lists of the Little White Ribboners reveal that a majority of those enrolled were babies of the WCTU members themselves. Surely in these cases, the enrolment would be redundant. For example, the first Little White Ribboner in an Edmonton Union was one of Nellie McClung's children.[52] The number of unions that had active LWRs was small, the names on the rolls were few, and the activities sponsored by the department were not well attended. It could be said that the success of the Little White Ribboners as a method of educating the population was minimal.

Loyal Temperance Union (LTL)

On the surface the Loyal Temperance Legion (LTL) should have been the most successful of departments. "The children's welfare should be our first consideration," according to the 1918 report, "the children of the home, the children of the community, the children of the nation — for the little ones of today are the men and women of the future."[53] The LTL was called "A Training School for Future Citizenship." It had both plans of work drawn up for conduct of meetings, and a lesson manual with hints and helps. Each meeting would study some aspect of temperance truths, the harm of alcohol, or the evil effects of tobacco, through a study book, an experiment, or a short talk. This was to be followed by an activity for the children, something to interest and hold them. Some suggestions were:

Make collections of scrap books which may be given to the Children's Homes or Hospitals. Lead a foot committee for crushing cigarette stubs. Have a membership contest for securing new members. . . . Spread Thanksgiving or Christmas cheer among the needy. Distribute literature for the mother WCTU. Act as ushers at public meetings of the Union. Train the boys and girls through songs, recitations, rally-cries, drills and playlets about the harm of alcohol and narcotics.

Public meetings, such as medal contests for the best temperance speech or pageants were also suggested as a method of educating the public through the temperance recitations and songs of the Legioners.[54]

The WCTU wanted the children to sign pledge cards, receive certificates, wear pins and get some instruction in temperance principles.[55] Organized LTL activities on the Prairies were varied. One union taught scientific temperance by means of coloured charts and debates. Another had the Tobacco Act printed upon large cards and displayed where tobacco was sold to minors. In some unions the LTL and the mother union worked together: the LTL might be entertained at an ice cream social or a picnic; in return the children sold tickets for medal contests or took part in the ladies' musical program.[56] Carlstadt, a Canadian Pacific Railway station northwest of Medicine Hat, was pleased to report a course of study with chemical demonstrations, the completion of a banner, a double medal contest and a picnic. "Even mischievous Jimmy — the bad boy of the town — is wearing the LTL colors."[57] In Vermilion the LTL was organized and conducted by a school teacher who held two medal contests and gave much temperance instruction.[58] Lethbridge appeared very happy: "The leaven of Edmonton in the form of a consecrated young teacher is working out and Lethbridge is making definite plans for thoroughly organized work in the schools."[59] Red Deer had an LTL membership of fifty in 1911 in the capable hands of Mrs. I.M. King, a teacher in the public school, who held the meetings at the close of school hours in the school room. Since she had begun using the school room to hold the meetings, membership and attendance had increased, she reported, probably because the denominational slant was not a cause of concern in the school as it had been when the meetings were held in a church, or church hall.[60]

However, most reports were not as optimistic as these. In one instance everything was in readiness and had to be abandoned at the last minute because the promised use of the schoolhouse had been denied the group. More than one school district refused to cooperate with the WCTU by not allowing them use of their facilities. In other districts unions indicated a willingness to do LTL work but hesitated because a mission band or some other juvenile society was organized and doing some temperance work. They felt to form an LTL would mean the depletion of one or the other.[61] Also mentioned as a reason for poor LTL work was the Red Cross and other patriotic activities which took so much time.[62] The influenza epidemic of 1918 interfered.[63] The Union at Greenshields reported a "wet" teacher who refused LTL meetings with the children.[64] In Whitla, southwest of Medicine Hat, the problem was many Catholic children, some of whom drank beer and whose parents were uninterested.[65] The LTL Report to the 1912 Alberta Annual Convention suggested the following as usual reasons for not working an LTL department: scarcity of leaders, children already overtaxed with schoolwork and other organizations, difficulty of gathering the children together, and lack of sympathy on the part of teachers and schoolboards.[66] The WCTU paid a great deal of lip service to the value of education outside the school; however, this rhetoric was not translated into LTL activity.

Young Women's Christian Temperance Union (YWCTU)

The third youth branch of the organization, the Young Women's Christian Temperance Union was probably the least successful of the three. The arguments for establishing "Y" unions were: that the "Y"s' were the future "W's" and must be prepared for the work or it would suffer;[67] that the young were lost in the senior union and a "Y" gave them a chance to run meetings and to learn organizational skills;[68] that they (the young temperance workers) could influence other young people as members of the older union could not;[69] and that a "Y" in existence in a town provided newcomers with the "right kind of friends." According to testimony from a "Y" member, belonging meant receiving moral and temperance instruction and practical or executive training. It meant learning about the dangers and drastic results that alcohol and narcotics had on the body. It meant public speaking, making motions, and leading meetings. It meant meeting an acceptable sort of young people. It meant "better friends, cleaner bodies and better thoughts and ideals."[70]

The meetings and activities advocated for the "Y" were many, including devotional, educational and social programs. They could contribute to patriotic service, help with LTL groups, hold debates, invite speakers and generally promote the moral welfare of their members.[71] They could become involved in Ruthenian and Indian work, learning the value of charitable as well as temperance works.[72] One Alberta local "Y" conducted "A Trip Around the World" in which four homes were each "decorated to represent some country, while the costumes worn by the young ladies receiving and serving as well as the refreshments served and program rendered were in keeping with the general theme." About 175 people took advantage of the "trip" to learn about different countries and to hear some temperance material.[73] In 1923 the provincial "Y" department organized an educational program to help members understand the great work of the WCTU. The course of study consisted of three books, *Alcohol in Experience and Experiment, Nicotine,* and *Studies in Government.* Each of these was to be studied carefully, an examination written, and a diploma awarded.[74] These kinds of programs did not seem to attract members to existing "Y" groups or to help unions start "Y" programs. Of forty-nine unions organized in 1923 in Alberta only six reported "Y" work, and even these six were not overly enthusiastic about the number of girls who regularly attended meetings, or the kinds of activities promoted. Saskatchewan reported no "Y" activity and did not even appoint a provincial superintendent for this work. Complaints of too many organizations for the young adult, the fact that churches and Canadian Girls in Training groups did temperance work and the lack of good leadership were cited as reasons why "Y" work was neglected. The problem with other youth organizations which gave temperance lectures and passed temperance resolutions was somewhat the same problem that the LTLs ran into with mission bands and other juvenile societies. The formation of a "Y" might deplete both groups and yet these others did not do the practical temperance work the "Y" espoused: pledge signing, training the temperance worker, holding meetings with a temperance theme, and sponsoring social gatherings in the interest of total abstinence.[75]

A pattern seems to have emerged. The WCTU had as one of its watchwords "educate" and in some years, education was stressed to the exclusion of other interests as the focus for the year's work. Much of the literature spoke of the importance of education, particularly the education of youth. And yet the three youth departments did not flourish. What had developed was a leadership which voiced the right sentiments, seemed to know what was needed, and suggested good pedagogical methods, and a membership which agreed with these sentiments, but for a variety of reasons had difficulty in making them work. There seemed to be a great divergence between theory and practice with regard to the formal as well as the informal educational work of the WCTU on the Canadian Prairies.

IV

There can be no doubt that the WCTU was convinced of the necessity of educating the youth of the country to temperance — their problem was how to do it. What was the best possible way of attracting the youth — not only to prohibition sentiments, but also to train them to become prohibition workers? The answer was that every avenue should be explored, every method should be tried, every age group should be contacted. Although the public school might be the best route to approach all children, there were hazards. The teaching and content were in the hands of strangers, some of whom would be uncommitted strangers. The women had little control over the public school classroom, even after a WCTU-approved textbook had been adopted. Centralized departments of education in the Canadian provinces were not very open to grass-roots input. And even when the policy concerning temperance was improved, implementation did not necessarily follow. Sunday school programs posed fewer hazards for the women. After all, the teachers were more likely pro-temperance. And it was easy to plug into the curriculum of an organized educational institution pedagogical techniques and programs for temperance. The material for the Sunday school was developed at the national level, leaving the local WCTU members with only the job of convincing temperance-prone churches to commit themselves to the course. Yet Sunday school work was slow to get moving, and critics argued that temperance teaching in the Sunday school was akin to preaching to the converted.

Like Sunday schools, youth groups could also be controlled by the temperance women. However, a well-run, successful youth group took initiative, planning ability, time and hard work. Attracting children, organizing entertainment, and teaching temperance principles to the young in informal settings were difficult, time-consuming tasks. The youth groups, made up of a variety of children of committed and uncommitted parents, were not a captive audience, and were not easy to run. In their educational departments the women were caught in a squeeze. The public school which reached all the children could not be controlled; the Sunday school reached only a portion, and that was more than likely a committed portion; and the youth groups attracted a still smaller population and required the most commitment in time and energy from the women themselves.

The operation of both their public school and their "out-of-school" educational programs reveals something of the character of the WCTU. First of all, for many, WCTU membership gave them their first contact with a non-sectarian organization, and they brought to it attitudes and experiences gained in church groups, such as the Women's Missionary Societies of the various denominations. In a majority of instances this meant fundraising through bazaars, teas, and sales; it meant collecting items of clothing and household goods to be shipped to the needy; and it meant carrying out the wishes of the ministers and male elders of the church. Some WCTU women, called upon to convince teachers and trustees, had only this experience to support their efforts. Going outside the organizational and financial role to personally contact children on Indian reserves, in "foreign" villages and at remote settlements was to extend their maternal role beyond their ability and experience. Given the less than radical nature of most members it is not surprising that they generally stayed closer to home.

Second, their experience with children affected the work they accomplished with youth groups. Women in the home were used to working daily with children, either as individuals or in small groups, and their audience was a captive one. A successful youth group needed a varied clientele, an entertaining program, and a weekly meeting. The leader needed to cope with a large and changing membership, and one that produced problems of language, discipline, and parental conflict. Although the time-consuming nature of organizing such a program was no doubt a factor in its limited role, the women's lack of experience in areas outside the home also has to be considered.

Third, the organizational framework of the WCTU, which allowed local members to choose their areas of activity, was an ingenious way of enticing members to follow their interests, but it had built-in flaws. Because members and locals could pick and choose which departments to emphasize, some were ignored altogether, others worked haphazardly, and little effort was given to the more unpleasant tasks. The small membership, the number of areas of interest, and the tendency to choose areas of work where the women had some knowledge or expertise meant that the numbers of children touched by the educational work of the WCTU was small.

This study raises a number of questions. Prohibition legislation in Alberta and Saskatchewan was introduced in 1916, long before the departments of education upgraded their programs, at a time when the Sunday school department was quite ineffective, and youth groups were small in numbers and in activities. Both provinces defeated prohibition and accepted government control of alcoholic beverages in 1924, at which time there was an attempt to upgrade the school programs and the Sunday schools became more active. This would suggest that schools and other educational agencies had little direct influence on either prohibition or its defeat, and the increased activities of the 1920s amounted to closing the barn door after the horse was gone.

And yet American research to date credits the WCTU-induced school programs with effecting the outcome of the Eighteenth Amendment. Perhaps what is needed is a revision of the work of Gusfield, Timberlake, Mezvinsky and others in relation to education, much of which appears to be based on WCTU rhetoric only. The recent trend in WCTU-related research which delves more closely into the records of local temperance groups could be applied here and the educational work approached both from the input of the WCTU and the actual output of the school.

A second question relates to the women themselves. Why did they keep appointing superintendents and making reports back to the annual convention when the temperance work was so ineffective? There are several possible answers. Any kind of activity, whether it produced results or not, provided a morale booster. It gave the women the illusion of accomplishment, allowed them to believe they were having an effect. It rallied the troops. It was an incentive to other less active locals and departments to match or better the work being done in a particular locale. The WCTU was not an introspective group. Its members did not spend a lot of time analyzing their activities, adapting national strategies to local needs, or assessing the effectiveness of local efforts. They did spend a great deal of time meeting, praying, talking and generally keeping busy. They did not stop to dwell on whom they reached, how many programs were effective, or on the reaction to their activities. What seemed to be important to them was activity itself.

The WCTU on the Canadian Prairies was a part of the international WCTU movement, of which the National WCTU in the U.S. was the originator and organizer. The rhetoric coming from the U.S. group in the form of literature, newspapers, periodicals, visiting organizers and speakers, and Canadian members with U.S. experience, preached that the educational program in most states was a fantastic success. Frances Willard, Mary Hunt and others who visited Canadian unions stressed the educational program. Mrs. Louise McKinney, president of the Alberta group for twenty-two years, had been a state organizer in North Dakota prior to settling in Alberta. She was convinced that the American success had to be duplicated in the West. Perhaps the leaders especially felt they had to follow the lead of the mother group. Maybe staying as closely tuned as possible to the national WCTU gave the women a collective sense of participation and strength. By running educational programs, no matter how small the results, the women were extending their roles outside the home and in the process educating themselves, learning first-hand to deal with departments of education and Sunday school officials, and with teachers and trustees. They gained experience in organizing programs, coping with various age groups and backgrounds, and with selecting materials and strategies. Although the stated goals of their work may not have been met, the WCTU did have these important results for the women involved.

The final question concerns women's experience as teachers and the effect this had on their educational work in voluntary associations. Did the fact that many WCTU women had had experience as schoolteachers enhance or detract from their chances for success? Although Geraldine Joncich Clifford has recently argued that one-room schoolteaching was at times productive of self-confidence and even rebellion,[76] the literature generally suggests that educational hierarchies tended to reinforce gender stereotypes with the women at the bottom of the hierarchy.[77] This may account for the difference between the educational theory propounded by the WCTU leadership and the educational activity carried out by members at the local level. Educational leaders within the WCTU who were former schoolteachers may have been those who had gained enough self-confidence to adapt their own educational theory and practice to the needs of the temperance campaign, while members at the local level, perhaps, were women whose educational experience made it difficult to carry out a program requiring them to approach male principals, trustees and department officials. Further research which attempts to identify the backgrounds of the general membership should help to clarify this issue. Perhaps, also, a look at the educational role of other women's associations may raise similar questions about the relationship of theory to practice.

Notes

[1]Andrew Sinclair, *Prohibition: An Era of Excess* (Boston: Little, Brown & Co., 1962); Joseph Gusfield, *Symbolic Crusade: Status Politics and the American Temperance Movement* (Urbana, Illinois: University of Illinois Press, 1963); James Timberlake, *Prohibition and the Progressive Movement, 1900-1920* (New York: Atheneum, 1970).

[2]Norman H. Clarke, *Deliver Us From Evil: An Interpretation of American Prohibition* (New York: W.W. Norton and Co., 1976).

[3]Jack Blocker, *Retreat from Reform: The Prohibition Movement in the United States, 1890-1913* (Westpoint, Conn.: The Greenwood Press, 1976).

[4]Ruth Bordin, *Women and Temperance: The Quest for Power and Liberty, 1873-1900* (Philadelphia: Temple University Press, 1981).

[5]Barbara Leslie Epstein, *The Politics of Domesticity: Women, Evangelism and Temperance in Nineteenth Century America* (Middletown, Conn.: Wesleyana University, 1981); and Meredith Tax, *Feminist Solidarity and Class Conflict, 1880-1917* (New York: Monthly Review Press, 1981). See also Aileen Kraditor, *Woman Suffrage Movement, 1890-1920* (New York: Doubleday-Anchor, 1965).

[6]Wendy Mitchinson, "Aspects of Reform: Four Women's Organizations in 19th Century Canada" (Ph.D. thesis, York University, 1977).

[7]"The WCTU: 'For God, Home and Native Land': A Study in Nineteenth Century Feminism," in Linda Kealey, ed., *A Not Unreasonable Claim: Women and Reform in Canada, 1880-1920* (Toronto: Women's Educational Press, 1979); and "The Woman's Christian Temperance Union: A Study in Organization," in *International Journal of Women's Studies*, 4 (Mar./Apr., 1981): 143-156.

[8]Marcia McGovern, "The Woman's Christian Temperance Union Movement in Saskatchewan, 1886-1930: A Regional Perspective of the International White Ribbon Movement" (M.A. thesis, University of Regina, 1977).

[9]Norton Mezvinsky, "Scientific Temperance Instruction in Schools." *History of Education Quarterly*, 1 (Mar., 1961): 48-57.

[10]Timberlake, *Prohibition and the Progressive Movement, 1900-1920*, p. 50.

[11]Quoted in the *Canadian White Ribbon Tidings*, Apr. 1920, p. 93 from *The Union Signal*. The Hon. P.P. Claxton made this statement in a letter to the National Temperance Council at its Prohibition celebration in Washington, D.C., Jan. 15-16, 1920. See also Timberlake, *Prohibition and the Progressive Movement*, p. 50.

[12]Gusfield, *Symbolic Crusade: Status Politics and the American Temperance Movement*, p. 86.

[13]North-West Territories, Council of Public Instruction, *Annual Report*, 1900, pp. 47-48, hereafter NWT CPI AR, 1900, pp. 47-48.

[14]North-West Territories, Department of Education, *Annual Report* , hereafter NWT Ed. AR, 1902, pp. 25-26. The Annual Reports included an appendix which listed the Public School Leaving Examinations. Standards I to V were the elementary grades; VI through VIII, the high school.

[15]NWT Ed. AR, 1902, p. 26.

[16]NWT Ed. AR, 1903, p. 54.

[17]NWT CPI AR, 1898, 1900, and NWT Ed. AR, 1903.

[18]William Nattress, *Public School Physiology and Temperance* (Toronto: William Briggs, 1893), pp. 14, 38, 79 and 90.

[19]NWT Ed. AR, 1903, p. 18. Perusal of the examinations appendix showed no "hygiene and temperance" examination. The other examination dropped was in "Principles of Reading."

[20] *Report of the Annual Convention of the Alberta-Saskatchewan Woman's Christian Temperance Union*, hereafter Alta.-Sask. WCTU AR, 1906, p. 42.

[21]See *Minute Book*, 1909, of the Strathcona Union of the Alberta-Saskatchewan Woman's Christian Temperance Union, Box 1, File 1, WCTU(B) papers, Glenbow; and *Edmonton Bulletin*, Apr. 27, 1916.

[22]See Alta.-Sask. WCTU AR, 1906, p. 42; Alta.-Sask. WCTU AR, 1908, p. 52; *Minute Book* of the Strathcona Union; Nanton District Minutes, WCTU, Jan. 8, 1920; and Alta. WCTU AR, 1920, pp. 66-67.

[23]President Tory of the University of Alberta, the Temperance and Moral Reform League, the Alberta Council of Education, the Local Council of Women of Calgary,

the Women's Institutes, the United Farm Women of Alberta, and the United Farmers of Alberta, as well as the Prohibition Association made appeals to the government and promised moral support.

[24]Alberta, *Programme of Studies, 1910, Standards I-V, Elementary* (mimeograph copy). Department of Education Archives, No. 1-A, and Alberta, Department of Education, *Course of Studies for the Public School.* (Edmonton: Government Printer, 1911).

[25]*Arithmetic, Elementary Science, Industrial Arts and Writing. Part II of the Course of Studies for the Elementary Schools of Alberta. Grades I to VIII inclusive.* (Edmonton: King's Printer, 1922), pp. 26-27.

[26]Alta. WCTU AR, 1925, p. 79.

[27]John W. Ritchie and Joseph S. Caldwell, *Physiology and Hygiene for Public Schools* (Toronto: The Educational Book Co. Ltd., 1922), pp. 170-187.

[28]Both the Glenbow-Alberta Archives and the Provincial Archives have the records of various school divisions. These include teachers' timetables and inspectors' reports on individual teachers.

[29]The author has a sampling of teacher biographies in her possession.

[30]Besides inspectors' reports on individual teachers (see footnote 28), the *Annual Reports* of the Department of Education also include a summary statement by the inspectors.

[31]Alberta. Department of Education. *Annual Report*, 1927 and 1929. See "Reports of the Normal Schools."

[32]Examination papers are available in the Legislative Library in Edmonton. See *Sessional Papers,* Legislative Assembly of Alberta, Vol. XIX, Part 2, 1924, and Vol. XX, Part I, 1925.

[33]*Programme of Studies for the Intermediate School: Grades VII, VIII and IX, 1935* (Edmonton: King's Printer, 1935), p. 885.

[34]*Report of the Annual Convention of the North-West Territories Woman's Christian Temperance Union,* hereafter NWT WCTU AR, 1904, p. 20.

[35]Alta.-Sask. WCTU AR, 1912, pp. 91-92, and Alta. WCTU AR, 1929, p. 73.

[36]Ibid., 1912, pp. 91-92.

[37]*Report of the Annual Convention of the Saskatchewan Woman's Christian Temperance Union,* hereafter Sask. WCTU AR, 1913, pp. 52, 53.

[38]Alta. WCTU AR, 1927, p. 31.

[39]Alta. WCTU AR, 1921, p. 73.

[40]Alta. WCTU AR, 1928, p. 36; *Canadian White Ribbon Tidings,* Nov. 1929, p. 224; and *The Northern Messenger,* Jan. 1930, p. 14.

[41]*The Northern Messenger,* Jan. 1930, p. 14.

[42]*The Canadian Girl* and *The Canadian Boy.* See Oct. 11, 18, 25, Nov. 1, 8 and 15, 1930 editions.

[43]1931 National Temperance Study Course for Sunday Schools. Board of Christian Education, Church School Administration. Temperance Lessons, 1931-40. B12, F80, United Church of Canada Archives.

[44]Alta. WCTU AR, 1918, p. 32.

[45]Undated, unsigned letter in WCTU files, Glenbow; possibly Mrs. Stewart to Mrs. McElroy, in the late 1920s, F3, B1(E).

[46]Alta. WCTU AR, 1927, pp. 68-69.

[47]*Memorandum* on Little White Ribboners' Department of Work adopted by Dominion WCTU, B8, F46(E).

[48]"Wise Words to Mothers and Fathers" concerning *Alcohol and Its Influence on Health* by Florence Stackpoole, B1, F16(E).

[49]Alta.-Sask. WCTU AR, 1905, pp. 33-34.

[50]Alta. WCTU AR, 1917, p. 60.

[51]Alta. WCTU AR, 1927, p. 68.

[52] Ibid.

[53]Alta. WCTU AR, 1917, p. 59.

[54]Loyal Temperance Legion of Canada (LTL) (constitution and suggestions for juvenile temperance work); and Lesson Manual with Hints and Helps. Mrs. A.E. Jones papers, Saskatchewan Archives Board, Regina.

[55]Alta.-Sask. WCTU AR, 1911, p. 81.

[56]Alta.-Sask WCTU AR, 1908, p. 50.

[57]Alta.-Sask WCTU AR, 1911, p. 67.

[58]Alta. WCTU AR, 1915, p. 47.

[59]Alta. WCTU AR, 1913, p. 56.

[60]Alta.-Sask. WCTU AR, 1911, p. 67.

[61]Alta.-Sask. WCTU AR, 1908, p. 50.

[62]Alta. WCTU AR, 1917, p. 48 and AR, 1919, p. 32.

[63]Alta. WCTU AR, 1919, p. 35.

[64]Alta. WCTU AR, 1920, p. 53.

[65]Alta.-Sask. WCTU AR, 1911, p. 66.

[66]Alta. WCTU AR, 1921, pp. 54-55.

[67]Alta. WCTU AR, 1921, p. 55.

[68]*Canadian White Ribbon Tidings*, Oct. 1929, p. 201 and *White Ribbon Tidings*, Aug. 1905, p. 416.

[69]Alta.-Sask. WCTU AR, 1905, p. 33.

[70]*Canadian White Ribbon Tidings*, Oct. 1929, p. 201. Although the "Y" was aimed at young women, men could become honorary members. They could not, however, hold office, because women needed at least one organization where by constitution they held office and learned how to run a meeting and make decisions. *White Ribbon Tidings*, July 1905, p. 392.

[71]Alta. WCTU AR, 1921, p. 55. The *White Ribbon Tidings* for Apr. 1921 listed twenty-seven activities a "Y" could do — from editing a temperance newspaper for Sunday schools and organizing a sunshine band to visit "shut ins," to putting Bibles and good reading matter in cabooses of freight trains and holding a newspaper clipping evening with prizes for the most temperance clippings.

[72]Alta. WCTU AR, 1920, p. 51.

[73]*Canadian White Ribbon Tidings*, Mar. 1928, p. 68.

[74]Alta. WCTU AR, 1923, pp. 61-63.

[75]Alta. WCTU AR, 1921, p. 56.

[76]Geraldine Joncich Clifford, "Teaching as a Seedbed of Feminism." Paper presented at the Fifth Berkshire Conference on Women's History, Vassar College, Poughkeepsie, New York, June 1981.

[77]Alison Prentice, "The Feminization of Teaching" in Susan Mann Trofimenkoff and Alison Prentice, eds., *The Neglected Majority: Essays in Canadian Women's History* (Toronto: McClelland and Stewart, 1977).

12

Public Schools and the Workers' Struggle; Winnipeg, 1914-1921

Bill Maciejko

The experience of western Canadian workers has been documented else-where.[1] In part, it is a history of people living and working in the worst of conditions, judged even by the harsh standards of the day; and, in part, it is a history of people seeking radical solutions, against entrenched and often ruth-less opposition.[2] Theirs was a struggle not only for better wages and working conditions, but often for the creation of a new social order consistent with their experience and ideals. For the radicals, it was a struggle over the basic values and ideals upon which Canadian society is structured. The purpose of this chapter is to present a critique of public schooling by the radical workers around World War I, and their attempt to assert the worth of the values and ideals of their working-class culture for the public education system in Win-nipeg. It was a contest for ideological control, entered into when the radical workers perceived public schools as being used to promote an ideology, that is, a systematic set of values and beliefs, in opposition to their own.

The radicalism of western Canadian workers is often seen to have crested in the years 1914 through 1921. The strikes of 1919 may even be interpreted as the high (or low) point of the radical movement.[3] Bryan D. Palmer, in surveying the history of Canadian workers, raised objections to the "excep-tionalist" interpretation of radicalism, and placed the movement in a long tradition of workers' struggle.[4] He found this tradition to be linked to, or part of, a working-class "culture marked off from that of its rulers."[5] In his *Work-ing-Class Experience,* Palmer outlined this culture as having an essentially independent community life including social norms and controls, leisure activities, a literature, and a press all created by, or used by, exponents of working-class values and aspirations. This culture was maintained in Winni-peg, led by people who had brought their working-class traditions from Ontario, Britain, and continental Europe,[6] and infused with the ideas and activities of the American workers' movement.[7] All this was reported weekly in Winnipeg by an active labour press, which at that time consisted of *The Voice,* replaced by the *Western Labor News* in 1918, and joined by the *O.B.U. Bulletin* in 1919. These papers were supported by individual subscription, and, when approved at a general meeting, by union locals which ordered copies in lots to be either re-sold or distributed free to members. *The Voice* and the *News* also carried paid commercial advertisements, apparently screening these so as to advertise only those businesses which treated employ-ees and consumers in a decent manner.

The labour press was an important vehicle for the ideas and campaigns of working-class leaders. These leaders, many of whom came from Britain where they were often "schooled in the militant and socialist environment of British working-class politics,"[8] became ascendant in the western Canadian workers' movement in the era of the First World War. R.B. Russell, a Scot machinist, brought with him ideas of syndicalism seen in his leadership of the One Big Union (OBU) and in the Winnipeg General Strike of 1919. After his release from prison for strike activity, Russell continued to lead the OBU and to be an active advocate of labour reform until the fifties. R.A. Rigg, an immigrant bookbinder who had trained as a Methodist preacher in England, was most active prior to the war. He was a member of the Socialist Party of Canada (SPC), and an executive member of the Winnipeg Trades and Labor Council (WTLC). When the influence and organization of the SPC began to decline, Rigg was instrumental in creating the Winnipeg branch of the then decidedly Marxist, Social Democratic Party (SDP). He was elected alderman in 1913 and an MLA in 1914, both on the SDP ticket. As worker militancy increased, Rigg responded by moving to the right. Because he opposed radicalism in 1919, he was granted only probationary membership in the Dominion Labor Party[9] and eventually withdrew his application for membership.[10] He served the interests of the conservative unionists against the OBU in the twenties, deserting the radical cause, and using what influence he had left to urge rank-and-file workers to rejoin the international unions, thus joining forces with the business interests of the city. Rigg, however, before this reversal was an active and effective opponent of capitalism.

Rigg was joined in the legislature of Manitoba in 1915 by F.J. Dixon. Dixon's career was the reverse of Rigg's. Prior to the war Dixon, a moderate, had opposed socialism, but as social injustice continued, and as the excesses of militarism and imperialism increased, Dixon became more and more radical. He organized many well-attended demonstrations against the war. In 1918 he was a founding member of the Dominion Labor Party (DLP). By 1921 he was too radical even for the DLP and led a splinter group of activists and politicians out of the DLP to form the Independent Labor Party (ILP). The ILP was loyal to the members and ideals of the OBU, and as evidence that even those workers forced to quit the OBU (by tactics of the conservative unionists, the bosses and the state) were supportive of the values and goals of the OBU, it was the ILP which survived at the polls, eclipsing the DLP, and becoming eventually the Cooperative Commonwealth Federation (CCF), when linked with the farmers' movement. Dixon continued to represent many of the workers' struggles, both in and out of the legislature, until he was forced to resign his seat in 1923, severely weakened by the cancer which eventually killed him.

A.W. Puttee, a printer by trade and a British immigrant, was a Lib-Lab MP, elected in Winnipeg in 1900. After 1904 Puttee was active on both the WTLC and on city council. From 1897 to 1918 he was editor of *The Voice,* in which capacity he campaigned against the war, against imperialism, and for the workers' struggle, supporting even his more radical opponents including the SPC and the Industrial Workers of the World (IWW) when they conflicted with the common enemy — the capitalists. Puttee, who did not support the principle of the general strike, lost support of many workers in 1918 because of his moderation. *The Voice* was then replaced by the *Western Labor News,* owned by the WTLC and edited by William Ivens, a social gospel preacher who joined with the radical workers in their opposition to militarism and in their social struggles. He was imprisoned for his part in the General Strike of 1919. Ivens, a founder of the Labor Church, continued to work for the OBU and the ILP, editing the *O.B.U. Bulletin* after the conservatives had recaptured the WTLC and the *News* late in 1919. Ivens was elected MLA while still serving his prison term in 1920. In the ILP Ivens was linked politically with J.S. Woodsworth, the longtime social activist who had become increasingly radicalized during the war and was also arrested in 1919 as a strike supporter. He too advocated the OBU. In 1921 he was elected as an ILP-endorsed candidate for parliament. He continued to represent a working-class riding in Winnipeg through the forties, eventually leading the CCF federally.

Woodsworth and other radical leaders acted against the suffering and exploitation of people in their communities. Many were linked directly or by association with both the social gospel movement and the radical unions. They often opposed war on principle, or specifically because they saw the war as unjust and unnecessary, being waged because of, and to the profit of, the capitalists. They came to see capitalism as a cause of war and of social deprivation in general. These leaders and others were part of the English-speaking workers' movement and were joined in spirit and often in action by non-English speaking radicals (i.e., people to whom English was a second language), including Finns, Poles, Ukrainians, Germans, Italians, and Jews of various nationalities. While they never formed a single party, or even a cohesive association, people such as these acted at the centre of an eclectic, loosely-defined, socialist, force which proposed an alternate vision for Canadian society.[11] This vision and the activities which proceeded from it were not confined to the radical few, although these were of course the most articulate and the most visible. By 1919 many rank-and-file workers expressed the same type of opposition to the capitalist order as their leaders. Literally thousands of people would participate in open-air rallies and demonstrations in support of radical principles and personalities. And, when questioned, many rank-and-file workers would declare the vision, ideals and struggles of the leaders to be their own.[12]

The labour press reflected the scope and the eclecticism of the workers' movement. The press was not exclusively the mouthpiece of the leaders. It provided a source of expression, inspiration and information for many individuals who wrote to the editors expressing their support of and opposition to the actions of the leadership. In every issue readers were informed of the activities and interests of their 'fellow workers' throughout the industrialized world, and were kept up-to-date on local concerns and actions, including their own athletic tournaments, social events, lectures, and meetings. The press provided an alternative view to the "dailies" that were seen to serve the interests of their opponents on almost every subject touching the community from international diplomacy to the price of bread at the corner store. One subject which received a good deal of attention in the workers' press was schooling. Workers were concerned not only with the availability of schools but with the essential social function of the schools; not only that children should read, but also with what they read. At this fundamental level, schooling was often perceived as conflicting with the values of working-class culture.

Just as the essence of schooling is not the buildings, materials or lessons in themselves, so the essence of culture, as a social rather than an "artistic" concept, is not the materials or practices in which culture is manifested. The essence of culture is an ethos, a base of ideas, values, and beliefs from which all else is constructed. It is at this basic level that culture provides the standard and the source for "the whole way of life" for a person or group of people.[13] Where the basic ethos of a society varies, its people often belong to separate cultural groups. Accordingly, Raymond Williams has defined "working-class culture" and "bourgeois culture," as follows:

> [Working-class culture] is not proletarian art, or council houses, or a particular use of languages; it is, rather, the basic collective idea, and the institutions, manners, habits of thought and intentions which proceed from this [collective idea]. Bourgeois culture, similarly, is the basic individualist idea and the institutions, manners, habits of thought and intentions which proceed from that [individualist idea].[14]

Because the essence of culture is an idea, it is not pre-determined by, but may be influenced by, birth, social position, or occupation. Working-class culture could attract members of the "lower, middle, or upper classes." Likewise, bourgeois culture could attract members of all 'classes.' Many members of the proletarianized classes, people categorized together by virtue of not owning or controlling the resources and tools of production, who believed their best chance for advancement lay in individualist pursuit, could adopt the bourgeois world view. They would then become culturally bourgeois, regardless of any actual change to their material or social condition.

Bourgeois reformers are those who seek to remove social inequity and injustice by "equalizing opportunity," often using the schools to help achieve their goals. Working-class reformers, by definition radicals, seek to remove and reconstruct the structures seen to create social inequity and injustice. Although some working-class activists denounce bourgeois school reform, others sanction such reforms as "band-aid solutions." All, implicitly or explicitly, contest the ideological and systemic functions of schooling.[15] The ideological contest over schooling was part of the radical workers' struggle in Winnipeg.

The ideas of working-class culture were demonstrated in Winnipeg in unions; in socialism as opposed to capitalism; in anti-imperialism, as opposed to chauvinistic patriotism and imperialism. Its beliefs were consistent with the working-class ideals of "international socialism," or "international working-class," and the notion of human brotherhood of some social gospel advocates. Even with the factionalism and internal disputes over doctrines and methods which so often impeded their actions, the radical workers maintained sufficient strength and commitment to figure largely in the history of the western labour movement. Their disputes centred on how best to attain their goals, not on the existence of those goals. It was over pursuit of those working-class goals and the expression of those collective values that the radical workers came into conflict with the function of the public school. They saw the school as an agency that too easily expressed bourgeois values.

Bourgeois culture, as defined above, was clearly demonstrated in Winnipeg in this same period. The politics, economy, and social life of the city were dominated by a loose association of businessmen which functioned as a single elite of capitalists,[16] who, according to Artibise, held "in common a certain set of values," exemplified by personal advancement through individual effort and "little concern with the goal of creating a humane environment for all the city's citizens."[17] Irving Abella described the elite as possessing the "fiercely individualistic . . . [ideas of] Social Darwinists."[18] When this bourgeois elite engaged a "social conscience," their efforts took the form of private charities and individual acts of philanthropy which did not entail systemic changes or any threat to their own advantage. In Dixon's "Land Values" column, which appeared weekly in *The Voice,* the question, "What is 'Philanthropy?'," was answered, in part, as follows:

> The men usually called "philanthropists," as a rule, uphold existing injustice but give money to relieve victims of the wrongs they uphold . . . These philanthropists may well be described as men who give money to repair a little of the harm they themselves helped to do or as Tolstoy has well stated: 'men willing to do anything to help the poor except get off their backs.' . . . [This is] the true nature of what is commonly called 'philanthropy.'[19]

Thus perceived, philanthropy is only another means which, by design or unplanned consequence, reinforces the power of the bourgeoisie while robbing the recipients of power. At the same time, the relationships of philanthropy reinforce social stratification and ranking. Moreover, philanthropy could even be profitable occasionally, as S.J. Farmer noted. In 1912 vacant lots in Winnipeg were being turned into garden plots under the direction and control of the Winnipeg Garden Club. Farmer, who later became an MLA and leader of the Manitoba ILP and CCF, wrote:

> It would be better to so arrange things that everyman could own his garden, instead of having to depend upon semi-charitable organizations. . . . The

members of the Winnipeg Real Estate Exchange, which is kindly cooperating with the the Garden Club . . . [will have] the value of their holdings . . . increased by the improvements resulting from the cultivation of 'their' vacant lots.[20]

The elite did not, of course, directly involve themselves in controlling the details of everyday life for all people in the city. Careless has found that most often the "elite in-group" left the running of civic affairs to a lesser group of politicians and professionals who shared their interests and values.[21] The elite did not directly manipulate the community, but, as Gerald Friesen has said, it was the elite "who 'set the tone' or established the rules . . . asserting the rule of law, the power of the church, the influence of the school lesson. . . .,"[22] It was therefore this elite, and those lesser bourgeoisie, with whom the radicals would have to contend in the contest over the function of schooling, for the social function of schooling was to perpetuate the social order "set" by the bourgeoisie.

Schooling is a social process, reflecting and re-creating social values and socially-valued knowledge. But society is not an independently existing organism capable of thinking, valuing, or choosing. People have to decide what "society" values, and what is of value to society. Like any particular expression of society, the school does not *naturally* exist, nor is any use to which it is put *natural*. The crux of the "social control theory" as it is applied to schooling is that a group of people have, or take for themselves, the right to decide these values and this knowledge, and then use the schools to inculcate, indoctrinate, or condition everyone else to adopt that knowledge and adapt to those values. But this involves power, and power is never absolute. Resistance is always possible. In viewing society, Talcott Parsons has defined power as ". . . the capacity of a unit in the social system, collective or individual, to establish or activate commitments to performance that contributes to, or is in the interests of, attainment of the goals of the collectivity."[23] In other words, power is the ability of a person or group to get others to agree to do as instructed or asked. If the others refuse to make this "commitment to performance," the leader is effectively powerless, regardless of position, title, or rank.

If schooling is a method by which people are taught to perform as the "controlling interests" want them to, the people may still refuse, and, more important, people can refuse to allow the school to be used in the manner desired by the leaders. Moreover, they may be able to use the school in a way consistent with their own aims and values. The contest between the radical workers and the bourgeoisie was a contest in power and resistance. The bourgeoisie occupied the decision-making positions in the school system. The problem for the radicals was to influence those decisions, and to have their own decisions actualized.

Education was clearly recognized by workers as being part of the struggle to change society. The radicals never contested the importance of schooling, only the nature of that schooling. R.A. Rigg, in 1913, while active in the SDP and the WTLC, wrote of "the place of education in the labour movement," as follows:

> Side by side with our [union and political] organizing let it never be forgotten that education is fundamentally more important. The incubus of capitalism can only be cast off by a working class whose intelligence has been aroused to realize that there must be a reversal of the present system of industry for profit, to one of industry for use.[24]

Schooling insofar as it provided literacy skills and an increased awareness was seen to be crucial to the radical movement. But schools are not the only place to learn to read or to learn about the world. Compulsory schooling, one of Rigg's goals, had another attraction for many workers in that it was useful in the campaign against child labour.

The labour movement had waged a long battle for the eradication of child labour, invariably linking this goal to compulsory education. When the Trades and Labor Congress of Canada convened in 1898 they demanded free, compulsory education, and the abolition of child labour.[25] In 1905, Daniel De Leon, an American socialist, a founder of the syndicalistic IWW, and an influence in western Canada, wrote of the "open cruelty of capitalism even against the defenseless child," one consequence of which was the denial of schooling.[26] In 1907 the Trades and Labor Congress held a national convention in Winnipeg, and put forth its "Platform of Principles," the first of which was "free, compulsory education."[27] The SPC in December 1911 campaigned in graphic but not exaggerated terms for the removal of children from the workplace, using their weekly, the *Western Clarion,* to ask of workers: "Do you glory in sending your children to work (instead of to school), to be sweated, to be crippled, to be ground to death to feed the children of idle parasites?"[28]

Two weeks after issuing the above challenge to workers to keep their children from the workplace, the *Western Clarion* reiterated the message, citing Eugene Debs, another American socialist known in Canada for both his political and his union activities. Debs wrote that child labour was "a crime against both the children and society," and concluded: "The triumph of Socialism will [provide] for the joy of healthy childhood, for education, and for everything else required in a truly enlightened age for the scientific rearing of the children. . . ."[29]

In 1912 the Trades and Labor Congress was dominated by the "radicalism that permeated Canadian labour."[30] At this time it launched a political campaign which included a "children's programme," including compulsory education, health protection, and "open air schools," all seen as part of the "wage earners' revolt."[31] *The Voice* joined with the Trades and Labor Congress and the American Federation of Labor (AFL), which dominated the Congress after 1902, in denouncing child labour in 1914, because of its destructive effects on children, which included the denial of "a chance to grow, a chance to learn, and a chance to dream."[32]

Manitoba enacted legislation to enforce compulsory school attendance in 1916. *The Voice* seconded the efforts of F.J. Dixon and R.A. Rigg, both then representing working class constituencies in the legislature, in supporting the government's action.[33] The 1916 Public Schools Act of Manitoba made schooling compulsory for children up to age fourteen, excepting those children excused by authority of the Department of Education. Such excuses could be issued for economic reasons, that is, if a child was needed to support the family he or she could be released from school. *The Voice* campaigned not only for free schooling, but for "an ample government endowment" which would enable all children to attend school, whatever the financial circumstance of their family.[34] Financial assistance was long a part of the workers' campaign for schooling, recognizing that legislating children into school was of little benefit if the children could not afford the necessary supplies, or if their labour was needed, in kind or in cash, to support their families.

In 1913 the WTLC had sent a delegation to the Winnipeg School Board asking for "something tangible in the way of free textbooks."[35] Apparently the WTLC felt that the availability of books, which consisted of readers to book IV, the first arithmetic book, and an atlas, was insufficient to encourage parents to send their children to school, since the rest of the supplies still had to be purchased. This same delegation asked the school board to initiate swimming lessons because of the many drownings in the Red River, and to install sanitary drinking fountains in all schools as many schools, especially in the older sections of the city, were using the unhealthy "cup and trough" system. Delegates were told that the board would establish a committee to investigate swimming lessons, but received no recorded reply to their other concerns.[36] The issue of free textbooks and supplies was again raised in *The Voice* in 1914. This time the school board was urged to use the money they had allocated for "soldiers' salaries" for the purchase of the "implements necessary for study," so that children of the poor would not be shamed into playing truant or seeking employment, "so as not to appear poor before their more fortunate companions at school."[37] Earlier that year the WTLC had sent a delegation to the board requesting that eye glasses be supplied at cost to children in need of them.[38] In 1918 the Dominion Labor Party (DLP) used the municipal election to publicize their commitment to the supplying of free textbooks for all grades,[39] presumably through the high school. The policy in 1918 was for the school to supply for loan only the first arithmetic book and the first four readers, the free atlases no longer being offered.

Through their unions and their political organizations, workers advocated not only easier access to schooling but also more schooling. Rigg and Dixon had campaigned for a minimum school-leaving age of fifteen in 1916, but had received little support in the legislature. In 1919, the Winnipeg DLP amended its platform to call for compulsory schooling up to age sixteen.[40] In January 1921 the DLP called for school leaving to be raised to age eighteen, with a concurrent change to the Factories Act of Manitoba to forbid employment of children below the age of eighteen.[41] The One Big Union (OBU), in

June 1921, called for the removal of work permits which allowed children to be excused from school, and called for a general increase in wages to enable workers to keep their children in school.[42] A school-leaving age of eighteen, and the financial resources to actualize it, would grant to all children a high school education, at that time the privilege of only the children of the wealthier citizens.

The efforts of those workers may be seen to comply with similar activities by bourgeois reformers, who also advocated more schooling for all children and the end of child labour. It was only on the surface, however, that such agreement was apparent. The radicals saw schooling as valuable for two reasons, only one of which was shared by some among the bourgeoisie. First, compulsory schooling was effective in combatting child labour, a cause shared with many among the bourgeoisie. Second, radical workers also hoped that education would advance their larger struggle, the struggle to change the capitalist system. Education was to be part of that "revolution." William Ivens, the radical social gospel preacher, only months before he was imprisoned for supporting the workers during the General Strike in 1919, referred to the workers' "demanding greater educational facilities for their children" as an "intellectual upheaval" necessary to realize the radicals' vision of society.[43] How fruitful this ambition would be would depend on what happened inside the schools. The concern for the education of children felt by the radical workers did not end with placing them in school, but also embraced the type of education children would receive.

Critical consciousness is inherent in an "intellectual upheaval" towards radical social change. Far from creating a critical consciousness, public schooling in Manitoba, as elsewhere, was designed from its beginning to produce a homogeneous consciousness with little or no potential for original, or divergent, thinking.[44] By 1902, Manitoba teachers were being exposed to Quick's *Essays on Educational Reformers* as part of their training, in which they were informed that "we are all agreed that morality is more important than learning."[45] For teachers who may have missed reading Quick's declaration, the *Educational Journal of Western Canada* in 1903 informed them "It is far more important to be able to manage a school well than it is to teach it, for the character of the future life of every pupil depends more upon management than upon thinking."[46]

The emphasis on moral training continued to be important in the public schools of Manitoba as in other parts of Canada.[47] In 1915, for example, the official organ of the Department of Education and of the Manitoba School Trustees' Association, the *Western School Journal,* told teachers that among the desired "virtues and habits" to be created in children, was the "right attitude toward work."[48] The next year, W.A. McIntyre, principal of the Manitoba Normal School, wrote that the duty of teachers was "above all" to create socially acceptable attitudes and behaviours in children.[49]

It might be considered of little threat to the workers' struggle that children be taught 'right attitudes' toward work, or be habitualized in certain "virtues," until it is realized in whose interest these virtues, habits, and attitudes were to be created. In 1917 the *Western School Journal* carried the message that teachers should satisfy the businessmen of Manitoba. The businessmen, having trouble with their employees, workers who had previously been students, had made a

> . . . serious indictment of the efficiency of our schools. . . . [They] frequently complain of incompetency, inefficiency, want of tact and adaptability, lack of application, conscientiousness, thoughtfulness and thoroughness in their work.[50]

From the perspective of workers organizing to resist "the bosses," the teachers were being told to create a harmonious and efficient workplace, where workers were loyal first to the boss and the boss's needs. This would, of course, weaken worker solidarity, or in cultural terms, the collectivity. In 1919, William Iverach, president of the Manitoba School Trustees' Association (MSTA), clarified this, stating that the duty of school teachers was to undo such collectivities as "[social] classes, . . . guilds, unions, etc."[51] In place of these working-class collectivities, loyalties were to be transferred to the country, or the empire. Moral behaviour was to become synonymous with patriotic duty, with compliance to the "will of the state." To many workers that state and the "boss" were one and the same, and a call to patriotic duty was viewed by these workers as a call to give up their struggle and acquiesce to the will of the capitalist. Loyalty to the state, however, was paramount among those in control of the school system.

In 1917 the *Western School Journal* informed teachers that the "first question in certifying a teacher should not be with regard to his scholarship and training, but with regard to his character and loyalty."[52] Later that year, the same journal reminded teachers that the role of the educator was to foster a "proper state and municipal spirit."[53] This spirit would be such that it would not threaten the established order with radical change. The 1920 convention of the Manitoba school trustees was addressed by Dr. Flint, principal of Cornell College, who told the trustees that the best weapon against revolution was proper education.[54] In all likelihood, Flint was only reinforcing what the trustees already believed. At that same convention they passed a resolution soliciting the aid of the Canadian Clubs and "other kindred associations" in an attempt to limit the franchise to prevent the foreign voters from being able to act "irresponsibly."[55] The foreign voters were often seen to be supportive of radical candidates at the polls, especially in the North End of Winnipeg, an enclave of "foreigners" which consistently returned socialists in elections. The intended restriction of democratic privilege was not a departure for the trustees. In 1919 Iverach told the trustees, and through them the teachers, that it was the duty of public education to channel freedom, to "see to it that democracy is going to be a safe thing for the world."[56] Here Iverach echoed the beliefs of many who controlled schools and governments in "liberal democratic countries." It is always those in advantaged positions who attempt to control democracy and to decide what is "safe" for the world they dominate. The radicals, had they gained control of the state and the school system, would have used their position to create an intelligence safe for their society, a society based on collectivism, cooperation and a greater level of economic, and therefore political, equality.

Those who sought to empower the workers to gain control of their lives and of their society recognized that the workers had, in general, been defined as politically unsafe, and unfit for government. At one point, *The Voice* carried an attack on a "college textbook" in which it was written that workers were "unfit for political administration," *The Voice* pointed out that:

> Stuff like this has been successfully crammed down the throats of labor men for a long time. They have been thoroughly saturated with the belief that their sole duty was to be humble and diligent hewers of wood and drawers of water.[57]

The article in *The Voice* went on to denounce any right of the capitalists to rule, noting that under capitalist guidance people had been led into poverty and war. The rule of capitalists was said to be only "proficient in keeping labor docile under oppression and thereby creating the appearance of social progress and order."[58]

One method of keeping people "docile" is to create loyalties to their rulers, thus the importance of fostering patriotic sentiments. Patriotism is contrary to the ethos and the function of working-class culture in at least two ways: patriotism entails first loyalty to a governing body removed from the local experience of the people; thus it destroys the effectiveness if not the existence of the local collective. And, it separates people into various national groupings, thus destroying the larger collectivity of common experience. Both these effects of patriotism were recognized by the radicals. *The Voice* described the "patriotism of the capitalist" as being seen in the encouragement of foreign labour by employers, during which they "more or less black-listed" the British worker because of his trade union tradition. But when the foreign worker organized, the capitalist, "adopted a new policy: race hatred. Its controlled sheets bellowed, only as capitalist newspapers know how, to the public that . . . strikers were 'foreigners,' and entitled to no consideration. . . ."[59] A testimony to the accuracy of this perception is found in Clifford Sifton's often cited 'sheep-skin-coats-and-stout-wives' speech, which claimed that the peasant immigrant

> [is] good quality. A Trades Union artisan . . . is, in my judgement . . . very bad quality. I am indifferent as to whether or not he is British-born. It matters not what his nationality is; such men are not wanted in Canada, and the more of them we get the more trouble we shall have.[60]

Sifton, as a businessman, an investor, and as chairman of the Conservation Commission of Canada, a nationally-funded body responsible for investigating, among other issues, urban reform and city planning, would have been as concerned with labour unrest as he would have been with opening up the West to farmers.

In August 1914, when war was declared, *The Voice* announced the event with a cartoon captioned "Three Cheers for War," the 'cheers' being skeletal figures labled "Death," "Debt," and "Devastation."[61] The workers' press never adopted the "rally 'round the flag, boys" attitude to the war, an attitude common in the bourgeois dailies. Throughout the war, men connected with the labour press, such as Dixon, Russell, Ivens, Puttee, and Woodsworth, kept up a steady campaign against "the capitalists' war." To them, the workers' "enemy was the boss, not the German."[62] After waging a long and unsuccessful battle against conscription, they turned their defeat against their opponents, and continued to demonstrate their feeling that the German worker was as much a victim as the Canadian by pointing out the hypocrisy of those who advocated the war. The radical workers contended that phrases like "Our Country" meant little to workers who were so "completely . . . expatriated economically, that few men owned their own homes."[63]

The workers who led the campaign against the war and against conscription were apparently not without some success. In early 1917, out of two thousand men registered in Winnipeg as being fit and able for military service, not one enlisted.[64] As only the radicals publicly encouraged and supported draft evaders, they must have had some influence on the decisions of many of the two thousand who refused to enlist. The radicals were well-known for their positions on the war, yet they were able to maintain the support of large numbers of workers throughout the war and after in both strike situations and at the polls. It is doubtful that they could have secured this support if their "lack of patriotism" was alien to a general sentiment among workers. While the war caused some workers to abandon the radicals, many were themselves radicalized by their wartime experience, and came to see as valid the radical call for fundamental social change.

In preparation for the war, and throughout it, however, the bourgeoisie used the schools to further their aims by creating moral-patriotic loyalties and, many of their opponents claimed, a militaristic spirit in children. In 1912 Dixon denounced the "vociferous heralds of the God of War" who were organizing patriotic demonstrations in Winnipeg.[65] The WTLC, fearing that those "vociferous heralds" were active in the schools, sent a delegation to interview Daniel McIntyre, superintendent of Winnipeg Schools, about their concerns over military drill in the schools.[66] The delegation was apparently unsuccessful, and in January 1914, *The Voice* announced that the capitalists,

> . . . have degraded our public schools into veritable training corps, where the innocence of youth is polluted with the military spirit of bravado and aggression, where . . . the implements of death are bandied about, and looked

upon as lightly as a football outfit. . . . Through military training he [the student] is reduced to a veritable automaton, "ready, aye ready," to obey the word of command, not only to shoot down his fellow man upon some foreign shore, but to do unto death his own kith and kin . . . when they may have the temerity to assemble together to assert their rights. . . . This is all done, with one end constantly in view, and that is, that the present status of Capital and Labor must not be changed.[67]

The perception of militarism in school and the potential threat to the workers which resulted were not the baseless fabrications of a few alarmists. On May 8, 1914, *The Voice* reported that Sam Hughes, the minister of militia, had boasted of using thousands of teachers to train 44,600 children as cadets in Canadian schools.[68] The cadets were seen as a first step toward military enlistment. It was the militia which was a threat to "kith and Kin" who might organize and strike. This fear was very real, especially as Sam Hughes had openly declared that he regarded any strike as "incipient civil war" to be dealt with in those terms.[69] Allowing people who shared Hughes' opinions to influence the public schools, *The Voice* said, had resulted in the creation of a "reactionary policy of poisoning and perverting the minds of Canadian school children."[70]

That influence was apparent in Winnipeg. In March 1914, the *Western School Journal* had encouraged teachers to take a special course to enable them to train students in military drill, which included having children learn first-aid, map reading, signalling, company drill, rifle shooting, and gunnery. In addition to being paid for taking the summer course, teachers were to be paid a dollar a head for every child recruited and trained in the cadets,[71] unusual bonuses to the teachers' normally small wages. In May 1914, the WTLC sent a delegation to the Winnipeg school board to again express its concerns about military training, but all they could report after their meeting was that the board had "signed an application for the formation of a cadet battalion."[72]

The workers who opposed military training in the schools were also anxious about the development of patriotic sentiments, in that it was usually patriotic duty that was used to justify the application of military skills. The schools of Manitoba, like those of other provinces, became active centres of war propaganda, teaching children that the cause of "their country" was just, that the war was totally the fault of the Germans and Austrians, and encouraging them to get involved with the war effort outside the classroom.[73] In 1915 Manitoba school teachers were again reminded that their duty was to prepare children for participation in the cause of Canada and the Empire, "to prepare them mentally, morally and physically for the great destiny which lies ahead of them."[74] This "great destiny" was for "even little children . . . to sacrifice . . . personal interests in . . . behalf [of the British Empire]."[75] That same year, Francis Beynon, a feminist leader active with Dixon and Woodsworth in the anti-war movement, wrote of her opposition to the schools being used to teach patriotism, as patriotism was a tool of the "clever defenders of the established order."[76]

The *Western School Journal* urged children to "do their bit" for the war by joining patriotic organizations such as the Boy Scouts and Red Cross,[77] and by selling the products of their manual training and domestic science classes.[78] *The Voice* saw such events and activities as "ominous," and even in 1917, claimed the "revival of patriotism" in the schools to be the result of "a mistaken emphasis and a false sense of value"; proper values to be taught, it suggested, were those of peace and cooperation.[79] The usefulness of patriotic and "moral" training did not end with the end of war. During the period of labour militancy after the war, the Manitoba School Trustees' Association met and planned to participate in the "National Conference on Character Education," to be held in Winnipeg, October 20-22, 1919. The conference was to facilitate the use of the schools in "making a higher type of citizenship in Canada," and Major C.K. Newcombe, who had earlier addressed the trustees with a "very thrilling account" of tank battles and refugees, was pointed out as an example of that "higher citizenship."[80] As the date for the conference approached, the *O.B.U. Bulletin* announced it under the title of "Dope the Kiddies," as being a "most sinister meeting so far as the education of the working class children is concerned."[81]

The conference resulted in the creation of the National Council of Education, a joint effort by prominent businessmen, religious leaders, government officials, and educators.[82] The conference called for Dominion grants to help meet "the necessity of the rapid and effective 'Canadianization' of the immigrants,"[83] at a time when they were being held responsible for the recent "workers' revolt" in the West. The recommended socialization process was to be controlled by the bourgeois elite, including Sir Edward Beatty, member of the Council and president of the C.P.R.[84] Beatty, when appointed chancellor of McGill in 1922, called for the increased use of education at all levels to teach people to make the "correct decisions," and to become "good and useful citizens," especially as education could affect the working class.[85]

In 1920 the OBU, seeing that the Winnipeg school board had joined with the Canadian Clubs to sponsor classes in the schools on patriotic ethics, alerted parents that such a program would result in "poisoning the minds of youth," and urged parents to,

> . . . warn their children of this pernicious campaign [and explain] . . . to them the true vision of International Brotherhood. . . . Explain to them how modern wars are caused by the desire for Imperial and Commercial expansion, and the aim of the rulers and capitalists of the world is to keep the workers apart.[86]

Perhaps taking as its example the case of New York school children who had struck against thirty-two schools considered to be anti-working-class, the report of which was carried in *The Voice,*[87] the OBU further advised parents to:

> Explain to [the children] what a strike is, and maybe some with a little more
> initiative may take what their parents call "direct action" and we may not
> be surprised to read that, becoming sick and tired of such twaddle and
> nationalistic poison the pupils of some Winnipeg schools would strike in the
> interests of International Brotherhood.[88]

While the OBU tried to alert parents to the "poison" of patriotic teaching, the Dominion Labor Party (DLP) monitored the Winnipeg school board on a regular basis, reporting to its membership any significant occurrences. In October 1920, the school board committee of the DLP attended a meeting of the school board in connection with "the war pictures shown to children."[89] No record has been located of any response made by the board.

The effects of the radicals' campaign against patriotic instruction and military training in the schools were certainly less than they would have desired. No immediate change in policy was made following their representations to the authoritative bodies which seemed content and secure in using the schools, consciously or otherwise, in opposition to the expressed values and ideals of working-class radicals. But, the radical critique of schooling was not completely without effect. On the issue of patriotism, at least, the radical workers were joined by dissident teachers.

The Voice provided a platform for "a rural school teacher" to express her (or his) conviction that the school was being used to implant a war-like mentality in children through the use of readers which were full of war stories and "heroes [who] are mostly professional murderers," including General Wolfe and Sir Francis Drake. The teacher also condemned history books and lessons for "placing before children a civilization . . . founded on murder, race hatred and revenge. . . ." The writer urged other teachers to remove from their lessons "the old blatant Rule Britannia type of patriotism" and replace it with "definite anti-war teachings," even if this meant subverting directions issued by the provincial Department of Education.[90]

In July 1918, William Bayley, the Winnipeg teacher and labour activist who became an MLA in 1920, criticized patriotic teaching, going so far as to attack the use of the national anthem in schools as nothing more than part of the effort to make children "believe that we are the envy and dread of the whole world." He suggested that "God Save the King" be replaced with "God Save the People," and that lessons in patriotism be replaced with "a class of social ethics."[91]

Members of the workers' movement campaigned actively for support from teachers. *The Voice* reported that, as in Britain, in Canada "there is a place of usefulness in the labor cause for teachers and [that] several of them are contributing their talents."[92] In an effort to forge links with teachers, and perhaps to influence what teachers did in the classroom, the workers would frequently champion the teachers' cause.

In 1917 *The Voice* printed a defence of a Winnipeg teacher who had been censured for criticizing the school system of the city. In this defence, *The Voice* advocated that teachers should be free to engage in critical activity, that "the only discipline which teachers should be subjected to is that of FREE-DOM [*sic*]," and that teachers should answer to the needs of the community, not the dictates of the board.[93]

Working-class candidates for school trustee in Winnipeg often used their platforms to publicize the concerns of teachers. In the 1919 school board elections several candidates, all of whom ran under the auspices of the DLP, became teacher advocates. Lawrence Pickup stated that labour representation on the board would ensure that teachers would receive better treatment as employees.[94] C.E. Beekin argued for reduced pupil-teacher ratios to facilitate the teachers' work and to reduce the spread of disease.[95] Edith Hancox, business agent for the radical Women's Labor League which organized support for strikers and hosted Russell's first speaking engagement when he was out on bail,[96] campaigned for the right of teachers to collective bargaining, higher salaries, and free textbooks.[97] None of these candidates was successful, but another DLP candidate, Rose Alcin, was elected. Prior to the 1919 election, the *Western Labor News* had advocated higher salaries for teachers, thus supporting the efforts of Deputy Minister of Education Robert Fletcher to retain good teachers in Manitoba,[98] evidence that the workers would support what they saw as good policy, no matter where it came from. Their struggle was over ideas, not necessarily peronalities.

Working-class candidates had run for the school board before 1919. In 1914 the Labor Representation Committee (LRC), an organization to aid any candidate who would advance the cause of socialism, was joined by the Political Equality League (PEL), a suffragette organization, in supporting the candidacy of Mrs. J.K. Brown.[99] When she won the election, the first woman to do so in Winnipeg, the workers' press rejoiced in the success of "their" candidate,[100] but much of her support may have come not because of the LRC but from the bourgeois supporters of the PEL.

Brown's record on the board is not known so it cannot here be determined if she upheld the interests of the LRC. The Political Equality League itself was not consistent in supporting workers' attempts to place their members on the board. In 1916 workers at the C.P.R. yards in Winnipeg nominated Ernest Robinson, a fellow railway worker, as trustee. Robinson, then president of local 147, International Brotherhood of Blacksmiths and Helpers, had been influential in organizing the Weston Forum, an extension of the People's Forum started by Woodsworth, Dixon, and Puttee as a platform for education and reform. Robinson was endorsed by the LRC.[101] His opponent in the election was Mrs. Hample, a founder of the PEL who enlisted the help of the prominent suffragette, Lillian Beynon Thomas, in her campaign.[102] Beynon Thomas, who was closely connected with Nellie McClung, once described Hample as "a great philanthropist."[103] Apparently bourgeois philanthropy did not always extend to allowing the working-class to represent their own concerns on the school board. Robinson lost to Hample. Hample eventually became chairperson of the board; Robinson became a Labor MLA.

It is reasonable to assume that the suffragettes may simply have wanted one of "their own" on the board. But it should be noted that Hample did not run in another electoral ward where there was no labour candidate and that the suffrage leaders are not on record as supporting candidates like Edith Hancox or Rose Alcin. This type of activity may have helped foster the belief among many workers that the Political Equality League was class-bound, and had nothing to offer working-class women, as *The Voice* once warned when it published a letter to that effect under the heading: "Topical Comments: Canadian Women's Suffrage Movement Dominated by the Wealthy Class."[104]

In 1920 the DLP fielded seven candidates for eight vacant trustee positions, leaving one seat in the North End for the SDP to contest.[105] In the 1921 school board elections, the DLP was again active.[106] In 1920 Rose Alcin was joined on the board by Charles E. Beekin, J. Simpkin, and Maude McCarthy as Labor trustees. The election of 1921 took place during the reorganization of labour politics in Winnipeg, as the Independent Labor Party broke from the DLP, the latter choosing to remain loyal to the conservative trade unionists. None of the DLP candidates was successful that year and the DLP, with no strong members and unable to hold rank-and-file support against the ILP, soon faded away.

With all this activity, the labour politicians were unable to get strong representation on the board, having at most four trustees on a board of fifteen. The *Western Labor News* noted in 1919 that there was a need for workers "to vitalize the School Board," and explained their inability to secure more positions on the board by the fact that they were "shut out because of the property qualifications."[107]

The property qualifications were an important means by which the bourgeoisie kept a tight grip on civic and school-board government in Winnipeg. From its incorporation, the city was governed by commercial interests. Only those people with substantial (though far from elite status) real estate investments could vote or hold office, and those with more property were able to vote more than once in the same election; the amount needed to qualify was raised and lowered to suit the needs of those in control.[108] Workers had little or no influence on the decisions of the civic leaders. The effect of the property qualification "was to allow a commercial elite to govern Winnipeg with but little regard for . . . the labour . . . vote."[109] The same process of exclusion which applied to civic politics applied to school board elections, so that the board was "in effect elected only by the wealthiest sector of the population."[110]

The qualifications which seem small by today's standard disqualified completely all lodgers and boarders, a common type of accommodation for many unskilled, clerical, and young workers of the day. Those who held freehold tenure to property assessed at $100, and those who rented property assessed at $200, were eligible to vote in 1918. In that year, as worker militancy was increasing, two changes were made to the qualifications: the tenants' qualification was doubled (from $100) and spouses of qualified voters were given the right to vote, whereas previously it had been only the actual owner or leaseholder who could vote. This last change would have almost doubled the number of voters of the "propertied classes."

The ratepayers may have contended that since they paid the bills it was their right to govern the city and the school board. But the workers' movement of the time was largely based on an awareness that it was the labour of the workers which produced the wealth and the property of the property owners. They would therefore have rejected any such claims of the bourgeoisie to have "earned the right to rule." Also, since the workers were affected by the policies of the schools and the city, they could have claimed a moral right to have a share in the control of the institutions which affected them.

Recognizing the barriers to working-class representation on the school board, their leaders turned their attention to having the property qualifications removed. In January 1919, the DLP sent William Ivens, "with the usual delegation to the legislature" in an attempt to have the provincial government remove the qualification.[111] The *Western Labor News* optimistically reported that after Iven's presention to the legislature, it was "fully expected that the request [would] be granted at once."[112] The request was not acted on, and in January 1920 the DLP sent a delegation directly to the school board to have the qualification removed.[113] A month later, the DLP authorized S.J. Farmer to follow up on the delegation's action by writing a letter, restating their request, to the board.[114] This still had no effect, and a month after Farmer's letter was to have been written, the lone DLP trustee in Winnipeg, Rose Alcin, tried to get the board to change its position. Alcin received no support from the other trustees who laid the matter aside.[115] In fact, Mrs. Hample, the "great philanthropist" and school trustee, reportedly joined other trustees in declaring that "the property qualification was not large enough in their opinion and should be increased."[116] The "non-political" administration of schooling in Manitoba was also effectively closed to members of the workers' movement. All official decisions about the content and activity of Manitoba schools were made by members of the Manitoba Educational Advisory Board, a provincially-appointed body with statutory powers to control textbook selection, course content, and teacher certification. The Advisory Board answered to the legislature, and was distinct from the Department of Education though it worked closely with that body. In practice, in matters of curriculum and instruction, and in staffing, the official power of the Board was absolute.[117]

The Advisory Board was dominated by a few influential educators, including Daniel McIntyre, superintendent of Winnipeg schools, and Robert Fletcher, deputy minister of education. With due regard to the "progressive" sentiments and rhetoric they shared with many of this period, both were able to remain well-connected with, and well-liked by, the business community of

Winnipeg,[118] the same community which so vehemently opposed the workers' economic and social demands. In 1917 the links between the commercial elite of Winnipeg and the Advisory Board were emphasized when Daniel McIntyre and Robert Fletcher were joined by W.A. McIntyre, principal of the Normal School, advocate of "progressive" education, editor of the *Western School Journal*, and member of the Advisory Board, on a special committee of the Winnipeg Canadian Club. The task of this committee was to implement a special patriotic instruction program, part of which was to glorify the participation of Canadians in the war.[119] This program was of the type radicals had long campaigned against, since such instruction was used by the bourgeoisie to foster its own values and ideals in opposition to those of the working-class radical movement.

In regard to schooling, at least, many workers in Winnipeg might agree that the statement "capital controls the pulpit, the school, and the press,"[120] was no exaggeration. Workers had no direct access to control the schooling of the young citizens of the society in which they lived. Public schooling was authorized by persons who expressed many intentions of using the schools to create values and belief in ideas supportive of their perceptions and advantaged position in society. But radical influence was not totally without impact. It was seen in the "rural school teacher" who campaigned for the subversion of official doctrine on patriotic instruction, urging others to follow a similar course of action against "a civilization . . . founded on murder, race hatred and revenge," and to replace this with teaching based on the collective ideals of internationalism and cooperation.[121] This same collectivism was demonstrated by William Bayley, the Winnipeg teacher and activist, who addressed the 1914 Manitoba Teachers' Convention on the need to use citizenship and civics classes to teach the effects of capitalism, and stated that "no-one should own" the essential resources necessary for production;[122] and who, in 1918 provided "an exhibition lesson on civics" at a public meeting in the Liberty Temple, Winnipeg, which demonstrated how the high school program might be adapted towards teaching "the fundamental truths of our industrial society."[123] It cannot be known from behind the closed door of the classroom how many teachers shared these perspectives and values, or if, or how, they might have translated such ideals into classroom practice.

The radical workers supported compulsory schooling as a method of ending child labour; but, more than this, they recognized that education was an essential part of their struggle to create a society based on the collectivism ethos of working-class culture. The public schools of Winnipeg, as elsewhere in Canada, were the creation of the bourgeoisie, who intended to use the schools as instruments to replicate a society consistent with the individualist ethos of bourgeois culture.

As part of the larger struggle for social control, the radical workers contested the control of schooling, as seen in the debate over patriotic instruction, militarism, and bourgeois morality in the public schools. In this contest the radicals were unable to breach to any significant degree, the political and social barriers to direct representation in the school system bureaucracy. Those persons in positions of authority in the school system gave no indication of being positively influenced by the critique of schooling offered by the radicals, and the schools continued to be used as instruments of instruction and training based on the ideology of the bourgeoisie. The legitimate avenues of power — authoritative position and influence — were effectively closed to radical reform. But people may still choose to use the school to meet their own ideals. Ultimately, the power of the radical rests in the ability of the individual to resist, to choose not to agree, to choose personal alternatives to the bourgeois ideals upon which the society and the school have been constructed, and then, without waiting for systemic changes beyond their power to effect, to initiate personal reforms. In this way schooling in a bureaucratic society may reflect values and ideals other than those of persons in authoritative positions. As, for example, it was declared during the workers' struggle in 1914:

> Of course, we realize that the public schools, like all . . . institutions under capitalism, necessarily express capitalist ideas, but even in such institutions we are glad to find that occasionally a little real and pregnable truth in the way of economics manages to creep in.[124]

Notes

[1]Among these are A. Ross McCormack, *Reformers, Rebels, and Revolutionaries: The Western Canadian Radical Movement, 1899-1919* (Toronto: University of Toronto Press, 1977); David J. Bercuson, *Fools and Wise Men: The Rise and Fall of the One Big Union* (Toronto: McGraw-Hill Ryerson Ltd., 1978); David J. Bercuson, *Confrontation at Winnipeg: Labour, Industrial Relations, and the General Strike* (Montreal: McGill-Queen's University Press, 1974); Norman Penner, *Winnipeg 1919: The Strikers' Own History of the General Strike* (Toronto: James Lorimer and Company, 1975).

[2]Irving Abella, *The Canadian Labour Movement, 1902-1960* (Ottawa: Canadian Historical Association, 1978), p. 5.

[3]David J. Bercuson, "Labour Radicalism and the Western Industrial Frontier: 1897-1919," in R. Douglas Francis and Donald B. Smith, eds., *Readings in Canadian History: Post-Confederation* (Toronto: Holt, Rinehart and Winston of Canada, Ltd., 1982), p. 157.

[4]Bryan D. Palmer, *The Working-Class Experience: The Rise and Reconstitution of Canadian Labour, 1800-1980* (Toronto: Butterworth and Co., Canada, Ltd., 1983), pp. 177-178.

[5]Ibid., p. 137.

[6]The antecedents of the Winnipeg workers' experience may be seen in Gregory S. Kealey, *The Toronto Workers Respond to Industrial Capitalism: 1867-1892* (Toronto: University of Toronto Press, 1980); G.S. Kealey and B.D. Palmer, *Dreaming of What Might Be: The Knights of Labor in Ontario, 1880-1900* (Cambridge: Cambridge University Press, 1982); G.S. Kealey and Peter Warrian, eds., *Essays in Canadian Working Class History* (Toronto: McClelland and Stewart Ltd., 1976); also, see Henry Pelling,

A History of British Trade Unionism (Harmondsworth, England: Penguin Books Ltd., 1971) for the British tradition.

[7]An idea of the radical tradition from continental Europe, which was felt in Winnipeg, is contained in Donald Avery, *'Dangerous Foreigners': European Immigrant Workers and Labour Radicalism in Canada, 1896-1932* (Toronto: McClelland and Stewart Ltd., 1979); for a discussion of immigrant radical leadership in Canada, see J. Donald Wilson and Jorgen Dahlie, eds., *Canadian Ethnic Studies: Special Edition: Ethnic Radicals* 10:2(1978); A.R. McCormack, *Reformers, Rebels, and Revolutionaries,* gives an indication of the exchange of ideas and personalities between the American and western Canadian radical movements.

[8]J.E. Rae, "The Politics of Class: Winnipeg City Council, 1919-1945," in Carl Berger and Ramsay Cook, eds., *The West and the Nation* (Toronto: McClelland and Stewart Ltd., 1976), p. 235.

[9]Dominion Labor Party, "Executive Minutes," Aug. 7, 1919; MG 10, A14-2: Box 2; File 5; Provincial Archives of Manitoba, hereinafter PAM.

[10]Dominion Labor Party, "Minutes," Sept. 10, 1919; MG 10, A14-2: Box 2; File 6; PAM.

[11]J. Donald Wilson and Jorgen Dahlie, eds., *Canadian Ethnic Studies* 10:2(1978); A.R. McCormack, *Reformers, Rebels, and as Revolutionaries*; and, D. Avery, *'Dangerous Foreigners'*, best demonstrate this eclectic character of the labour movement; perspectives of the impact of immigration on western Canadian working-class society, and politics, may be seen in Frances Swyripa and John Herd Thompson, eds., *Loyalties in Conflict: Ukrainians in Canada During the Great War* (Edmonton: Canadian Institute of Ukrainian Studies, University of Alberta, 1983); J. Herd Thompson, *The Harvests of War: The Prairie West, 1914-1918* (Toronto: McClelland and Stewart Ltd., 1978); Alan F.J. Artibise, "Divided City: The Immigrant in Winnipeg Society, 1874-1921," in Gilbert A. Stelter and Alan F.J. Artibise, eds., *The Canadian City: Essays in Urban History* (Toronto: McClelland and Stewart Ltd., 1977), pp. 300-336; and, D. Avery, "The Radical Alien and the Winnipeg General Strike of 1919," in C. Berger and R. Cook, eds., *The West and the Nation*, pp. 209-231; J.E. Rae, "The Politics of Class," in C. Berger and R. Cook, eds., *The West and the Nation*, pp. 232-249.

[12]G.S. Kealey, "1919: The Canadian Labour Revolt," *Labour/Le Travail* 13 (Spring, 1984):12.

[13]Raymond Williams, *Culture and Society, 1780-1950* (London: Chatto and Windus, 1967), pp. xvii-xviii.

[14]Ibid., p. 327.

[15]A parallel argument is seen in the debate between the "impossiblists" and other socialists over the issue of trade unions. The impossiblists held that such devices only strengthened the system by co-opting discontent and pacifying workers; others thought that these could be agencies toward the eventual creation of a socialist society, even though most of the leadership of the international unions had early in their history renounced radical social change. The theme of this debate recurs throughout McCormack's *Reformers, Rebels, and Revolutionaries.*

[16]Alan F.J. Artibise, *Winnipeg: A Social History of Urban Growth, 1874-1914* (Montreal: McGill-Queen's University Press, 1975), p. 23; and J.E. Rae, "The Politics of Class," p. 245.

[17]Alan F.J. Artibise, *Winnipeg: A Social History*, p. 23.

[18]Irving Abella, *The Canadian labour Movement*, p. 5.

[19]"What is a 'Philanthropist?'," *The Voice*, Aug. 1, 1913, p. 6.

[20]S.J. Farmer, "The Winnipeg Garden Club," *The Voice*, Apr. 12, 1912, p. 3.

[21]J.M.S. Careless, "Aspects of Urban Life in the West, 1870-1914," in G. Stelter and A.F.J. Artibise, eds., *The Canadian City*, p. 132.

[22]Gerald Friesen, *The Canadian Prairies: A History* (Toronto: University of Toronto Press, 1984), p. 286.

[23]Talcott Parsons, "Evolutionary Universals in Society," in Leon H. Mayhew, ed., *Talcott Parsons On Institutions and Social Evolution: Selected Writings* (Chicago: The University of Chicago Press, 1982), pp. 309-310.

[24]R.A. Rigg, "The Place of Education in the Labor Movement," *The Voice*, Oct. 3, 1913, p. 4.

[25]Bryan D. Palmer, *Working-Class Experience*, p. 158.

[26]Daniel De Leon, *The Preamble of the Industrial Workers of the World*, (Edinburgh: Socialist Labor Press, 1907), p. 17. [an address given by De Leon in Minneapolis, July 10, 1905].

[27]Trades and Labor Congress, "Platform of Principles," in *Twenty-Third Annual Convention of the Trades and Labor Congress of Canada* (Winnipeg: TLC, 1907), p. 1. R.B. Russell Collection, MG 10, A14-2; box 15; PAM.

[28]*Western Clarion*, Dec. 9, 1911.

[29]Eugene V. Debs, "Children of the Poor," *Western Clarion*, Dec. 23, 1911.

[30]Desmond Morton and Terry Copp, *Working People: An Illustrated History of the Canadian Labour Movement* (Ottawa: Deneau Publishers, 1980), p. 98.

[31]"The Wage Earners Revolt," *The Voice*, Sept. 27, 1912, p. 1.

[32]"Condemns Child Labor," *The Voice*, June 5, 1914, p. 3.

[33]"Current Events: Some Legislation on Education," *The Voice*, Feb. 11, 1916., p. 1.

[34]"Current Events: Why Ask For More?," *The Voice*, Feb. 18, 1916, p. 1.

[35]"The Trades and Labor Council: Teach Swimming," *The Voice*, Sept. 19, 1913, p. 5.

[36]Ibid.

[37]"Jottings form Billboard," *The Voice*, Sept. 11, 1914, p. 1.

[38]"Trades and Labor Council: Communications," *The Voice*, Apr. 17, 1914, p. 1.

[39]"Dominion Labor Party," *Western Labor News*, Nov. 1, 1918, p. 1.

[40]Dominion Labor Party, "Minutes," Jan. 22, 1919, MG 10, A14-2, Box 2, File 6, PAM.

[41]Ibid., Jan. 26, 1921.

[42]"Exploited Children," *O.B.U. Bulletin*, June 18, 1921, p. 2.

[43]William Ivens, "Signs of the Times," *Western Labor News*, Jan. 17, 1919, p. 8.

[44]Neil G. McDonald, "David J. Goggin: Promoter of National Schools," in David C. Jones, Nancy M. Sheehan, Robert M. Stamp, eds., *Shaping the Schools of the Canadian West* (Calgary: Detselig Enterprises Ltd., 1979), p. 24.

[45]Robert Herbert Quick, *Essays on Educational Reformers* (New York: D. Appleton and Co., 1901), p. 492. [copy inscribed, "Manitou 1902" Manitou, Manitoba was then site of Normal School classes].

[46]*Educational Journal of Western Canada* 4(Jan. 1903):272, cited in Richard N. Henley, "The Compulsory Education Issue and the Socialization Process in Manitoba Schools: 1897-1916," (M.Ed. thesis, University of Manitoba, 1978), p. 90.

[47]William Bruneau, "Opportunism and Altruism in Official Moral Education, 1880-1939: The Examples of France and Canada," *History of Education Review,* 14, (1985):25-39.

[48]"Editorial," *Western School Journal,* 10:3(Mar. 1915):78.

[49]W.A. McIntyre, *Talks and Discussions with Young Teachers: An Introduction to Pedagogy* (Toronto: The Copp, Clark Co. Ltd., 1916), p. iii.

[50]"Trustees' Bulletin," *Western School Journal,* 12(Feb. 1917):50.

[51]William Iverach, "Address to the Convention," *Proceedings of the Thirteenth Annual Convention of the Manitoba School Trustees' Association* (Winnipeg: MSTA, 1919), p. 17.

[52]"Education and Democracy," *Western School Journal,* 12(Apr. 1917): 158.

[53]"Editorial," *Western School Journal,* 12(Sept. 1917):255.

[54]*Proceedings of the Fourteenth Annual Convention of the Manitoba School Trustees' Association* (Winnipeg: MSTA, 1920), p. 8.

[55]Ibid., p. 13.

[56]William Iverach, "Address to the Convention," MSTA, 1919, p. 15.

[57]"Current Events: Labor and Two Professors of Economics," *The Voice,* Feb. 5, 1915, p. 1.

[58]Ibid.

[59]John Gabriel Saltis, "Foreigners, Etc.," *The Voice,* July 27, 1917, p. 5.

[60]Clifford Sifton, "The Immigrants Canada Wants," *Maclean's Magazine,* 35:7(Apr. 1, 1922):16.

[61]"Three Cheers for War," [cartoon] *The Voice,* Aug. 7, 1914, p. 1.

[62]David J. Bercuson, *Fools and Wise Men,* p. 58.

[63]Scott Nearing, "Our Country," *The Voice,* Apr. 27, 1917, p. 5.

[64]Robert Craig Brown and Ramsay Cook, *Canada, 1896-1921: A Nation Transformed* (Toronto: McClelland and Stewart Ltd., 1974), p. 220.

[65]F.J. Dixon, "The Jingoes on the Firing Line," *The Voice,* Sept. 20, 1912, p. 8.

[66]*The Voice,* July 19, 1912, p. 5.

[67]George Scott, "The Coming Conflict," *The Voice,* Jan. 2, 1914, p. 7.

[68]"Boasts of Training Cadets," *The Voice,* May 8, 1914, p. 6.

[69]"Jottings from Billboard," *The Voice,* May 15, 1914, p. 1.

[70]"Boasts of Training Cadets," *The Voice,* May 8, 1914, p. 6.

[71]"Summer School for Cadet Instructors and Male Teachers' Military and Physical Drill," *Western School Journal,* 9(Mar. 1914):5-6.

[72]"Labor Men at School Board," *The Voice,* May 15, 1914, p. 3.

[73]John Herd Thompson, *Harvests,* pp. 39-43.

[74]J.H. Mulvey, "President's Address," *Western School Journal,* 10(May 1915):156.

[75]Ibid.

[76]cited in Ramsay Cook, "Francis Marion Beynon and the Crisis of Christian Reformism," in Carl Berger and Ramsay Cook, eds., *The West and the Nation,* pp. 197-198.

[77]W.A. McIntyre, "The Year That Has Gone," *Western School Journal,* 112(Dec. 1917):421-422.

[78]"Patriotism and Production in the Public and High Schools of Manitoba for 1917," *Western School Journal,* 12(Sept. 1917):270-272.

[79]"Our Educational Forces and the Problem of War and Peace," *The Voice,* Mar. 9, 1917, p. 6.

[80]*Proceedings of the Thirteenth Annual Convention of the Manitoba School Trustees' Association,* (Winnipeg: MSTA, 1919), p. 9.

[81]"Dope the Kiddies," *O.B.U. Bulletin,* Oct. 4, 1919, p. 2.

[82]Alf Chaiton, "Attempts to Establish a National Bureau of Education, 1892-1926," in Alf Chaiton and Neil G. McDonald, eds., *Canadian Schools and Canadian Identity* (Toronto: Gage 1977), pp. 121-122.

[83]H.T.J. Coleman, "The Winnipeg Conference on Moral Education," *Queen's Quarterly,* 27(Jan.-Mar. 1920): 317.

[84]Alf Chaiton, "Attempts to Establish a National Bureau of Education," p. 122.

[85]John Boyd, "The University's Role," *The Canadian Magazine,* 58(Jan. 1922):218 and 221.

[86]"Poisoning the Minds of Youth," *O.B.U. Bulletin,* Oct. 16, 1920, p. 1.

[87]A. Vernon Thomas, "N.Y. Mayorality Election and the Gary School System," *The Voice,* Nov. 2, 1917, p. 5.

[88]"Poisoning the Minds of Youth," *O.B.U. Bulletin,* Oct. 16, 1920, p. 1.

[89]Dominion Labor Party, "Executive Report, Minutes," Oct. 13, 1920, MG 10, A14-2, Box 2, File 6, PAM.

[90]E.D., "Start With the School Children," *The Voice,* May 19, 1916, p. 7.

[91]"Bayley's Vancouver Speech," *The Voice,* July 19, 1918, p. 2.

[92]"Current Events: Bayley On Another Mission," *The Voice,* June 21, 1918, p. 1.

[93]"Current Events: Teachers are Servants of the City," *The Voice,* Apr. 20, 1917, p. 1.

[94]"Ward Two Fight Begins," *Western Labor News,* Oct. 31, 1919, p. 8.

[95]"Blumeburg Off to a Good Start in Ward Six," *Western Labor News,* Oct. 31, 1919, p. 8.

[96]"Women's Labor League," *O.B.U. Bulletin,* Sept. 20, 1919, p. 3.

[97]"Good Meeting at Argyle School," *Western Labor News,* Nov. 7, 1919, p. 1.

[98]"Manitoba Teachers are Underpaid," *Western Labor News, Sept. 5, 1919, p. 1.*

[99]*"A Woman as Candidate for School Board," The Voice,* Nov. 13, 1914, p. 4.

[100]"Labor Won in Keen Contest," *The Voice,* Dec. 18, 1914, p. 1.

[101]"For School Trustee," and, "L.R.C. Endorses Robinson," *The Voice,* May 5, 1916, p. 8; "School Trustee Election," *The Voice,* May 12, 1916, p. 8.

[102]"School Trustee Election," *The Voice,* May 12, 1916, p. 8.

[103]Lillian Beynon Thomas, "Manitoba Women Voted First," [typed draft, n.d.], "Articles, Short Stories, Radio Scripts, c.c. 1914-1961," Lillian Beynon Thomas Collection, P 191, PAM.

[104]"Topical Comments: Canadian Women's Suffrage Movement Dominated By the Wealthy Class," *The Voice,* Jan. 9, 1914, p. 1.

[105]Dominion Labor Party, "Minutes," Nov. 3, 1920, MG10, A14-2, Box 2, file 6, PAM.

[106]Ibid., Oct. 31, 1921.

[107]"School Board," *Western Labor News,* Mar. 14, 1919, p. 4.

[108]Alan F.J. Artibise, *Winnipeg: A Social History,* pp. 38-42.

[109]Ibid., p. 41.

[110]John Pampallis, "An Analysis of the Winnipeg School System and the Social Forces that Shaped It: 1897-1920," (M.Ed. thesis, University of Manitoba, 1979), p. 48.

[111]Dominion Labor Party, "Executive Minutes," Jan. 29, 1919, MG 10, A 14-2, Box 2, File 5, PAM.

[112]"Labor Party," *Western Labor News,* Feb. 7, 1919, p. 1.

[113]Dominion Labor Party, "Minutes," Jan. 14, 1920, MG 10, A 14-2, Box 2, file 6, PAM.

[114]Ibid., Feb. 25, 1920.

[115]"D.L.P. Notes," *Western Labor News,* Mar. 26, 1920, p. 5.

[116]"Lawyers on School Board Cling to Property Qualifications," *Western Labor News,* Mar. 26, 1920, p. 1.

[117]Alexander Gregor and Keith Wilson, *The Development of Education in Manitoba* (Dubuque, Iowa: Kendall/Hunt Publishing Co., 1984), pp. 49-50.

[118]John Pampallis, "Winnipeg School System and the Social Forces," p. 47.

[119]Winnipeg Canadian Club, "Fiftieth Anniversary of Confederation," April 16, 1917, "Correspondence," T.C. Norris Collection, MG 13, H 1, Number 844, PAM.

[120]"Capital Controls Pulpit, Schools, and the Press," *O.B.U. Bulletin,* May 14, 1921, p. 1.

[121]E.D., "Start With the Children," *The Voice,* May 19, 1916, p. 7.

[122]"Social Democratic Party: Socialism and Schools," *The Voice,* Dec. 18, 1914, p. 3.

[123]"Labor Party Column: Can Children Understand," *The Voice,* May 31, 1918, p. 8.

[124]"Social Democratic Party: Socialism and Schools," *The Voice,* Dec. 18, 1914, p. 8.

Policy-Making and Legislation

13

Transfer, Imposition or Consensus?
The Emergence of Educational
Structures in Nineteenth-Century British Columbia

Jean Barman

During the third of a century between 1849 and 1886 the geographical area we know as British Columbia was transformed from an isolated British colony to a Canadian province directly linked by rail with the rest of the country. Educational structures similarly altered from a simplistic approximation of the British class-based denominational model to a free non-sectarian system similar to that desired, if not always in place for religious and political reasons, elsewhere across North America.

The alteration in educational structures is most readily explained in terms of the larger political shift: British Columbia became a Canadian province; therefore, its educational structures should as a matter of course come to resemble those already in place elsewhere in Canada.[1] Closer assessment of events suggests that such an explanation is simplistic, overemphasizing the influence of external forces on the province's development. Until the completion of the railroad, British Columbia remained geographically separated from the rest of the Dominion. Even when ideas came from elsewhere, they were worked through and very possibly modified to accommodate social and economic priorities in British Columbia.

Such was the case with education. Institutions were not imposed by a minority group within British Columbia; nor were those already in place elsewhere merely reproduced. Rather, educational structures emerged out of the needs of families living in British Columbia for schools that were universally accessible by virtue of being non-sectarian and free of cost. While this growing consensus of opinion was usefully informed by events elsewhere, in particular the geographical areas from which settlers came, it rapidly acquired its own impetus and direction in response to conditions within British Columbia.

Three stages leading to the consensus realization can be distinguished. The first years of white settlement, from 1849 to the early 1860s, witnessed the transfer of structures approximating English practice with their clear class and religions divisions between schools. Dissatisfaction with fee-based denominational education developed during the decade prior to entry into Confederation in 1871. While led primarily by settlers from within British North America and opposed most fervently by British Anglicans, the emerging consensus soon became more broadly based, resulting in new forms of schooling being enacted into law first on Vancouver Island in 1865 and then by the new province's Legislative Assembly. The third period, 1872 to 1886, saw the consensus implemented. Not only were its central premises firmly entrenched, but attempts by the major denominational groups to secure special treatment were repulsed. As well, the role to be accorded non-public schools was defined. The consequence was an educational consensus so well-suited to the particular conditions of British Columbia that it would endure virtually unaltered for almost a century.

I

White settlement on the southern tip of Vancouver Island was initiated by the decision of the Hudson's Bay fur trading company to move its western North American headquarters northward from the Oregon territory, as a consequence of the 1846 boundary settlement between the United States and Britain. The handful of Englishmen and Scots in charge of the new British colony at Victoria quite naturally continued familiar patterns of behaviour, living so far as possible as if in Britain itself. To quote a contemporary, a "fairly rigid class structure" quickly developed, with clear social divisions existing between the Company's officers and "servants," as well as among the handful of settlers who came to work Company farms.[2] Schools were expected to reinforce these divisions.

In the new colony as in England, education was perceived as having two prime functions: preparation to maintain existing place within the social order, and inculcation of denominational religious beliefs. Children from poor families were best prepared to accept their own inevitably inferior position by being given only rudimentary literacy training. Conversely, children in families of high status had to be extensively educated were they to take their expected position at the forefront of their generation. In England opportunities for poor children were limited to denominational charity schools of great simplicity, while families able to afford the fees could choose between local grammar schools and a variety of private-venture schools, generally under the oversight of clergymen of the state Church of England, or Anglican church.[3]

The Hudson's Bay Company traditionally delegated responsibility for the education of officers' children to its chaplain. Thus, the Rev. Robert Staines, an Anglican cleric who arrived from England in 1849, was to receive two hundred pounds, or $1,000, a year for serving as Company chaplain, and another $1,700 for maintaining a fee-based boarding school with both beginning and advanced studies.[4] The education of "the children of the labouring and poorer classes" was a different matter. Governor James Douglas, who soon had charge of both Company and colony, proposed in late 1851 that they be provided with "one or two elementary schools" run by individuals "of strictly religious principles" and offering "a good sound English education and nothing more."[5] A young labourer who had acted as school master during the outward voyage of a group of settlers was hired to open a modest day school in Victoria for the sons of the "Company's labouring servants," with pupils supplying their own books and stationery, as well as contributing a $5 annual fee to supplement the teacher's salary. In 1853 a similar school was opened at Nanaimo, about seventy miles north of Victoria, for the children of English miners working Company coal deposits, and a third district school began a year later at the Company's agricultural settlement of Craigflower west of Victoria.[6] When a new Hudson's Bay chaplain, the Rev. Edward Cridge, arrived in 1855 he was, like his predecessor, expected to "take charge of a Boarding School of a superior class," and very soon was also given oversight of the three district schools, then enrolling about eighty pupils.[7] In addition, for Hudson's Bay servants who were French-Canadian, an alternative existed from time to time when a visiting Catholic priest would offer their children lessons. At least two private-venture girls' schools also operated, perhaps briefly.[8]

In 1858 the tranquility of this isolated British outpost of perhaps five hundred non-Natives was shattered by the discovery of gold on the adjacent mainland.[9] The news having reached California just as its gold rush was in decline, the port of Victoria was inundated over the next several years with miners and entrepreneurs moving north from San Francisco as well as by adventurers from Britain and British North America. In 1858 alone some 25,000 individuals passed through Victoria on their way to the gold fields. By the end of the year the city's stable white population had reached 3,000.[10] The British Crown moved quickly to assert administrative control. Hudson's Bay oversight of the mainland was terminated and a new Colony of British Columbia created on August 2, 1858. The Company's grant to Vancouver Island was not renewed at its expiry on May 30, 1859, and that area also passed under direct administration of the Colonial office.

The immediate effect of the gold rush on education was to extend fee-based denominational structures. The Catholic church moved most quickly. A girls' school was begun in June 1858 by the young, dynamic Quebec order of the Sisters of St. Ann, invited to the west coast by the local bishop. Its first prospectus stated boldly that "difference of religion is no obstacle to admission," and early pupils included not only "English, American and German" boarders with parents in the gold fields but various "girls of Victoria's upper social class."[11] Of fifty-nine boarders who enrolled during the first nine months of 1860, twenty-two had typically Jewish surnames, the majority giving their home address as "California."[12] By 1861 nearly a hundred girls were in attendance, day pupils assessed $35 to $60 a year in fees. Catholic boys' education fared less well: the apparent inability of the French Oblates, who dominated missionary activity, to teach in English meant that most efforts were somewhat sporadic until 1863 when Irish Oblates arrived.[13]

The Church of England was not about to be left behind. No sooner had an Anglican bishop to the two British colonies arrived in early 1860 than he was denouncing "the zealous Church of Rome," so "forward in the matter of education." Bishop George Hills reported home: "Boys of the upper class go at present to the Roman Catholic Bishop's school. . . . The case is therefore urgent." Similarly, "the whole question of Female agency in the mission is most important, in order to prevent the sapping of the very lifeblood of the future population with unsound religion and infidelity."[14] The Anglican church therefore acted quickly both to maintain religious control over the district schools and to establish fee-based schools on a par with its Catholic competition.

While three district schools continued under the supervision of the Rev. Cridge, with their operating subsidy now provided by the government, Bishop Hills personally ensured that they adhere to Anglican doctrine. For example, a "farmer" who protested he "did not wish his children to be taught such trash as the Catechism" was given no alternative but to withdraw them. Use of school buildings was denied such groups as the Quakers and Jews "on the grounds that we never allow our educational or religious buildings to be used for any religious objects not in connection with the Ch[urch] of England." At the same time, these schools remained, to quote the bishop, "old fashioned & inferior"; the Rev. Cridge termed them "in an imperfect and elementary state."[15] Pupils came and went with great rapidity: during the first half of 1861, for instance, the three schools enrolled 111 pupils, of which forty-two had arrived during the time period and thirty-six departed.[16] Despite population growth, additional district schools were opened very slowly, one at Cedar Hill just north of Victoria in 1863 and another a year later at a small settlement in the Cowichan Valley between Victoria and Nanaimo. Little incentive existed to improve or expand these schools, for they were, to quote a contemporary description of Vancouver Island, "designed for families unequal to the expense of a first-class education."[17] As Bishop Hills noted in his diary, he and the colonies' governor agreed that such "schools were only for charity children."[18]

The Anglican church focused its attention on establishing new schools 'for the better classes." Collegiate School for Boys opened on May 28, 1860, and a female complement in September of the same year. Intended "for girls of the middle & upper sort," Angela College offered "careful religious training, in combination with a solid English education, and the usual accomplishments," including "music, singing, drawing, French, Italian, German & Spanish." Collegiate School was, according to its original prospectus, unique "along the shores of the Pacific." "Conducted on the principles of a superior English Grammar School" and intended "to fit the rising generation, as well for commercial and professional pursuits, as for the Universities," the school offered subjects ranging from classics and modern languages to advanced mathematics and architecture. As assessed by an English visitor of 1861, "boys receive a first class education, second only to that of our highest Public Schools."[19]

Although day pupil fees at the two Anglican schools ranged from $60 to $120 a year, they had immediate appeal. As one original Collegiate pupil, son of a Hudson's Bay surgeon, recalled, "All boys whose parents could afford it were immediately sent on the opening of the institution."[20] Among the school's first pupils were also a number of Jewish boys, sons of local businessmen, attracted by the assistant head's teaching of the "Holy Scriptures in Hebrew."[21] In similar fashion, Angela College served "the young ladies of the colony — those requiring the best education."[22] Some four dozen boys and half as many girls were enrolled by the end of 1860, the lesser appeal of Angela College probably due to the competition of St. Ann's Academy and of several private venture schools for girls. About four years later, an educational census was taken of Vancouver Island: of five hundred children in school only a quarter were attending the subsidized district schools, the remainder preferring in roughly equal proportions Anglican, Catholic and private-venture alternatives.[23]

II

Even as fee-based denominational structures of education were seemingly being entrenched on colonial Vancouver Island, opposition was emerging. Centred among arrivals from within British North America, it reflected larger discontents. The historian Allan Smith has argued that by this date Ontarians already possessed a "sense of community and self-consciousness" which came "increasingly to encompass all of British North America in their vision of the national future."[24] Many Ontarians and Maritimers of relatively modest background had come to the west coast with the gold rush, only to discover in this far corner of British North America a self-contained and self-confident social order centred around the original Hudson's Bay families, which they could neither penetrate nor, indeed, provoke into confrontation. However much Amor De Cosmos, the Nova Scotian who established the *Colonist* newspaper in Victoria in December 1858, railed against the Island's monopolistic "Family-Company-Compact," he and his Canadian compatriots remained outsiders, even as newcomers from Britain were being absorbed into the established social life and coopted into administrative positions.[25] Social and religious tensions intertwined. The Church of England had over the last two centuries become a bastion of the privileged due to the disaffection of large numbers of the lower-middle and working classes to the Non-Conformist denominations of Presbyterianism, Congregationalism and Methodism. The Anglican church's base of support was similar in British North America, where it was also identified with the dominant socio-administrative structure. Newcomers from Ontario and the Maritimes belonging for the most part to Non-Conformist, or Evangelical Protestant, denominations almost all favoured greater state intervention in education to create structures intended in common for all the children in a community.[26] Across the United States and British North America, their contemporaries had repeatedly initiated "common" schooling along the frontier.[27] Such activity was consonant with their beliefs for, unlike the Anglicans and Catholics who considered good works and sacramental worship concomitants of salvation, Evangelical Protestants believed salvation possible only through personal conversion. Consequently, less need existed for children to be educated into ritual than for them to grow up adhering to basic Christian morality.

At first advocates of common schooling in British Columbia played within the rules established by the dominant society and created their own fee-based common schools. In August 1861, John Jessop, a Methodist school master from Ontario, opened co-educational Central School with yearly fees of about $30 to $35.[28] "Conducted exclusively on non-sectarian principles" and based "on the admirable system of Canada West [Ontario]," Central School aimed, according to its founder, at "placing the common school system here on a satisfactory basis."[29] The next spring a school run as "the Common Schools of Canada are conducted" was begun at the mainland capital of New Westminster by a missionary sent west by the Canadian Presbyterian church.[30] The schools' limitations soon became evident. For them to be truly "common" to all children necessitated the financial support of government, preferably at levels obviating fees. The New Westminster school early sought a government subsidy, and on its receipt was reorganized as a district school, still charging relatively high fees of $30 and then $18 a year.[31] As such, it continued through the 1860s, complemented in that small mainland community of several hundred white residents by fleeting private ventures, two abortive efforts of the Anglican Church, and small Catholic schools established by the Sisters of St. Ann and the Oblates.[32] By mid-decade small government-subsidized schools were also in operation at nearby Sapperton and in the more distant communities of Langley, Douglas, Lillooet and Yale.[33]

Victoria's first "common" school survived about three years as a private venture. Early enrolments reached some hundred pupils for reasons found reprehensible by Bishop Hills. The private and district schools under Anglican supervision had resisted pressure by white American Southerners settled in Victoria to exclude the offspring of "coloured" families also arrived from the United States. Jessop however agreed, and enrolments boomed. Buoyed by success, he began major physical expansion, a project which, given the school's low fees, became financially disastrous once enrolments stagnated, probably due to the general economic decline which set in as the gold rush ran its course. The school closed in March 1864.[34]

The demise of Jessop's Central School coalesced a consensus of public opinion that was by now expanding beyond its Evangelical Protestant North American origins to include numerous individuals of other backgrounds, both North Americans and Britons, who either out of principle or because of their limited financial means did not support the colony's class-based denominational system of education. The proportion of total population such individuals comprised is impossible to determine. Perhaps 7,500 whites resided on Vancouver Island in 1864, over half in Victoria.[35] Neither is the proportion non-British in background known, although in 1865 a British naval officer did report that half of the two colonies' 14,000 white residents were "foreign."[36] Due to a gender imbalance in the non-Native population, the proportion of families with children was considerably less than would normally be the case:

shortly after Central School's closure, the Rev. Cridge had found five hundred children in schools across Vancouver Island, four hundred of them in Victoria.[37] Other children received no formal education. In Victoria alone, fifty to a hundred were, according to contemporary accounts, "running through the streets," "acquiring street education that will prepare many of them in after years for every description of crime and depravity."[38]

The concern felt by Victoria residents for the education of their children amidst growing economic recession was evident at a public meeting called shortly after Central School's closure in March 1864. Fully five hundred residents, with "every element in the community pretty thoroughly represented," turned out to "demand the establishment of a free Common School in a central position, efficiently conducted, open to all classes of the community and non-sectarian in the strictest sense of the term." Some five hundred signatures had been collected on a petition calling on the Island's Legislative Assembly to act. At the meeting only Collegiate School's principal and the Rev. Cridge dared defend the existing situation. Both were immediately denounced, the Rev. Cridge for having as head of the district schools "done nothing toward promoting education" but "come forward now and oppose the movement." One parent reminded him caustically that "the District School is as full as it can hold." Another related how, to quote the *Colonist*, "he had a large family, and that if he sent them to the Collegiate School, it would cost him from $900 to $1,500 for the same education which in Canada was free."[39]

Speakers at the meeting were especially dissatisfied with the hold exercised by denominational schools in a city as cosmopolitan as Victoria had become since the gold rush. One father stated that, although he "was a member of the Church of England, and was strongly in favour of bible teaching, . . . in a mixed community like this, where Jew, Turk, Roman Catholic and every other denomination was represented, a school system must be totally devoid of any religious teaching." Another parent added "that for his part he would wish to see denominational schools in every part of the colony and government aid extended to them all, but we must do here what can be done; in the present state of the colony an entirely non-sectarian system of education was necessary."

The next year witnessed vigorous debate both in and out of the Legislative Assembly over what, according to the *Colonist*, had become "the two great principles — free schools and a non-sectarian system of education."[40] The debate's religious component was summed up by a Non-Conformist English minister:

> The clergy of the English Church have been loud in agitation for the introduction of the Bible in the proposed Common Schools; but the bulk of the inhabitants are unwilling to accede to that arrangement in consequence of the mixed character of the community. There are individuals of every race, and members of every religious persuasion in the colonies; and it is maintained ; as in Canada and the United States — that it would be unjust to

Jews, Catholics, Buddhists, and Mohammedans, to adopt exclusively the text-books of any one religion.[41]

Consensus on the denominational issue was difficult to attain, its adherents assuming that, "as an integral portion of the English state, we, a small and remote colony," must adopt the structures in place in the mother country: "Since Vancouver [Island] and [British] Columbia are British colonies, let them be truly British in all their institutions; and perchance we shall enjoy domestic happiness and general prosperity."[42] Opponents countered that "the instruction of youth in new countries is valued much [more] highly than it is in Great Britain," where overall educational levels were relatively low.[43] In that case, so responded a proponent, properly complete the denominational system now partially in place:

> In this city there are already schools for the children of Catholics and Episcopalians [i.e., Anglicans]. There is now an excellent opportunity for one of the other [Evangelical Protestant] denominations to secure one in which, most probably by the admission of the bible, they could all unite; the Jews from their wealth and numbers would hardly be behind as regards a schoolhouse for their children. With these four schools, established by and the property of the separate parties, let the government give to each such a portion of the grant to which, from the number of their scholars, they are entitled.[44]

Probably decisive in tipping the balance was Arthur Kennedy, the colony's new British governor who within days of his arrival in late March 1864 had made clear to an Anglican delegation headed by the Rev. Cridge that he preferred to replace the district schools under the cleric's control with "a nonsectarian system" which "included Roman Catholic and all denominations." "Don't you think that in a country like this, where men are thrown much together, it would be better that they should be educated together?"[45]

The public debate over free schools rapidly became the more critical of the two, centred as it was on the key issue of what should be the nature of society in the British colony. The proponents of continued pupil fees argued for the maintenance of the same clearly-defined class divisions as existed in the mother country, while those favouring free schools stressed their important role in bringing together all classes within the community in a single institution, as was occurring in the "Canadian schools."[46] As the *Colonist* pointed out, so long as fees existed, whether or not disallowable on grounds of inability to pay, they "brought in those invidious distinctions between the rich and the poor, so inimical to the growth of independence, and so detestable in a young community like our own."[47]

By October 1864, when a "Free Schools Bill" was introduced into the Vancouver Island Legislative Assembly, its members were publicly agreed "to legislate for the majority of people."[48] The chairman of the committee which brought in the bill was Dr. Israel Wood Powell, an Ontario physician and Anglican, who summed up popular opinion in his formal proposal "that there should be established in this colony a system of free schools, conducted by thoroughly competent trained teachers, wherein the intellectual, physical and moral training would be such as to make the schools attractive *to all classes of the people.*" It therefore followed logically, so continued Dr. Powell, "that in a community such as this, where religious opinions are so diversified, and where the benefits of a well-devised educational system should be extended to all, the reading of the bible or the inculcation of religious dogmas in free schools would be inadvisable."[49] In the Assembly debate, Dr. Powell vigorously defended use of the word "free" in the wording of the bill as standing "in contradistinction to charity schools," such as existed in England. "The object of the committee was to establish schools free to all, and where the system of education under thoroughly trained teachers would be such as to attract all, both rich and poor." Nonetheless, he soon suffered a tactical defeat when a bare majority in the Assembly decided, apparently in the interests of discretion, to substitute "common" for "free."[50]

This concession on form probably helped unite Assembly members when the bill, passed by them, came under attack from the Legislative Council. Unlike the Assembly which was elected, the second legislative body was appointed by the governor and tended to reflect his position which, while favouring non-sectarianism, did not extend to free schools. The bill was returned, amended so as to give the General Board of Education in charge of implementation "power to regulate the amount of School fees payable for Educational purposes in any Common School so, however, that the same do not exceed fifty centimes per month for each scholar." The Assembly was outraged at the action of Council members: "They had murdered the bill." Sent back unchanged, the bill was again amended by the Council, and again the Assembly rejected this challenge to "the very principle of the bill which had been distinctly enunciated as a free school measure." An Assembly member had no hesitation in attributing class motives to the Council:

> The fifty cents a month would at the best bring in but a paltry revenue, while on the other hand the discretionary powers of remitting fees would tend to make distinctions of the most invidious character among the pupils, sapping the foundation of the children's independence.[51]

This time the Council acquiesced, and the bill became law as "An Act respecting Common Schools."[52]

The triumph was short-lived. Even as non-sectarian free schools under direct government control were opening — most notably a revived Central School under Jessop enrolling over two hundred pupils — opposition was strengthened by both the continued poor state of the economy and the appointment of a forceful new governor even more committed than his predecessor to fee-based education. To save money, the two colonies of Vancouver

Island and British Columbia were amalgamated in 1866 as the Colony of British Columbia under a single legislative body, a Legislative Council half or more of whose members were appointed by the governor and therefore amenable to his will. Within days of the union having received royal assent on August 6, Vancouver Island's General Board of Education was notified by the government that no expenditures, including teacher salaries, would be guaranteed "beyond the 31 of August, instant." Frederick Seymour, the new governor appointed to the united colony, concurred, since "the whole system of the public schools required reforming."[53] He soon elaborated his position, referring to himself in the third person:

> He thinks that any man who respects himself would not desire to have his children instructed without some pecuniary sacrifice on his part . . . else it may happen that the promising mechanic may be marred, and the country overburdened with half-educated politicians or needy hangers-on of the Government.

Unnecessary education, likely if it be free, would only result in individuals unhappy with their destined place in the social order. "The system he would desire to see," while containing "a public school open to all denominations" teaching "children to read, write and go through the simpler forms of arithmetic" at a fee of perhaps $6 a year, would encompass "Denominational Schools, also, to which the Government contributed, but in a moderate degree." Under such a plan, it would probably be the case, so argued the governor, that the "Denominational Schools, though more expensive to the parents, absorbed the greater number of children."[54]

The governor's public position on education gave new heart to the powerful supporters of a class-based denominational system of schooling. As a pupil at Collegiate School recollected, his classmates in these years were the sons of "the very earliest pioneers of our beloved city of Victoria and the Pacific Coast," including leading Hudson's Bay families.[55] Angela College was headed by a sister of the Attorney General and then by the sister of a leading Hudson's Bay official, both from Britain.[56] While families of comparable social status resident outside Victoria could not maintain educational exclusivity as easily, opportunities did from time to time arise. The Anglican rector in Nanaimo reported in 1868: "The mornings I devote to teaching my own boys, and those of the better class of parishioners who are not satisfied with the associations and the *non-religious* education of the public school."[57] Not surprisingly, when the governor's appointed Executive Council was asked its views on the educational situation in 1867, members responded that the state's role should be limited to establishing "a cheap general common school of an elementary description in each Town or district where at least a certain limited average number of pupils can attend winter and summer, on the plan of so much per head." Denominational schools also ought to be supported, if "at a much lower rate per head," so that their clientele "who contribute their full quota to the taxes and revenue but who consciously object to what they consider 'godless' Schools will derive some benefit." "On no account should absolutely Free schools be supported."[58]

Although outmaneuvred politically, the consensus in favour of free, non-denominational schooling remained intact, as was indicated by a public meeting called in Victoria in August 1867 to endorse the General Board of Education's declaration to the governor "that the system of free education established in Vancouver Island is in accordance with the wishes of the community." Whereas at mid-decade, prior to the passage of the Common Schools Act, just a quarter of the Island's five hundred pupils had been attending subsidized schools, now fully half of the eight hundred children receiving a formal education were in free schools. After Dr. Powell, chairman of Vancouver Island's General Board, reviewed its troubled history, considerable discussion ensued. Aware both of "the present financial embarrassments of the Colony" and of the board's inability "to re-open the schools owing to a want of funds," participants debated at some length whether or not a fee ought temporarily to be charged. The position of the great majority was reiterated by a Methodist missionary from Ontario:

> The age of exclusiveness was passing away, and if Britain expected to continue great she must make every effort to educate the young or she would go behind. We are here to found a new State, and it was the interest of every State to educate its children. It was not alone the interest of parents — it was the interest, the *duty*, of the State to furnish free education. [prolonged applause] . . . Let this meeting speak out loudly and unhesitatingly in support of Free Schools and in denunciation of the system attempted to be enforced by the Government.

Other participants were more succinct, one merely pointing out that among parents "there were a good many here who could not pay. Adopt the fee system and you send half the children into the streets to become worse than Siwashes [Chinook term for halfbreeds]." The only declared supporters of denominational schools were "two Catholic gentlemen," and the meeting virtually unanimously supported the Vancouver Island board's actions."[59]

This consensus of popular opinion gained new adherents from both Vancouver island and the mainland as a consequence of the unworkability of new, more stringent school legislation enacted in early 1869. During the debate in the Legislative Council, the free-schools principle had received primary attention. Opponents argued, much as did members of the Executive Council, that

> The system of free education was most vicious; it was burdensome to those who contributed to denominational schools, who did not desire free school education, and it destroyed that stimulus to exertion which would exist were the scholars required to pay something towards the cost of education.[60]

Among the supporters of school fees was John Robson, an Ontario Presbyterian who since 1861 had edited the New Westminster *British Columbian* newspaper. While Robson had repeatedly editorialized that schools should be "free from sectarian domination and exclusiveness" and "placed within the reach of all," he had never favoured their being free of cost to pupils.[61] Now he asserted:

> To throw free education open to everyone was a serious principle, it caused people to forget the advantages that were bestowed on them and rendered the parents careless as to the attendance of the children at school. There could be no doubt that making the parents pay one-half the cost of educating their children was the true principle.

Outnumbered in the Council, the proponents of free schools still pressed their case. The bill, they argued, proposed that "certain of the people were supposed to be worthy of charity, and thus class was set against class." As a model for British Columbia to follow, "it would be better to be taught by Canada or the United States, where education was understood to be the right of all and not that of a class." One of the most vocal defenders of free schools was J.S. Helmcken, an English physician brought out by the Hudson's Bay Company who had married Governor Douglas' eldest daughter. Dr. Helmcken pointed out that, particularly in rural districts where families "were struggling to get their farms into a state of cultivation," teachers would simply not be paid under the proposed system by which the government would provide half their salaries, but only after the remainder had been collected in the locality, "whether by voluntary subscriptions, Tuition fees, or General Rate."[62] In the end the bill passed with little real opposition, due both to the Legislative Council's composition and to members' primary concern during this period with the even more divisive issue of whether or not the colony should join the new Canadian Confederation.[63]

Implementation of the 1869 act proved as difficult as its detractors had forecast. While at least twenty localities scrambled to meet its rigorous demands, most soon found themselves in an intolerable situation, even after levying pupil fees of $6 to $18 a year, in addition to taxes. Reporting to the governor in early 1871, the Inspector General of Schools appointed under the act, who had been its principal supporter in the Council, acknowledged that only fifteen schools were managing to operate and that the equipment in all but two was "of the scantiest description" with many buildings "small and inconvenient." Local school boards were simply unable or unwilling to enforce collection of school taxes. The situation would improve only when the government took a bigger role by levying and collecting the necessary taxes, possibly with an exemption "made in favour of those who support private or denominational schools" which were "certified to be efficient by the Inspector approved by the government."[64]

III

British Columbia entered Confederation later in 1871, by which time the deteriorating educational and economic situation of the last half-dozen years had amply reconfirmed the need for free non-denominational schooling. The opposition had been discredited: according to the *Colonist*, in the election for the first provincial legislature, "no candidate, be his private opinions what they might, volunteered to say a word against this form of education." "No measure was more distinctly or more unanimously demanded."[65] Almost immediately, without disagreement on principle, the Assembly passed a bill "for the establishment, maintenance, and management of Public Schools throughout the Province of British Columbia," whose provisions were based both on the 1865 act and on systems being put in place in Ontario and across the United States. The critical issue of finance was resolved by the annual allotment out of general revenue of a specified sum "for Public School purposes," the amount accorded the first year being virtually triple that allowed just a year previous. The act dealt explicitly with the denominational issue: "All Public Schools established under the principles of this Act, shall be conducted upon strictly non-sectarian principles."[66]

The non-sectarian provision, reflecting the social and economic conditions of British Columbia, distinguished this act from recent legislation elsewhere in Canada and in England. The English Education Act of 1870, while establishing non-denominational state board schools, also recognized existing church schools as a fundamental part of the subsidized state system of elementary education.[67] Similarly, the British North America Act had safeguarded "any Right or Privilege with respect to Denominational Schools which any Class of Persons have by Law in the Province at the Union."[68] As a consequence, separate Catholic schools officially recognized in Ontario or elsewhere at Confederation had been brought under their provincial systems. The case for recognition had been made several times in colonial British Columbia: Governor Seymour had been in favour, as had members of his Executive and Legislative Councils as well as the Inspector General of Schools in 1871. During the debate on the 1869 bill, one of several proponents of financial support for the colony's denominational schools had even cited the situation "in Canada" to make his case. About the same time, the religious orders operating Catholic schools had petitioned the Legislative Assembly for financial assistance.[69] All these moves had either been rejected or simply not acted upon, and the British Columbia legislation therefore did not even mention, much less take responsibility for, denominational or other non-public schools.

British Columbia's educational consensus did not immediately become, to quote the *Colonist*, "acceptable to all and good enough for all."[70] First, each of the principal religious groups in the province — Anglican, Catholic and Evangelical Protestant — had to be rebuffed in their efforts to secure special treatment. The Anglican attempt to coopt educational structures may have existed primarily in the perceptions of others, reflecting larger distrusts. Union with Canada had been purely economic, the new province emerging from negotiations with debts paid and the promise of a transcontinental railroad. As the last colonial governor had reported home, "the most prominent Agitators for Confederation are a small knot of Canadians."[71] The Anglican bishop still considered, for instance, that since "the great heart of the people beats with that of England so fervently," the preferred course would have been "the closer union and protection of the mother country."[72] At the same time, many Canadians viewed Confederation as both a vindication of their discontents and the guarantee of a new, more acceptable status deemed theirs by right in a geographical entity now itself Canadian. Any suggestion of opposition became a deliberate affront, as witnessed by a letter in the *Colonist* of April 1872 from "Citizen" concerning a rumour that the Anglican rector in Nanaimo, a community characterized by a contemporary as having "a divided line betwixt the aristocracy and the democracy," might open a parish school:

> Now to establish a denominational school in such a community is nothing more than to keep up caste distinctions in a country where "Jack is as good as his master" — where we are supposed to ignore the old fogy teaching of the old country where children are taught to regard the squire and the parson with dreadful and deferential awe.[73]

Confrontation occurred almost immediately after the education bill's passage. Lieutenant-Governor Joseph Trutch, despite having been appointed for his acceptability to both Britons and Canadians, requested reconsideration of the act by the Assembly after receiving a petition from sixty-eight Victoria residents opposed to a clause prohibiting appointment of a clergyman as Superintendent of Education.[74] The *Colonist* was furious: given "the present condition and circumstances of the Province," such an appointment, especially if it went to an Anglican cleric, would be met "with distrust and disappointment."[75] The Assembly was equally incensed, and the bill was returned unaltered for the lieutenant-governor's signature. Less than two weeks later, the *Colonist* again charged interference. Certain individuals were refusing to sit on the provincial Board of Education, "thus seeking to block the wheels of the new School Act." The newspaper stated that the government had "confined the invitations chiefly to those who are in reality at heart enemies of the system," men it termed "Canada haters."

The spate of letters which followed made clear the antagonism existing between Evangelical Protestant Canadians and Anglican Britons. Among the most vocal was "Non-Conformist," who wrote that of the first six men invited on to the board, five were Anglicans, of whom "four are unbelievers in the free, nonsectarian system." Anglicans totalled less than a third of the province's population, "but I suppose the Cabinet being formed exclusively of members of the Anglican Church, it is considered proper that the Board of Education should be composed of similar material."[76] While the appointment shortly thereafter of longstanding common schools' proponent John Jessop as Superintendent of Education diffused suspicions, tensions did not completely disappear, as evidenced by an attack a few years later on the board's class assumptions:

> Having arrived here with the prejudices against popular education of England of twenty years ago, they have retained their opinions and are at present only tolerant of the system of public education established here because of political pressure.

The writer further charged that board members were "of too high a social rank to condescend to have their children taught with Tom, Dick and Harry" but rather educate "their children in private schools."[77]

Such a course became increasingly less feasible, for Anglican education was in decline, and with it disappeared what supporters of the province's educational consensus perceived to be a major threat. The Anglican church's difficulties were largely self-induced: for over two decades after Confederation, the church in British Columbia remained under the direct oversight of the Archbishopric of Canterbury, through which came personnel, finance and direction.[78] Thus, attitudes formed when the province was still a British colony received constant reinforcement. The church continued to believe that British Columbia was a class-based society, and that parishioners gave the same priority as at home to the maintenance of social distinctions through education. In 1878, for instance, the Englishwoman heading Angela College opened a separate "subsidiary" for "girls of poor parents" so as "to give a religious training to all classes" while still reserving the school itself for "girls of the upper and middle classes."[79] When a founding bishop was appointed to the new mainland Diocese of New Westminster created in 1879, one of his first acts was to set up local church schools. That conditions in British Columbia might differ from those of Britain had not even crossed his mind: months "before I ever set foot in the country I occupied myself in laying plans for the education of both boys and girls."[80]

So far as the Church of England in British Columbia was concerned, common education was to be disparaged. As late as 1891, Bishop Hills was condemning the public system, noting that its "depressing and atheistical character" would certainly result "in criminality increasing by leaps and bounds."[81] The lack of fees at the public secondary level caused special alarm: "the lesson of the dignity of labor" would be taught the poor "not by Free High Schools, full of Latin and Greek and the Higher mathematics and Dancing and Deportment, but by Free Industrial and Technical Schools, which will turn out clever mechanics and artisans and agriculturalists, and good wives."[82] Education's function was to ensure the maintenance of class distinctions from generation to generation.

In reality, important socio-economic differences had separated Britain and British Columbia since the 1860s. As reports to the church's London headquarters acknowledged, "there are no wealthy people in British Columbia belonging to the Church," "no resident proprietors with means and leisure at their disposal."[83] The experience of the Bishop of New Westminster pointed up the harsh reality. Having expended even his private income on the diocese's church schools, he was especially "disappointed at finding Church children sent indiscriminately to Roman and to free schools, while our own are left to languish for want of support."[84] Soon his schools had to be closed for lack of pupils. While Victoria did contain numerous established families still favouring class-based denominational education, even this support gradually dissipated, due in part to a theological dispute erupting in 1874 between Bishop Hills and the Rev. Cridge. The city's longtime cleric promptly established the Reformed Episcopal Church, taking with him many Hudson's Bay families and the staff of Angela College.[85] His subsequent creation of competing church schools diminished the prestige of all the institutions, and enrolments fell. In 1880 Angela College became a private venture to be closed in the next economic recession. Collegiate shut its doors in 1885.[86] Long before then, most Anglicans had reconciled themselves to the province's public system.

Acceptance of the province's educational consensus by Catholics, whose theological commitment to denominational education was even greater than that of Anglicans, also took time. Their desire for tacit recognition and financial support similar to that given Catholic schools in Ontario came to a head in 1876 over a proposal in the provincial Assembly to levy a $3 annual school tax on all adult males, the cost of education having up to this time come out of general revenue. Although the measure was directed against the province's growing Chinese population — "the present tax would really be a saving to the white population of some $17,000, which sum would now be paid by Chinamen" — it was Catholics who protested. A petition signed by sixty-four Catholic residents of Victoria, including the bishop, argued that Catholics should be exempted since "your Petitoners cannot in conscience send their children to the socalled unsectarian schools, wherever they have schools of their own." The *Colonist* opposed the Catholic initiative as threatening once again to "draw the lines of sectarianism." As participants in the Assembly debate pointed out, "there are other denominations besides the Catholics that objected to secular education." "If the Catholics were to be excepted, the Jews and in fact every other sect would claim the same privilege." The bill passed unaltered, and Catholics thereafter turned their principal attention to the maintenance of their own private institutions.[87]

And, unlike Anglican church schools, Catholic institutions remained strong, continuing to service the 15 to 19 percent of the white population of that faith. Impressive new physical structures existed in Victoria and New Westminster. In 1873 the Oblates began a boarding school in the Cariboo offering a "Thorough English and Commercial Education." Three years later, the Sisters of St. Ann joined them. A girls' school opened in Nanaimo in

1877. In 1880 the two orders jointly established a school in the interior settle-ment of Kamloops in anticipation of the transcontinental railroad, with additional schools being established as settlement warranted.[88]

Neither were all Evangelical Protestants wholly satisfied with the prov-ince's educational consensus, and they attempted cooptation through redefining the concept of "non-sectarianism" in the Public Schools Act more closely toward their particular religious tenets. In spring 1876, a Presbyterian min-ister was appointed principal of the new Victoria High School, the first public secondary institution in the province. Although Alexander Nicholson ren-ounced his ordination before taking up the post, trouble erupted.[89] A letter from "Father" in a local newspaper shortly after the school opened comprised a single sentence:

> Will you inform me why the Master of the High School (in contravention of the Public School Act) is allowed to perform the duties of Minister in one of our churches and also religious services at the school supposed to be non-sectarian?[90]

The subsequent outrage showed that public sensibilities were offended. Both Victoria newspapers argued that such a practice would favour Protestants over Catholic, "Israelite," or "Spiritualist." "In the general rivalry of the sects for their share of the material patronage, the Free School system would soon receive its death-blow." While maintaining he had spoken in church as a layman, Nicholson was forced to resign the principalship to defend his posi-tion that "a simple non-sectarian prayer to God" be allowed in the schools.[91] Shortly thereafter school exercises were officially "limited to the Lord's Prayer and Ten Commandments, and it is optional with the various Trustee Boards whether the same shall be used or not."[92]

Even as these efforts by the major religious groups to secure special treat-ment were being repulsed, Jessop and his successors as superintendent of education were implementing an educational system which would endure vir-tually unaltered for a century. As the biographer of Jessop has noted, he was indefatigable in establishing free non-sectarian common schooling across British Columbia.[93] By the time of his forced departure from office for polit-ical reasons in August 1878, the young province of 10 to 15,000 whites possessed fifty-one common schools as well as the high school in Victoria, together enrolling 2,200 pupils.[94] At the railroad's arrival eight years later, eighty-three existed, including three high schools, with enrolment at 4,500.[95]

By then, the role to be accorded non-public education within the consen-sus was also defined. The Catholic issue had reaffirmed the intention of the 1872 legislation not to provide financial support to denominational schools, a demand which lost much of its force once the Anglican schools with their more politically powerful supporters collapsed. Jessop had made clear that private schools would remain unsupervised. His annual reports virtually ignored these institutions which had once so bedevilled him. Only once, writing in 1877 about conditions in New Westminster, did he reveal any lingering antipathy:"There are several denominational and private schools in this city competing for pupils with the public school, notwithstanding which, the latter is decidedly gaining in attendance and the confidence of parents."[96] After 1883 for virtually a century, the annual reports did not even acknowledge, much less attempt to monitor, non-public schools.[97]

*   *   *

In 1886 British Columbia began a fundamental transformation as the long-promised transcontinental railroad finally arrived, and the province was for the first time directly linked to the rest of the nation of which it had thus far been a part primarily on paper. In the case of education, however, this change was not critical for the consensus which had first coalesced during the mid-1860s favouring free non-denominational education was firmly in place. Not until the late 1970s, when private schools would be accorded official recognition and financial support (see Chapter 16), was there fundamental alteration of the system which had emerged in response to social and economic conditions in British Columbia from 1849 to 1886.

Notes

I am grateful to J.D. Wilson and Neil Sutherland for their incisive comments on an earlier version of this essay.

[1] For this perspective, see F. Henry Johnson, "The Ryersonian Influence on the Public Schools System of British Columbia," *BC Studies* 10 (Summer 1971): 26-34.

[2] John Sebastian Helmcken, *The Reminiscences of Doctor John Sebastian Helmcken*, Dorothy Blakey Smith, ed., (Vancouver: University of British Columbia [hereafter UBC] Press, 1975), pp. 114-16, 293.

[3] On England, see Brian Simon, *The Two Nations & the Educational Structure, 1780-1870*, v. 1 in his *Studies in the History of Education* (London: Lawrence & Wishart, 1981), esp. pp. 277-367. On British Columbia, see Donald L. MacLaurin, "Education before the Gold Rush," *British Columbia Historical Quarterly*, hereafter BCHQ, 2 (1938): 247-53; and his "The History of Education in the Crown Colonies of Vancouver Island and British Columbia and in the Province of British Columbia" (Ph.D. thesis, University of Washington, 1936). Examination in the Provincial Archives of British Columbia, hereafter PABC, of MacLaurin's primary manuscript sources confirms his research on colonial British Columbia to have been exhaustive, inclusive and exact. Therefore, sources are cited from MacLaurin to facilitate access by other researchers.

[4] Recollecton of Roderick Finlayson, quoted in Alexander Begg, *History of British Columbia From Its Earliest Discovery to the Present Time* (Toronto: Ryerson Press, 1894, reprinted 1972), p. 212. See also C. Hollis Slater, "Rev. Robert John Staines," BCHQ, 14 (1950): 187-240. On education provided by the Hudson's Bay Company at Fort Vancouver, see G. Hollis Slater, "New Light on Herbert Beaver," BCHQ, 6 (1942): 13-29; and Juliet Pollard, "Growing Up Metis: Fur Traders' Chil-

dren in the Pacific Northwest," in J. Donald Wilson, ed., *An Imperfect Past: Education and Society in Canadian History*, (Vancouver: Centre for the Study of Curriculum and Instruction, UBC, 1984), pp. 120-140.

⁵James Douglas to Archibald Barclay, Hudson's Bay governor, Oct. 8, 1851, in Douglas' letter book, PABC, quoted in MacLaurin, "History," pp. 12-13.

⁶See MacLaurin, "History," pp. 13-20.

⁷"Memorandum of Salary Allowances for a Clergyman for Vancouver's Island," PABC, quoted in MacLaurin, "History," pp. 12-13; and "Minutes of the Council of Vancouver Island," quoted on pp. 22-23. The minutes have been published in *Journals of the Colonial Legislatures of the Colonies of Vancouver Island and British Columbia, 1851-1871*, 5 vols., James E. Hendrickson, ed., (Victoria: PABC, 1980). For this reference, see v. 1, pp. 16-17. See also J. Forsyth, "Early Colonial Schools on Vancouver Island," parts I-III, *Times* (Victoria), Mar. 1922, located in Vertical File, PABC. The evidence suggests that, while Mrs. Cridge ran a school for girls, a complement for boys was never opened.

⁸See MacLaurin, "History," pp. 12-14, 24 and 26.

⁹G.P.V. and Helen B. Akrigg, *British Columbia Chronicle, 1847-1871* (Vancouver: Discovery Press, 1977), p. 59; and W. Kaye Lamb, "The Census of Vancouver Island, 1855," BCHQ, 4 (1940): 51-58.

¹⁰*Times* (London), Jan. 19, 1859.

¹¹Reprinted in *Colonist* (Victoria), Apr. 21, 1908; see also Sister Mary Margaret Down, *A Century of Service, 1858-1958: A History of the Sisters of Saint Ann and Their Contribution to Education in British Columbia, the Yukon and Alaska* (Victoria: Sisters of Saint Ann, 1966), pp. 28-41.

¹²"St. Ann's Convent, Register, Victoria, B.C.," in Vertical Files, PABC. For one Jewish girl's account of her experience, see *A Chaplet of Years: St. Ann's Academy* (Victoria: Colonist, 1918), pp. 29-35.

¹³Kay Cronin, *Cross in the Wilderness* (Vancouver: Mitchell Press, 1960), pp. 99-101, 53 and 134. See also Down, *A Century of Service*, pp. 23-27, 42-45; and *Colonist*, Sept. 1, 1863; Nov. 3, 1863; and May 3, 1925.

¹⁴Anglican Church, Columbia Mission, *Special Fund Obtained During a Ten Months' Appeal by the Bishop of Columbia* (London: R. Clay, 1860), p. x; and Angl. Ch., Columbia Mission, *Occasional Paper*, June 1860, pp. 14-16. See also Frank A. Peake, *The Anglican Church in British Columbia* (Vancouver: Mitchell Press, 1959); and Rev. George Hills, Bishop of Columbia, Diary, 1860-69, excepting 1867-68; typescript copy in British Columbia Provincial Synod Archives, Anglican Church of Canada, Vancouver School of Theology, UBC, esp. entries for Sept. 3, 1860, and Nov. 7, 1861.

¹⁵Hills, Diary, Apr. 25, 1861;. Report of Rev. Cridge to Colonial Secretary on Colonial Schools, Aug. 27, 1861, PABC, reprinted in MacLaurin, "History," p. 38; and *Colonist*, Apr. 11, 1864. See also Hills, Diary, Jan. 30, 1860; Aug. 20, 1860; and Sept. 10, 1860. On fees, see Mar. 10, 1863.

¹⁶1861 report, reprinted in MacLaurin, "History," p. 37.

¹⁷Matthew MacFie, *Vancouver Island and British Columbia* (London: Longman, Green, 1865), p. 84.

¹⁸Hills, Diary, Mar. 10, 1863; see also Mar. 8, 1861.

¹⁹Ang. Ch., Dioc. Of Col., *Annual Report*, 1860, pp. 85 and 95; *B.C. Directory*, 1863, pp. 134 and 138-39; *Colonist*, May 22 and 24, July 7 and 10, and Dec. 25, 1860;

Hills, Diary, Sept. 29, 1860, and Jan. 19, 1863; and Dorothy Blakey Smith, ed., *Lady Franklin Visits the Pacific Northwest* (Victoria: PABC, 1974), pp. 16 and 36.

[20]*Colonist,* Apr. 26, 1925; see also Apr. 6, 1919.

[21]Ang. Ch., Dioc. Of Col., *Annual Report,* 1860, p. 84, and *Colonist* Apr. 26, 1925.

[22]Smith, *Franklin,* p. 16.

[23]Undated report from Rev. Cridge for 1864 or 1865, PABC, reprinted in MacLaurin, "History", pp. 41-43, and in F. Henry Johnson, *A History of Public Education in British Columbia* (Vancouver: Publications Centre, UBC, 1964), pp. 29-30. One report puts the number of private venture schools in Victoria in 1863-64 at eighteen. *Colonist,* May 2, 1876.

[24]Allan Smith, "Old Ontario and the Emergence of a National Frame of Mind," in F.H. Armstrong, H.A. Stevenson and J.D. Wilson, eds., *Aspects of Nineteenth-Century Ontario* (Toronto: University of Toronto Press in association with the University of Western Ontario, 1974), pp. 197 and 209.

[25]Margaret Ross, "Amor de Cosmos, a British Columbia Reformer" (M.A. thesis, UBC, 1931), offers a vigorous defence of De Cosmos' position. See also James Gordon Reid, "John Robson and *The British Columbian*," (M.A. thesis, UBC, 1950); and F. Henry Johnson, *John Jessop: Goldseeker and Educator* (Vancouver: Mitchell Press, 1971), p. 31; Helmcken, *Reminiscences,* pp. 174-78; and Hills, Diary, Jan. 9, 1860. Despite the *Colonist*'s visibly pro-Canadian sympathies, even after De Cosmos' departure as editor in 1863, it is an invaluable source of contemporary information concerning events in early British Columbia. As well, its editorials provide a useful guide to Canadian attitudes toward particular issues.

[26]See MacFie, *Vancouver Island,* p. 83; and Alexander Rattray, *Vancouver Island and British Columbia* (London: Smith, Elder, & Co., 1862), p. 171.

[27]See, for instance, David Tyack, "The Kingdom of God and the Common School: Protestant Ministers and the Educational Awakening in the West," *Harvard Educational Review,* 36 (1966): 447-69; and Timothy L. Smith, "Protestant Schooling and American Nationality, 1800-1850," *The Journal of American History,* 53 (1967): 679-95. On Canada, see Neil McDonald and Alf Chaiton, eds., *Egerton Ryerson and His Times* (Toronto: Macmillan, 1978), and Alison Prentice, *The School Promoters: Education and Social Class in Mid-Nineteenth Century Upper Canada* Toronto: McClelland and Stewart, 1977).

[28]*Colonist,* Jan. 10, 1863, and Oct. 19, 1864.

[29]John Jessop to E. Ryerson, Victoria, Aug. 16, 1861, quoted in Johnson, *Jessop,* p. 38; see also pp. 36-43 and *B.C. Directory,* 1863, p. 137.

[30]Margaret Lillooet McDonald, "New Westminster, 1859-1871" (M.A. thesis, UBC, 1947), pp. 356-58.

[31]Ibid., pp. 358-59; and *Columbian* (New Westminster), Sept. 2, 1864, quoted in Reid, p. 116.

[32]McDonald, "New Westminster," pp. 353-67; Angl. Ch., Dioc. Col., *Annual Report,* 1870, p. 16; Down, *A Century of Service* p. 62; and *Columbian,* Jan. 18, 1926, and June 19, 1965. On population, see McDonald, "New Westminster," pp. 69-70; Margaret A. Ormsby, *British Columbia: a History* (Toronto: Macmillan, 1958), pp. 201 and 209; and Akrigg, *Chronicle,* p. 200.

[33]See MacLaurin, "History," pp. 60-61.

[34]Hills, Diary, Mar. 27, Apr. 20, and June 13, 1862; Mar. 18, 1860; Feb. 18 and Mar. 21, 1861; and, Jan. 20, 1862; *Colonist,* Jan. 10, 1863, and Mar. 22, 1864; and

Angl. Ch., Dioc. Col., *Annual Report,* 1861, p. 26, and 1863, p. 10. On the Catholic attitude to race, see Down, *A Century of Service,* pp. 48-50. On the various schools' positions on race, see also Smith, *Franklin,* p. 10.

[35]See Hubert Howe Brancroft, *History of British Columbia* (San Francisco: History Co., 1887), p. 592, who probably based his estimate on contemporaries' recollections. Population figures for the early 1860s are sparse. One estimate puts Victoria's white population in February 1861 at 2,500, another that of 1862 at 5 to 6,000. See I.J. Benjamin, *Three Years in America 1859-1862,* vol. 2 (Philadelphia: Jewish Publication Society, 1956), p. 142; and R. Byron Johnson, *Very Far West Indeed: A Few Rough Experiences on the North-West Pacific Coast,* 5th ed. (London: Sampson, Low, Marston, Low & Searle, 1873), p. 34. A letter in the *Colonist* on Apr. 4, 1864, gave the city's population as 7,000. See also Ormsby, *British Columbia,* pp. 169, 209 and 239. As well as whites and Indians, the city and colony contained numerous adult Chinese males and a handful of black families.

[36]Rear-Admiral the Hon. Joseph Denman to the Secretary of the Admiralty, Esquimalt, June 3, 1865, Public Records Office, ADM 1/5924, cited in Akrigg *Chronicle,* pp. 319-20. Benjamin stated that Victoria contained about a hundred Jews in 1861. In his general research on Jewish life in British Columbia, Cyril Edil Leonoff evidently encountered no information on early Jewish education. See his *Pioneers, Pedlars, and Prayer Shawls: The Jewish Communities in British Columbia and the Yukon* (Victoria: Sono Nis, 1978).

[37]1864/65 report, quoted in MacLaurin, "History," pp. 41-43. Cridge's list did not include Central School but referred to a small successor school founded under Presbyterian auspices in April 1864. See *Colonist,* Apr. 6, 1864. The male/female ratio in both an 1868 Victoria area census and an 1870 Vancouver Island census was approximately 3:2. *Colonist,* Oct. 6, 1868, and H.L. Langevin, *Report* (Ottawa: I.B. Taylor 1872), p. 152, also reproduced in Akrigg, *Chronicle,* p. 404.

[38]*Colonist,* Apr. 4, 1864.

[39]Ibid., Apr. 11 and 12, 1864. For evidence of this meeting's direct effect on subsequent legislation, see Dec. 13, 1908.

[40]Ibid., May 23, 1865.

[41]MacFie, *Vancouver Island,* p. 84.

[42]*Colonist,* Oct. 21, 1864, and May 9, 1864.

[43]Ibid., Oct. 14 and 21, and Apr. 13, 1864.

[44]Ibid., Apr. 19, 1864.

[45]Ibid., Apr. 4, 1864. On the various deputations soliciting the new governor's favour, see Mar. 27 and 31 and Apr. 1, 1864. For evidence of the Rev. Cridge's continuing authority, see Apr. 9, 1864. On Kennedy, see Cecil Gilliland, "The Early Life and Early Governorships of Sir Arthur Edward Kennedy" (M.A. Thesis, UBC, 1951); and Robert L. Smith, "The Kennedy Interlude, 1864-66," *BC Studies,* 47 (Autumn 1981): 66-78. Gilliland suggests that Kennedy was early influenced by Utilitarianism in his view that state-supported schools should be non-denominational, but offers no evidence dating prior to Kennedy's arrival on Vancouver Island to back up his assertion. See pp. 19-20 and 382-83.

[46]*Colonist,* Oct. 19, 1864. By contrast, American precedent was very seldom cited in discussions.

[47]Ibid., Apr. 13, 1865.

[48]For the chronology of this and a previous bill introduced in the 1864 session, see *Journals,* v. 3, pp. 591-92.

[49]*Colonist,* Oct. 8 and 12, 1864. On Dr. Powell, see B.A. McKelvie, "Lieutenant-Colonel Israel Wood Powell, M.D., C.M.," BCHQ, 11 (1947): 33-54. Italics in original.

[50]*Colonist,* Oct. 19 and 26, 1865. On the bill's progress through the Assembly, see *Journals,* v. 3, pp. 201-02, 204-06, 208-10, 213, 229, 238-41 and 243-45.

[51]*Colonist,* Oct. 26, 1864, and Mar. 17 and Apr. 13, 21 and 27, 1865. On the disagreement between the two bodies, see *Journals,* v. 3, pp. 289, 294, 298, 304-06, 308, 311, 368; and v. 1, pp. 289-90, 292-93, 301-03, and 307-08.

[52]Reprinted in MacLaurin, "History," pp. 44-46. No evidence was encountered explaining the Council's reversal. On the two bodies' authority, see "The Constitutional Development of Vancouver Island," *Journals,* v. 1., pp. xxvi-vlviii.

[53]See MacLaurin, "History," pp. 51-52 and 63-90; and Johnson, *Jessop,* pp. 53-61.

[54]Speech of Jan. 24, 1867, reprinted in *Journals,* v. 5, pp. 43-44, and in MacLaurin, "History," pp. 65-68; and comment of Apr. 19, 1867, quoted on p. 74. On Seymour's upper-class background and career, see Margaret A. Ormsby, "Frederick Seymour, The Forgotten Governor," *BC Studies,* 22(Summer 1974): 3-25.

[55]*Times,* Jan. 30, 1939. See *Colonist,* Aug. 21, 1949, on pupils attending Angela College. See Angl. Ch., Dioc. Col., *Annual Reports,* and Hills, Diary, for development of the two schools.

[56]Angl. Ch., Dioc. Col., *Annual Report,* 1869, p. 76; Harriet Susan Sampson, "My Father, Joseph Despard Pemberton: 1821-1893," BCHQ, 8 (1944): 121-22; and *Colonist,* Aug. 21, 1949.

[57]Angl. Ch., Dioc. Col., *Annual Report,* 1868, p. 85. Italics in orginal.

[58]Views of members of Executive Council, Apr. 12-18, 1867, PABC, reprinted in MacLaurin, "History," pp. 71-74.

[59]*Colonist,* Aug. 12, 1867; and Arthur Harvey, *A Statistical Account of British Columbia* (Ottawa: G.E. Desbarats, 1867), p. 24, which states that in 1867 404 pupils were enrolled in the ten Vancouver Island common schools, with another 419 spread between the two Anglican and two Catholic schools and eight private ventures, all in Victoria. Harvey also observed that mainland facilities were sparse.

[60]*Colonist,* Feb. 5, 1869.

[61]*Columbian,* July 18, 1861, and Dec. 16, 1866, quoted in Reid, "John Robson," p. 114. See also Feb. 27, 1862, and Apr. 6, 13 and 23, 1864, cited on pp. 114-15.

[62]Since mid-decade the white population had apparently declined by almost half to about 8,500. See Langevin, *Report,* p. 152. Harvey, *Statistical Account,* p. 9, put the population of Vancouver Island in 1867 at about 5 to 7,000 whites, Chinese and blacks, that of the mainland at perhaps 10,000. He also noted that the latter was "very fluctuating," with many miners leaving each winter for Vancouver Island or California. On the other hand, settlers were "steadily increasing in number."

[63]"An Ordinance to establish Public Schools throughout the Colony of British Columbia," reprinted in MacLaurin, "History," pp. 93-98. On the debate, see *Journals,* v. 5, pp. 198, 210, 217, 221, 223 and 233-34; and *Colonist,* Feb. 5, 8-9, 11-12 and 17-18, 1869.

[64]See MacLaurin, "History," pp. 103-27.

[65]*Colonist,* Apr. 23 and May 5, 1872.

⁶⁶"An Act Respecting Public Schools," Apr. 11, 1872, reprinted in British Columbia, Superintendent of Education, *Annual Report*, 1875, Appendix A. On passage, see *Colonist*, Mar. 12, 14, 20 and Apr. 7, 9, 11 and 12, 1872.

⁶⁷See Simon, *Two Nations*, p. 365; also pp. 337-67.

⁶⁸See J. Donald Wilson, "Education in Upper Canada: Sixty Years of Change," and "The Ryerson Years in Canada West," in J. Donald Wilson, Robert M. Stamp and Louis-Philippe Audet, eds., *Canadian Education: A History* (Scarborough: Prentice-Hall, 1970), pp. 190-240.

⁶⁹Executive Council session of Feb. 27, 1869, in *Journals*, v. 4, p. 115.

⁷⁰*Colonist*, May 5, 1872.

⁷¹Anthony Musgrave to Earl Granville, Oct. 30, 1869, quoted in Ormsby, *British Columbia*, p. 242.

⁷²Angl. Ch., Dioc. Col., *Annual Report*, 1868, p. 102. Bishop Hills was in England on leave 1869-71 and so came back to a *fait accompli*.

⁷³*Colonist*, Apr. 13, 1872, and Apr. 29, 1867.

⁷⁴Ibid., Apr. 7, 1872. See Ormsby, *British Columbia*, p. 252, on Trutch's appointment; and Hills, Diary, Dec. 5, 1884, on Trutch's attitude to Canadians.

⁷⁵*Colonist*, Apr. 9, 1872; see also Apr. 11 and 12, 1872.

⁷⁶Ibid., Apr. 23 and 24, 1872; see also Apr. 25 and 26, 1872.

⁷⁷Ibid., May 7, 1876; see also May 9, 1876.

⁷⁸The Anglican church in Canada amalgamated in 1893. Walter N. Sage, "The Early Days of the Church of England on the Pacific Slope, 1579-1879," *Journal of the Canadian Church Historical Society*, 2 (1953): 1-17; Peake, "The Anglican Church"; and Angl. Ch., Dioc. Col., *Annual Report*, 1883, pp. 37-38. On Bishop's Hills' opposition to the consolidation of the church in Canada, see Hills, Diary, June 25, 1891; on Canadian indifference to the church in British Columbia, see Nov. 10, 1892.

⁷⁹Angl. Ch., Dioc. Col., *Annual Report*, 1878, p. 18; see also 1871, p. 72, and 1872, p. 8.

⁸⁰Rev. Robert H. Gowen, *Church Work in British Columbia, Being a Memoir of The Episcopate of Acton Windeyer Sillitoe, D.D., D.C.L., First Bishop of New Westminster* (London: Longmans, Green, and Co., 1899), p. 71, also pp. 77 and 93; *The Churchman's Gazette and New Westminster Diocesan Chronicle*, 1883, p. 283; Angl. Ch., Diocese of New Westminster, *Quarterly Paper*, 1 (1884): 10-12, and 2 (1884): 8-10 and 29-35.

⁸¹Angl. Ch., Dioc. Col., *Annual Report*, 1891, pp. 33-34.

⁸²*Churchman's Gazette*, 1891, p. 823; see also Angl. Ch., Dioc. N.W., Synod, *Address*, 1899, pp. 6-10; and *Churchman's Gazette*, 1886, p. 298; 1887, pp. 397 and 406-07.

⁸³Angl. Ch., Dioc. Col., *Annual Report*, 1868, p. 9; 1874, p. 29; 1876, p. 13; and 1884/85, p. 7.

⁸⁴Gowen, *Church Work*, pp. 137-39; and Angl. Ch., Dioc. N.W., *Quarterly Paper*, no. 6 (1885): 12-13. See also 4 (1885): 13-14, 7 (1886): 11-13; and *Churchman's Gazette*, 1883-1888.

⁸⁵*Colonist*, Dec. 30, 1874; *Guide to the Province of British Columbia for 1877-78* (Victoria: T.N. Hibben & Co., 1877), p. 270; and Hills, Diary, 1874-1875, esp. Nov. 1 and 4, 1874. See also Jan. 3 and 6, and Dec. 19, 1877.

[86]Angl. Ch., Dioc. Col., *Report,* 1881, pp. 15 and 30; 1883, p. 17; 1885, p. 12; 1886, p. 10; 1887, pp. 1-11 and 18; 1889, p. 18; and 1895, p. 15. See also *Colonist,* Aug. 31, 1892; Aug. 29, 1893; and Aug. 21, 1949; and *Victoria Illustrated* (Victoria: Ellis & Co., 1891), pp. 26-27.

[87]*Colonist,* Apr. 28, 1876; see also Apr. 29-30 and May 2 and 3, 1876.

[88]See Edith Down, *St. Ann's: Mid Twin Rivers and Hills, 1880-1980* (Kamloops: Sisters of St. Ann, Victoria, 1980); Down, *A Century of Service,* pp. 66, 68-69, 74-79, 82-87 and 92-96; Cronin, "Cross in the Wilderness," pp. 108-120, 134 and 136; *Colonist,* Nov. 21, 1879, Aug. 25, 1901, Aug. 28, 1907, Apr. 21, 1908, Apr. 19, May 3 and Aug. 9, 1925, Aug. 27, 1930, Apr. 14, 1940, Nov. 3, 1960, and May 9, 1976; *Province* (Vancouver), May 28, 1938, and June 1, 1968; *Columbian,* Jan. 18, 1926; *Nanaimo Daily Press,* Mar. 15, 1962; *Cowichan Leader,* Oct. 26, 1939; and *Kamloops Daily Sentinel,* Feb. 4, 1967.

[89]On the passage of the new act, see *Colonist,* May 4, 6, and 11-13, 1876.

[90]*Daily Standard* (Victoria), Sept. 7, 1876. See also *Colonist,* Aug. 8 and 22, and Sept. 15, 1876.

[91]*Colonist,* Sept. 6, 7, 9, 15 and 16, 1876; and *Daily Standard,* Sept. 2, 5-8, 11 and 12, 1876.

[92]British Columbia, Superintendent of Education, *Annual Report,* 1876, Appendix B.

[93]See Johnson, *Jessop.*

[94]British Columbia, Superintendent of Education, *Annual Report,* 1878, p. 179. The first national census to include British Columbia, taken in 1881, put the white population at 19,448. *Census of Canada,* 1881, v. 1, pp. 298-99 and 394-95.

[95]British Columbia, Superintendent of Education, *Annual Report,* 1886, p. 135.

[96]Ibid., 1877, p. 20.

[97]Ibid., 1876, p. 91; see also 1872, p. 31; 1874, p. 7; and 1883, p. 92, for the last mention. For more detail on the history of private education, see Jean Barman, *Growing Up British in British Columbia: Boys in Private School* (Vancouver: University of British Columbia Press, 1984).

14

Schools and Social Disintegration in the Alberta Dry Belt of the Twenties*

David C. Jones

In the tumultuous land rush years before the First World War prairie society witnessed an overexpansion into marginal and dry areas. Unprecedented wheat prices and two mammoth harvests in 1915 and 1916 led farmers to overextend themselves, to double their equipment, and to brush aside the somewhat safer policy of mixed farming. As land prices escalated immediately following the war, a prolonged drought began in 1917 followed by a severe post-war depression starting in 1920. The cost of living rose and crop prices plummeted.

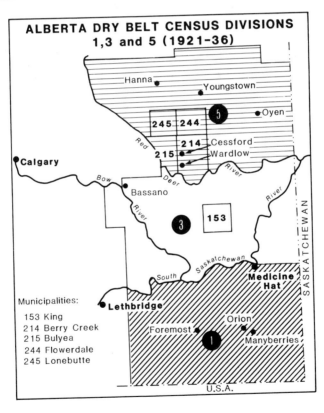

ALBERTA DRY BELT CENSUS DIVISIONS 1,3 and 5 (1921-36)

Municipalities:
153 King
214 Berry Creek
215 Bulyea
244 Flowerdale
245 Lonebutte

*This chapter, with additions, is reprinted from *Prairie Forum*, 3 (1978): 1-19, with permission.

Everywhere the depression and drought of the early twenties was serious, but in the marginal areas it was catastrophic. These regions in Interlake Manitoba, portions of southwest Saskatchewan, and the dry belt of southeastern Alberta were the last settled and least stable regions of the Prairies. The most extensive of these regions and the hardest hit was the Alberta dry belt.

Until recently, western Canadian historiography has been strangely silent on the matter of the Alberta dry belt society of the twenties. Little was known about the magnitude of the calamity, about its effects on people or institutions. In particular, nothing systematic was written about the dry belt school, its teachers, or their relationship with the land.[1] Since the school was perhaps the most vital and powerful institution in that society and since it survived the catastrophe of the twenties, it is a most instructive means of viewing the disintegration which occurred. This chapter will try to clarify the extent of the disaster, to show how the school was affected by the economic hardship and depopulation, how the determination to maintain schools greatly intensified the sense of social dislocation and anxiety, and how teacher training, curriculum and social conditions further agitated this sense by moulding an institution alienated from rural life and unrelated to the fundamental agricultural activity of the land.

Significantly this interpretation of the school as a source of conflict, community discord, and social anxiety runs counter to the traditional view of the school as a community centre and a source of integration. Except where otherwise noted, specific school districts to be examined were among the sixty-seven which eventually became the Berry Creek Consolidation in 1933. Centred in the municipality of Berry Creek, south of Hanna, the region extended both east and west of that jurisdiction.

Consider first the extent of the dry belt problem. Between 1921 and 1926 the three census divisions constituting the dry regions lost 21 percent of their population. This figure greatly underestimates the exodus in the hardest-hit regions. The local improvement district surrounding the towns of Manyberries and Orion, south of Medicine Hat, declined from 940 inhabitants to 531 in the same period. Further north, the adjoining municipalities of Berry Creek and Bulyea dropped from 1,369 to 534 and from 830 to 336 respectively. The municipality of King, between Brooks and Medicine Hat, literally wasted from 815 to 153.[2]

Accompanying this exodus was a dramatic decrease in the number of farms. The number in Manyberries district, for example, dropped from 213 to 96; that in King municipality dropped from 217 to 61; and that in Berry Creek dropped from 463 to 148.[3] Simultaneously farm abandonments rose. About two-thirds of the province's vacant and abandoned farms in 1926 were concentrated in the dry belt which involved only three of Alberta's seventeen census divisions.[4] The magnitude of the calamity in the twenties can be appreciated when one realizes that there were more abandonments then in both the province and the region than at any time during the Great Depression.[5]

Farm sizes in the stricken area increased markedly. By 1926 the percentage of farms in census divisions 1 and 5 over 480 acres was roughly twice the provincial mean.[6] While 71 percent of Albertan farms in 1926 were totally owned, only 56 percent of farms in the dry belt were totally owned. Some municipalities, of course, were much worse off. The most striking example, perhaps, was Bulyea where of 122 occupiers only 44 were complete owners.[7]

In view of these statistics, it is little wonder that no fewer than five major investigations were made into portions of the dry belt in the twenties. One by the Federal Department of the Interior indicated that of 2,386 resident farmers in the area roughly between the Red Deer and South Saskatchewan Rivers east of the town of Tilley, only 645 remained at the end of 1924.[8] An Albertan study, known as the Tilley East Commission, estimated in early 1926 that there were then "well under 500" remaining. The commission also estimated that no less than three thousand parcels of land, approximating 450,000 acres of 784,000 acres taken up, were in the process of forfeiture.[9]

The economic catastrophe was accompanied by a series of nightmarish plagues — infestations of grasshoppers, Russian and Canadian thistles, army cutworms, pale western cutworms, wireworms and even rabbits. For farmers smitten by these, the drought and the hail, the destitution and the loss, it must have seemed that nature had run amok.[10] In the dry belt of the twenties, indeed, the essence of life was this very sense of shattering uncertainty.

Under these conditions a crucial question was whether schools could exist. Clearly the costs of schooling were a major burden which threatened the community itself. By 1922 the story was grim. Inspectors at Hanna, Oyen, Irvine, Brooks and Foremost all remarked on the poor crops; in fact, by then their annual reports were more like economic resumes than pedagogical essays.[11] Tax collections in Hanna inspectorate for the year probably typified the dry belt as a whole — 5 to 40 percent of the amount levied.[12] Generally, the greater the disintegration of community, the less collected. The next year, Inspector J.F. Boyce of Bassano noted of his dry area that "the people still residing in some of these districts are so discouraged that there is little evidence of inclination" to meet tax obligations. In the areas of worst depopulation, Bulyea and Berry Creek, twelve of the forty districts "failed even to requisition the Municipal Secretary for the annual levy in 1923."[13]

The demoralization noted by Boyce, however, usually occurred after persistent local effort to maintain the schools. School taxes were often collected more speedily than other forms of debt. At Chinook, east of Hanna, for example, Inspector J.W. Yake reported that ratepayers in some distressed municipalities had paid "70 percent and even 100 percent of their school taxes." Frustratingly for schoolmen and locals, the monies were often poured into a common fund and used as security for municipal loans incurred at local banks.[14] Recognizing the propensity of locals to support the schools, municipalities even began to make school levies exceeding those required by local school boards in order to generate funds.

The effort to maintain the schools involved several strategies. All were problematic, all involved tradeoffs, and all generated anxiety.

The first ploy entailed applying for loans. The experience of the Creole Belle school district, extending into both Bulyea and Berry Creek municipalities, typified what happened when the municipalities failed to advance monies for school operations as required under the Rural Muncipality Act. On April 7, 1919, the secretary of the school board was instructed to write the Department of Education concerning "the neglect of the Bulyea Municipal Council to supply our school with our estimate on time. . . ."[15] A month later the secretary was asked to write again indicating "that the Board will be obliged to close the school unless it is forthcoming at once."[16] In August the secretary tried, apparently unsuccessfully, to arrange with the inspector a loan of $400 from the Department.[17] On November 1 the chairman and secretary were asked to interview the Bank of Toronto at Cessford, in Berry Creek municipality, "to try and arrange a loan for $100 on a note for 60 days."[18] At a special meeting two weeks later more insistent pressure was placed on the inspector to provide a loan "as soon as possible. . . [19] A week after, frantic and still unaided, the board decided to return to the bank at Cessford to sign a note for $225 in the names of the chairman and secretary and to have "the other members sign as collateral."[20] After receiving a pittance, the board again begged the inspector, first for $500, then for $550.[21] Beleaguered and unsatisfied, the board decided on May 29, 1920, after a few dollars trickled in, to pay the chairman and secretary "instead of paying Miss Ellsworth," the teacher. Ellsworth was "instructed to wait."[22] Over the next few months, the unnerving pressure increased. In March 1921, the Berry Creek municipality failed to supply the money for schools, and on May 1 the disconsolate board turned the school management over to an official trustee.[23]

Certain larger districts were more successful in exacting government assistance while the school board still operated. Efforts sometimes involved calling the government's bluff. Perhaps typical was the case of Bow Island, east of Taber. With poor crops and escalating costs, the school board held a special meeting on September 29, 1919, to consider finances. Since the Department of Education would not loan the money and since the town could not meet the requisition, the board decided to close the schools. The teachers and government were to be notified, and correspondence with the latter was to be published. A week later Inspector Williams informed the board that he was recommending a government loan of $1,965 to maintain the schools to the end of the year. Shortly thereafter Chief Inspector Gorman appeared on the scene, urging the town to assume responsibility for the schools. When the council refused, the government provided the assistance. The procedure was repeated in August 1920, involving this time the inspector, the chief inspector, and the deputy minister. Again, only after assurance that the Department would finance the schools till taxes came in, did the locals "consent" to operate the schools.[24]

By 1921 when the severity of the problem became more apparent, the flow of loans increased. The relief was shortlived, for the next year, under insistent financial pressure, the government instituted retrenchments and loan cutbacks.[25] As a call to the locals to dig deeper, it was sometimes successful. "It would appear," said Inspector Cartwright of Irvine in 1922, "that substantial loans previously made had a tendency in many cases to cause ratepayers to make less effort to pay their taxes and school boards to exercise less pressure."[26] Inspector Scoffield of Foremost stated that "the refusal to grant increasing loans to School Boards, far from effecting the closing of schools, has been the means of rousing boards to increased activity in tax collection and in reducing operating expenditures."[27] The result was not everywhere the same, for Lethbridge Inspector A.J. Watson noted "more schools being closed during the fall term than at any other time since I have been in this district" — a period of five years.[28] The trouble with the government policy, as with all policies meant to apply to a vast region with districts in varying degrees of distress, was that it was never quite clear who the truly destitute were. While the locals sometimes blurred the distinction by painting a picture unduly black and by bluffing closure too often, over and over districts went through the terrifying process of discovering the limits of their ingenuity to provide funds. Few ever wanted to close the schools, but it began to dawn on the most resilient and forebearing that the harder they worked the less likely the government would help.

A second strategy involved the addition of territory in an effort to widen the tax base. Most districts liked the idea, and many were even encouraged by inspectors to implement it. Unfortunately, school districts uniformly opposed giving up territory.[29] Village boards particularly resented the fact that by the thirties they educated perhaps 75 percent of the children with an assessment of roughly 35 percent of the total. Whenever predatory districts swooped down on them, hoping to lop off revenue-paying real estate, they reacted with pent-up fury.[30] Whenever new districts were carved out of adjoining ones, the result was bitter squabbling among the contenders for the territory, followed usually by acute internal strife in the heart of the "winner."

In the fourth year of drought the new district of Forcina decided to build a $2,170 school.[31] The consequences were devastating, as adjoining districts lost population and taxable land and the new district submerged in debt. Month after month the board struggled — seeking loans everywhere, attempting to extend the period of debenture call, supplicating for the renewal of notes and the postponement of the teacher's salary.[32] Things hardly improved. Ten years later, as the secretary reviewed 1929 and thought of the future, he wrote dejectedly, ". . . I think to commence this term we really have nothing."[33]

A more viable solution to the problem of finance was the short term school. Thus the Arlington school board ruled on January 20, 1923, "that no levy be made this year." "Owing to the term being short last year," the secretary wrote, "there is enough money left to run the school seven months this year."[34] The Brown school board decided to engage a teacher four months only in 1923, opening school "on or about the 16th of April."[35] Sometimes more than finance was involved in the creation of short term schools. Thus the Jennings school board decided on February 10, 1919, that "owing to the fact that all children were small . . . to hold school seven months and more if [the] weather stayed good."[36]

While the short term school, generally open through summer, may have been a practical option for the locals and a means of maintaining local control, it was viewed by inspectors as the bane of the rural school, one of the chief reasons why rural education could never hope to approach urban education. Throughout the twenties, as schoolmen sought to remedy the rural school problem, they increased teacher certification requirements and length of normal school service and moved to terminate the "summer schools." Chief Attendance Officer D.C. McEacherne perused teachers' contracts and warned districts about violating regulations. "As . . . the School Act does not permit any board of a rural school district to grant more than ten weeks vacation during the entire year," he wrote the dry belt district of Keystone, "your board has no authority to grant a summer vacation as stated in paragraph five of the agreement submitted."[37]

By the late twenties, two or three lawsuits had occurred which local trustees lost when they defied attendance regulations in sections 182 and 191 of the School Act. "I would suggest that your Board fall in line with the said sections," wrote Inspector J.F. Boyce of Bassano to L.E. Helmer, secretary of the Britannia school board, on December 26, 1927. "If it is the desire of the Board of trustees of Britannia to close down for the winter months please give me the details of their reasons, such as the size of the children, the number and names of the grades, the distance of the children from the school and their means of reaching the school, the number of pupils above grade V and the state of the finances of the district."[38] The reference to grades was motivated by an official belief that where there were high school grades, or where the grade spread was such that the little children or the older ones might unduly suffer, or where there were many grades, the task of teaching was harder and the need for a longer term greater. The point of Boyce's letter was that the financial condition of the district was no longer enough to warrant a summer school. The letter indicated increased government attention as the traditional form of local control failed. For local trustees who survived, sometimes by dint of herculean effort, government standardization moves constituted a *coup de grace*. While professional schoolmen deeply felt that summer schools threatened the future of rural children and that a new form of administration was desperately needed, official intervention sometimes completed the breaking of the local spirit which the depression and drought had begun.

A fourth strategy for maintaining the rural schools in the dry belt involved the enforcement in 1923 of the Tax Recovery Act, the object of which was to bring in tax arrears from farmers, mortgagees, and loan companies.[39] The operation of the Act had the same result as other forms of government intervention. Successful in continuing the operation of many schools which otherwise would have closed in the Lethbridge and Medicine Hat inspectorates, the Act did much to destroy what was left of the local community.[40] Providing a speedy means of securing some unpaid taxes, it also assured widescale abandonment by the hardiest farmers still on the land. A single notice in the *Alberta Gazette* in 1923, for example, listed 36 percent of the total land area in King municipality under threat of forfeiture.[41]

The most common strategy of the locals was to try to cooperate. While some effectively managed cooperative schools, either jointly run or jointly used by two to four districts, the experience generally eroded the sense of community and set up a host of differences and antagonisms which were often difficult to eliminate. Districts which "cooperated" did not want to sell their school houses and did not want to change the district name.[42] Those who wanted to send their children into a neighbouring school had to await a report from that school regarding possible overcrowding and the always contentious issue of cost.[43] The decision of whether to send one's children to another school and renounce all further local control, or to operate one of the schools jointly and maintain a semblance of board input, was difficult to make.

The experience of the Arlington school district was typical. In February 1927, the board called a meeting to discuss the advisability of cooperating with Square Deal or Jennings districts "with the idea of reducing taxes." One trustee, F. Rudge, objected to school in either of these districts since the distance was too great for his children to walk. At the same time, the secretary presented figures which must have seemed very threatening to Rudge. The cost of running the Arlington school for a year, including teacher's salary, fuel, stationery, and audit was $740. The direct tax was $468. By cooperating with another district, costs including half the teacher's salary, half the fuel, and rental of the school house, were $425. The direct tax was only $153.[44]

With difficulty the board decided against cooperation. The minutes, however, reflected an uneasiness and lack of decisiveness. At a meeting in January 1928, the board deemed "that as long as the number of children as at present remain . . . it would be advisable to run our own school."[45] Exactly one month later, the board reversed its stand and decided "to cooperate with the Jennings School district for 1928. . . ." It also decided to move the school house.[46] In January 1929, as the cooperation was extended another year, the board reported that Mr. Rudge had left the district.[47] While it was by no means clear that these school troubles had caused his departure, local histories of this period in the dry belt are sprinkled with cases of families moving in search of better schooling for their children. Also, as high school became more important toward the end of the decade, many families were split by the need to board sons and daughters in distant communities with high school facilities.

Not surprisingly, statements in board minutes like "Nothing was decided on," were common.[48] Yet decisions had to be made, and the process was often agonizing. Once something was settled, it had to be reconsidered each year. Thus the Connorsville trustees agreed to pay the Corinth board 25¢ per day per pupil for the education of Connorsville children in 1923.[49] But a few years later, the Connorsville people considered the cost "a little high."[50] As well, agreements were often jeopardized by the inability of boards to pay for the tuition of their children in outside districts. When the board of Moccasin Flat failed to pay the tuition of Una Hornby for the term ending June 30, 1919, at the Creole Belle school, the Creole Belle trustees decided five days later not to "consider entering into an agreement for the tuition of the children of Moccasin Flat . . . until the said bill be paid."[51]

It was the sad truth that the urgent need for money fragmented the community in every conceivable way. On October 7, 1922, the secretary of the Crocus Plains school board wrote an area resident:

> Some time ago we wrote you about your account with this district, but have received no answer.
>
> This school cannot be kept running without funds, so we have decided to give you until the end of October to pay this account. If it is not paid by then your children will be expelled.[52]

A sixth and sometimes terminal strategy for maintaining the schools in the burnt-out areas involved the assumption by inspectors of the role of official trustee. In 1923 Chief Inspector Gorman reported ninety school districts in the province in the hands of official trustees, "the greater proportion of which were in the southern inspectorates."[53] Official trustees were appointed when there were no locals left to govern, or they did not want to govern, or they could not operate because of unremitting debt or internecine quarrels. Sometimes they were appointed where there was a particularly determined board which had stayed through thick and thin and discovered in the end that its self-preservation formula of summer school or low salaries for teachers was unacceptable to government. Offical trustees were the means by which control over schooling was transferred, sometimes wrested, from despondent, pathetic, bickering, fearful, and sometimes courageous locals. Trusteeships in the dry belt, however, were not the results of some conspiracy by professional schoolmen to impose a new system of administration involving consolidation upon unsuspecting or reluctant locals. [54] They were the results of an official policy, buttressed by local sentiment, to stablize local school districts, to regenerate collapsing school boards, and to restore the status quo before the drought.[55]

Unfortunately, many local school boards could not be resurrected. As Inspector Scoffield of Foremost said, "In a few cases successive crop failures have so broken the spirit and interest of these people that they will not stand for election to the school board nor attend school meetings."[56] Significantly when the official trustees were appointed they used the strategies that they as inspectors had devised in concert with the locals and that the locals had fashioned on their own. Thus they perpetuated the dramatic new alignments, fluctuating student dormitories, makeshift boundaries, and floating schools — ploys which were exceedingly disruptive and unsettling and which caused no end of disputes. The school might be retained, the official trustees began to see as the locals and the tax collectors had seen, but only by destroying the community.

In all the grasping to maintain dry belt schools, the interrelationship between floundering locals and paternal government was profoundly complex. Occasionally, the locals made threats they had little intention of carrying out, sometimes they cried and no one heard, sometimes as with the short term school they were willing to do with less than official policy permitted. For the government, extreme crises demanded extreme measures and some, like the Tax Recovery Act, were self-defeating. As well, chaos demanded order, and some forms of government order, like standardized attendance regulations, stultified local self-determination.

From all this, what can one infer about the dry belt state of mind? Almost for sure, the locals did not know what to make of government attempts to help. The government swore that it was dedicated to the restoration of local control, but that rarely happened. The government promised to maintain the schools, but few provincial moves were as disconcerting for the locals as the one to reduce loans. Government policies regarding individual districts were *ad hoc* decisions, dependent upon inspectors, or official trustees, or provincial finances, and thus were never certain, never definite. These qualities were part of the legacy of strategies to keep the schools.

If these strategies heightened the lines of community division, the sense of anxiety and break-up, the divisiveness was reinforced by the nature of what happened in the school, of the teachers, and of the circumstances under which they lived — all of which helped to produce an institution largely unrelated to the fundamental agricultural activity of the land and out of touch with rural life. Notwithstanding all the agonizing effort of government schoolmen and locals to provide schools, the kind of school provided was in a basic sense apart from the people, apart from the land, and apart from the community.

To understand how this happened, one must review briefly the nature of teacher preparation in the period, contemporary curriculum reform, and teachers' living experiences in the dry belt.

The purpose of eight months of normal school training in the early twenties was the preparation of teacher trainees for instructing all subjects on the elementary school curriculum. A major weakness of teacher training institutions in Alberta, as elsewhere, was that they failed to prepare teachers for rural conditions. "The teachers being trained here," said W.A. Stickle, principal of Camrose Normal School in 1921, "will nearly all teach in rural schools, yet they get no opportunity to observe or to practise in a rural school." Without such practice, he concluded, trainees did not learn how to compose multiple graded timetables, how to group classes, how to keep students busy on different projects, or how to grade, teach or test such classes.[57] Principal E.W. Coffin of the Calgary Normal School, meanwhile, was pleased that his institution had an arrangement with two rural schools. Since only one was a single room school and since that meant that of the fourteen apprenticeship schools connected with the normal school only one was a bonafide country school, Coffin's elation was doubtlessly tempered.[58]

The next year unprecedented numbers of trainees flooded the teacher training institutions in response to a number of factors — the depression and lack of clerical jobs, departmental pressure to induce permit teachers to take regular training, and rumours that the government loan to students was to be withdrawn and that the normal school course was to be lengthened to two years.[59] Inundated at the height of drought in the dry belt, Coffin regretted that "we cannot hope to give every student the opportunity of apprentice work in either of our two rural schools."[60] At Camrose, Stickle again noted the "anomaly of training rural school teachers without observation or practice in a rural school — especially considering the fact that "quite a large percentage of our students are wholly ignorant of the problems of the rural school or the rural community. . . .[61] Indeed, he stated that with the massive increase in enrolment and only twelve public school rooms available, each room would have twenty-one student teachers in the 1922-23 school year![62] Hamstrung, Stickle did what he could "to put the students into touch with movements which concern the rural districts. . . " Special speakers gave addresses on school fairs, the public health nurses, tree culture, municipal hospitals, Junior Red Cross, and organized girls' work. "Students are encouraged," he said, "to identify themselves with rural organizations which aim to improve conditions, and to be real members of the community."[63]

What was needed was a broad knowledge of rural life, a spirit of enlightenment and willing leadership. Camrose Inspector J.W. Russell characterized the need well in 1921. "There is not sufficient effort being made by our teachers in leadership in community work," he said, "the majority being content . . . to accept the type and standard of community activity prevalent, rather than to aspire to leadership and to shape community life and activity."[64]

These exhortations and earlier ones from the normal schools, summer schools, and inspectors since before the war had been accompanied by demands that the curriculum be expanded. Significantly, the disaster in the dry belt of the twenties occurred just as the most concerted attempt in prairie and national history to enhance agriculture on the school curriculum bogged down. Promoters of the subject had argued that school gardening and school-supervised home gardening would bring the school and community together by engaging students and teachers in the essential activity of the land, by accentuating the dignity of labour and the work of the soil, and by encouraging farm children to stay on the land. In Alberta and other western provinces, school gardening peaked around 1916, and in five years it was all but forgotten.[65] Many tragedies befell gardens in the period — drought, hail, frost, gophers, maggots, lack of summer care, and lack of leadership.[66] Generally, however, school gardens were worst where field crops were worst — in the dry belt.

The story of Miss Speiran exemplified what happened in dry belt school gardens. Arriving from Ontario in 1916, fresh from normal school and eager to plant a garden in the coming spring, Speiran went to a district near Oyen, just then beginning the long drought. At her school in the spring of 1917, she carefully built elevated rows where her students planted their seeds. The notion of elevating seeds was current in Ontario where there was danger of flooding. Unhappily, in the dry belt the major dangers of the next decade would be drought and soil drifting. Despite massive intervention on behalf of students lugging water to the garden, the plants were victims of the gophers and the hot winds. My mid-June she had abandoned the project.[67] Once was often enough. As Inspector M.E. Lazerte of Bassano wrote, "I have noticed that if the school garden is a failure the first year it takes a long time to win back the sympathy and cooperation of the parents. . . ."[68]

Closely tied to school gardening was the school grounds beautification movement. Properly-kept school grounds were part of the plan to bring school and home together by making the school a local shrine and by providing carefully-landscaped models for home grounds maintenance and esthetics. "The natural features of the site and its surroundings," a departmental bulletin said in 1916, "should be attractive and lend themselves to a landscape treatment that would cultivate a taste for the beautiful and make the school centre a place of which the district may be proud."[69] Nowhere in the province, however, were these purposes so thwarted as in the dry belt. There, upkeep was neglected, no playground equipment was bought, and fences were left down. No trustees ever illustrated the negation of the beautification movement better than the Lyman school board. None ever so poignantly depicted what the school meant to the sinking dry belt community. The scene was a meeting on September 25, 1926, the mood was deliriously comical, and the occasion was a sort of Last Supper, strangely jovial and insanely sardonic. The trustees began to talk of painting the school.

> Then followed a very heated discussion as to the colour, each trustee insisting on his national colours. Owing to the great diversity of opinion and the apparent hopelessness of arriving at an agreement, it was decided on the suggestion of the chairman to paint the school yellow, with the view of its blending with any deposit made on the door step or nuisance committed in the vicinity. Further that a white elephant to be painted on the front. [*sic*] This suggestion met with great enthusiasm and was immediately carried unanimously.[70]

The dry belt school and its grounds were neither a shrine nor a model, nor were they beautiful or enviable. For these tired trustees they were mostly a burden. Less than four months later, there were only ten ratepayers in the district. On March 17, 1930, Lyman fell into the hands of an official trustee.[71]

Also related to school gardening and to grounds beautification, but much more successful, was the school fair. Instituted in 1916 under the guidance of the School of Agriculture at Olds, school fairs spread rapidly across the province in the early twenties. By 1921 there were 89 school fairs, and by 1922, 129.[72] Principal J.C. Hooper of Claresholm School of Agriculture explained that the purpose of fairs was "to stimulate in the children an interest in the activities of the farm and the home, to increase their knowledge of the principles and practice of farming and home-making, to encourage the teaching of agriculture and home economics in the rural schools, [and] to increase the interest of parents in the work of the school.[73] As R.M. Scott, principal of Youngstown School of Agriculture (established in 1920) said, "They have promoted . . . loyalty to home and community."[74]

This role was enhanced in the dry belt when the regular fairs were cancelled and the agricultural societies died out.[75] For a time, in communities such as Orion, Manyberries, Irvine and Youngstown, school fairs took the place of the agricultural fairs as the major community celebration.[76] When drought cancelled the agricultural fair at Youngstown in 1922, for example, the secretary of the agricultural society reported that the society was banding "behind the school fair [to] . . . make it a success in every way."[77] Why school fairs could be held when agricultural fairs could not is explainable partly through the fact that exhibits of penmanship, manual training, or domestic science were less susceptible to the weather than purely agricultural products. As well, both the government and the locals were more determined to maintain the schools than the agricultural societies.

For several reasons, school fairs never completely supplanted the agricultural fairs in the dry belt. First, most school fairs in the region became the responsibility of the new schools of agriculture at Raymond, Gleichen and Youngstown. Agricultural instructors had no sooner taken over the organization than the government closed the Gleichen and Youngstown schools in 1922.[78] Crop failure had reduced enrolment to unacceptable levels, and the institutions created to combat farming difficulties in the dry areas fell victim to the problems they were to solve. Second, in May 1923, as an economy measure, the staff of school inspectors for the province was reduced from forty to twenty-five.[79] Since an integral part of the inspector's job was the adjudication of school fairs, the staff reduction at a time of fair expansion meant that the remaining inspectors were hard pressed to cover the fairs. As A.R. Gibson, inspector for Red Deer, said, "the Inspector's work is now heavy and his being held responsible for . . . school fair work interferes with his itinerary. . . ."[80] With less inspectoral interest, especially in the dry areas where problems of finance became critical, teachers had less incentive to participate. Third, the success of school fairs still depended largely, though not completely, upon good crops.[81] As Inspector John Scoffield of Foremost lamented, "On the eastern side of the Inspectorate the dry season of 1923 affected few school activities more seriously than the school fairs. Field and garden crops were a failure and no fairs were held."[82] Finally, those who taught for short terms had no time to prepare exhibits, and sometimes their schools were not open when the larger fairs were held.

School fairs did not perish in the dry belt of the twenties, but they were increasingly limited to the bigger centres where the quality of agricultural exhibits was often pathetic. Under such circumstances, the festivity could be a discouraging display of the land's intransigence, of man's subservience to nature. Clearly the fact that the school fair had a strong non-agricultural component allowed it to continue in the dry lands. It survived partly because it represented enterprises which were *not* related to the fundamental activity of the land. That is, the kind of fair which emerged in the dry belt could not inspire children with signs of progress, could not exact pride in the work of the soil, could not genuinely interest children in farm life, and could hardly speed their return to the land. Even in that school activity ostensibly most related to agriculture and rural life, there was thus a basic irrelevance, a counter-productiveness.

There was also something about the living conditions of school teachers which promoted the sense that the school was somehow apart from the people. Inspector F.L. Aylesworth of Oyen wrote in 1924 that

> the rural teacher is presented with perhaps only three really serious problems: (1) The location of a suitable boarding-house; (2) How to avoid being entangled with different factions, and in petty disagreements and quarrels rife under present economic conditions; (3) How to provide herself with suitable and adequate recreation and entertainment without acquiring the habit of attending six or more barn dances a week.[83]

Concerning only the first problem was there any real attempt at solution. When money was provided in 1919 for the construction of teacherages, it was hoped that the residential difficulties of teachers would be solved. Two years later, however, Inspector Dobson at Hanna felt that the "Departmental plan has not met with much success . . . since many teachers prefer to board."[84] The explanation for this preference is beginning to emerge from teacher biographies of the period and later. These show a life of hardship in the "residences" — stories of snow-laden roofs caving in, of infestations of mice and vermin, of fear of "foreigners" in immigrant districts, of social isolation and abject loneliness.[85] Moreover, in the dry belt where funds were shortest, facilities were skimpiest, and improvements were often put off indefinitely. Teachers might renovate, of course, but at their own expense. At Creole Belle district in 1919, the teacher was "allowed to buy [wall] paper for the residence," providing she "put it on" and agreed "to be paid . . . when there are sufficient funds available."[86] Characteristically, the teacherage more resembled a bare and secluded cloister than the headquarters of a community leader.

For those who boarded there was companionship — and suffering of another sort. The district of Crocus Plains had to "bear the loss in having bought furniture for the teacher's shack . . . when the teacher decided not to use the same."[87] In times of poverty, teachers might regret such decisions. Sometimes local penury was so pervasive that the teacher had to board on a rotational scheme with every family in the district. While it was possible to know virtually everyone at least superficially, the scheme involved continual adaptation to changing routines, expectations, and degrees of destitution.

When the gardener, Miss Speiran, came to the Oyen district, she boarded with an English family in 1917. Farming on only a quarter section, the family was eager to board the teacher as a means of supplementing their income. Speiran ate in a separate room from the four children since there was not enough "quality" food to go around. Favoured, she recalled her guilt as the children gazed ravenously at her plate. To reach her bedroom with its uncomfortable straw mattress, she had to pass through the main bedroom where the couple and their four children slept.[88]

Ten years later, Norman Jackson Pickard began his teaching career in a German settlement sixteen miles south of Irvine. Following a diphtheria outbreak, Pickard contacted Inspector Carr who ordered him to close the school. The locals, however, countermanded the order, voting to keep the school open. After a second outbreak, Pickard took no chances and appeared on the scene with a Mounted Policeman to enforce the order. As Pickard's biographers have noted, the incident demonstrated the difficulty faced by young, inexperienced teachers in attempts to provide the enlightened community leadership the normal schools and inspectors advocated.[89]

In circumstances like these, the school was in charge of one who was forced to live a very restricted life, who often had the best interests of the locals at heart but who frequently knew nothing of their lifestyles, who had been exhorted to join the community but who remained in the end an outsider.[90] In a very real way, the school with its alien tutor was the symbol of what was left of the burnt-out dry belt. It had been favoured over the community by government and locals alike. If the community was reeling from desertion, the first thought was to save the school, but repeatedly that meant either realigning it with the remnants of other localities or tearing it from its community body altogether. It usually did not mean keeping it on the community's terms — if those involved intermittent operations or the endless extension of debts. In that the school had not linked itself permanently with the fundamental activity of the community and the land, it survived. Its inability to become relevant was simultaneously the mark of its success and failure. Any educational institution designed to deal directly with or to improve life as it then existed on this dying land was doomed. The agricultural schools at Gleichen and Youngstown proved that. The school survived precisely because it represented a world far from the scorching wind, the dust and the thistles, away from the back-breaking labour, the hopelessness and the destitution.

As the relief in groceries, coal and seed escalated in the southeast in amounts which in some districts dwarfed similar measures during the Great Depression, the railroads were called in to assist the exodus.[91] By the end of 1926, 1,851 families totalling 3,179 carloads had been freighted out — some to Saskatchewan, many to the wetter west, and a few to the newer north. The experience of these and thousands of others who left in a more private manner, often with less, was utterly demoralizing.

This chapter has argued that the kind of school that survived in the Alberta dry belt of the twenties contributed to the social malaise of the period and region. The fanatical determination to maintain the schools meant that they would exist in a way which heightened uncertainty, fear, dislocation, in essence, the Durkheimian sense of "anomie." The issue of schooling — when, where, with whom, and how — tore districts apart, neighbours apart, and families apart. Teacher training in the period bore little relationship to rural life in general, and curricular reforms involving agriculture suffered grievously in the dry belt. These factors and social conditions intensified the teacher's determination to be gone after an apprenticeship in what must have seemed like purgatory. They thwarted many attempts at self-sacrifice and service. The rotational boarding schemes left the schoolmarm in a constant state of stress and pity for her penniless hosts and herself, with variations to be heard on the lament of the farmer and new routines to be learned each month or two. Training, conditions and often background had made the teacher an outsider, hardly capable of integrating a society which the school itself had done so much to fracture.

The experience of local school districts in the Alberta dry belt of the twenties set the scene and justification for the larger school districts in the thirties, for the Berry Creek area was the first major rural consolidation in the province.[92] Not surprisingly, Alberta pioneered the establishment of large school divisions, and the first nine were in the dry areas.[93] These grand jurisdictions were to become part of the administration of enormous tracts of wasteland which Alberta euphemistically called the "special areas."

The decade of the twenties in the dry belt witnessed the beginning of these areas, the consequences of the overexpansion of prairie society, horrendous personal loss, and the accommodation of schools to a new social and demographic reality. The accommodation foreshadowed accurately the fate in store for much of the Prairies during the Great Depression.

Notes

I thank Nancy M. Sheehan and Robert M. Stamp for their constructive comments.

[1]Since the appearance of this article in 1978, I have continued the examination of the dry belt problem. See David C. Jones, "A Strange Heartland: The Alberta Dry Belt and the Schools in the Depression," in D. Francis and H. Ganzevoort, eds., *The Dirty Thirties in Prairie Canada* (Vancouver: Tantallus, 1980), pp. 89-109; Jones, "We'll All Be Buried Down Here in This Dry Belt. . . ." *Saskatchewan History,* xxxv (Spring 1982): 41-54; Jones, "The Canadian Prairie Dry Belt Disaster and the Reshaping of 'Expert' Farm Wisdom," *The Journal of Rural Studies* 1:2 (1985): 135-146; Jones, "An Exceedingly Risky and Unremunerative Partnership: Farmers and the Financial Interests Amid the Collapse of Southern Alberta," in David C. Jones

and Ian MacPherson, eds., *Building Beyond the Homestead: Rural History on the Prairies* (Calgary: University of Calgary Press, 1985, pp. 206-227); Jones, ed., *We'll All Be Buried Down Here in This Dry Belt: The Prairie Dryland Disaster, 1917-1926,* (Alberta Historical Society, forthcoming); Jones, *Empire of Dust — Settling and Abandoning the Prairie Dry Belt,* (forthcoming).

²*Census of the Prairie Provinces 1926* (Ottawa: King's Printer, 1931), pp. 518, 561-2. For relevant studies see Jean Burnet, *Next Year Country* (Toronto: University of Toronto Press, 1951); A.M. Pennie, "A Cycle at Suffield," *Alberta Historical Review,* II (Winter 1963): 7-11; James H. Gray, *Men Against the Desert* (Saskatoon: Modern Press, 1967); W.A. Mackintosh, *Economic Problems of the Prairie Provinces* (Toronto: Macmillan, 1935); Wilfred Eggleston, "The Old Homestead: Romance and Reality," in Howard Palmer, ed., *The Settlement of the West* (Calgary: Comprint, 1977), pp. 114-29.

³*Census of Canada 1921,* vol. V. Agriculture, (Ottawa: King's Printer, 1925), pp. 168-69; *Census of the Prairie Provinces 1926,* pp. 711-12; *Census of Canada 1931,* vol. VIII, Agriculture, (Ottawa: King's Printer, 1936), p. 672.

⁴*Census of the Prairie Provinces 1926,* p. 702.

⁵*Census of the Prairie Provinces 1936,* p. 1174.

⁶*Census of the Prairie Provinces 1926,* pp. 711-712.

⁷Ibid., p. 716.

⁸B. Russell and W.H. Snelson, *Report on Southern Alberta Drought Area* (Department of the Interior, Dec. 17, 1924), p. 6. The other studies included: Saskatchewan, *Royal Commission of Inquiry into Farming Conditions* (Regina: King's Printer, 1921); Alberta, *Report of the Survey Board for Southern Alberta* (Edmonton: King's Printer, 1922); Report of the Commissioner on Banking and Credit with Respect to the Industry of Agriculture in the Province of Alberta, Nov. 1922, W.N. Smith papers, Glenbow, hereafter G; Tilley East Commission, 1926, BR 143, G. See also Appendix B, "Problems of a Retrograde Area in Alberta," in Mackintosh, *Economic Problems of the Prairie Provinces,* pp. 291-94.

⁹Tilley East Commission, pp. 11, 17.

¹⁰See Helen D. Howe, *Seventy-Five Years Along the Red Deer River* (Calgary: D.W. Friesen and Sons, 1971), pp. 152-53; Pendant d'Oreille Lutheran Church Women, *Prairie Footprints* (Val Printing, 1970), p. 96; Shortgrass Historical Society, *Long Shadows* (Bow Island: Commentator Publishing Co., 1974), pp. 33, 71, 191, 192; Sunshine Women's Institute History Committee, *The History of the Border Country of Coutts* (Lethbridge: Southern Printing Co., 1965), pp. 74, 84; Bow Island Lion's Club Book Committee, *Silver Sage: Bow Island 1900-1920,* (1972), pp. 301, 311, 461; Alberta, *Annual Report of the Department of Agriculture 1920,* pp. 9, 35, 36; hereafter ARA; ARA 1931, p. 7; ARA 1933, p.7.

¹¹Alberta, *Annual Report of the Department of Education 1922,* p. 58, hereafter ARE.

¹²ARE 1922, p. 58.

¹³ARE 1923, p. 72.

¹⁴ARE 1921, p. 57; ARE 1922, p. 60. Re speedier collection of school taxes note the Parr district minutes of Oct. 7, 1922, which instructed the secretary to "write to each of the ratepayers in the Parr S.D. and request the rate-payer, should his taxes be in arrears, to pay his school taxes at least, in order to keep the school in operation." (Berry Creek School District, box 9, folder 51, hereafter BCSD, G.

[15]Creole Belle school board minutes, Apr. 7, 1919, BCSD, box 4, folder 15, G.

[16]Ibid., May 3, 1919.

[17]Ibid., Aug. 23, 1919.

[18]Ibid., Nov. 1, 1919.

[19]Ibid., Nov. 14, 1919.

[20]Ibid., Special Meeting, Nov. 26, 1919.

[21]Ibid., Dec. 8, 1919.

[22]Ibid., May 29, 1920.

[23]Ibid., May 1, 1921.

[24]*Silver Sage,* pp. 175-76.

[25]The 1921 provincial deficit of $14.6 millions was the greatest deficit in the period 1913-37. (*Royal Commission on Dominion Provincial Relations,* Province of Alberta, Comparative Statistics of Public Finance, Appendix J. p. 8) The outstanding debt in the province in 1921 was $96.1 millions. In 1925 it was $116.1 millions, highest of all provinces in the West and second only to Ontario in the country. (M.C. Urquhart and K.A.H. Buckley, *Historical Statistics of Canada* (Toronto: Macmillan, 1965), p. 221) For a good study of Alberta finances in the period see "Financial Position of Alberta," in Stewart Bates, *Financial History of Canadian Governments* (Ottawa: 1939), pp. 256-83.

[26]ARE 1922, p. 60.

[27]ARE 1923, p. 71.

[28]Ibid.

[29]Dry Coulee school board minutes, Jan. 14, 1926, BCSD, box 4, folder 21, G. Connorsville school board minutes, Mar. 16, 1921, BCSD, box 3, folder 13. G.

[30]Cessford school board minutes, June 26, 1931, BCSD, box 3, folder 10, G.

[31]Forcina school board minutes, May 12, 1920, BCSD, box 5, folder 22, G.

[32]Ibid., May 12, 1920-June 25, 1921.

[33]Charlie McLay to L.A. Thurber, Jan. 27, 1930, Forcina school board correspondence, Ibid.

[34]Arlington school board minutes, Jan. 20, 1923, BCSD, box 1, folder 1, G.

[35]Brown school board minutes, Feb. 9, 1923, BCSD, box 2 folder 9, G.

[36]Jennings school board minutes, Feb. 10, 1919, BCSD, box 6 folder 30, G.

[37]D.C. McEacherne to C.F. Patterson, Mar. 10, 1925, Keystone school board correspondence, BCSD, box 6 folder 33, G.

[38]J.F. Boyce to L.E. Helmer, Dec. 26, 1927, Britannia school board correspondence, BCSD, box 2 folder 7, G.

[39]See Alberta, *Statutes 1922,* An Act to Provide for the Recovery of Taxes 1922, ch. 25. See also Alberta, *Annual Report of the Department of Municipal Affairs, 1922,* p. 7.

[40]ARE 1924, pp. 57, 51; see also ARE 1923, p. 71.

[41]*Alberta Gazette,* vol 19, May 31, 1923, pp. 668-71.

[42]Cessford school board minutes, Jan. 14, 1922, BCSD, box 3 folder 10, G.

[43]Connorsville school board minutes, Jan. 14, 1922, BCSD, box 3, folder 13, G.

[44]Arlington school board minutes, Feb. 24, 1927, BCSD, box 1, folder 1, G.

[45]Ibid., Jan. 13, 1928.

[46]Ibid., Feb. 13, 1928.

[47]Ibid., Jan. 14, 1929.

[48]Connorsville school board minutes, Dec. 2, 1922, BCSD, box 3, folder 13, G.

[49]Ibid., Mar. 20, 1923.

[50]Ibid., Jan. 22, 1927.

[51]Creole Belle school board minutes, July 5, 1919, BCSD, box 4, folder 13, G; see also Homestead Coulee school board minutes, Apr. 16, 1928, BCSD, box 6, folder 27, G.

[52]Crocus Plains school board minutes, Oct. 7, 1922; BCSD, box 4, folder 17, G.

[53]ARE 1923, p. 72. See also ARE 1924, p. 79.

[54]This is an important point deserving amplification. The noted American historian David Tyack has identified a movement to "take control of the rural common school away from the local community and turn it over to the professionals. . . ." "The impetus to consolidate rural schools," he says, "almost always came from outside the rural community." (*The One Best System,* (Cambridge: Harvard University Press, 1974, p. 25) A close look at the period in which the sixty-seven districts of Berry Creek came to consolidation suggests that the impetus often came from *within* the community, that official trustees tried again and again to regenerate the local school boards, and that by the time consolidation had come in 1933, the natives generally recognized that local school governance was for reasons quite apart from official propaganda for large administrative units, simply impossible and against their best interests.

[55]ARE 1923, p. 72; ARE 1924, p. 72.

[56]ARE 1924, p. 81. See also Burnet, *Next Year Country,* ch. 7.

[57]ARE 1921, p. 45.

[58]Ibid., p. 38.

[59]ARE 1922, pp. 43-44.

[60]Ibid., p. 43.

[61]Ibid., p. 45.

[62]Ibid., p. 44.

[63]Ibid., p. 45.

[64]ARE 1921, p. 93.

[65]See ARE 1913, pp. 56, 57; ARE 1914, p. 82; ARE 1916, pp. 47, 56. See also G.V. Van Tausk, "Development of School Agriculture in Alberta," *The Agricultural Gazette of Canada,* 10 (Mar.-Apr. 1923): 145-47, hereafter *TAG*; Van Tausk, "High School Agriculture in Alberta," *TAG*, 10 (Sept.-Oct. 1923): 453-54; "School Gardens: Alberta," *TAG*, 3 (Feb. 1916): 170-74.

[66]See ARE 1915, p. 122; ARE 1916, p. 93; ARE 1917, p. 44; ARE 1918, p. 37.

[67]Jim Devaleriola, Teacher Biography, June 1978, in author's possession. For similar results in Hanna inspectorate see ARE 1918, p. 47; and in Jenner inspectorate see ARE 1919, p. 80.

[68]ARE 1915, p. 133.

[69]*School Buildings in Rural and Village School Districts,* Bulletin, (Edmonton: King's Printer, 1916), p. 8.

[70]Lyman school board minutes, Sept. 25, 1926, BCSD, box 8, folder 43, G.

[71]Ibid., Feb. 4, 1927; Mar. 29, 1930.

[72]ARE 1921, p. 28; ARE 1922, p. 30.

[73]ARA 1921, p. 152.

[74]Ibid., p. 161.

[75]See for example W. Holdsworth to Secretary, Manyberries Agricultural Society, Mar. 23, 1927, box 29, folder 234; Holdsworth to D.W. Nattress, Jan. 23, 1930, Agricultural Societies of Alberta 1887-1955, hereafter ASA, G. See C.W. Whitney to W. Holdsworth, Sept. 25, 1927, indicating the windup of the Foremost Agricultural Society, ASA, box 15, folder 118, G. See also P.W. Johnson, Secretary, Dept. of Agriculture, Report re Irvine Agricultural Society, Apr. 15, 1930, ASA, box 21, folder 171, G.

[76]ARA 1922, p. 162.

[77]E.E. Maxwell to Alex Galbraith, July 4, 1922, ASA, Box 48, folder 409, G.

[78]See E.B. Swindlehurst, *Alberta's Schools of Agriculture, A Brief History* (Edmonton: Queen's Printer, 1964), pp. 78-82.

[79]ARE 1923, p. 52.

[80]Ibid., p. 79.

[81]See for example ARA 1921, p. 161; ARE 1924, p. 83.

[82]ARE 1924, p. 84.

[83]Ibid., p. 70.

[84]ARE 1921, p. 67.

[85]Ted Hellard, Teacher Biography, Apr. 1978; Anne Gagnon, Teacher Biography, Mar. 1978, in author's possession.

[86]Creole Belle school board minutes, Oct. 4, 1919, BCSD, box 4, folder 15, G.

[87]Crocus Plains school board minutes, Jan. 12, 1920, BCSD, box 4, folder 17, G.

[88]Devaleriola, Teacher Biography.

[89]Fran and Tom Cormack, Teacher Biography, June 1978, in author's possession.

[90]For further evidence on the outsider theme see Jones, "A Strange Heartland," and Robert S. Patterson's ch. 6 of this book.

[91]Re relief see *Story of Rural Municipal Government in Alberta: 1909 to 1969,* nd., p. 82, *et passim; Silver Sage,* pp. 302-11; *Statutes of Alberta, 1922,* "The Drought Relief Act," ch. 8.

[92]Note also the much smaller Turner Valley consolidation, and the earlier Warner area consolidation.

[93]ARE 1938, p. 56.

15

"Our Boys in the Field": School Inspectors, Superintendents, and the Changing Character of School Leadership in British Columbia

Thomas Fleming

Unlike in the United States where local communities have appointed their own school superintendents since the early nineteenth century (1830s), school boards across Canada have not generally been empowered to select their own chief school officers until recent decades. In British Columbia, the employment of superintendents remained a provincial matter until 1974 when the New Democratic Government broke with the past and granted the province's seventy-five school districts permission to hire school leaders of their choice, provided they met certain criteria.

The local employment of superintendents signalled an important change in British Columbia public school administration. It meant, for one thing, that district superintendents were no longer "the Department of Education's men-in-the-field" or "servants of the Crown," as they had been for the best part of a century. For the superintendents, local employment meant that their allegiance was now to their immediate political masters, the school boards who hired them, and to the local communities they represented. The shift from provincial to local employment also marked the break-up of the small administrative group or "family" of school professionals who had risen through the ranks to become school inspectors and, later, superintendents, and who had long been seen as the most visible symbols of the provincial government's presence in schools.

The advent of local control over senior administrative appointments in the mid-1970s also reflected important social and educational changes that had taken place in British Columbia since the end of World War II, most notably, rising demands by various constituencies for greater school board autonomy, the actions of powerful special-interest groups in education, and the general politicalization and pluralization of school policy-making in the years after mid-century. Widespread public and professional discussion in the late 1960s and early 1970s about such matters as administrative decentralization, accountability, and broadening the school's mandate also gave further impetus to the drive for locally-appointed school leaders.

Within the context of such events, this chapter will explore some of the major forces which brought about and shaped the development of the local superintendency in British Columbia. More specifically, it will examine from a historical perspective how the superintendent's role evolved from that of the school inspector; how attempts by the Department of Education to redraw educational jurisdictions in the 1930s and 1940s precipitated a need for school executives to operate at the district level; how various social, political, and professional forces coalesced in the period from 1950 to 1970 to create a climate receptive to local employment; and, finally, how the transition from provincial to local employment changed the vision and character of public school leadership in this province.

The School Inspectors: Agents of Provincial Control

To understand the emergence of the local superintendency, and the radical break with the past it represented, it is necessary to understand the strong tradition of central control that existed in provincial education from the early 1870s to the mid-1970s. British Columbia, as educational historian F. Henry Johnson pointed out, "entered Confederation with the most centralized school system on record."[1] And, for much of the first century of public schooling in this province, this pattern of central decision-making was evident. Government in Victoria, through the Council of Public Instruction and the Department of Education, controlled many aspects of school district operations. Provincial authorities determined the extent to which schools would be financed, the number of school boards that would exist, the organizational and administrative structures for the delivery of services, the character of the school curriculum, the nature of testing and standards, and criteria for teacher certification.[2]

Provincial leaders also controlled the selection and appointment of school supervisors above the rank of principal. Early attempts by British Columbia municipalities to follow the American example and appoint their own chief educational officers were met by government resistance and, eventually, resulted in failure and frustration. In the closing years of the nineteenth century, for example, the growth in size and complexity of urban school systems prompted the Vancouver school board to seek provincial permission to hire its own senior school official. Despite misgivings about the divided allegiances that an appointment of this kind might promote, the provincial government acquiesced in 1901 and authorized Vancouver to appoint a city superintendent as the "administrative head of the schools," provided, of course, that the appointment and the salary it carried were first approved by the Council of Public Instruction.[3]

This experiment in local autonomy proved short-lived. After some differences with local officials about the tasks assigned to principals, provincial authorities decided in 1912 to reassert their control over local operations and to change the title of "city superintendent" back to that of "municipal inspector of schools," a position more closely aligned with government in Victoria and subject to the supervision of provincial inspectors assigned to report on the condition and progress of schools in the municipality.[4] Not surprisingly, this action on the part of the provincial government exacerbated tensions between provincial and local leaders and, ultimately, led to the resignation of then-superintendent W.P. Argue. He complained that the role of municipal inspector was one of mere clerkship and that the government's intention was "to destroy local control in the management of schools and to centre everything in the department at Victoria."[5]

Argue's assessment of the government's objective was correct. The school management and supervision system that emerged with the establishment of public schooling in the 1870s was highly centralized and based on the notion that the provincial government, and no other authority, should control what went on in provincial schools. Faced with the problem of administering and supervising schools in an area of over 360,000 square miles, and in a province already noted for its cultural as well as geographic diversity, the government sought to ensure some uniformity in school operations by tightly monitoring the system through its staff headquartered in Victoria.[6]

The task of overseeing schools scattered across a vast territory, however, was too great a burden for the provincial superintendent of schools to handle alone. Consequently, legislation was passed in 1879 which empowered the Lieutenant-Governor-in-Council to appoint a school inspector to assist the superintendent. This office was not filled until 1887, when David Wilson, principal of Boys' School in New Westminster, was appointed as the first inspector, a position he held for twenty-one years. At the time of his appointment, there were 5,345 pupils in the provincial system, 118 teachers, and ninety-two high school students.

The inspectorate was gradually enlarged by the addition of other inspectors in 1892 and 1897. By the time of Putman and Weir's survey in 1924, the Department of Education had a well-organized supervisional contingent of two high school inspectors, Arthur Sullivan and J.B. DeLong, sixteen elementary inspectors, and four municipal inspectors.[7] From the founding of the inspectorate in 1887 until 1958, when the inspector's position was superseded by that of the government-appointed district superintendent, 118 men and one woman served as the province's agents and the chief instruments by which Victoria administered British Columbia schools.[8] Margaret Strong, the only woman to serve in this capacity, was appointed by the New Westminster school board as a municipal inspector and held this position from 1913 to 1915.

Over these seven decades, during which the school population grew from about 5,000 to roughly 260,000 pupils, the inspectors came to be recognized as the most prominent representatives of government authority. One early twentieth-century educational observer wrote, "the central controlling power of the system" was not the Council of Public Instruction, as defined by the School Act, but really "a suite of offices in the parliament buildings at Victoria, presided over by the superintendent of education, assisted by the school inspectors. . . ."[9] And, it was the "Education Office," this observer contended, which exercised a form of "benevolent despotism" over trustees and teachers alike.

A comprehensive description of the inspector's role and formidable powers was provided in 1918 by George Hindle, a school teacher in Trail who wrote a study of education in British Columbia for his doctoral degree in pedagogy at the University of Toronto. To quote Hindle:

> In practice, each room or division of a graded school and each non-graded school is visited twice a year by the official inspector, who usually spends half a day in the room, during which he examines the order, discipline, methods of teaching, etc., and reports on these and the general progress of the school. It is his duty to discuss with teachers all matters which may promote their efficiency, and the character and usefulness of the school. Furthermore, it is his duty to furnish teachers and trustees with such information as they may require regarding the Public School Act and the performance of their respective duties. In addition to the work of inspecting schools, the inspector must render aid and direction to new school districts in the process of formation. He is often detailed to visit a locality petitioning for the establishment of a school district, or an assisted school, and the fate of the petition depends almost wholly on this report. It is his duty to encourage the establishment of schools where none exist by holding public meetings in the localities. He has power to appoint trustees in all cases where the ratepayers have neglected to do so at their annual meeting.[10]

It is not surprising that principals and teachers and, occasionally, even trustees, viewed inspectors' visits with some trepidation. Often, informal networks developed within school districts to advise of an inspector's coming. Warnings were relayed by messengers on foot and on horseback, by agreements reached in collusion with friendly boarding-house owners in whose premises inspectors might lodge, and, in later years, by frantic telephone calls alerting others to an inspector's arrival. Johnson tells the story of one principal who informed his staff of the inspector's presence by sending them a note with a quotation of Tennyson: "The curse is come upon us/Said the Lady of Shallott."[11]

Teachers had reason to be apprehensive about the semi-annual or annual reports inspectors would file on their classroom proficiency, knowing, no doubt, that failure of their pupils to pass the inspector's muster would be attributed, as John Jessop put it, "to inefficiency in imparting instruction." One observer recalled the harsh judgements rendered by inspectors in the pre-World War I period: "The faults of the teacher in discipline and method are the subject of pitiless review and a high standard of excellence is demanded of him. One fears that the critical and offical aspects of the work are too much in evidence."[12] Little, it seemed, escaped the watchful eye of the inspectors. With cold detachment, inspectors noted the "mechanical" character of a teacher's style, the lack of "real teaching," the absence of "order, discipline, and control," and, for the least fortunate, the conclusion that "results for the past few years have been very disappointing." Reports such as these, filed in triplicate (one copy to the teacher, the school board, and the superintendent's office in Victoria), sometimes brought a sudden and merciless end to a teacher's career.

This is not to say, of course, that inspectors were always critical of teachers, or that they always adhered to standards in an inflexible manner. Stories abound of inspectors turning a blind eye to the fact that certain schools were not enrolling sufficient pupils to remain in operation. In some cases, inspectors were known to count infants, or even family pets to arrive at a school population of ten — the number required to keep a school open. Likewise, many inspectors were known for their acts of kindness to teachers in various kinds of trouble, as well as their willingness to bring news of the outside world to those in isolated schools. For every inspector who sprinkled cologne on a handkerchief to avoid smelling unwashed children, there was someone like High School Inspector J.B. DeLong, a fine instructor himself, who might whisper to a sports-minded teacher the latest World Series score gleaned from a radio which he listened to between classes.[13]

Apart from reporting on teacher performance, inspectors were also responsible for preparing annual reports on their districts. These documents formed the basis of the Department of Education's own annual reports on the condition of provincial schools. In collecting such information, inspectors became the province's leading educational experts, and provided the statistical data necessary for Victoria to maintain its administrative expertise, and, thereby, its hegemony over the development of the school system.

Prior to the Great Depression, inspectors and the administrative staff to which they reported were particularly concerned with quantitative assessments of the overall state of the schools. Preoccupied with efficiency — a theme which dominated the social and educational thought of the late-nineteenth and early-twentieth century — the inspectors, like school leaders elsewhere, sought to improve statistical methods which would allow them to gauge such things as pupil absenteeism and retention rates, pupil and teacher performance, enrolment increases, and school operating costs. They believed, as one writer put it, that "an accurate body of educational statistics is one of the greatest possible utility to the teacher, to the parents of children at school, to the trustees or committees of management, to the nation at large, and still more to the children themselves."[14]

Not everyone agreed with the zealousness with which statistics were assembled for the annual reports. Criticisms of diligent number-gathering were countered with arguments like that of Superintendent Stephen Pope, who said only "those who study these statistics with a view to obtain a knowledge of the condition of the schools are properly prepared to give an intelligent opinion as to the value and character of the work accomplished."[15] It did not worry inspectors or their superiors that knowledge revealed by such studies remained something of a private preserve. After all, they were the professionals, charged with administering and controlling provincial schools in a rational and impartial manner..If others did not understand the necessity for manage-

ment information of this kind, they did, and they used it to help design a
system of schooling whose benefits seemed self-evident.

The Social and Educational Character of the
Provincial Inspectorate, 1887-1958

Despite the authority vested in the inspectors and the unquestionable
influence they enjoyed in managing and shaping the provincial system, the
qualifications required to hold their position were never outlined in school
legislation, as they were for teachers or trustees. In practice, however, the
career path leading to the job of inspector was relatively straightforward, and
remained constant over time. Inspectors invariably began their careers as
teachers, and, having distinguished themselves in that capacity, then moved
on to become vice-principals and principals. They were recruited into the
inspectorate when an inspector was impressed with their administrative performance and advised them to apply for a vacant position within the ranks.
Candidates for the inspectorate were thus "hand-picked" by seasoned inspectors, and this process of succession, in itself, testified to the closed nature of
the "old boys' network" controlling provincial schooling. As one former
inspector described it, civil service leaders sought men who were "bright,
loyal, and ambitious — men who would advise government, fight for what
was right, and who would administer in accordance with their conscience":
more humourously described, it was a commitment to "poverty, chastity, and
obedience."[16] For many, the job became the most important thing in their
lives.

Failure on the part of principals to heed a superior's recommendation to
enter government service might end or stall an administrative career. Those
who for family or financial reasons were reluctant to join the inspectorate
(inspectors were paid considerably less than principals) were warned of the
negative consequences such refusals could have on their futures. One principal, who contemplated rejecting a promotion to inspector, was cautioned:
"there are a lot of Siberias out there where you could never be heard from
again."[17]

Prior to the Great Depression, most of the inspectors were born and educated outside the province — in the Maritimes, Ontario, and the British Isles
— and had come to British Columbia as teachers during the large migration
into the province after Confederation. They were described by a turn-of-the-
century popular press as gentlemen, scholars, and individuals of high character who took great pride in the province's educational development and the
quality of school leaders it attracted.[18] Indeed, the early inspectors were a
group of learned men, certainly when compared to others at this time. Twenty-
eight out of the first thirty-eight individuals to become inspectors held either
B.A. or M.A. degrees, and four held an LL.D.[19]

Frank Eaton, who headed Vancouver schools in. 1903, exemplified the
high academic standing characteristic of many of these men. Born in Kent-

ville, Nova Scotia, he taught in that province before becoming a principal. Recipient of a B.A. degree from Harvard and an M.A. from Acadia, he also taught at the Boston Latin School and at the Massachusetts Institute of Technology. Twice he travelled to Europe where he studied the educational systems of Great Britain and Germany. He had also owned, edited, and published two newspapers prior to his career as chief of Vancouver's schools.[20]

Inspectors of the post-1925 era differed somewhat from their predecessors. In the main, they were born and educated in British Columbia. They attended provincial schools, enrolled in Victoria or Vancouver Normal School after graduation, began teaching, and, finally, earned a degree at the University of British Columbia — usually by taking summer school courses over a long period of time. Compared to earlier inspectors, they were less likely to have had a classical, liberal education or to have had educational or work experiences outside the province. However, they were seen to be educational experts and men of practical affairs by public and professionals alike, although few were ever formally trained in administration. There was a belief, at least among some inspectors, that administrative theory "wouldn't help much with the problems at Bella Coola."[21] Overall, the period 1925 to 1970 might generally be described as the age of the school practitioner — notwithstanding the fact that inspectors such as Harold Campbell, Bill Plenderleith, Cliff Conway, John Gough, Patrick Grant, Jack Kirk, Frank Levirs, and others contributed scholarly articles on diverse subjects to learned and professional journals. For the most part, these men were more interested in performing school administration than in theorizing about it.

The inspectors' right to provide educational leadership was assured not only by their educational credentials and school experience, but also by what was seen to be an experience in command. Many had served in the armed forces during World Wars I and II.[22] T.G. Carter, for example, fought overseas in World War I and joined the Royal Canadian Air Force in 1941, where he served with distinction for four years. Carlyle Clay was a member of the Royal Flying Corps in 1918; Alex Turnbull earned the Military Cross for his valour in France between 1914 and 1918; C.J. Strong was a lieutenant-colonel in the Canadian Army; Harold Campbell, later deputy minister of education, served with the University Battalion in World War I; and Daniel Mackirdy earned the Distinguished Flying Cross with the RCAF in World War II. These men, and other inspectors who had entered the armed forces, carried into the inspectorate traditions and values learned in the military. Their transition from military to government service was, therefore, not difficult. They were proud of this period in their lives and many of them, in fact, continued to use their armed forces rank as an honorific long after the wars were over.[23]

For such men, allegiance to a central governing authority in education was much in keeping with their own traditions of military service. They saw themselves, according to Harold Campbell, as "educational legionnaires," or "colonial officers above reproach" and, more practically, Joe Phillipson noted, as "educational expediters" — men who would find ways to get the school work of the province done.[24] In joining the inspectorate, they took an oath to uphold the policies of the Crown and the Department (the Department of Education was itself formally organized in 1920), a loyalty symbolized in the crest of the government-issue briefcases they carried on their rounds. As Colonel John Burnett observed: "We were the Department's men, selected by the Department, employed by the Department, and responsible to the Department."[25] And, these sentiments of fidelity were reciprocated by super-intendents of education and their senior staffs in Victoria who typically referred to the inspectors as "our boys in the field," and who made it plain that valiant and faithful service would be rewarded. The Department would not leave its men "in the wilderness," either literally or figuratively. "We don't want to hear from you," senior Inspector C.J. Frederickson informed a young inspec-tor prior to his first assignment. "If we don't, we'll know you're all right. But, if we do, we'll be behind you."[26] Such bonds of support and friendship, or seeing themselves as "part of the system," as one put it, characterized the inspectorate and sustained the inspectors in their endeavours. The strength of this relationship can be measured to some extent in the length of time inspec-tors spent in service. Of more than one hundred individuals who worked as inspectors from 1919 to 1958, most remained with the government until retirement, as inspectors, as members of normal school staff, or as senior administrators in Victoria.[27] Of this group, only a handful resigned to take up careers outside of education, and these resignations were generally not prompted by differences with the Department over policies or practices.

Of course, a career as inspector offered not only job security, but also opportunities for administrative advancement, for playing a larger role in the provincial school system, and for travel. After teaching assignments in iso-lated, ungraded schools, or administrative positions in small-town high schools, few principals could resist the lure of the open road. Many inspectors saw themselves as outdoor enthusiasts, students of nature, or "twentieth-century mountain men." For this reason alone, the job appealed to them. The natural obstacles of rock slides, washouts, and heavy snowfalls presented exciting challenges to be overcome, challenges that frequently became the substance of stories recounted later at length before colleagues and friends. In many respects, the nature of the inspectors' work was defined by the travel they did and by the seasons of the year that allowed them to travel. For the latter reason alone, inspections usually took place in the spring and fall when roads were passable and journeys less arduous. Even into the late 1950s, inspectors were obliged to travel thousands of miles annually under primitive conditions to remote mountain hamlets, or to villages sited on treacherous coastal inlets. Quite often, getting to the schools required more time and energy than the task of inspection itself.

However, the inspector's work life was not always solitary. In addition to the strong system of professional support within the Department, there were also social ties among inspectors and their superiors. Until the 1950s, marking "departmental" exams, for example, became a much-anticipated annual event. During the early summer when time was set aside for this task, inspectors throughout the province travelled to Victoria with their wives where they all stayed at the same hotel, usually the Sussex. While inspectors read papers and exams or conducted other departmental business, their wives would meet each morning for tea, shopping, bridge, or similar activities. In the course of such rituals, it was not unknown for inspectors' wives — many of whom had been teachers themselves — to take cues on dress or matters of deportment from the chief inspector's wife.[28] Occasions like the annual marking session were also punctuated by one or more formal dinners with the chief inspector and provincial superintendent. Events of this kind not only strengthened social and professional bonds among provincial schoolmen but, in addition, compensated somewhat for the rigours of travel and the sacrifices made by inspectors' families. In 1958, when the "new" Public Schools Act took effect and changed the title of "inspector of schools" to that of "district superintendent," Chief Inspector of Schools Frank Levirs, expressed a sentiment no doubt shared by many of his colleagues when he wrote: "The passing of a time-honoured designation must be viewed with some regret. . . ."[29]

Structural Changes Within the Provincial System, 1925-1958

The eventual breakup of the school inspectorate in 1958, and the subsequent evolution of the modern superintendency in British Columbia — a two-stage development beginning with the establishment of the district superintendency in 1958 and the local superintendency in 1974 — was brought about by several important changes to the organization of provincial schooling between 1925 and 1958. Events that ultimately led to local employment for superintendents were first set in motion in 1924 when J.D. MacLean, minister of education, appointed J.H. Putman, senior inspector of schools for Ottawa, and George Weir, a professor of education at the University of British Columbia, to survey provincial schools and to recommend ways to improve their curricula and systems of finance and administration. The Putman-Weir report, presented to government in 1925, had far-reaching effects, not the least of which was a proposal that many of the province's seven hundred school districts be consolidated into larger units in the interest of efficiency.[30]

By 1933, the Department of Education was prepared to undertake a series of experiments with large units of school administration. The first took place in the Peace River region, where sixty-three isolated districts were collapsed into one large Peace River Educational Administration Unit during the years 1933 to 1937.[31] The experiment did not attempt to consolidate schools in this sparsely-populated rural area; instead, administrative services were brought together into four divisions, each comprised of six to fourteen former districts. Inspector Bill Plenderleith was appointed director of school operations, as well as official trustee, and was assisted by an area advisory council and by local school committees composed of former school board members. Plenderleith's appointment and the danger it appeared to present to local autonomy provoked a sharp reaction among Peace River residents. Some called the action "arbitrary, undemocratic, coercive, despotic, fascist," and, even, "un-British." A petition sent to the minister of education demanded the "public schools of the district be returned to the elected school boards of the people."[32] Despite such protests, however, similar experiments were carried out in the Matsqui-Sumas-Abbotsford area in 1935, and in rural areas surrounding Nanaimo and Ladysmith in 1942.

Concerns with educational efficiency were also expressed in other forms, especially in government-inspired attempts to recalculate the basis of school finance. In June 1934, just as the Peace River consolidation plan was being framed, the government empowered a commission to study school finance. Heavily influenced by its technical advisor, Major H.B. King, who later became chief inspector of schools, the commission published a 230-page document in 1935 entitled *School Finance in British Columbia*.[33] This document, known as the "King Report," offered a number of radical proposals for restructuring the organization and finance of provincial schools.[34]

Although the commission's recommendations embarrassed the government — and the report was generally ignored — the idea of bringing greater order and efficiency to rural schools persisted. By 1944, provincial conditions favoured a comprehensive review of school organization and finance. Since the depression years, it had become increasingly apparent to community and government leaders, as well as to leaders of the British Columbia Teachers' Federation (BCTF), that management structures for rural schools were cumbersome and ineffective. Of the province's 650 school districts, 590 had a combined pupil population of only 23,000; 392 rural districts, headed by their own boards, operated no more than a single, one-room school; and 213 districts functioned without boards and were under the care of an official trustee, who was usually the inspector of schools assigned to the area.[35] What all this meant, of course, was that many of the province's sparsely-populated districts could not offer educational services comparable to those found in urban or more developed areas. Neither the grant-per-teacher allowance provided by Victoria, nor tax revenues generated locally, was sufficient to sustain more than the barest school programs, or to overcome existing disparities in educational opportunity, particularly at the secondary level where, in many cases, there were too few youngsters to justify schooling past grade 8.[36]

For these reasons, in 1944 the Hart Government appointed Maxwell Cameron, a professor of education at UBC, to conduct a one-man inquiry into financial and organizational problems facing provincial schools. In his report, tabled the following year, Cameron proposed that the province "undertake a thorough reorganization of its school districts" so that each administrative unit would be "large enough to justify a reasonably adequate schooling from grades one to twelve."[37] He recommended that the province's 650 districts be reduced to seventy-four; that a standard assessment rate be levied against all property for school support; and that the provincial government bear increased responsibility in financing basic education programs throughout the province.[38]

The translation of Cameron's recommendations into a legislative bill, and its subsequent passage in 1946, marked a watershed date in British Columbia school history, not just in terms of reconstituting the basis of school finance, but also in the way it reshaped the role of school inspector. Prior to implementing Cameron's plan, the Department of Education called the inspectors and other government officials together on several occasions to "trouble-shoot" potential problems arising from the transition to larger units of administration. It became clear that inspectors would be obliged to take on other tasks in addition to their supervisory and reporting functions. For one thing, they would be more closely aligned with local authorities than in the past. From now on, they had to assist boards in developing transportation systems to serve broader territories, to help boards interpret and apply provincial policies, and to advise boards on how districts should be organized and administered. In effect, with the creation of seventy-four large districts, each inspector became the general superintendent of instruction for a number of local school systems — a change of role that would be formally recognized in 1958.[39]

Other structural changes were occurring in school systems during the 1930s and 1940s which also underscored the need for stronger administrative leadership at the local level. Over the first half of the century, schools themselves had become complex organizations, growing in size and specialization, and expanding the scope of their operations. By the late 1940s and 1950s, not only were there greater numbers of youngsters in schools, but they were attending more regularly and remaining in school longer. The consolidation of small schools (more than 200 of the province's 1,100 or so schools were closed between 1942 and 1947) as well as the development of the combined junior-senior high school contributed further to school size.[40] At the same time, the formal and informal elements of the curriculum had become more comprehensive since the introduction of the "new education" early in the century. Throughout the 1920s, 1930s, and 1940s, course offerings multiplied and new consideration was given to such things as counselling and guidance problems, "ability grouping," and provisions for individual differences among pupils. Obviously, the problems encountered in providing and coordinating such educational and social services called for a system of school management far beyond what school inspectors could provide as itinerant supervisors.

Changes in the teaching force also pointed to the need for more professional administration in schools. The trend to strengthen teacher qualifications, which had begun with the normal schools in the early 1900s, continued to grow in the period between the two world wars. Radical changes were proposed to "upgrade" teacher education and to extend preparation programs. Across the province, teachers increasingly saw themselves as members of a profession — and this profession was not as acquiescent as it had been half a century before. Beginning in the late 1930s, the BCTF earned important concessions from government: they secured the right to compulsory arbitration in 1937; they made it possible for married women to continue teaching in 1945; and, almost a decade later, they ensured that women received equal pay for equal work.[41] In addition, in the years leading up to mid-century the Federation made it clear they sought greater involvement in determining other aspects of teachers' lives, most notably in the areas of curriculum-making and professional certification. In short, new tensions and new divisions were making their presence felt in the relationship between teachers and the Department of Education and between teachers and the boards who employed them. Again, such developments suggested inadequacies in existing provisions for school management and underlined the need for local school trustees to have the advice and assistance of their own senior educational administrators on a continuing basis.

Finally, another factor which contributed to closing the inspectorate in 1958 and to the emergence of the district superintendent's office had to do with changing perceptions of the inspector's role. In 1925, Putman and Weir had distinguished between supervision — whose primary purpose was constructive personal service — and inspection, whose purpose was to judge worth and efficiency. The notion of "inspection" that grew out of a late nineteenth-century need to control rapid educational development became somewhat dated by the end of the 1930s, both in Canada and elsewhere. The autocratic and authoritarian practices which frequently marked school management in the first quarter of the twentieth century, in fact, gave way by mid-century to a more liberal and democratic approach to administration. By the 1940s and 1950s, progressive ideas about the value of constructive criticism and non-punitive supervisory techniques had gained acceptance in educational circles, as well as in the world of business and industry.

In British Columbia, such ideas became popular at a time when the inspector's role was already being transformed and, indeed, broadened by closer affiliation with local authorities. As one former inspector observed, in the years following the Cameron Report, the task of "inspecting" teachers became distasteful to many government men-in-the-field.[42] They no longer wished to "report" on other human beings: their role, as they now saw it, was closer to that of director of instruction. They wished to be educational statesmen, not judges dispatched to rule on the pedagogical proficiency of others. By the mid-1950s, school supervisors across western Canada were conversant with the view that "the improvement of teaching is not so much an activity of the inspector in which pupils and teachers participate as an activity of teachers and pupils in which an inspector participates."[43]

Pressures for Autonomy and Participation After Mid-Century

The struggle for local control of schools and for the local appointment of school leaders intensified in the post-1945 era for several reasons. To begin with, the end of hostilities meant that national and provincial attention could return to matters of domestic policy and to issues left unresolved by the outbreak of war. In the quarter of a century after the Allied victory, rising birth rates, the enrolment of veterans in educational institutions, and new views about the value of developing human resources and the nation's intellectual capital made public education a larger and more visible enterprise than ever before. In British Columbia, for example, this growth was evident in the following statistics. In the twenty-four year period from 1947 to 1971, there was a thirty-five-fold increase in educational expenditures: in 1970-71, the money spent on education equalled the entire provincial budget only nine years earlier. During this same period, school enrolments almost quadrupled from 137,827 to 527,106 pupils, and secondary enrolments increased by a factor of nearly five. The growth in the teacher population in these years was no less impressive: between 1947 and 1971, the number of teachers rose from 4,833 to 22,301. This was brought about by a combination of circumstances, including higher grade-to-grade retention rates, growth in secondary schooling, the swelling of administrative ranks, and a declining pupil-teacher ratio (the average classroom size for all schools dropped from about twenty-eight to twenty-four pupils in this twenty-four-year period).[44]

With this growth, however, and the massive public investment in education, there was also serious criticism. Hilda Neatby's 1953 volume, *So Little For The Mind,* raised disturbing questions about the quality and substance of what she referred to as "progressive schooling," as did the public debate on pedagogy that followed in the wake of the Sputnik launching in 1957. Uncertainties about the state and direction of the schools led to the establishment of royal commissions of inquiry into education in Ontario, Nova Scotia, Manitoba, and Alberta between 1950 and 1958. In 1958, British Columbia also followed suit by appointing its own royal commission headed by Sperrin Chant, dean of Arts and Science at UBC, to "inquire into, assess and report upon the provincial educational system to university level."[45]

Although the Chant Commission proved to be of little consequence in changing the administrative structure of British Columbia schools, it provided a timely forum for the expression of long-held resentments against tight provincial control of education. Moreover, the hearings afforded the BCSTA and the BCTF a welcome opportunity to present publically their case for the local control of schools, and indeed, for the local appointment of school superintendents.

The Trustees' Association, in particular, had emerged in the post-war era as a powerful and politically sophisticated organization and had shown itself to be increasingly inclined to do battle with provincial authorities over the issue of school district autonomy. District amalgamation gave school trustees a larger political base from which to assert their independence and to make known the needs of their constituents. By the mid-1950s, individual trustees and their Association were openly challenging the provincial government on a variety of fronts, especially those concerning school finance.

The emergence of government-appointed superintendents in 1958 was viewed as a positive change by the BCSTA, but they contended that a superintendent in the service of the province could not fully address local needs for school leadership. What was most required, they believed, was a change in the locus of administrative control. The Trustees' Association advised the Chant Commission that the district superintendent "must be closely identified with the school system" and, therefore, each board of school trustees "should be permitted to appoint its own superintendent who would fulfil the function of chief education director and whose line of authority would emanate from the school board with certain specific responsibilities to the Department of Education."[46] The BCTF submission expressed many of the same concerns, and recommended that the district superintendent be appointed as "chief executive officer of the school board."[47]

Despite these strong appeals for district autonomy in hiring superintendents, the Chant Commission did not propose major changes when they tabled their report to government in 1960.

From Provincial to Local Control in the 1970s

Neither the creation of the district superintendent's office in 1958 nor the findings of the Chant Commission in 1960 quieted mounting demands for local control over senior administrative appointments. Through the 1960s and early 1970s, the provincial government continued to be pressured by the BCSTA, the BCTF, individual school boards, and by the superintendents themselves to decentralize administrative authority and to grant school boards autonomy in selecting their own educational leaders.

These demands, in part, reflected broad social changes taking place elsewhere in Canada and the United States. The 1960s were years of dramatic change, a time when traditional values and beliefs were being questioned, when the practices of social institutions were being challenged as perhaps never before. New political alignments were replacing older liberal and conservative forces, new tensions were created by a culture that increasingly saw itself as pluralistic, and new expectations were expressed by parents and other community members demanding participation in educational affairs.

Political and social change were not the only factors influencing the roles of district superintendents in British Columbia. Since Cameron's reorganization of district boundaries in 1946, the Department's field personnel had been troubled by the question of allegiance. Their increasing involvement with local authorities raised the issue of whether their loyalty lay primarily with the government in Victoria, or with the school boards with whom they now closely worked. Furthermore, the shift in position from that of school inspector to district superintendent in 1958 seemed to signal that, in the future, their careers would be shaped more directly by local rather than provincial developments. Unfortunately, however, their roles and responsibilities remained ambiguous. Each level of government held its own expectations of what superintendents should do, its own agenda of tasks and priorities, and its own concept of what constituted sound educational leadership, and, frequently, such things were in conflict.

The issue of loyalty, of course, was also intertwined with other issues. Terms of employment, for example, were a matter of increasing importance to superintendents in the 1960s and early 1970s.[48] Some individuals who were willing to forego the security offered by the civil service argued for school board control over senior administrative appointments, believing that such a change would enhance both their professional status and financial position. In fact, to many superintendents the issue of money was really an issue of status; salaries reflected one's place and value in the system. Others, however, saw great risks in local employment and questioned the ability of school boards to choose educational leaders, as they were inexperienced in such matters and, perhaps, not altogether conversant with the educational needs of the province as a whole.[49]

A final resolution to this issue came in a decisive manner with the electoral victory of the NDP in 1972. The new government was committed to the idea of administrative decentralization, not only in education but also in other areas of public administration. Prior to her appointment as minister of education, Eileen Dailly had served on the Burnaby school board, and had advocated local employment of superintendents during her term of office.[50] She believed the "the people out there," as one ministry official put it, should control administrative appointments, as well as other aspects of public schooling. Her views in this regard corresponded closely with positions the BCSTA and the BCTF had been promoting, at least since the time of the Chant inquiry. The Federation, in particular, had taken an active role in the campaign of 1972, believing that an NDP government would be amenable to the idea of local control as well as to teacher aspirations for greater participation in educational policy- and decision-making.

The seventy-year struggle by local communities to appoint their own school leaders ended on April 18, 1973, when the Legislature approved An Act to Amend the Public Schools Act which gave school boards of districts with an enrolment of twenty thousand pupils the right to hire superintendents to "advise and assist" them.[51] This legislation further provided for local choice in employing assistant superintendents and outlined in broad terms superintendents' duties and responsibilities, as well as the terms under which they could be discharged.

Even before the NDP's victory, the character of the Department of Education had begun to change. During the previous decade, the Department had been forced to "consult" more with outsiders, while the system of career advancement and reward that had existed in the Department since its earliest beginnings had started to collapse. In 1965, Neil Perry, an economist and academic administrator at the University of British Columbia, was brought in as the first "outsider" to become deputy minister of education. When Perry resigned in 1970, Joe Phillipson, who was serving as assistant superintendent of administration, was promoted over then-Superintendent Frank Levirs to become deputy minister.[52] With the election of the NDP government in 1972, Phillipson was removed, and Jack Fleming, formerly of IBM and who had served as a Burnaby school trustee, was appointed by Minister Eileen Dailly as deputy minister.[53] Within the Department, combined effects of the recent legislation and the new appointments were immediately apparent. The "old guard" had begun to lose control.

At conferences and other meetings of superintendents throughout the 1970s, the focus shifted from relations with the Department of Education to more pressing concerns about how to deal with emerging political constituencies, parental involvement, accountability, special interest groups, and how to create strategies for professional survival.[54] Community activism had become evident in the efforts of informally-constituted interest groups to enlarge the mandate of the school and to pressure school systems into providing an array of new services, especially in the areas of special education, compensatory and remedial programs, social development, and schooling for the gifted. In future, superintendents would have to accept the fact that school policy-making had become a battleground for the resolution of competing social and political ideologies, that special interest groups — and not educational professionals — were to have greater impact on the course of decision-making, that the once-united profession of education had become factious and factionalized, and that old concepts of authority and legitimacy had been eroded by growing community pressure for full participation in school affairs.

The Changing Character of School Leadership

The beginning of local employment for school superintendents in 1974 marked the end of an era in British Columbia educational history. With the closing of the inspectorate in 1958, and the breaking of the Department's grip on the superintendency a decade and a half later, the government in Victoria lost much of its influence in shaping the character of school leadership in the province — influence it had enjoyed since the late nineteenth century. This decline was brought about not only by the advent of local employment, but as a result of other factors, most notably the retirement or resignation of certain key figures within the Department itself, or the decision of veteran schoolmen to leave government service to seek local appointments. These schoolmen had not only guided the affairs of the Department, in some cases since the 1920s and 1930s, but had also engineered the provincial system itself and played an instrumental role in the movement to expand public schooling in British Columbia.

Empowered by an unwritten public consensus about the virtue and value of schooling that endured throughout their professional lives, they were not uncomfortable in framing the goals of education, or in deciding how the public good should be served. Their work as inspectors and superintendents had made them part of an administrative fraternity whose views about education were respected and rarely challenged by the provincial community they served. They were expected to be neutral, to take the long view, and, above all, to express the provincial viewpoint about education. And these things they did.

In contrast, the men and women of the 1970s who became the first generation of superintendents and assistant superintendents to be locally employed inherited an educational world in turmoil, one often in disagreement over the direction schools should take. They became chief executive officers for school boards just as the tide of public support for education was beginning to ebb, and just as community skepticism about the effectiveness of all institutions and experts was on the rise. Unlike the inspectors and government superintendents they replaced, they would not be protected from the hurly-burly of school board and community politics by the talisman of Department authority. They assumed their roles as school leaders not as members of a team headquartered and reinforced in Victoria, but as individuals largely dependent on their own experience, wisdom and skill.

The changes of the 1960s and 1970s, together with the coming of local employment, focused the attention of school superintendents on the broad responsibilities of managing large and complex organizations. By the 1970s, the system of public education had been built. The major battles for universality in schools had been fought and won by earlier generations of schoolmen. What was left for the school leaders of the 1970s was to manage parts of a system already constructed, to refine methods of local operation, and to find ways to cope with restless public and professional constituencies. The new tasks of public education were, perhaps, less grand in vision than those of the past. But so, perhaps, was the age.

Notes

[1] F. Henry Johnson, *A History of Public Education in British Columbia* (Vancouver, British Columbia: University of British Columbia Publications Centre, 1964), p. 88.

[2] Ibid., pp. 88-98.

[3] Ibid., p. 96.

[4] George Hindle, *The Educational System of British Columbia* (Trail, British Columbia: Trail Printing and Publishing Company, 1918), pp. 32.

[5] *Vancouver Daily World,* June 12, 1912, 1.

[6] Hindle, *Educational System of British Columbia,* pp. 14-15.

[7] J.H. Putman and G.M. Weir, *Survey of the School System* (Victoria, British Columbia: King's Printer, 1925), p. 237.

[8] British Columbia Department of Education, *One Hundred Years: Education in British Columbia* (Victoria, British Columbia: Queen's Printer, 1971), pp. 106-109.

[9] Hindle, *Educational System of British Columbia,* p. 29.

[10] Ibid., p. 83.

[11] Johnson, *A History of Public Education in British Columbia,* p. 155.

[12] Hindle, *Educational System of British Columbia,* p. 87.

[13]Interview with Harold Campbell, Victoria, Dec. 8, 1983.

[14]British Columbia, *Annual Report of the Public Schools, 1879-1880* (Victoria, British Columbia: Queen's Printer, 1880), p. 320.

[15]*Annual Report of the Public Schools, 1888-1889,* p. 215.

[16]Interview with Les Canty, Victoria, Oct. 28, 1983.

[17]Interview with Joe Phillipson, Victoria, Dec. 8, 1983.

[18]*British Columbia: From Earliest Times to the Present* (Vancouver, British Columbia: S.J. Clarke Publishing Company, 1914), pp. 994-995.

[19]Fred Smith, "The Inspectors: The Men Behind the Title" (Unpublished paper, University of British Columbia, 1984), p. 4.

[20]*The Colonist,* Jan. 12, 1908, p. 21.

[21]Interview with Roy Thorstenson, Vancouver, Dec. 17, 1983.

[22]British Columbia Ministry of Education, Card File on Field Personnel (Victoria, British Columbia: Field Services Division, 1971).

[23]Among the inspectors who were usually referred to by their military rank were individuals such as: Colonel W.N. Winsby; Colonel A. Graham; Colonel J. Burnett; Colonel T.G. Carter; and Major H.B. King.

[24]Interview with Harold Campbell; interview with Joe Phillipson.

[25]Interview with John Burnett, Vancouver, Dec. 14, 1983.

[26]Interview with Bill Lucas, Vancouver, Dec. 7, 1983.

[27]British Columbia, Department of Education, *One Hundred Years,* pp. 106-109.

[28]Interview with George and Melva Nelson, Victoria, Dec. 22, 1983; Interview with Harold Campbell.

[29]British Columbia, *Public Schools Report, 1957-1958* (Victoria, British Columbia: Queen's Printer, 1958), p. 35.

[30]Putman and Weir, *Survey of the School System* pp. 241-242.

[31]F.A. McLellan, "The Development of the Superintendency in the Large School Unit," in W.A. Plenderleith, ed., *The Canadian Superintendent,* (Toronto: The Ryerson Press, 1961), pp. 9-10.

[32]Alan H. Child, "A Little Tempest: Public Reaction to the Formation of a Large Education Unit in the Peace River District of British Columbia," *B.C. Studies,* 61(1972):24.

[33]H.B. King, *School Finance in British Columbia* (Victoria, British Columbia: King's Printer, 1935).

[34]Statistics Canada, *A Century of Education in British Columbia: Statistical Perspectives, 1871-1971* (Ottawa: Information Canada, 1971), p. 24.

[35]Maxwell A. Cameron, *A Report of the Commission of Inquiry into Educational Finance* (Victoria, British Columbia: King's Printer, 1945), p. 83.

[36]Johnson, *A History of Public Education in British Columbia,* p. 126.

[37]Cameron, *A Report of the Commission of Inquiry,* pp. 86-87.

[38]McLellan, "The Development of the Superintendency," p. 14.

[39]Mollie Cottingham, "A Century of Public Education in British Columbia," Paper presented to the First Annual Meeting of the Canadian College of Teachers, Niagara Falls, Aug. 11, 1958, p. 12.

[40]British Columbia Department of Education, *One Hundred Years,* p. 76.

[41]Johnson, *A History of Public Education in British Columbia,* pp. 162-190.

[42]Interview with Frank Levirs, Victoria, Oct. 28, 1983.

[43]Treffle Boulanger, "The Changing Role of the School Inspector," Paper delivered May 15, 1956, at the CEA-University of Alberta Short Course, p. 5.

[44]British Columbia Department of Education, *One Hundred Years,* pp. 68-90.

[45]British Columbia, *Report of the Royal Commission on Education* (Victoria, British Columbia: Queen's Printer, 1960), p. 1.

[46]British Columbia School Trustees Association, "Brief to the Royal Commission on Education," Apr. 1959, p. 28.

[47]British Columbia Teachers' Federation, "Brief," p. 31.

[48]W. McCordic, "From Civil Service to Local Board Employment," in *The Local Employment of Superintendents,* pp. 8-27; and E.J. Ingram, "Locally Employed Superintendents of Schools: The Alberta Experience," in *The Local Employment of Superintendents,* pp. 29-46.

[49]Interview with Walt Hartrick, Vancouver, Nov. 1, 1983.

[50]Interview with Joe Phillipson.

[51]British Columbia, *An Act to Amend the Public Schools Act,* 1973.

[52]Interview with Harold Campbell; Interview with Les Canty.

[53]Interview with John Meredith and Harold Campbell, Victoria, Nov. 16, 1983; Interview with Joe Phillipson.

[54]John Andrews, "Role Changes in the Superintendency," in *The Superintendency at the Crossroads: Conference for District Superintendents,* 1974 (Victoria, British Columbia: Faculty of Education, University of Victoria, 1974), pp. 2-10.

The Aid-to-Independent-Schools Movement
in British Columbia

L.W. Downey

The action of the British Columbia government in enacting Bill 33, The Independent Schools Support Act of 1977 was, in many ways, a landmark event in Canadian education. Until that time, the B.C. educational system had been stubbornly maintained as a unitary non-denominational system, the only one of its kind in Canada. But in Bill 33,* the Government served notice that it intended to recognize alternatives, to support some freedom of choice in education, and to assist the private sector in becoming more competitive in the delivery of educational services.

John F. Kennedy once observed:

> The essence of ultimate decision remains impenetrable to the observer . . . often, indeed, to the decider himself. . . . There will always be the dark and tangled stretches in the decision-making process — mysterious even to those who may be most intimately involved.[1]

Kennedy's claim may have a good deal of validity. But today, eight years after the event, it does seem possible at least to cast Bill 33 in historical perspective. It may even be possible to remove some of the mystery from the "dark and tangled stretches" in the processes that led to the major shifts in public policy that Bill 33 represented. To attempt to do so is the purpose of this chapter.

Background and Setting

Elsewhere in this volume (see Chapter 13), the story of the early development of the British Columbia school system is traced in some detail. That story provides the historical background for the policy issue to be examined here. The important features of the setting in which the aid-to-independent-schools movement emerged were as follows:

---

*Bill 33, after enactment became The Independent Schools Support Act. Later, it became the Schools (Independent) Support Act. For simplicity, and because in British Columbia the Bill, the Act, and indeed the event is referred to as Bill 33, I shall retain the term Bill 33 throughout this Chapter.

1. In the Free School Act of 1865, and again in the Common School Ordinance of 1869, the principle of a unitary, non-denomination school system was firmly established.
2. When British Columbia entered Confederation in 1871, no denominational schools existed, in law. Hence, Section 93 of the British North America Act, which was worded in such a way as to protect denominational schools that existed at the time of the union, was not relevant.
3. The first Public Schools Act of 1872 reaffirmed the principle of non-sectarianism in public education.
4. For several decades after the union, the public school system grew and developed, largely unchallenged by supporters of other forms of education.

But over the same period, two major types of non-public schools developed in British Columbia, each with a value base quite at variance with the public school system. The denominational schools, which pre-dated confederation, grew and multiplied; they followed the view that religion should permeate all aspects of education. The private, non-denominational schools developed as another kind of alternative; they found their support among clients who opposed the concept of mass education and favoured, instead, a kind of educational elitism.[2]

Non-public schools developed slowly from their beginnings in 1849, when there were only two, to 1939 when their number had increased to forty-nine. But after the war, from 1945 to 1978, sixty-five additional schools were added for a total of 180 schools enrolling 24,000 students.

The major denominational group was the Catholic School Trustees' Association which developed sixty-six schools serving 13,000 students. Other denominational schools, however, were created by the Society for Christian Schools (nineteen schools and 2,000 students), by the Seventh Day Adventists (1,000 students), by the Mennonite Educational Institute (480 students), and by other so-called fundamentalist groups (2,000 students). Ten prestigious, private, non-denominational schools, enrolling about 3,500 students, developed and formed the Independent Schools Association.[3]

In view of these early developments in B.C.'s educational history, one cannot be much surprised by the support-for-independent-schools movement which began to take shape in mid-century. The Roman Catholics, where numbers warranted, formed private schools akin to the parochial schools of the United States. They felt discriminated against, of course, because most other Canadian provinces accorded Catholics the right either to form their own publicly-supported, separate school system or, through special administrative arrangements, to operate schools that were, in fact, Catholic schools. Supporters of the "elitist" grammar-school type of education, initially, simply formed and financed their own schools, only to find later that the costs of maintaining such schools could become burdensome, even for their clients.[4]

Furthermore, by the 1960s, the concept of alternative education had become popular. Even within the public school system, efforts were made to create alternative forms of education and alternative schools to cater to the wishes of particular client groups.

In the early 1950s, the simmering resentment of the Catholics broke into the open. The supporters of elitist schools began a search for political power. The public school system soon came under criticism from a number of sources. And society, on a binge of multi-culturalism, became increasingly prepared to see and to support alternatives which were conceived and developed by individuals and groups rather than the state.

The stage was set. The movement for public support of non-public schools was underway.

Early Concessions — The Thin Edge of the Wedge

The "ideological alternative" to public education, which the independent schools purport to be, was four and a half decades in the shaping. The first move for formal recognition of that alternative was in 1932, when the Catholic schools and independent schools joined forces to petition the government for exemption of their properties from municipal taxation. The argument was that, since the non-public schools saved the state the expense of educating some 4.5 percent of its young citizens, the state ought to subsidize them in some modest way. But the municipal committee of the legislature rejected the petition, declaring that private schools ". . . should pay taxes like any ordinary profit-making business. . . ."[5]

For forty-five years thereafter, the issue of whether or how to recognize or support the independent alternative was never far from the centre of political activity in British Columbia. The Catholic schools case became one of economic justice: double payment, both taxes and fees, for educational services. The independents were more concerned, initially, at least, with recognition or accreditation by government. So as the case unfolded, essentially as a series of sub-issues and incidents, the religious schools and the independent schools attempted to chip away, incrementally, at the resistance of government.

During the election campaign of 1941, the Roman Catholic Lay Organization made four demands:

    i.   extension of health services to parochial school children;
    ii.   provision of free textbooks;
    iii. establishment of Catholic College in affiliation with the University of British Columbia; and
    iv. exemption of private school properties from municipal taxes.

At the time these requests were rejected. And although governments attempted to maintain a consistent posture in treating the independent schools as private, profit-making businesses, circumstances and persistent pressures caused them to yield to requests one by one.

1. *Textbooks*

For years, the independent schools argued that their students should have the same right as public school students to free, government-issued textbooks up to grade six and to participation in the government-sponsored book rental scheme in effect in the secondary schools. In 1951, the government yielded to this pressure, but was cautious to point out that its concession was to individuals, not to schools. Education Minister Straith justified the decision in the following terms:

> Our department does not look at it from the aspect of assistance to schools, but rather having in mind the principle that there should be equal opportunity for education for all children of the Province. . . .[6]

Clearly, there is a tinge of protection-of-the-child-by-the-state ideology in this statement. Implied is the notion that, if the parent makes an unwise decision on behalf of the child (i.e., sends him to an inadequately equipped school), then the state has the right or responsibility to apply some corrective measure on behalf of the individual child.

2. *Health Services*

Up to 1951, health and dental services were provided in parochial schools by the Catholic Health Services Offices, which, in turn, were funded by the Community Chest. But then the Chest withdrew its support, claiming that an organization which depended on voluntary contributions from the public should not support a health service for children of one school system (the parochial) when the same service was provided by government for the children of another school system (the public).

When the fund withdrew its support, the Catholic Health Services Offices folded. Committed as it was to the policy of early immunization and detection through the schools, the government simply had no alternative but to step in and fill the void. Interestingly, no official action was taken; through an informal gentlemen's agreement, services were restored. Whether or not shrewd tacticians saw in this simple incident a procedural precedent is difficult to say. But as we shall note later, the tactic of withdrawing services was subsequently used in a much larger and much more controversial incident.

3. *Pupil Transportation*

By the early 1950s, when large-scale school consolidations had been implemented across the province, the bussing of students had become a significant factor in school operations. Indeed, most local school authorities operated fairly elaborate bus systems. When the Catholic schools requested that their students be given the right to use these services, the government passed the buck to the local school boards.

Minister of Education Straith announced that, although the provincial government contributed 60 percent of the costs of pupil transportation, it regarded the management of the transportation system as a local school board matter. so he said: ". . . We have laid down that, if seats are available on the regular school buses, private school children can use them. . . "[7]

Not surprisingly, this move had the effect of decentralizing the conflict. In many communities, school boards refused to be governed by the apparent intent of the minister's policy. They refused to allow parochial school students to ride their buses, claiming that they could never be sure when their empty seats might be required by their own students. As a result, Catholic school supporters frequently requested the minister to intervene.

Premier W.A.C. Bennett attempted to assert the government's position: the bussing of private school students, he suggested, "should be in the same category as a textbook rental scheme,"[8] that is to say, a service to individual students, not to schools, and a service which local authorities should extend, when feasible, in the interests of improving the educational opportunities of students who choose to attend private schools. But despite the admonitions of the government, throughout the 1960s, the issue generated a good deal of heat at the local level and gave impetus to an emerging grassroots movement.

4. *Other Issues Still to Come*

Later, other issues were to re-emerge and be similarly resolved: (1) request for exemption of private school properties from municipal taxation was finally granted in 1957; (2) public funding of a Catholic university was granted to Notre Dame University in 1967; and (3) permission for private schools to negotiate directly with Ottawa for participation in the federal government's support program for bilingual education was granted in 1972. But these concessions followed and were a part of the story of various power-seeking moves by the non-public schools. We shall take stock of these moves in the next section.

In summary, however, it seems reasonable to conclude that the non-public schools were embarked upon a step-by-step, thin-edge-of-the-wedge attempt to gain recognition and support. Though their ultimate aim, their ultimate "ideological alternative," had not yet taken form, they were clearly penetrating the consciousness of people in the educational system, of society, and of the government.

The Quest for Power: Coalitions and Confrontations

The story of the bid by the non-public schools for power and influence is classic. It began with the revitalization of the B.C. Catholic Education Association (BCCEA) and its adoption of a grassroots and labour-union-style move for influence. It proceeded to a confrontation with government in an incident which could not have been more prudently selected from a political point of view. It moved to the formation of a coalition and the inevitable counter-coalition — informal, though nonetheless very real. It proceeded to political activity, thereby creating or revealing breaks in party solidarity. And it produced a series of further concessions for the non-public schools as well as a clearer articulation of what had come to be known as the independent school alternative.

1. *The Revitalization of the BCCEA*

In 1951 (the year in which textbooks, health services and transportation were granted to non-public schools), the British Columbia Catholic Education Association underwent an executive reorganization. Mr. Pat Power became president and Mr. Reg Paxton the first full-time executive secretary. Under their leadership, the Association grew into a large, active protest group. Drawing upon his experience as a union organizer, Power promoted education rallies in the various communities, the purpose being to increase membership, to spread the cause of the Catholic schools, and to encourage members to become politically active.

The Association came alive; the movement gained momentum. Indeed, something of a competition developed among parishes to sell the ideas of and membership in BCCEA. In one rally at St. John the Apostle parish in Vancouver, it was reported that: ". . . the group attending set forth plans to contact every member of the parish, and be the first to bring in a 100 percent parish associate membership in the BCCEA."[9]

The Association also became a very active political lobby group, sending delegates to Victoria to petition the minister for concessions on the various issues (transportation, health services, taxation, and so on). Furthermore, members were encouraged to bring the concerns of the Catholic parents to the attention of their MLAs and cabinet members.

Two other figures are noteworthy in this movement: Mr. Ray Perrault and Archbishop William Duke. Perrault was very active in BCCEA politics; later he became leader of the B.C. Liberal Party, which gave early support to the concept of government assistance to independent schools. Archbishop Duke of the Vancouver Diocese, always outspoken on educational matters, never hesitated to use the pulpit to help rally Catholics to the cause of the BCCEA. In his closing address to the Diocesan Congress in 1951, for example, he said:

> Since so many of our people are here together today, I take the occasion to draw attention of all to the question about which we are all so deeply concerned. That is the double school tax which we have to bear. Catholic working men and their families feel they cannot support it any longer. . . .[10]

On another occasion, at Nelson, B.C., he closed his sermon with the statement of faith that ". . . in God's good time, British fair play will be obtained, and Catholic schools for our little ones will be duly recognized by the Province."[11]

2. *The Maillardville Confrontation*

Whether by design or by coincidence, the efforts of Power, Paxton, Perrault, Duke and others were given a great deal of impetus and publicity by a confrontation between the parochial schools and the public schools of Maillardville, a small community in the municipality of Coquitlam which has a comparatively high proportion of French Catholics in its population. In April 1951, the Catholic School Board simply closed two schools, Our Lady of Lourdes and Our Lady of Fatima, and instructed the 840 students attending these schools to register in the already-overcrowded public schools of the Coquitlam school district. The schools remained closed for a year and a half, making it necessary for the public school system, very quickly, to expand its staff and facilities to accommodate the new students.

No doubt, the reason for this action on the part of the Catholic schools was a lingering resentment over a number of issues, primarily taxes. The spark that ignited the affair, however, was the refusal of the school board to allow parochial students to use the school buses, and the government chose to believe that this was at the heart of the matter. Education Minister Straith dismissed the matter, saying that ". . . the question of transportation is a local problem. . . ."[12] Premier Bennett, though not inclined to intervene directly, urged that local boards comply with the government's permissive guideline and provide transportation for Catholic school students.

Pat Power saw the Maillardville affair in a positive light, inasmuch as it brought the independent school issue to the public attention:

> For the first time in the history of this Province the school question has been effectively raised and things will never be the same. . . . Maillardville has done a splendid job of advertising to the people of this Province and the whole of Canada how narrow the education laws of British Columbia are. . . .[13]

The Catholic schools of Maillardville reopened in September 1952 with the textbook and health care concessions their only two victories. But the affair was not over. In 1953 and again in 1954 and 1955, the Catholic schools of Maillardville declined to pay their property taxes to the municipality of Coquitlam, forcing the municipality to face an unpleasant dilemma: whether to ignore the confrontation, thereby losing valuable tax revenue and, in the process, establishing a dangerous precedent; or to seize the Catholic schools for non-payment, thereby aggravating an already volatile situation and, likely, adding to mounting public sympathy for the Catholic schools.

Once again, the "plight of the Catholic schools" was in the media; once again, pressure was on the government to redress their grievances. Premier Bennett saw in the Maillardville affair something of a political time bomb, a potential for problems more serious than his government had yet faced in the non-public school issue. So he determined to defuse the issue, in 1957, by amending the Municipal Act.

3. *The Tax Exemption Issue*

The requirement that non-public school supporters not only pay taxes in support of public education, in addition to operating their own schools, but also pay property taxes on their own school properties "like any ordinary profit-making business" was the one that continued, for decades, to irk them and add to their hostility toward the system. Only in Vancouver were non-public schools exempt from municipal tax because of a clause in the Vancouver City Charter which granted exemptions to "incorporated seminaries of learning." During the Depression of the thirties, the Vancouver city council considered having this exemption removed (to increase the property tax revenue by $57,000) but refrained when it realized that the cost of operating the schools would far exceed the potential tax revenue that would result from removal of the exemption.[14] The existence of this exemption in Vancouver served as something of a precedent which other non-public schools wished to utilize; the reasons city council did not attempt to have the exemption removed became the reason why non-public schools in all other areas claimed they, too, should be exempt.

As indicated, the closure of the Maillardville schools, with the suddenly-imposed and, then, just as suddenly removed, burden upon the Coquitlam public school system — along with the subsequent withholding of property taxes by supporters of Maillardville Catholic schools — impressed Premier Bennett with the vulnerability of the provincial government, as well as local school boards. So at the 1957 sitting of the legislature, major revisions to the Municipal Act were introduced, including the exemption of all educational institutions from municipal property tax.

Though the premier saw the inevitability of the measure, and though he doubtless considered it politically expedient to proceed, he apparently did so with some trepidation. On two previous occasions, in 1956 and 1957, the legislative committee on municipal affairs (composed of a majority of Social Credit MLAs) had rejected government-sponsored amendments to exempt private schools. So this time, the proposed amendment did not go to committee; indeed, it did not even go to caucus, a most unusual procedure.

The premier explained his failure to follow procedures by claiming that it was essential to introduce the bill without delay.[15] No doubt, however, he anticipated resistance, not only from the Opposition but also from his own party. As it turned out, six Socred members did vote with the Opposition after applauding CCF party leader, Robert Strachan, when he stated:

> . . . We would not deny to anyone the right to send their children to a private school of their choice, if they so desire . . . but once anyone makes that choice, we feel the individual parent should be prepared to pay the necessary costs of maintaining their children in such a private school and that maintenance costs include payment of taxes.[16]

When the bill passed, the issue of property taxes on non-public schools ended as a major victory for the independent schools. In the process, the CCF took a stand against public support of private schools — a stand which it maintained, with some exceptions, thereafter. The Liberal Party came out on

the side of the private schools. And the Socreds split with the majority following the party line but with a few (six) openly declaring their opposition —
despite the political wisdom displayed by their very powerful leader.

4. *The Coalition: The Federation of Independent School Associations*

Though the Maillardville affair no doubt hastened the tax exemption
amendment of 1957, it also had some very negative effects upon the Catholic
schools movement. The closure of the Catholic schools imposed a serious burden upon the public school; the confrontation tactic of the closures eventually
generated a backlash of resentment and hostility. Even many Catholic school
supporters disavowed the tactics of their leaders and withdrew their support.

By the early sixties, the BCCEA seemed to have lost much of its early
impetus. Its image was tarnished. It was then realized that an organization
was needed to represent *all* private schools, not just the Catholics. So in 1964,
a meeting was held by all private school organizations: the Independent School
Association, the Catholic Schools Trustees' Association, the National Union
of Christian Schools, and representatives of non-affiliated schools such as the
Mennonite Educational Institute. A founding committee was formed to
develop a constitution, the major points of which were: (1) a federation of
associations rather than schools, so that no one could dominate; (2) voting
power on policy matters would be evenly distributed among member associations, though fees would be assessed on a per-pupil basis; and (3) the name
would be the Federation of Independent Schools Associations (FISA). The
federation was created under the B.C. Societies Act in 1966 and made its
first representation to government a year later.

The aim of FISA was to create a political climate in the province hospitable to the existence of independent schools and supportive of their public
funding. Its major techniques were the dissemination of information and
political activism. For example, the federation established a constant presence
at educational and political conferences; its members joined political parties
and became active in the support of independent schools in those parties; and
they wrote letters to editors, appeared on open-line shows and generally
attempted to raise the level of public awareness and support. Mr. Gerard
Ensing was appointed full-time executive director to coordinate the efforts of
the federation and to serve as its official spokesman.

5. *Parties and Politicians*

The support-for-independent-schools movement in B.C. posed a difficult
problem of accommodation for political ideologies. One, reflecting the values
of the Catholic Church, was promoted throughout the 1950s and 60s by the
BCCEA; it was essentially a common-man, grassroots organization, employing promotional tactics not unlike those of a labour union. The other ideology,
reflecting elitist values (cultural, if not economic) was promoted, initially by
the Independent Schools Association, as an alternative to mass, public education. In short, the one ideology found its basis in religious imperatives; the
other, in cultural alternatives. Ultimately, as we have noted, the two strands

of the movement came together with the creation of the Federation of Independent School Associations, after which (as we shall note later) the ideology of the movement was more clearly articulated.

But meanwhile, provincial political parties and persons in power were continuously forced to take positions and to search for a rationale for dealing with the movement in politically feasible ways.

The Social Credit Party under W.A.C. Bennett did grant a number of concessions to the non-public schools, some of them (health services, textbooks, transportation) allegedly for the purpose of equalizing opportunities for children, but others (exemption of private school properties from municipal taxes) clearly out of political expediency. Yet until he was defeated in 1972, Premier Bennett and his government maintained the policy established at Confederation: a unitary, non-sectarian system of public education, with no public support of non-public schools.

During the election campaign of 1972, when the issue appeared to be a politically important one, Premier Bennett declared his party's position in these terms:

> . . . people have the right to go to private schools if they want to, but public policy is to encourage people to go to public schools. Our policy is integration not segregation, and make no mistake about it.[17]

But Bennett did not enjoy the same kind of party solidarity on the non-public schools issue as he did on most other matters. Indeed, he was opposed in caucus, and even in the House, for being both too compromising and too adamant on the issue. Six backbenchers voted against him in his amendment to the Municipal Act, a major concession to the non-public schools. But it was a Socred member, Herb Capozzi, who in the same sitting criticized the government for neglecting Catholic children and who requested some form of support for their schools. Similarly, it was a Socred MLA, Dudley Little, who in 1971 introduced a private member's bill to give recognition to independent schools.

The significance of W.A.C. Bennett's policy on non-public education in the election of 1972 is difficult to determine. But he appears to have completely misread the evolving mood in the core of his party, namely, the Evangelicals, the Pentecostals and the Fundamentalists, who by then were prepared to align themselves with the Catholics. He appears also to have misread the mood of the voters; though he promised them policy reviews in all other major areas, he said that Socred policy with respect to private schools was one area he would not review. His intransigent position, despite the shifting mood of his party and of society, no doubt contributed in some degree to his defeat.

In 1973, a year after the defeat, the Socred convention reversed the party's policy and declared its intention, when re-elected, to introduce legislation that would extend legal recognition and financial support to independent schools. That declaration was in fact, incorporated into the party's platform for the 1975 election; and, no doubt, along with other educational matters, played a part in the Socreds' return to power.

So it happened that, over the course of two decades, the Social Credit Party moved first from adamant opposition to any competition to the public school system to a series of concessions to non-public schools, and finally, to a declaration of recognition of and financial support for the non-public education sector.

It should be noted, however, that in the final stages of that turnaround, the ranks of the Socred caucus were augmented by the defection of certain influential individuals from the Liberal Party. One of these was Dr. Pat McGeer, who throughout his entire political career had advocated recognition of and public support for independent schools.

The New Democratic Party (NDP), under Robert Strachan, took a stand against any kind of support for non-public schools. Strachan opposed the amendment to the Municipal Act in 1957, claiming that parents who choose to send their children to private schools must be prepared to pay for that choice. That position was reaffirmed in 1967 when Robert Williams, speaking for the NDP, opposed Capozzi's request for aid to private schools.

During the election campaign of 1972, the new NDP leader Dave Barrett equivocated slightly, saying that his position on aid to independent schools at the moment was negative, but that he might be prepared to change his mind after the upcoming NDP convention.

Some evidence of a softening of the NDP position emerged during the party's brief term in office from 1972 to 1975. First, the government allowed the Federation of Independent School Associations to negotiate directly with the federal government for grants in aid of bilingual programs in independent schools. Second, Premier Barrett appointed a cabinet committee to examine what "basic services" ought to be provided by government to these schools. The committee's recommendations were simple: that the government provide transportation for non-public school students and that the Library Commission undertake to provide supplementary services for children in the non-public sector. Nothing happened to these recommendations, for the NDP government was defeated a few months later.

Finally, while Bill 33 was before the House for a full five-month period, the NDP was so divided on the issue that it simply could not deal with it. The bill did not get to the floor of the party convention. There were no public statements of party position. And when the bill came up for second reading, the party boycotted the session, on a matter of procedure, not principle.

The Liberal Party had maintained a consistent position for years, favouring some form of aid to non-public schools. In 1957, the Liberals supported the Socreds in their proposed amendment to the Municipal Act. In 1967, Liberal Member Pat McGeer spoke out in support of Socred MLA Capozzi when he proposed aid to private schools. (Indeed, at that time, McGeer's suggestion was a direct refund to the parents of private school students of a percentage of tuition fees.) In 1968, McGeer called for grants to private schools, claiming that every child educated in the non-public sector represented a saving to the B.C. taxpayer of $440 per year. In 1971, Garde Gardom, in debate with Education Minister Donald Brothers, argued that the government should provide operational grants to qualified private schools on the same basis as it did to public schools. In 1972, new Liberal leader David Anderson pledged that, if elected, the Liberals would pay grants covering 60 percent of the operating costs of any non-public school offering a regular curriculum. Finally, in 1975, the new Liberal leader, Gordon Gibson, endorsed funding for independent schools.

It should be noted here that the two articulate spokesmen for the Liberal policy, McGeer and Gardom, subsequently defected to the Socreds and ultimately became the architects of the Socred plan. The Conservative Party was not a force in the independent school movement. In 1969, Conservative leader John DeWolf proposed $100 per student grants to non-public schools because, in light of increasing costs, there was a real danger that some private schools might have to close, thereby releasing up to twenty-five thousand students upon the public schools. In the 1972 campaign, the Conservatives declined to adopt a position, agreeing instead to keep the question open. In 1975, Conservative leader Scott Wallace came out in support of legal recognition of independent schools and some funding.

Clearly by 1975, when a closely-fought election campaign was about to be waged, all the political parties had decided that traditional postures toward non-public education would no longer be accepted by the electorate. The two strong contenders, however, differed markedly in their platforms. The NDP under Dave Barrett pledged to extend transportation and library services, but not to support independent schools as any kind of serious alternative to public education. The Socreds, under their new leader William Bennett, Jr., pledged formal and legal recognition of the private education sector along with a direct government subsidy, either to the schools or to their children.

Other educational issues no doubt influenced party positions on the matter, and very likely affected the outcome of the election as well. During the previous 1972 election, the B.C. Teachers' Federation had mounted a mammoth campaign against the Socreds and in favour of the NDP. This action generated lingering resentment among Socreds toward "the public school establishment"; perhaps some of this resentment remained in 1975. Also, the BCTF's attempt to flex its political muscle in 1972 probably increased both the public's disillusionment with the public schools and, correspondingly its tolerance for a non-public alternative. It is possible, too, that the hasty and short-lived coalition between the BCTF and the NDP served ultimately, to weaken both in the arena of public opinion.

In any case, during the events leading up to the election of 1975, the Federation of Independent Schools had consolidated its ideological position and had injected it into the mainstream of political debate. Similarly, the opponents of the movement, led by the BCTF, had reaffirmed a counter-ideology and attempted to convince the people and the politicians of its appropriateness.

Legislation [18]

After the election of 1975 and the return of the Socreds to power, it seemed certain that some kind of government aid to non-public education would soon be forthcoming. What remained uncertain, however, was the form that aid might take and exactly who might receive it. Three general possibilities had been discussed during the election campaign:

i.   A program of subsidies for special services such as libraries, laboratories, and so on, probably to be administered through a so-called "adoption" scheme whereby the local school board would serve as the distributor of services and/or funds;

ii. Direct operating or instructional grants to private schools; or,

iii. Direct aid or rebates to students and parents, in the form of income tax credits, property tax exemptions, tuition grants, or educational vouchers.

Bill 33, which became The Independent Schools support Act, took ten different forms before it finally became law. The first seven of these were working drafts, prepared behind closed doors, largely by the minister's policy adviser and the legal offices, but with confidential advice and reaction from ministry personnel and from a few carefully-selected outsiders. The eighth draft was introduced for first reading; the ninth and tenth incorporated amendments brought about by reactions from the public and from lobby groups, by reconsiderations in caucus, by legislative committee hearings, and by parliamentary debate.

The initial phase of legislation-drafting was largely a technical one, though it also produced a significant attitudinal change in ministry personnel. No doubt, initially, the whole concept of public aid to non-public education was anathema to the minister's staff, just as it was to most of the public education establishment. But over the four- or five-month period during which the bill was being shaped, there was something of a turnaround in the ministry from grudging acceptance of the minister's directives to a fairly genuine commitment to his objective.

Also at this stage there were some consultations with FISA. The government was not disposed to accept all the federation's earlier recommendations; nor, however, did it intend to introduce the funding at a level which might have a shock effect on the public. So, during the first drafting phase, FISA was given the opportunity to contribute and to be informed on a confidential basis.

In the process, there were literally hundreds of changes, most of them fairly trivial. Some, however, were quite significant to the shape of the aid program.

1. *Constitutional Concerns*

Concerns over potential constitutional implications troubled shapers of the bill throughout. Legal advisers cautioned that to treat the independent schools as a dissenting, a minority, or a separate system, might just be to lock British Columbia into the terms of section 93 of the B.N.A. Act so that, in the event that the government decided to eliminate or reduce aid, appeals based upon the constitutional provisions for "dissident systems" might be possible. Since B.C. had, for over a hundred years, been unique in its exclusion from that constitutional requirement in education, the government was determined to retain its exemption. Hence, it was decided to deal in legislation with the concept of aid to *institutions,* not to systems.

2. *Qualifying Authority*

As an alternative to the concept of "system," it was decided to deal in "qualifying authorities"; but that idea too caused problems. Initial drafts required that each qualifying school be established as an "authority" under the Societies Act and be a non-profit organization.

FISA reacted negatively, suggesting under certain circumstances (the parochial schools of a large city, for example), there would be a number of schools operating under one authority. Also, it was discovered that some non-public schools were not operating under the provincial Societies Act, but rather under federal statutes.

Hence, the definition of "qualifying authority" kept changing, even up to the legislative debates, with the shapers of the bill attempting to accommodate all private schools without jeopardizing B.C.'s positions with respect to the constitution.

3. *Conditions of Aid and Desire to Participate*

One issue which proved difficult at the time was that of qualification for aid. The government was aware that most schools wanted to receive aid but it also knew that some schools did not, for they were afraid that aid would erode their independence. So the question became: how might the legislation accommodate both "qualification" and "desire to participate"? The first inclination was to "license" all schools, but this idea was rejected, as government had no desire to deal with any school not wishing to participate. The term "classification" was then considered, but rejected for the same reason. Finally, it was decided that the term "qualification" was the appropriate one. Schools would be allowed to apply for qualification, or alternatively ignore the program, as they wished.

4. *Time and Experience Qualifications*

Exactly what waiting period for qualification should be prescribed caused argument. The drafters of the bill wanted to avoid making the aid program an incentive for fly-by-night operators to establish private schools. FISA had suggested a three-year waiting period; the government decided on five. But the bill was originally written in such a way that any school which had not been in operation a full five years at the time of enactment would be required to wait another five years before qualifying.

Not surprisingly, FISA caught this, and argued for a maximum three-year waiting period. Drafters of the bill admitted their error, and reduced the waiting period to five years, but would not accept FISA's proposal of a three-year period. (Four years later, however, the waiting period *was* reduced to three years.)

5. *Qualifications of Teachers*

Issues involving the certification of teachers proved quite controversial. Some wanted, originally, to incorporate a clause making the possession of B.C. teacher certification a factor in a school's qualification. FISA argued, however, that often the non-public schools (particularly the elitist, independent schools) had on their staffs outstanding scholars, artists, and athletes; to require such individuals to return for teacher training would be ridiculous, in fact, might mean losing them to the teaching profession. Traditionalists in the profession, and particularly the BCTF, countered that to admit such unqualified persons would be to deny the very existence of a teaching profession.

The first effort to overcome this problem was to introduce in the legislation a "grandfather clause," which would allow individuals with longstanding experience in the private schools to live out their careers. But that was not the kind of grudging concession the independents wanted. Part of the alternative they saw in their service is the use of teachers who are not prepared and socialized in the traditional mode.

They prevailed. The legislation presented for first reading included a provision for the minister to appoint independent schools teacher certification committees, and for the inspector of independent schools to grant certification.

Another issue related to certification was that of membership in the B.C. Teachers' Federation. As one can infer from the issue of certification, it was originally intended that private school teachers be "brought to the fold," as it were. But later, as the more independent alternatives prevailed, membership in the professional association was no longer assumed. So the architects of the act wondered how to allow optional membership, specifically deny required membership, and yet studiously avoid, as one person expressed it, allowing the matter to emerge as a "red flag" in the legislation.

Legal counsel suggested that the matter be ignored, advising that optional membership, as already provided for in the Public School Act, would remain operative and that compulsory membership could not be inferred from the new act. But in order to avoid future controversy, of a legal case on the matter, a clause was inserted expressly excluding private school teachers from compulsory membership in the BCTF.

The Bill was introduced for first reading on March 30, 1977. After about a six-week public debate, it was given second reading on June 13. The official Opposition attempted to stop the bill on procedural grounds, but refused to debate the ideological issues involved. Clearly, the Opposition was divided, as it boycotted the session.

The *Colonist* reported the final September 10 session on the bill as follows:

> The storm raging around Bill 33 — independent school funding legislation — blew itself out with a less than potent final gust Wednesday as the bill passed its test in the legislature.

Analysis and Conclusions

The *Colonist's* somewhat plaintive, final comment of Bill 33 seems suggestive of the central question in the case: in a province such as British Columbia — a province which, from its beginnings, had staunchly rejected any alternative to public, non-sectarian education — how could a Bill 33 succeed? Undoubtedly, there were a number of contributing factors: the leadership and determination of Education Minister McGeer; the effective functioning of the supporting lobby and the not-so-effective functioning of the competing lobby; divisiveness in the ranks of the Opposition; and, a decided shift in the public mood. The story would not be complete without some analysis of these factors.

1. *Leadership*

Dr. Pat McGeer became minister of education after the Socreds were returned to power in 1975. He immediately began advocating aid to independent schools. Indeed, he became the chief architect of Bill 33 and the strategist who maneuvered the new policy through society, through the Opposition, and through the Legislature.

In all tasks, he displayed the skills and determination required to win policy battles. He articulated the new policy in terms comprehensible and attractive to society; he displayed a certain doggedness, touched with a willingness to compromise; he brought to his mission individuals and groups willing to be helpful, but effectively excluded those who were not; he coped with opposition, for the most part with scorn for their unwillingness to debate and their inability to oppose in unison; and he did not hesitate to use his considerable power and prestige to achieve his ends.

2. *Lobbies*

It is interesting, in retrospect, to speculate about the behaviour and probable influence of the two major lobby groups — the supporting one centred in FISA, and the competing one in the BCTF. The supporting lobby struck a low-key, but nevertheless persistent posture. It perceived the minister as powerful and treated him with deference; it perceived the issue to be a novel one in B.C. and so proceeded to do much of the "homework" needed to inform the minister and his staff; and it perceived the balance of public opinion to be shifting in its favour and so proceeded to nudge the shift gently. Its perceptions were accurate. Its actions paid off.

The competing lobby, in contrast, perceived *itself* to be powerful and so did not hesitate to confront the minister, vigorously and in public. It believed the proposed policy change to be out of step with social opinion and proceeded to oppose it in the public arena. Its perceptions were inaccurate and its actions unsuccessful.

3. *Divisiveness in the Opposition*

The issue of public support for non-public education is not one which takes shape along the lines of traditional party ideologies. Indeed, the NDP party, the official Opposition throughout this case, was clearly divided over the issue. Many party members were clients of Catholic or independent schools. On second reading, the Opposition did oppose the bill — but on procedural, not substantive grounds. And when its opposition on procedural grounds failed, the NDP, rather than get caught in a debate over ideological issues, boycotted the session and allowed the bill to pass.

4. *The Mood of Society*

Over the few decades prior to 1977, there appears to have been a gradual shift in public attitude toward schooling. As a result of a growing diversity in the society and a corresponding acceptance of pluralism in values, hostilities toward non-public schools had given way to greater tolerance. Indeed, surveys conducted during the development of Bill 33 indicated that a majority of British Columbians favoured aid to independent schools — provided the aid was not excessive, and provided independents were not allowed to deviate too far from the established curriculum.

(These two provisos ultimately became the guidelines of the aid program: so-called Class 1 schools, those that agreed to provide the core curriculum and meet certain other requirements, were funded at a level of 30 percent of the costs of the public school in the districts in which they were located; Class 2 schools, those that did not offer the full core but met other minimal requirements, were funded at 9 percent.)

British Columbians appear to view these arrangements as being just about right. Opposition to aid to independent schools has been all but silenced. But wherever the funding formula produces an increase in grants to independent schools and a decrease in grants to public schools (enrolment statistics have tended to produce this result), outcries inevitably follow.

A spokesperson for the NDP Party recently acknowledged that aid to independent schools in B.C. is here to stay — provided it stays at its current level and provided the qualifications for aid are not diluted.

Notes

[1]John F. Kennedy, as quoted in G.T. Allinson, *Essence of Decision: Explaining the Cuban Missile Crises* (Boston: Little, Brown and Co., 1971).

[2]Some of my reactors have objected mildly to my use of the term "elitist" to describe these schools. With apologies I shall persist, for I can find no better description for the kind of non-mass-education ideology which characterizes them.

[3]By 1985, eight years after Bill 33, enrolment had increased rather dramatically as indicated by the following statistics from the March, 1985 FISA *Monday Bulletin.*

Enrolment Statistics
British Columbia Independent Schools

Year	CPS-ISC Catholic	ISA Private	SCS-BC InterDen	AMG Mixed	FISA Total	Non-FISA Total	Total
77-78	13,264	3,559	2,471	1,357	20,651	3,040	23,691
78-79	13,395	3,556	2,702	1,411	21,064	3,492	24,556
79-80	13,226	3,667	2,946	1,273	21,140	3,687	24,827
80-81	13,712	3,661	3,239	1,498	22,110	4,204	26,314
81-82	14,077	3,839	3,436	2,056	23,408	4,528	27,936
82-83	14,620	3,872	3,592	2,002	24,086	4,194	28,280
83-84	15,516	3,935	3,745	1,518	24,714	4,404	29,118
84-85	15,421	3,886	3,969	1,756	25,032	—	—
Percent increase over 1977	16.2	9.1	60.6	29.4	29.2	22.9	44.8

CPS-ISC:	Catholic Public Schools Inter-Society Committee
ISA:	Independent Schools Association
SCS-BC:	Society of Christian Schools in British Columbia
AMG:	Associate Member Group
FISA:	Federation of Independent School Associations

[4]I use a number of terms to describe the schools and school systems under review — and deliberately so. For all of the terms were in use, each with a subtle connotation, during the debates. It may be useful, however, to place the terms in perspective here.

There are in Canada four major types of schools. They might be classified as follows:

	Public	Private
Denominational	1	2
Non-Denominational	3	4

Cell 1, the public-denominational schools are, elsewhere in Canada, referred to as "separate schools." The Cell 3 schools are the public, non-denominational schools — the only type recognized in B.C. prior to the movement described in this report.

Cells 2 and 4 include the schools of concern here. They are private; they are both denominational and non-denominational. As the debate proceeded, the term "private" was often used to imply profit-making; the terms "denominational" and "Catholic" were used to imply religious separatism. Today, all the Cell 2 and Cell 4 schools are referred to as independent.

[5]*Victoria Daily Times,* Mar. 17, 1933.

[6]*B.C. Catholic,* XX: 19 (1951): 1.

[7]J.V. O'Reilley, *Independent Education in B.C.* (Vancouver: The Knights of Columbus, 1972), p. 7.

[8]*Vancouver Sun,* Apr. 13, 1951.

[9]*B.C. Catholic,* XX: 36 (1951): 1

[10]*B.C. Catholic,* XX: 28 (1951): 1.

[11]*B.C. Catholic,* XX: 47 (1951): 3.

[12]O'Reilley, *Independent Education in B.C.,* p. 7.

[13]*B.C. Catholic,* XX : 48 (1951).

[14]*Vancouver Province,* Sept. 9, 1937.

[15]*Vancouver Sun,* Mar. 6, 1957.

[16]*Victoria Colonist,* Mar. 21, 1957.

[17]*Vancouver Province,* May 29, 1972.

[18]The data used as the bases of this section came from two sources:

i.   The government's confidential files, covering this phase of the development, were turned over to the researcher, in complete and unedited form, with only one caveat to govern their use — namely, that he "exercise reasonable discretion" in the use of the informal communications.

ii. Persons involved in the process were interviewed — sometimes to clarify the meanings of materials, sometimes to clarify sequences of events, and sometimes to ascertain intent or background thinking.